The Other Side of Coexistence

The Other Side of Coexistence

AN ANALYSIS OF RUSSIAN FOREIGN POLICY

Albert L. Weeks

Pitman Publishing Corporation

NEW YORK • TORONTO • LONDON • TEL AVIV

Contents

The Other Side of Coexistence

Introduction

"What do we do next?"

Leonid Brezhnev was overheard uttering this question inadvertently into an open microphone atop the Lenin Mausoleum in a hectic moment just before the start of the May Day 1969 ceremonies.[1] Although the General-Secretary of the Communist Party of the Soviet Union was actually referring to arrangements for a parade, his question had ironic relevance beyond the problem of the route to be followed by the marchers in Red Square. Soviet foreign policy is presently at a crossroads. "What do we do next?" is precisely the question.

The Soviet economy needs peace, but the U.S.S.R. feels threatened militarily on both its western and eastern flanks, particularly on the latter, where the potential adversary is Communist China. In this situation the Soviet Union has two alternative courses of action: (1) to go it alone, putting an even greater strain on its peacetime economy while relying to a limited extent on its Warsaw Pact allies or (2) to rebuild the old World War II alliance with the Western powers, including the United States. The second alternative necessitates an entire recasting of its ideology in order to fit "American imperialism" into a "strange alliance" with Soviet Russia. This is one of the major crossroads at which Russia presently stands. The course of action that it finally chooses will in great part be determined by the precedents that have been established in Russia's diplomatic history.

The purpose of this book is to examine the various courses of action which Russia—pre- and postrevolutionary, Tsarist and Soviet—has chosen to take in its relations with other nation-states in the world; and to analyze the motives for these chosen policies. For over 200 years, the United States has loomed large in Russian foreign policy decisions and is therefore given special attention in this book. As the world's most powerful country, the United States shares an unconstituted dyarchy over large areas of the world with the second most powerful country, the Soviet Union. Russia's relations with the United States have been crucial to the destinies of both countries before and since 1917.

Given today's nuclear-tipped Intercontinental Ballistic Missiles, one principle that operates in the relations between the U.S. and the U.S.S.R. is of enormous importance: peaceful coexistence—namely whether science

3

doth make cowards of us all, whether the destructiveness of modern weapons will persuade the two superpowers to coexist in the world and not resort to mutual destruction. The problem of *coexistence* or *coextinction* is central to much of the discussion that follows in these chapters.

Peaceful coexistence is like a square number that factors easily into its roots. In looking for the square root of peaceful coexistence, two primary elements may be factored out:

1. *the terms* upon which peaceful coexistence will be carried out (theory)
2. *the behavior* of both halves of the double relationship (practice)

The first problem of *upon whose terms* and *whose philosophy* peaceful coexistence will be realized involves each country's grand strategy. Suppose one side considered the policy of peaceful coexistence a merely temporary device with which to gain time, perhaps to prepare for some later non-peaceful action. Or suppose peaceful coexistence were being used only as a tactic by one of the two sides in order to achieve world domination, exploiting peaceful coexistence as a slogan to make that nation more popular and attractive to the world's masses, but in no positive or meaningful way to apply the principle to the other half of the relationship.

The behavior on both sides of the coexistence relationship obviously determines what kind of peaceful coexistence it is going to be in practice. There are several types of coexistence; although all of them are peaceful, they differ strikingly in other respects. For example, one may speak of "active" and "cooperative" coexistence, on the one hand, or "passive" and "limited" coexistence, on the other. There is even a mutated form which, for lack of a better term, might be called "unbalanced" coexistence—a relationship under peaceful coexistence in which one of the two halves takes more initiatives than the other toward making coexistence peaceful, workable, and long lasting.

In the discussion of peaceful coexistence and the other problems confronting the two superpowers, the focus of this book is centered on the "other side" of this double relationship: namely, How do the *Russians* regard peaceful coexistence and the other principles governing Russo-American relations? What are the Soviets' terms for getting along with the American half of coexistence?

Before taking apart the Russian doll-puzzle of Tsarist and Soviet policy before and since 1917, let us take a "distant shot" of the problem.

The vagaries of Soviet foreign policy are an inexhaustible source of puzzlement and conflicting interpretation in the West. Newspapers apply, often too hastily, a simplistic scale of "hard" and "soft" to describe, say, the latest speech by a Soviet leader. Some observers think they see an enigmatic or utterly meaningless pattern of zigzags etched in the international arena by the leaders in the Kremlin. Others attempt a profounder analysis by deciphering an alleged "Code of the Politburo." Scholars, who presumably are more deliberate in their speculations and who are, hopefully, better versed in Soviet foreign policy than the general run of newspaper columnist or editorial writer, isolate a number of modalities operating in Soviet foreign policy-making. These factors may include Communist ideology, Russian messianism, the special Soviet conception of international law, Russia's basic geopolitical position, the Tsarist and 50-year Soviet inheritance and experience of Russian diplomacy, and so on.[2]

It is, indeed, a difficult task to make sense out of a nation's, any nation's, foreign policy. For one thing, the policy-makers are gamblers. Since events proceed in the international arena in an unpredictable way, policies must be tried or withdrawn similar to the way chess players make gambits and "middle-game" adjustments as the "situation" changes. The resultant total picture may display a pattern (to the degree it does) of trial and error, of attack and retreat, of partial success or no success at all in the defense of the national interest.

Another complication stems from the fact that the policy-makers and the historians of diplomacy seldom agree among themselves on whether the country's national interest has been served in the long run by this or that major foreign policy decision. It is difficult to analyze the pluses and minuses of a nation's effort on the international front; success in diplomacy cannot be conveniently evaluated within the columns of some huge Kafkaesque ledger.

Descriptions and expositions of Soviet foreign policy often include a discussion of a number of factors determining that policy. However, the specialists by no means agree among themselves on just what these factors may be. When they do agree on some of them, they may disagree on their relative importance. Despite disagreement, however, the state of the art is enhanced by the fact that many of the scholars do argue their cases well and with considerable documentation.

Some Western specialists are inclined to stress the more traditional motivations allegedly operating upon the leaders in the Kremlin. Russia's geopolitical position, they maintain, is a function both of modern technology and basic, "eternal" geography; geopolitics appears to them to be the crucial determiner of foreign-policy decisions. Likewise, these geographically and geopolitically inclined observers emphasize the factor of Russian national security about which Tsars and Commissars have displayed extreme anxiety.

A second group of scholars proceeds somewhat differently, stressing ideology rather than national interest and national security per se. The fact that the U.S.S.R. is committed to Communist ideology, including especially the messianic goal of World Revolution, strikes these scholars as being of cardinal importance in the study of Soviet foreign policy. According to them, national interest may even be sacrificed at times on the altar of the holy writ of Marxism-Leninism, Russia's new Orthodoxy. A branch of this school adds the historical factor of Russia's century-old Pan-Slav tradition which, as enunciated by Danilevsky, Dostoyevsky, and others, has influenced pre- and postrevolutionary Russian foreign policy as surely as the German *Volk* romanticists of the Herder school had influenced German foreign policy.

Permit this author to attempt to bring some order into the discussion of Soviet foreign policy by the use of a working typology; call it a set of handles or "regulating principles" *à la* Kant, if you wish. Treated metaphorically, these *modes* of policy resemble an arrangement of stops on the console of a pipe organ and are labeled as follows:

NATIONAL SECURITY

IDEOLOGY   LEADERSHIP   ECONOMICS

Extending the metaphor, the "score" becomes the Kremlin leadership's assessment and interpretation of the world of international politics, in general and with reference to a given place and time. The "organist," a plural instrumentalist under today's "collective leadership" in the Kremlin, is the Politburo; in former times, the Tsar, Lenin, or Stalin were the one-man performers. Depending upon how the organist wants the "music" to sound, the stops are set at various intensities. The result is harmony if the *national interest* is served, disharmony if it is not.

These four modes—*National Security, Ideology, Leadership,* and *Economics*—figure to one degree or another in the determination of Russian foreign policy, depending at the same time on external circumstances and the leaders themselves who make the assessments. In a given case, only one or two modes may be involved. For example, Soviet Middle East policy need not necessarily involve Ideology. Quite the contrary. The Communist Party is outlawed in most of the dozen key Arab states; in any case, the Moslem religion is scarcely compatible with official Soviet atheism. For these reasons, the Kremlin organist, in designing a policy for expanding Soviet influence in the Middle East, obviously does not engage the stop labeled "Ideology." Instead, Ideology is deemphasized while traditional Russian National Security and the desiderata of Economics are brought into play. Another example of stop settings is illustrated by the "events" in Czechoslovakia in August 1968. Here, interestingly, *all* modes were involved, but to varying degrees. Although the Soviet decision on Czechoslovakia was orchestrated with a combination of all four modes of Soviet response, it is this author's contention that two modes in particular were most crucial: National Security and Leadership.

The National Security mode is switched on, as in the Czechoslovak case, whenever Russian policy-makers deem an international situation, most often adjacent to Russian borders, to be an alleged threat to the integrity, security, and welfare of the empire. Depending upon who the leaders are making the decisions, response within the mode of Russian National Security will be effected in (1) a radical or (2) a subdued fashion. This is why, in considering Czechoslovakia, it is necessary also to discuss the factor of Leadership.

Under the party leadership of the *primus inter pares*, Leonid Ilyich Brezhnev, the post-Khrushchev alliance of various interest blocs (heavy industry, defense industry, professional party *apparatchiki,* and the "Young Turk" faction) constitute, in fact, a group of political leaders who are defending not only their country's national interest as they see it, but also their personal careers, positions of power in the hierarchy, and their various interlocking "vested interests." The replacement in October 1964 of Nikita Sergeyevich Khrushchev, who had been taking Soviet policy along a strikingly moderate course, is of immense importance. More radical and uncompromising Soviet actions on the foreign front in the post-Khrushchev period—and not only with respect to Czechoslovakia but also to Vietnam, the Middle East, and elsewhere—cannot be understood without considering the emerging policies under Khrushchev's leadership in the closing months of his ten-year reign.

Within the mode of National Security, as was mentioned earlier, either a *radical* or *subdued* response is a possible course of action. If radical, the armed forces are given their marching orders by the civilian politicians; if subdued, various kinds of pressure will be applied—diplomatic, economic, and sometimes the implied threat of military intervention. For reasons to be discussed later, the radical course was chosen for Czechoslovakia in the summer of 1968 and for coping with Red China's alleged "border intrusions" in 1969.

What to do?—*Shto delat?*—the perennial Russian question—has always confronted Russian leaders in a particularly agonizing manner in their assessments of the world situation at any given moment.* But uppermost

---

*Often repeated in Russian literature, even in titles, *Shto delat?* is as common a phenomenon on the Russian cultural scene as, say, the garrulous Rudins, the ingenuous Tatyanas, or the auto-frustrated Oblomovs. For example, it was the title of a famous novel by Chernyshevsky, an equally famous essay by Lenin, and a less known but nonetheless trail-blazing pamphlet by the "first Bolshevik," Peter Nikitich Tkachev. In Russia, the mere asking of the question implies a situation that has too long floundered without remedy. Often the remedy which is recommended by the reformers is therefore radical, the situation having become radically intolerable. The most recent political example of this came at the end of the reign of Khrushchev in 1964 when a bleak picture confronted Khrushchev's conspiring associates. And, as it turned out, Khrushchev's successors were to make some radical readjustments.

in their minds has been the preservation and augmentation of Russian power on the Eurasian Continent and especially in areas immediately adjacent to Russia's borders. A complex of concerns involving National Security and ultimately national interest has always been paramount in the answer to the question What to do? in crucial situations—whether Russia was ruled by a half-mad martinet, Paul I; an idealist and mystic, Alexander I; a "family man" with *extra-domo* ambitions for his Mother Russia, Nicholas II; or a scheming political adventurer and non-Russian named Djugashvili (Stalin). Despite the differences in their characters, their times, and their policies, all of these leaders were conscious of the enormous power represented by the Russias conceived against the background of Russian geography and Russian geopolitics.

NOTES

1. *Newsweek* (May 12, 1969), p. 52.
2. Three cogent treatments of the problem are Kurt London (ed.), *The Soviet Union—A Half-century of Communism* (Baltimore: Johns Hopkins Press, 1968); Adam B. Ulam, *Expansion and Coexistence—The History of Soviet Foreign Policy, 1917–67,* (New York: Praeger, 1968); and DeVere E. Pentony (ed.), *Soviet Behavior in World Affairs: Communist Foreign Policies* (San Francisco: Chandler, 1962). There are, of course, many others. See Bibliography at the end of the present book.

PART ONE

DIVERGENCE

CHAPTER I

Grounds for Divergence

There are at present two great nations in the world which seem to tend towards the same end, although they start from different points. I allude to the Russians and the Americans . . . Their starting point is different and their courses are not the same, yet each of them appears to be marked by the will of heaven to sway the destinies of half the globe.

— ALEXIS DE TOCQUEVILLE, Democracy in America (1840)

The two countries, the United States and the Soviet Union, live in separate worlds—geographical, political, cultural, economic, and geopolitical. In terms of longitude, the U.S.S.R. is 180° or halfway around the globe from America; the boy who thinks he is digging a hole to China in his backyard in America is instead aiming in the direction of Russia. This geographical remoteness is only partially compensated by the fact that the two countries narrowly miss touching each other at the top of the world, where the U.S.-Soviet border slips between Big Diomede Island (U.S.S.R.) and Little Diomede Island (U.S.) in the Bering Strait. But even at this point of encounter in the Arctic, the two do not actually touch; they merely reach out toward each other like Jehovah pointing at the outstretched hand of Adam in the fresco by Michelangelo. In terms of latitude, the southern border of the U.S.S.R. corresponds roughly to the U.S.-Canadian border. A line drawn due west from the Russian capital of Moscow intersects the North American Continent through the middle of Hudson Bay!

Despite these and other geographic and climatic differences, the United States and the Soviet Union are sometimes thought to resemble each other in several respects. Both are large industrialized nation-states with a federative structure. Both have populations over the 200 million mark. Both are said to have a "frontier spirit" ingrained in their national characters, Siberia serving as the analogue to the American Far West. Some even allege that the sheer enormity of the two countries—the U.S.S.R. is the world's largest country, the U.S., the third largest—has introduced a common ingredient into the character of their citizens: in the American, a marked tendency toward love of "vastness" and exaggeration, or ballyhoo; in the Russian, the same penchant,* summed up by the Russian term for it, *vranyo*. The alleged similarities are multiplied further.

The comparison-makers, sad to say, are given to naive wishful thinking. Although both New Yorkers and Muscovites stop on the red and go on the green,** and the cars crossing the intersections resemble their transworld counterparts, these and other likenesses are largely superficial. The fact is that the two countries are profoundly dissimilar, even in the very areas in which well-meaning people think they see similarities.

The American and the Russian Economies

To say, for example, that the Soviet Union, like the U.S., is an industrialized nation is true, so far as the statement goes. But to imply that any meaningful socio-economic or "psycho-social" similarity can thereby be established is patently false. For one thing, Soviet industrialization is not as extensive as the American (see Table 1).

The Soviet gross national product is about half that of America's; the G.N.P. of eleven northern states of the U.S. surpasses that of the whole U.S.S.R. The Soviets themselves admit in their statistical handbooks that productivity on their kolkhozes and sovkhozes (collective and state farms) is only about a third of what it is on American privately owned farms. Even the highly touted mechanization of Soviet farms leaves much to be desired despite official Soviet *vranyo* about the "world's greatest production of tractors and modern agricultural machines" and the advantages of socialized agriculture.[1] The fact is that the large Soviet production of agricultural machines has had surprisingly little effect on the productivity of the Soviet farm employees (all citizens are, in a sense, employees of the state) or on the standard of living in the village. Negligence of the machines and shortages of spare parts put fully a quarter of them out of action for long periods. Nearly half of the villages still lack electricity as well as other essential facilities that are taken for granted even in the Ozark

---

*Hence, naively, Sorokin states: "Psychologically, this continental character favors broad mental horizons, vast perspectives . . . [There is] mutual mental, cultural, and social congeniality between the two nations"—(Pitirim A. Sorokin, *Russia and the United States* (New York: Dutton, 1944). Written when "strange-alliance" friendship of the U.S. and U.S.S.R. was in full swing, Sorokin's book is full of such examples of congeniality including alleged American and Soviet "agreement" on the definition and application of democracy.

**The Chinese Red Guards have demanded that mainland China dispense with the Soviet-American "bourgeois" custom of red/stop, green/go, proposing instead green/stop, red/go—red presumably being a forward-looking color.

TABLE 1.   Annual Output of Selected Industrial Commodities in the U.S.S.R. (actual or planned) and the U.S. (1967)

	U.S.S.R.		U.S.	
	1968	1969[a]	1970[a]	1967
Electricity (thou. mill. kwh)	638	687	800	1,384
Oil (mill. tons)	309	327	345	435
Gas (thou. mill. cu. m.)	170	186	215[b]	514
Coal (mill. tons)	600	595	665	511
Iron (mill. tons)	79	–	94	78
Steel (mill. tons)	107	113	124	118
Plastics (thou. tons)	1,293	c1,500	1,800[c]	5,680[d]
Chemical fibers (thou. tons)	554	–	700[e]	1,700
Mineral fertilizer (mill. tons)	43	47	62	62
Cement (mill. tons)	88	92	100	67
Motor vehicles (thou.)	801	847	1,360	10,330[d]
Passenger cars (thou.)	280	344	600[f]	8,598[d]
Tractors (thou.)	423	449	600	331[d]
Cotton fabrics (mill. sq. m.)	6,115	–	9,000[g]	8,400
Refrigerators (mill.)	3	–	5–6	6[h]

NOTES: [a]Planned figures.
[b]Revised target: originally 225,000 mill. cu. m.
[c]Revised target: originally 2,200,000 tons.
[d]Data for 1966.
[e]Revised target: originally 780,000 tons.
[f]Revised target: originally 700,000 passenger cars.
[g]Revised target: originally 9,500 mill. sq. m.
[h]Data for 1965.

SOURCES: *Pravda*, October 11, 1967, and December 11, 1968; *Izvestiya*, January 26, 1969; *Bulletin* of the Institute for the Study of the U.S.S.R., February 1969, p. 27; *UN Statistical Yearbook 1968; Statistical Abstract of the United States 1968.*

Mountains.* Likewise, mail delivery to these areas is slow. The horse and wagon is still a common means of travel in the Russian countryside, as a province party official on a routine "inspection" explained recently in the journal *Partiinaya Zhizn* (*Party Life*). The irate "Inspector General" reported that it had taken him three days to get to a certain village, N-sk, 200 miles away.

One of the earmarks of industrialization and modern urban culture in general is the automobile. And yet the rush hour in any one of the half dozen large cities of European Russia, as I can personally testify, lasts all

*A delegate to the Twenty-third Party Congress (1966), a milkmaid, complained that during the course of a single shift, she often had to carry as much as one and a half tons of cow feed because the automatic seed conveyers were out of order.

of twenty minutes. At other times one sees a fair number of buses and trucks, but very few taxicabs, and only a miniscule number of ordinary automobiles, most of which in any case are chauffeur-driven "official" limousines. Not only do the Russians have probably the shortest and lightest European rush hour, they also have a very low per capita ownership of automobiles (almost the lowest in all of Europe). They produce 250,000 private motor cars for a population of 240 million, or about one car per 1,000 people (contrasted to the U.S. figure of one car per every 23 people).* Moreover, total Soviet road mileage is only about a quarter of U.S. mileage, although the U.S.S.R. has a territory about two and a half times as large.[2] A current Soviet joke (*anekdota*) concerns the limited use of automobiles in the U.S.S.R.:

> TROLLEY-BUS CONDUCTOR: Step to the rear, please, gentlemen. Step to the rear.
>
> PASSENGER: We are not gentlemen. We're Comrades.
>
> TROLLEY-BUS CONDUCTOR: That is impossible. Comrades don't ride on trolley-buses. They ride in big black limousines.

The U.S. and the Soviet Political Systems

As to the federative structure of the Soviet Union, the U.S.S.R. is perhaps best characterized as a *pseudo*-federation, as one U.S. Soviet expert has put it.[3] First, unlike the American federation, the U.S.S.R. is multinational. Several whole national Republics are included within its borders. For example, the Uzbek Soviet Socialist Republic contains mostly Uzbeks; Kazakhs live in the Kazakh S.S.R.; Tadzhiks in the Tadzhik S.S.R., and so on. But even here the apparent "national autonomy" is illusory. The Great Russians, Ukrainians (Little Russians), and Belorussians in that order dominate the party and government hierarchies in these Republics, as they do in the lesser political and administrative subdivisions throughout of the U.S.S.R. (see note, p. 15). This occurs despite the fact that in many cases these three national groups constitute only a tiny minority within a given area under their authority.

Josef Stalin conceptualized the idea of pseudo-national autonomy quite candidly when he said that the essence of the Soviet state lies in its *Great Russian ruling core*** and that no national Republic could be expected to

---

*The cars, to the degree they are available, are expensive. The Volga, the equivalent of a Ford Falcon, costs 5,602r (a Falcon costs about half that), a Soviet worker's salary for almost five years!

**Shortly after V-E Day (May 8, 1945), Stalin, at a Kremlin banquet on May 24 (according to PRAVDA, May 25), proposed the following toast: "I should like to drink a toast to the health of our Soviet people and, above all, to the Russian people. I drink first of all to the Russian people because they are the most outstanding nation of all

secede from the Union because "the principle of self-determination must be an instrument in the struggle for Socialism and *must be subordinated to the principles of Socialism*" (italics mine).[4] And, of course, none of the "great Soviet family" has dared or been permitted to run away from home. Nor has any Republic officially requested any additional autonomy.

The application of the Stalinist nationality principle is illustrated within the central government apparatus as well. The all-Union Supreme Soviet is divided into two houses. The lower house, called the Council of the Union (767 members), is based on proportional representation regardless of nationality. But the upper house or Council of Nationalities (750 members) is allegedly "representative" of all nations composing the U.S.S.R., no matter how small. Unfortunately, the whole democratic scheme is vitiated *de facto*, since the Supreme Soviet itself has no substantive power, meeting for only a few days twice a year, and rubber-stamping what the party-controlled regime "proposes" to it, including especially matters pertaining to foreign affairs. This is the aspect of the Soviet system that one U.S. scholar and Soviet specialist describes as "counter-weighting," in which "democratic *form* is counterweighted with totalitarian *controls*."[5] A popular *anekdota* lampoons the U.S.S.R. Supreme Soviet as a body consisting of people "half of whom are totally incapable while the other half are capable of everything."

If by federation is meant the government of a nation in which significant and substantive prerogatives are reserved to the "states" (the 15 Republics in the U.S.S.R.) within the federation vis-à-vis the "center," then the Soviet Union is far less federative than it is *centralistic*. In no meaningful way, in fact, does the Soviet structure resemble the system in the U.S. The contrasts in the political sphere have an important bearing upon the degree and type of U.S.-Soviet divergence in general.

None of the 15 Soviet Republics enjoys any significant autonomy over crucial matters touching its citizens, as is the case, for example, in the U.S. federation. Textbooks and curricula are rigidly standardized, both for elementary and secondary schools and colleges and universities; educational policy is the monopoly of the central party and government apparatus in Moscow. (In the U.S., of course, application of the federative principle of division of powers causes educational policy to be decentralized, accruing to individual institutions or to school boards and local and state administrations.) In the important area of civil, criminal, and pro-

---

the nations forming a part of the Soviet Union . . . the leading force among all the peoples of our country." For an excellent discussion of the disproportionate number of Great Russians, Ukrainians, and Belorussians in the ruling organs of the party and government in non-Slav areas (and of Great Russians in the Ukraine and Belorussia), see T. H. Rigby, *Communist Party Membership in the U.S.S.R. 1917–1967* (Princeton, N.J.: Princeton University Press), 1968, chapter 12, pp. 364–399.

cedural law, the corresponding three types of codes are standardized from one end of the U.S.S.R. to the other and are patterned after the R.S.F.S.R. (the Russian Soviet Federated Socialist Republic), the largest and preponderantly Great Russian and most influential "founder" Republic of the U.S.S.R. Moreover, major economic decisions are made in Moscow. The central government's monopoly over important areas of Soviet life ensures and protects the equally monopolistic control of Moscow over the State's foreign policy.

A peculiar feature of the quasi-federative Soviet system is the fact that each of the 15 Soviet Republics possesses a Ministry of Foreign Affairs. Such an institution, were it viable, would be more characteristic of a *confederation* rather than a federation, where the central government has the sole power to conduct foreign relations. But as it turns out, the foreign offices in the Soviet Republics appear to have nothing to do. Which raises the question, Why does the "Stalin Constitution" give each of them such a ministry? One Western scholar has hypothesized that Stalin assigned the ministries to the then 16 Soviet Republics in 1944 in preparation for the Soviet demand that the U.S.S.R. be awarded 16 seats in the United Nations, then in the planning stage.[6] Another possibility was that Stalin was banking on the popularity the Soviet system would allegedly have with neighboring states in Asia; with a ministry, each of the Central Asian Republics of the U.S.S.R. could undertake various interstate matters (which, however, would be of little practical importance in the all-Union sense— minor border affairs affecting tourists, for example).[7]

Needless to say, none of the states of the United States has any authority in the *administration* of foreign affairs, because, in a federation foreign relations are monopolized by the central government. However, in the U.S. Senate, where each of the 50 states is equally represented, the 100 senators have a strong voice (power to "advise and consent") in the area of foreign affairs. These prerogatives of the senators from each of the states likewise dovetail with the semi-autonomous nature of the states within the U.S. federative system, and results in a high degree of "decentralized" discussion and criticism of an Administration's foreign policy.

Perhaps the greatest dissimilarity between Soviet and American politics, however, lies in the area of the Soviet's one-party dictatorship (provided in Article 126 of the U.S.S.R. Constitution). This institution immediately distinguishes the totalitarian Soviet regime from liberal democracies in the non-Communist world, where two or more political parties freely compete with one another. The "core of all organizations," social and political, is the 13-million-member Communist Party of the Soviet Union (C.P.S.U.). The C.P.S.U. is actually a machine for knitting the red thread of the party line ubiquitously into the policies of schools, factories, farms, editorial offices, theater and dance groups, the Republics and soviets (or local governing councils), and the ministries (including, of course, the foreign ministry). Moreover, the C.P.S.U. Politburo, consisting today of eleven full members, acts as a powerful "kitchen cabinet" for setting policy, foreign and domestic, within the all-Union party and government structures, although it is not mentioned at all in the Soviet Constitution.

"Anthropological" Differences

Another of the alleged similarities between the Soviet Union and the United States has an anthropological or, better, *pseudo*-anthropological flavor: the notion that Americans and Russians have common traits of character which would lead them to see eye to eye on most problems. One of these traits, a free-wheeling "pioneering spirit" and "wanderlust," is supposed to stem from the similar frontier environments represented by the American Far West and Russian Siberia. This trait is often referred to in exuberant expressions of American and Soviet friendship, an example of which was during Apollo 8 commander Col. Frank Borman's nine-day visit to the U.S.S.R. in July 1969, when the American space man spoke of the two nations' mutual "pioneer" experiences in settling their countries. Unfortunately, the comparison is weak at several points.

First, the American West acted as a strong magnet to the pioneers,* who undertook their journey *spontaneously*, sometimes in search of gold, sometimes in pursuit of a new life. Whatever their individual motivations, the pioneers viewed the West as the proverbial pot of gold at the end of the rainbow. Not so the Russian settlers to Siberia.** Not even the rich deposits of Siberian gold belonged to them.

Siberia was—and is—for the most part a forbidding place. Its winter lasts eight months with temperatures dropping at times to as low as —80°F! In the days of the Tsar, it was the location of countless places of exile. Moreover, most of the settlers who went there were Cossack soldiers or civilians sent on government assignment. As to gold: whereas the gold of the American West belonged to private prospectors who panned it themselves, Siberian gold belonged to the Tsarist state mines. In the Soviet period, under Lenin

---

*The Russians have even had to borrow our word "pioneer" to manufacture the Russian word *pionyer*.

**Siberia (*Sibir* in Russian) apparently stems from the name of a tribe of Huns called Sibiri or Seberi who lived beyond the Urals. "Siberian" (*Sibirnii*) sometimes carries in Russian the meaning of "penal" or even "evil." Cf. A. G. Preobrazhensky, *Etymological Dictionary of the Russian Language* (New York: Columbia University Press, 1951), p. 283. For an interesting and illustrated account of Siberia, see Dean Conger, "Siberia—Russia's Frozen Frontier," *The National Geographic*, Vol. 131, No. 3 (March), 1967, pp. 297–347.

and Stalin, and to a lesser extent their successors, Siberia brings to mind for Soviet citizens labor camps and exile. There is a sense in which Dostoyevsky's *Memoirs of the House of the Dead* (1862) leads with terrible continuity to Solzhenitsyn's *A Day in the Life of Ivan Denisovich* (1962), written exactly a hundred years after Dostoyevsky's equally horrifying description of Siberian exile.

Not all of Siberia, of course, is a trackless wasteland. Exceptions are parts of western Siberia, south central Siberia around Lake Baikal, and the Maritime Province area in the southern portion of Russia's Pacific littoral. Numerous Russians have volunteered to settle in these areas or have been assigned there in recent years for the purpose of opening up virgin lands or taking jobs in the comparatively new or ever-expanding industrial complexes at such remote places as Komsomolsk, Khabarovsk, Tselinograd, Novosibirsk, Irkutsk, and so on. But, as revealed in various press reports, letters to the editor, and conversations with Soviet citizens, some of the initially enthusiastic volunteers going to settle in Siberia (say, for example, to work on the Virgin Lands project in Tselinograd Province) soon became disillusioned by the appalling lack of provisions in the new settlements or by the harsh climate, or by both. Feedback to relatives and friends apparently has not created in the folks back home much of a desire to seek a new life in remote Siberia.*

Except for the rare but nonetheless thickly settled oases in the Siberian "white desert" (for example, in western and south central portions, and in the Maritime Province), Siberia remains a very thinly populated area which, by no stretch of the imagination, can be compared to the American Far West. The West was settled *en masse* and soon underwent extensive and intensive development.

To say to a Russian, "Go *east*, young man!" would be tantamount to leveling an insult at him.

As for the other anthropological fancy about the alleged mutual American and Russian penchant for, respectively, ballyhoo and *vranyo*, can anyone seriously maintain that this particular habit—if, indeed, it is endemic to Americans and Russians—is a monopoly held by these two large countries alone? Feelings of intense national pride and the extravagance that accompanies them are surely not the function of a nation's size—or so this author has observed on his travels to foreign countries. Quite the contrary. The Irish, the Italians, the English—all of whom live in countries of modest square mileage—are surely good matches for the citizens of larger countries

---

*One recent exception, according to the Soviet press, were the many border guards who volunteered to leave their various posts in European Russia for reassignment to the Pacific Maritime Province area and the Soviet-Manchurian border where the bloody clashes took place between Chinese and Soviet troops on March 2 and 15, 1969.

in their expression of national pride. If boastful patriotism and a sense of national *grandeur* were guarantees of mutual friendship, the Israelis and Egyptians or the Irish and the English would be the best of friends!

In any case, quite the opposite phenomenon has been noticed by Russian-speaking travelers and exchange students sojourning in the U.S.S.R.: namely, a marked tendency for Russians to write off their country for dozens of years since 1917, or at least to discard these years, on the grounds that they were times of intense and needless suffering (during the purges, periods of starvation, collectivization, forced resettlement, political Stalinism, and so forth, the victims numbering into the millions). Hardly a foundation upon which to build an intense love of country!

Despite their awareness of the many "negative phenomena" (a current euphemism used in the U.S.S.R.) during the half-century of Communist rule, however, most Russians are undoubtedly patriotic if scratched deeply enough. But to say that because of the vastness of their country, Russians engage in patriotic *vranyo* and that therefore they are "like us" is plainly false. Both Americans and Russians may tell tall stories, build tall buildings, and display a kind of vastness about their own countries. But it is doubtful that this has stemmed from the fact that the U.S. has four and Russia eleven time zones within their borders. Moreover, size in no way promises friendship and sympathy either between these two countries or other large ones.

As a matter of fact, rather than developing self-confidence or a "superiority complex" in the Russian, the tremendous lateral extent of his country and the various elements in his country's history have, if anything, *encouraged deep-seated feelings of insecurity*. This in part results from Russia's precariously exposed location on the Eurasian Continent (see below, pp. 25–26. By contrast, the United States is well situated and well protected on both its western and eastern marches by nothing less than the two largest oceans in the world.

American and Russian History and Culture

Well-meaning comparison-makers have further maintained that both Russia and the United States are "young" countries; this supposedly has created grounds for "common understanding" and convergence. The comparison is established apparently on the basis of the "mere 50-year history" of *Soviet* Russia since 1917 compared to the "mere 175-year history" of America since its Revolution. But here again the procedure is faulty in several respects. In the first place, Russian history is far too old for a post-1917 chronological framework to suffice. Russia, dating back to Kievan

Rus in the ninth and tenth centuries, is some 1,000 years old and has a rich and variegated history with traditions that in most respects bear no resemblance whatsoever to American history (see Table 2). In fact, if one considers America's European forebears and their history to be crucial for an understanding of America history per se,* then the history of Russia must be further distinguished from that of America. Russia is part of the *Eastern Byzantine civilization,* and until the eighteenth century—in other words, for most of its history—it was cut off from Central and Western European influences.

Capsulized** in Table 2 are some of the contrasts between American and Russian civilization, the bases for divergence, which largely stem from Russia's relatively long isolation from the rest of Europe. It would go far beyond the scope of this book to delve deeply into the many contrasting features of Russian and American (and Western) culture and the arts. A few examples may at least illustrate the gulf which separates the two worlds in these areas.

Henri Bergson has said that music is the most accurate sensor of the inner feelings of people. That being so, the "Russian soul" is indeed strikingly different from the American soul. There is simply no analogue in the U.S. or the West generally for the work of Modest Petrovich Moussorgsky— for example, his opera *Boris Godunov* and piano suite *Pictures at an Exhibition* are not only unique *sui generis,* but uniquely Russian. The same might be said of Tchaikovsky's *Fourth Symphony,* Scriabin's *Prometheus: a Poem of Fire,* Stravinsky's *The Rite of Spring* and *Petrushka,* Prokofiev's *Scythian Suite* and his film score and oratorio *Alexander Nevsky,* and the *Fifth* and *Thirteenth Symphonies* of that quintessential Russian composer, Dmitri Shostakovich.

In the literary field the Russian genius is equally specialized and unique. Gogol, Dostoyevsky, Tolstoy, Turgeniev, and Chekhov, to name only a few, have produced works of uniquely Russian feeling and inspiration. Chekhov, for example, is so "Russian" that his plays for this reason are often hard to interpret on Western stages. The poems of Pushkin, Lermontov, Blok, Mayakovsky, Pasternak, Tiutchev, or even Voznessensky and Yevtushenko are so permeated with Russianisms (in language and spirit) and an indescribable Russian irony that they are nearly untranslatable.

Needless to say, the religious art of Russia is totally without Western

*The philosopher of history who wisely said that "the present is the oldest time" might also say that America is extremely "old" in the sense of representing an accumulation of many centuries of development and a maturing of many processes derived from prior European civilizations. Thus, Gertrude Stein once observed that America is the world's "oldest country."

**For extensive treatments of Russian history, see recommended readings in the Bibliography.

TABLE 2. Contrasting American and Russian Historical Experiences

AMERICA	RUSSIA
Its history begins with the Jamestown settlement in 1607.	Its history dates back to the establishment of Kievan Rus in the ninth and tenth centuries.
Religion is most commonly Protestant; after the mid-seventeenth century the church is increasingly separate from the state and many religious sects are permitted to develop.	Russian (Greek) Orthodoxy is incorporated into the Caesaro-Papist Byzantine state in which the Tsar is a divine ruler who dominates the church through the secular-appointed Procurator-General of the Holy Synod; only one religion is tolerated.
After the adoption of the Constitution in 1787, and with steady although agonizingly slow progress, America advances down the road to liberal democracy including political freedom, free press, separation of powers, rival political groups and parties, *habeas corpus* and due process of law, and so on.	The three principles of Tsarist government (crystallized in the works of the Tsarist spokesman K. P. Pobedonostsev) are *Orthodoxy, Autocracy,* and *Nationality*. These three principles are transformed under Soviet rule after 1917 into *Communist Orthodoxy, One-party* or *One-man Rule,* and *Great Russian Nationalism*. The secret police (founded by Ivan the Terrible) serve as the protectors of absolutism whether Tsarist or Soviet with all the attendant police-state institutions of labor camps, internal spy and informer network, censorship and jamming, and so on.
The United States, although apparently "young," represents ripened Greco-Roman and Judaeo-Christian Western civilization. The Protestant Reformation and the political turmoil accompanying and following it eventually abet the development of democracy, especially as it is cultivated in North America. Thus, by the time the Industrial Revolution spreads from England to the European Continent and to America, an important degree of liberal-democratic government has already been implanted in the various Western political systems. The result is that the capital *vs.* labor struggles accompanying the later stages of industrialization are fought, in these countries, primarily by ballot rather than by attempted "workers" *coup d'états,* mass violence, or "revolution."	Russia, geographically isolated from much of Europe and distinct in its spiritual development, remained largely cut off from Western civilization, especially from the crucial Renaissance and post-Reformation political developments (e.g., Huguenot attacks on absolutistic government in France). "The giant that came last, the U.S.S.R., thus becomes industrialized in the twentieth century *before* passing into a "bourgeois" phase of political freedom and the attendant civil rights of a liberal-democratic system. The U.S.S.R. becomes an industrialized titan with a quasi-eighteenth century political structure of updated "Bourbonism"[a] including censorship, absolutism, and a privileged stratum; but instead of hereditary monarchy, a self-perpetuating oligarchy.

[a]The comparison with the Bourbons can be found in Boris Pasternak's *Doctor Zhivago*.

counterparts. Russian icons are a special product of the Russian genius and religious outlook, as an examination of the work of the monk Andrei Rublev (*ca.* 1360–1420) reveals. In modern times the secular paintings of Vrubel (1856–1910), to cite only one artist, reflect Russian legend and folklore as well as the wild demonic element one so often finds in Russian art, whether in music, literature, or the dance.

Russian essay or "publicistic" writing is peculiarly national in form and content and finds no counterpart in the works of such Western essayists as, for example, Addison and Steele, Swift, Voltaire, or Emerson. Moreover, the theological and philosophical tracts of Vladimir Soloviev (1853–1900) and Nicholas Berdyaev (1874–1948) are so characteristically Russian in their conceptions as to be instantly recognized upon the reading of, say, two unidentified paragraphs of their works. The same may be said of Alexander Hertzen (1812–1870), Vissarion Belinsky (1811–1848), Nikolai Chernyshevsky (1828–1889), and the contemporary Soviet scientist and essayist Andrei Sakharov (1921–   ).

American and Soviet Foreign Policy

In foreign policy few, if any, current comparison-makers have found or even sought any meaningful likenesses between the two countries, aside from the visible accoutrements of the superpower status of the bipolar leviathans. Instead, one may find numerous differences in their political instrumentalities and environments, not to mention differing geopolitical and historically determined circumstances. These in turn react upon the foreign policies of the two countries, often in the direction of aggravating their mutual divergence.

"A deep love of peace is the common heritage of the people of both our countries," said President Franklin D. Roosevelt during World War II. "On questions of maintaining peace, the U.S.S.R. and the U.S.A. can find a common language," said Soviet Foreign Minister Andrei Gromyko in mid-1969. Yet, the fact that both peoples yearn for peace is an obviously more important factor within a largely responsive liberal-democratic system like that of America. A well-known Western Soviet specialist has correctly observed that the "Soviet government, precisely because it remains a closed, dictatorial regime, enjoys a privilege denied to its Western opponents: the freedom to correct the results of political failure [as in Czechoslovakia] by brutal military action. . . . A regime that denies the right of opposition in principle, as the Soviets do, can retrieve a political failure by brute force far more easily than can a democratic regime."[8]

An anti-Bolshevik anarchist, about to die by a Soviet firing squad, cries out: "These new *oprichniki* [security troops of Ivan the Terrible], these master executioners of the new torture chambers. . . . Posterity will pillory the Bourbons of the Commissarocracy."

This is not to say that the human aspects of the 50-year history of Soviet foreign relations, either in its peaceful or violent modes, are a matter of utter indifference to Soviet policy-makers. Far from it. The Soviet leaders are definitely *not* devoid of national feeling or indifferent to the fate of their nation and its citizens. Indeed, it is undoubtedly true that the leaders in the Kremlin—especially in the post-Stalin period—have been sensitized and made security conscious *in the extreme* by the many grimmer aspects of past Soviet history, on both the foreign and domestic fronts (see, for example, Table 3 showing Soviet war casualties in the twentieth century).*

TABLE 3. Russian Military Engagements (Involving Casualties) in the Twentieth Century

Direct Involvement		Deaths
Russo-Japanese War	1904–05	90,000
World War I	1914–18	9,150,000
Finnish Civil War	1918	50,000
Engagements in the Baltic countries	1918–19	110,000
Civil War and intervention	1918–20	3,000,000
Soviet-Rumanian border conflicts	1918–20	(unknown)
Russo-Polish War	1920	3,000
Invasion of Georgia	1921–22	20,000
Sino-Soviet border conflicts	1929	(unknown)
Russo-Japanese border conflicts	1937–39	30,000
Russo-Finnish "Winter War"	1939–40	400,000[a]
Russo-German War (in World War II)	1941–45	20,000,000
Russo-Japanese War (in World War II)	1945 (one week)	(unknown)
Sino-Soviet border conflicts	1960–present	50–100 (approx.)
"Proxy" Involvement		Russian Casualties
Korean War	1950–53	none
Vietnam War	1964–present	none

NOTE: [a]Total casualties. Russian deaths, about 50,000; Finnish deaths, about 20,000.

SOURCES: I. A. Kurganov, *Novoye Russkoye Slovo*, November 5, 1967; *Malaya sovetskaya entsiklopediya* (3rd ed.); *The World Almanac and Book of Facts*; E. H. Carr, *The Bolshevik Revolution—1917–1923*, 2 vols. (New York: Macmillan, 1951).

*Professor I. A. Kurganov estimates that domestic travail in the U.S.S.R. (deaths in periods of starvation, during collectivization and the purges, in concentration camps, etc.) took 20,000,000 lives, or as many Soviet citizens as perished in World War II. A Russian word-frequency dictionary published in the U.S.S.R. in the 1960s throws some light on Russian consciousness of war and peace, suffering and tragedy. For example, using broadcasts, newspapers, plays, films, novels, etc., to count the frequency of adjectives, pronouns, verbs, and nouns, the Russian researchers found that "war" is a much more frequently used noun than "peace" and "happiness" in the Soviet materials; "toil," "war," "world," "history," and "order" are all used more frequently than "joy," "peace," and "freedom." Lest the reader draw too many hasty conclusions from these examples, he is invited to examine the dictionary closely himself: E. Shteinfeldt (ed.), *Chastotnii slovar sovremennovo russkovo literaturnovo yazyka* (Word Count in Modern Literary Russian) (Moscow: Izdatelstvo 'Progress,' n.d.).

On the obvious assumption that a considerable share of their motivation stems from national pride and desire for accomplishment and glory in ministering to the national interest, the Soviet leaders can be expected to seek to reduce the factor of human sacrifice by their own nationals in the international arena to the barest minimum. Accordingly, Foreign Minister Andrei Gromyko boasted to the U.S.S.R. Supreme Soviet in 1968 that the Soviet government was leading its people into their *third* consecutive "serene" and warless decade. Soviet listeners to the Foreign Minister's address (which was carried nationwide on Soviet TV) undoubtedly perceived that Gromyko was actually striking a not-so-subtle contrast with certain other foreign states whose people *have* been (or still are) involved in war, and were so engaged more than once since the end of World War II.* The great furor stirred up in the Soviet press over the 90-plus deaths of Soviet border guards in the skirmishes with Communist China on March 2 and 15, in May and June and on August 13, 1969, is a reflection of this Soviet concern for the lives of *Soviet* soldiers lost in international clashes.**

The essential problem in foreign affairs confronting the Soviet leaders since Stalin's death, in fact, has been not only (1) how to strengthen the security of the Soviet borders and internal security and (2) how to ensure the loyalty of Russia's various contiguous satellites, but also (3) how to extend Soviet influence throughout the world *without directly involving the U.S.S.R. and its own soldiers in combat.* (Incidentally, note that this list of three post-Stalin objectives as a whole finds no clear analogy in U.S. foreign policy.) As will be demonstrated later in this book, it is this intense Soviet preoccupation with national security on the one hand and the expansionist thrust often accompanying it on the other which cause the deepening of the channels of divergence separating the Soviet Union and the United States.

*Involvement by the U.S. in each of the two major wars since World War II with large attendant casualties (the Korean and Vietnam Wars) is the largest in scale for any country in any conflict since 1945. These two wars have lasted far longer than any of the others in the postwar period—the Korean War three, the Vietnam War over eight years dating from January 1961. They have also been far more costly in human life and property than any of the other postwar conflicts. Note that the U.S.S.R. was careful to keep out of these two wars while at the same time underwriting them and regarding them as "proxy" wars serving Soviet interests. There have been some 70 conflicts since World War II.

**Upon his return to the U.S. after a nine-day stay in the U.S.S.R. in July 1969, U.S. astronaut Col. Frank Borman referred to the "medical conservatism" of Soviet space-flight doctors who have apparently shown more reluctance than their American counterparts in approving more advanced types of manned space flights (for example, of the Apollo type). This conservatism may well stem from a Russian hypersensitivity about risky enterprises which might result in loss of life of Russian cosmonauts, two of whom have already perished, one on a space flight. The Soviet moon shot on July 13, 1969, just three days before the successful U.S. Apollo 11 manned moon mission, was unmanned.

Geopolitical Differences

We have already mentioned that Russia is 180° around the globe from the United States. This fact need not in itself establish any important divergence between the two countries. Australia, after all, is 130° around the world from the United Kingdom, but no major divergence exists between these two English-speaking members of the British Commonwealth. However, a closer look at Russia's *geographical* and *geopolitical* setting reveals a number of significant differences between Russia and America which *do* bear upon their diverse behavior in the modern world.

Russia is a semi-Asian (geographically, two-thirds Asian), semi-European multinational state. It is composed today of more than 100 nationalities, some 80 linguistic groups, and a population of 240 million. But as has already been mentioned, Russia is ruled essentially by only three of these many nationalities—the Great Russians, the Ukrainians, and the Belorussians. These groups compose about 55 percent, 20 percent, and 5 percent of the total population, respectively.* Besides living together in large entities in European Russia from ancient times to the present, they are today distributed from one end of the U.S.S.R. to the other (in some places as tiny minorities) and hold the key positions in the party and government in all 15 Soviet Republics.

Russia is positioned at the top and middle of Eurasia. Wrapped around 6,000 miles of latitude, the country resembles a huge crown of the Eurasian "tooth" whose roots are the Indo-China Peninsula, India, and the Arabian Peninsula. The twin-headed eagle of the Tsarist insignia—one of its heads looking west, the other east—symbolized this crucial midposition and latitudinal spread of Russia on what Mackinder correctly called the "World-Island."

Like its Tsarist predecessor, the U.S.S.R. is the largest single and continuous intercontinental empire in the world.[9] "It is not a state," runs an old Russian proverb, "but a world." Which involves hazards: the world's longest and most exposed frontiers, and the additional liability of there being only limited access to or protection by the sea.

The American geographer Chauncey Harris once told his class at the University of Chicago (of which I was a member) that Russia is "landlocked *by* the 'C's' and *from* the seas." The first "C" is iCe. Only a few Russian seaports remain open all year round—for example, on the Black Sea, in some Pacific inlets, and at Murmansk in the Arctic. Unfortunately, these ports possess mostly second-rate harbors and are, in any case, located far from the main centers of Russian civilization.[10] Furthermore, where

*An interesting amalgam of the three national groups may be found in the Politburo and Central Committee of the C.P.S.U. in Moscow in post-Khrushchev Russia.

Russia *can* exit to the sea without striking ice, there are foreign powers holding the keys to the gates. Constantinople (Turkey) stands at the exit from the Black Sea into the Mediterranean; Copenhagen (Denmark) watches over the exit from the Baltic Sea; the Caspian Sea (U.S.S.R.) is an inland body of water with no exit; the Chosen Strait (Korea), an exit south from the vital Russian seaport of Vladivostok to the Chinese littoral and beyond, is guarded by the North Koreans and Japanese. Thus, Russia is "land-locked by the 'C's.'"

Russia's geographical and geopolitical predicament has caused a number of characteristics to enter its basic grand strategy. Under both Tsars and Commissars, Russia has traditionally sought egress from its land-based imprisonment. This in turn has caused its foreign ministers to build any number of "bridges" or steps to the outside world. Whether by exerting pressure (sometimes military as well as diplomatic) or courting favor by offering various economic inducements, Russia has sought ways to penetrate the ice-free Mediterranean with its exits into the Atlantic and through the Suez Canal south into the Indian Ocean; to gain access to the Pacific Ocean (at Japan's and China's expense); and to control the Baltic Sea. Much of contemporary Soviet policy in the Near East and along the whole Mediterranean littoral bears the stamp of this traditional Russian effort, which in turn is prompted by its geographical/geopolitical predicament. The same may be said of the Soviet's jealous guarding of its Pacific Maritime Province in the face of the threat represented by mainland China, which is presently rattling its sabers and assuming an irredentist posture with respect to the almost 600,000 square miles of Soviet territory that it claims belongs to China. In some ways, Soviet Russia's extraordinary advances in rocketry (the U.S.S.R. put in orbit the world's first artificial satellite) may be attributed to the fact that intercontinental rockets over-leap boundaries, oceans, and landmasses, and represent in themselves a form of egress.

Russia's extensive frontiers with its many foreign neighbors present a mixed picture of assets and liabilities—a total geographical and geopolitical picture that makes a striking contrast to that of the United States, which borders on only two (friendly) countries. On the asset side, long stretches of Russia's southern border—for example, in Soviet Central Asia—are well protected by scorching deserts or chains of lofty mountains with few passes cutting through them. The 4,592-mile* serpentine border, excluding the nearly 2,500-mile southern frontier of the Soviet puppet state of Outer Mongolia (the Mongolian People's Republic), which separates the U.S.S.R. from mainland China is, at present, *more of an asset to Russia than to*

---

*After the appearance in the Western press of many differing figures for the length of the Sino-Soviet border, Soviet Foreign Minister Gromyko (on July 10, 1969) finally gave the authoritative mileage shown here (in kilometers, as stated by Gromyko, it is 7,395 km.).

China. The reason for this is that Russia is highly industrialized, whereas China is not. Russian rocket and conventional forces and military equipment are presently superior in quality to those of the Chinese, both as a whole and specifically with reference to the border area, although Chinese ground forces may outnumber those of the Russians. Consequently, Soviet defense of its side of the long Far Eastern frontier (both in the Central Asian and Manchurian sectors) is immeasurably stronger than China's defense of its side. In Central Asia, China is disadvantaged by the fact that its sensitive nuclear installations at Lop Nor in Sinkiang Province are 500 miles from the Soviet Kazakhstan border. (As a result, the Chinese are said to be moving their Lop Nor plants 300 miles further to the south, to Tibet.)

Still, Russia and China face a common disadvantage. Mostly flat land areas are situated between them at many points of contact in the Far East. This lack of barriers makes it easier for either country to penetrate the other. Moreover, the Chinese capital of Peking is located a scant 340 miles south of the southern border of the Soviet puppet state of Outer Mongolia. Furthermore, the strategic Chinese province of Manchuria adjoining the Soviet Maritime Province can be penetrated by merely crossing the Amur and Ussuri rivers or their tributaries (the Argun, the Sungari, and others).

The meandering Amur, called by the Russians the "Volga of the East,"* is 2,690 miles long (only six other rivers in the world are longer) and varies in width from 700 yards to from one to three miles at its widest point upriver from Khabarovsk. Flowing at a leisurely two-mile-an-hour rate, in subzero temperatures the river freezes over for some five months out of the year, at times solidly enough to permit vehicular crossings, including armored divisions.

The Ussuri, 560 miles long and the scene of the serious and bloody Sino-Soviet border clashes of March 1969, is similar to the Amur in several respects and is equally strategic. Because the Ussuri's gradient is low, it possesses a weak current, and hence it too freezes over solidly for almost half the year. However, it is sandier than the Amur, and has undergone cutting and filling to such an extent that numerous islands have been built up on either side of or athwart its *thalweg* (the middle of the main channel, which constitutes the boundary line between states). It was on one of these one-mile-long uninhabited silt deposits, Damansky/Chenpao (Treasure) Island, that the border clashes took place in March 1969. Casualties on both sides are believed to have numbered into the hundreds. (Damansky is presently garrisoned by the Russians.)

The Ussuri River possesses as much strategic importance as the Amur, perhaps even more. It forms the Chinese-Russian border adjacent to the crucial stretch of the Trans-Siberian Railroad after it bends south from Khabarovsk on its way to the terminus at the vital ice-free port of Vladi-

---

*The Amur was once known as the "River of Friendship" in the palmy days of ostentatious Sino-Soviet friendship, before the Sino-Soviet cold war set in after 1960.

vostok. The most important industrial, defense, and population centers of the entire Soviet Far East are, in fact, located either along the lower reaches of the Amur River or along the entire length of the Ussuri. Similarly, China's own sensitive industrialized region of Manchuria is bordered on the north and east by these river boundaries.

It is no wonder that rivergoing Soviet gunboats of up to 1,000 tons gross patrol the Ussuri River and the wide reaches of the Amur River from their bases at Khabarovsk[11] or that both the Chinese and Soviet border guards keep their carbines, automatic rifles, mortars, and even artillery and tanks, at the ready lest a major violation of the river borders be initiated by the other neighbor.

At the present time, the Soviets appear clearly to have the commanding position in the Far East and Central Asia relative to China. Illustrating this is a contemporary *anekdota* that I heard recently in the U.S.S.R. as told to me by a young aspirant for the Soviet diplomatic service. It goes like this:

SOVIET BORDER GUARD (peering through binoculars): What are those Chinese tanks maneuvering near our border?

CHINESE BORDER GUARD: They are our first-line defense.

SOVIET BORDER GUARD: And that single tank coming up from the rear?

CHINESE BORDER GUARD: That is our reserves.

Not an uproariously funny story surely—Soviet *anekdoty* rarely are—but one that does indicate, verbally at least, erstwhile Soviet unconcern about the present-day status of Chinese Far Eastern and Central Asian defenses. We shall consider later whether a similar pooh-poohing attitude toward China may be found within the Soviet Politburo itself. Recently, Soviet *anekdoty* about China have become more serious-minded, less ridiculing with respect to China. One goes like this. Peking wants to surrender tens of millions of its own soldiers to the Russian army. Mao sends an ultimatum: "Surrender or else." Twenty-four hours later 10 million Chinese soldiers cross the Soviet border and lay down their arms. Then the Soviet Politburo receives a new ultimatum: "Give in immediately or tomorrow another 50 million soldiers will surrender to you." Jokes aside, Mark Gayn of *The Chicago Daily News* reported from Moscow in September 1969 that he heard from a high-ranking diplomat of another Communist country that Brezhnev had informed Gomulka that the Chinese *actually* had such a strategy—to produce a breakdown of the Soviets' food supply and housing facilities, which are already marginal.

On Russia's western flank is the low-lying central Russian plain bordered on the north, west, and south by nearly a dozen different foreign states—a formidable liability of geography for Russia. Under both Tsars and Commissars, Russia has chosen to cope with this problem more often than not, as we shall presently see, by transgressing the norms of international law. Just as often, too, its geographical liabilities (the *Yin* and *Yang* or possibly "dialectics" of history?) have often been converted into sizable assets by Russian leaders, especially in times of war or threat of war.

These "indefensible" Russian lowlands have undergone attack and subjugation from all directions over centuries of Russian history. But on these same plains, the invaders were not only eventually driven back; *the counterattacking Russians with arms in hand succeeded in expanding Russian sovereignty, domination, or influence even farther than before the attack.* At the same time, the Russian state, centered in either St. Petersburg or Moscow, enjoyed a spin-off from the alleged or actual outside threats in the form of increased political stability and centralization at home.*

Securing the central Russian plain has been a major preoccupation of pre- and postrevolutionary Russian foreign ministers. In the last two world wars, World I and and the "Great Fatherland War" (World War II), not to mention the Fatherland War of 1812, Western enemies penetrated deeply into European Russia. One of the factors motivating Stalin's deals with Hitler (1939–1940), his occupation of Finland and Poland in 1939 and 1940, and the Soviet takeovers in the Baltic States and Northern Bukovina and Bessarabia in Rumania in 1940 may have been this concern for Russia's vulnerable western flank. The postwar establishment by the Soviets of a large East European sphere of influence and their jealous protection of it (for example, in Czechoslovakia in 1968) are similarly motivated in part by Soviet security-consciousness. Hand in glove with this pre- and postwar Soviet military and economic penetration of Eastern and Central Europe went the traditional Russian pattern of security-mindedness *coupled with extension of Soviet influence or control.* *

NOTES

1. Statement by I. F. Sinitsyn, U.S.S.R. Minister of Tractor and Agricultural Machinery Construction, in *Selskaya Zhizn* (*Village Life*), May 15, 1966.

*Aspaturian, in Pentony, ed., *op. cit.*, pp. 53–54, makes the accurate point: "A divided Russia invites attack, but a united Russia stimulates expansion in all directions. . . . In each crisis, after surviving the initial assault from without, she embarked on a campaign designed to carry her beyond her self-declared national frontiers." There are a few cases in Russian history, however, where political *instability* has resulted at home from abortive foreign adventures. The Russo-Japanese War (1904–1905) is an obvious example. The backlash from the Soviet invasion and occupation of "fraternal" Czechoslovakia in 1968 is another. See Chapter X of the present book.

**In another of the books dating back to the balmy wartime period of U.S.-Soviet friendship, we find this statement: "Both countries [the U.S. and Russia] have sought national security rather than foreign conquest or colonial possessions"—in Foster Rhea Dulles, *The Road to Teheran—The Story of Russia and America, 1781–1943* (Princeton, N.J.: Princeton University Press, 1944), p. 2. Writing in 1944, the author is in too optimistic a mood to imagine that the Soviets might soon revert to Tsarist expansionism and carve out a whole new sphere of influence—indeed, an empire—in Eastern, Central, and Southeastern Europe and in the Far East as they did in 1945–1948.

2. Ellsworth Raymond, *The Soviet State*, (New York: Macmillan, 1968), p. 354.
3. Richard Pipes, " 'Solving' the Nationality Problem," *Problems of Communism* (September–October 1967), p. 128.
4. J. V. Stalin, *Sochineniya* (Works), 1st ed. (Moscow: State Publisher, 1946–1952), vol. 4, pp. 31–32. From a speech by Stalin at the Third All-Russian Congress of Soviets in 1918.
5. John N. Hazard, *The Soviet System of Government*, 3rd ed. (Chicago: University of Chicago Press, 1964), p. 10.
6. Hazard, *op. cit.*, p. 94.
7. *Ibid.*
8. Richard Lowenthal, "The Sparrow in the Cage," *Problems of Communism*, (November–December 1968), p. 28.
9. Vernon V. Aspaturian, "The Geographic and Historical Inheritance," in DeVere E. Pentony (ed.), *Soviet Behavior in World Affairs: Communist Foreign Policies* (San Francisco: Chandler, 1962), pp. 51–52.
10. Raymond, *op. cit.*, pp. 3–4.
11. Erich Thiel, *The Soviet Far East—A Survey of Its Physical and Economic Geography* (London: Methuen, n.d.), pp. 225–230. The Chinese insist upon calling Khabarovsk by its ancient Chinese name, Poli. Similarly, Vladivostok is called Haichenwei by the Chinese.

CHAPTER II

Early Soviet Expansion

If you like a foreign province and you have enough force, take it immediately. As soon as you have done this, you will always find enough lawyers who will prove that you were entitled to the occupied territory.

— FREDERICK II OF PRUSSIA

This recurring phenomenon in Russia history—namely (1) protection of national security from real or imagined enemies by means of arms which (2) results in further expansion of Russia's borders—is shown in Table 4. Since 1939, for example, the U.S.S.R. has annexed outright four of its former neighbors ringing the central Russian plain, has seized territories from seven more countries, and has made territorial demands on two others.[1] A total of 264,200 square miles of territory including (at the time of occupation) 24,-396,000 people were acquired by the U.S.S.R. during this period. Add to this list those countries that were brought under varying degrees of Soviet domination (excluding China), and the totals become 1,321,200 square miles and 123,657,000 people. Forcibly acquired territories were added to the Soviet empire by means of war or the threat of war. These blows of the hammer and sweeps of the sickle have given the insignia on the Soviet flag more than symbolic importance.

As for the other bordering states, only Afghanistan—a mountain-locked Central Asian buffer state, whose main exports are horsehides and lambskins, and with a per capita annual income of about $50 (45r)—has not yet been forced to cede territory to Russia. Like Finland and Austria, Afghanistan has been sufficiently "neutralized" to satisfy the Soviet-made laws of political physics for orbiting satellites and quasi-satellites.

The Soviet Doctrine of Expansion

Going back to before 1939 and to the inception of the Soviet regime, Russian foreign policy under Lenin and the Bolsheviks from the very beginning

TABLE 4.   Territories Acquired or Dominated by the U.S.S.R. Since 1939

Territories	Area (sq. km.)	Population
Rumanian provinces	50,200	3,700,000
Estonia	47,400	1,122,000
Latvia	65,800	1,951,000
Lithuania	55,700	2,957,000
Northern East Prussia	14,000	1,187,000
Eastern Czechoslovakia (Carpathian Ruthenia)	12,700	731,000
Eastern Poland	181,000	11,800,000
Finnish provinces	45,600	450,000
Tannu-Tuva	165,800	65,000
Former Japanese possessions (Southern Sakhalin and Kurile Islands)	46,100	433,000
TOTAL	684,300	24,396,000

Territories Under Soviet Domination or Influence

East Berlin and East Germany	111,121	18,807,000
Bulgaria	110,900	7,160,000
Czechoslovakia	127,700	12,463,000
Hungary	93,000	9,224,000
Poland	311,800	24,500,000
Rumania	237,200	16,007,000
Outer Mongolia	1,621,100	2,000,000
North Korea	125,600	9,100,000
TOTAL	2,738,421	99,261,000

NOTE: Austria was under Soviet occupation until 1955; North Korea may be a joint sphere of influence shared by both Communist China and the U.S.S.R.; China is, of course, not dominated by the U.S.S.R. and is thus excluded; North Vietnam is both a Chinese and Soviet sphere of influence; Albania is not under the domination of the U.S.S.R. and neither is Cuba. (All data are for status at time of establishing Soviet domination, not the population at present.)

displayed many of the attributes of its Tsarist forerunner—above all expansionism. Take the task of *reconstituting the old Russian empire* under the new Red flag of Soviet rule. Were the former forcibly ruled lands within the Tsarist empire to be set free from the empire after the revolution? Were the Transcaucasus, Turkestan, Outer Mongolia, the Ukraine, and so on, to be permitted to enjoy genuine national independence apart from the Great Russian center? *If so*, what of Lenin's prerevolutionary vision of a "worldwide union of the proletariat"? *If not*, what of the sincerity of the Bolshevik-supported concept of the right of nations to self-determination?

Despite his homage to "proletarian internationalism," Lenin appears to have had some deep-seated, perhaps unconscious biases smacking of Great Russian chauvinism. Before 1917 Lenin's strong Russian bias was evident in his Russia-as-the-first-revolutionary-spark concept.* Likewise, after the Revolution, Lenin promoted the doctrine that the "*Russian* Revolution" (that is, the Bolshevik *coup d'état* of November 7, 1917) and the policies accompanying it should serve as the model for Communist parties in other capitalist countries, with minor adjustments being made for local particularities and contingencies. Moreover, Lenin seems to have conceived of a reconstituted Tsarist empire ruled by the Great Russians under the Red flag, including who knows what other additional nations, together forming what he called a gigantic "Union of Soviet Socialist Republics of Europe and Asia."[2]

Stalin was more specific about restoring the borders of the former Tsarist empire. Writing in 1920, he said:

Central Russia, that hearth of World Revolution, cannot hold out long without assistance from the border regions [formerly within the Tsarist empire], which abound in raw materials, fuel, and foodstuffs. The border regions of Russia in their turn are inevitably doomed to imperialist bondage unless they undergo the political, military, and organizational support of the more developed Central Russia.[3]

"Clear, one would think," as Stalin used to say upon making an oracular pronouncement.

Lenin's rather more general pronouncement on the "further merging of nations" had implications for the small nations, formerly part of the Tsarist empire, which sought independence after the March Revolution in Russia in 1917 (Lenin's following remarks were made in 1917): "The proletarian party strives to create as large a state as possible, for this is to the advantage of the toilers. It leads to closer ties between nations and to the further merging of nations."[4]

The essential Marxist formulation that the proletariat's home is the entire world (Marx in *The Communist Manifesto*: "The worker has no country") was construed by Lenin and his associates to mean, in Russian terms, a "Soviet" of the proletarians of the whole world. Scholars debate as to whether Lenin himself condoned the more obvious neo-imperialist policies and actions of his own appointed Commissar of Nationalities, Stalin. However, the latter made no bones about the fact, either before or after 1917, that he supported a policy of coercion applied to the borderlands to rejoin them to the empire around the Great Russian center ruled by the Bolsheviks. It is hard to believe that Lenin could have been blind to Stalin's and others'

*Lenin also considered Russia's prerevolutionary "socialist intelligentsia" to be far more dedicated than their Central and West European counterparts, who tended, said Lenin, to act like "Judases" or be too corrupted by Western bourgeois society, which had existed for a far longer time in the West than in Russia.

maneuvers and endeavors toward restoring the empire after the Bolshevik *coup d'état*. In any case, the *Vozhd*, Lenin, did nothing to stop the step-by-step reacquisition of the Tsarist colonies, a process that was largely completed by the Red Army and the Cheka (security police) before Lenin died in 1924.

One of the characteristics of this early Tsarist-like policy of expansionism by the Bolsheviks, which eventually carried the Red flag and strong Soviet influence beyond the borders of the Tsarist empire (see Table 4), was the appeal addressed to Russian national security. This argument was offered by some of the top officials in Lenin's cabinet, the Council of People's Commissars.

We have already referred to Stalin's statement in 1920 that the center "cannot hold out long without assistance from the border regions." Similarly, several other top Bolsheviks after 1917 voiced concern about the "necessity" (in terms of Russian national security) of bringing the borderlands within the Great Russian orbit. Both this idea and an updated "dialectical" interpretation of the "white man's burden" are suggested by the following statement made by a member of Lenin's Politburo, Grigory Yevseyevich Zinoviev: "We cannot do without the petroleum of Azerbaijan or the cotton of Turkestan. We take these products which are necessary for us, not as former exploiters, but as older brothers bearing the torch of civilization."[5] Another characteristic explanation given by the Soviet leaders for this early period of Soviet expansion (1918–1922) was the conception of Russia as the savior and giver of progress to underdeveloped regions.

Some undoubtedly would point to these apologias for Soviet expansion as examples of Russian messianism, perhaps even refurbished Pan-Slavism. However labeled, they frequently accompanied not only Red Army-supported restoration of the empire, but also post-1939 Soviet penetration of Eastern and Southeastern Europe, at one time an area of Tsarist probing as well.

In the center of Europe, of course, there could be no reference to "borderlands," least of all reassertion of Tsarist legitimacy even as applied to Bulgaria, where the Tsars had been particularly active for centuries.* Instead, the apologetic keynote became "liberation." The Soviet armies had "liberated" the peoples of Eastern and Southeastern Europe, say Soviet pamphlets and history books, bringing to them a higher civilization. The following quotations from Soviet sources convey this idea:

*When it came to the former Tsarist possession of the Kurile Islands, Stalin was not above reclaiming the islands on the basis of prior Tsarist suzerainty. As the Yalta agreement asserted, "The former rights of Russia violated by the treacherous attack of Japan in 1904 shall be restored" (U.S. Department of State, *Foreign Relations of the United States: The Conferences at Malta and Yalta 1945*, U.S. Government Printing Office, Washington, D.C., 1955, p. 984).

The rise of the states of People's Democracy was assured by the averting by the Soviet Army of Anglo-American interference and civil war.[6]

The Soviet Army, which did not allow the bourgeoisie to seize power and which helped the toiling masses seize power in their hands. . . . [7]

The armed might of the great Soviet Union . . . smashed the landlords' and capitalists anti-popular state power. . . . Relying on the Soviet Union, our people began building the foundations of Socialism.[8]

Stalin had predicted exegetically in 1934 that the spread of world war throughout Europe would definitely change the postwar political complexion of the Continent in favor of Communist civilization. As he told the Seventeenth Party Congress in Moscow on January 26, 1934:

The war will certainly unleash revolution and put in question the very existence of capitalism in a number of countries, as was the case in the first imperialist war [World War I]. . . . Let not the bourgeoisie blame us if on the morrow of the outbreak of such a war they miss certain ones of the governments that are near and dear to them, and who are today happily ruling by the grace of God. . . . There is no doubt that a second war against the U.S.S.R. will lead . . . to a revolution in a number of countries of Europe and Asia and to the overthrow of the bourgeois-landowner governments in these countries.

Some Case Histories of Soviet Expansion

We have reviewed Soviet doctrinal and propaganda treatment of both pre- and post-1939 Soviet expansion. Now let us examine chronologically several case histories of this mode of Russian behavior toward foreign nations, more particularly toward *neighboring* countries. In some instances, the assumed or actual threats to Russia's national security—a rationalization often accompanying restoration of the empire—are offered as excuses by the Soviets for the given expansion. Note also that in most cases the expansion has been a phase of a larger strategic plan, whether defensive or offensive in nature, as applied to an area of actual or impending military conflict.

The history of this Soviet expansion, the subject of the case histories which follow, is important for understanding, first, the diplomatic divergence that developed between the United States and the Soviet Union after World War II and, second, the brief period of "strange alliance" in that war. Even earlier, before Soviet involvement in the war, when the Stalin-directed Communist International (dissolved in 1943) ordered Communists in the U.S. to "sabotage" the American war industry, U.S. public opinion and the policy-makers in Washington found plenty in the Soviet record—dating all the way back to 1917—on which to base an anti-Soviet position.

Finland

"The secession of Poland and Finland [from the Russian Empire] after the victory of Socialism can only be of very short duration," wrote Lenin in 1916.[9] As it turned out, Lenin was partly right, if one counts the mere 22 years between 1917 and 1939, which was a period of nearly complete independence for Finland. He was partly wrong in that the Lenin government had made strong efforts to preclude secession and to incorporate both Finland and Poland into the Soviet Republic immediately after November 1917, but had failed. More prophetic in terms of future events—that is, the Bolsheviks' failure ever *fully* to restore Finland and Poland to the empire—were these words by Lenin before 1917:

There are two nations in Russia which are most cultivated and, in virtue of a whole series of historical and social conditions, most differentiated, and which could most easily and 'naturally' exercise their right to separation [from the empire] . . . Finland and Poland.[10]

After the Bolshevik *coup d'état* in November 1917, Russian troops were still in Finland. But so was a bourgeois government, which immediately reminded the new government in Moscow of its right to national independence on the basis of the Bolshevik Decree on Self-determination. Thereupon the Council of People's Commissars issued a special decree on December 31 recognizing Finland's independence. Commissar of Nationalities Stalin, however, appeared to be something less than satisfied with this course of events when he remarked to the All-Union Central Executive Committee:

The fact is that the Council of People's Commissars against its will gave freedom, not to the people, but to the bourgeoisie of Finland, which by a strange confluence of circumstances has received its independence from the hands of Socialist Russia. The Finnish workers and Social Democrats found themselves in the position of having had to receive freedom not directly from the hands of Socialists but with the aid of the Finnish bourgeoisie.[11]

Stalin added that this was a "tragedy of the Finnish proletariat."

Evidently encouraged by this and other statements by Soviet officials, the Finnish Social Democrats, at the time under the leadership of radicals, attempted to seize power by means of a Bolshevik-style coup in January 1918. They failed, but not before a civil war was unleashed throughout the little country. Soviet military forces, now loyal to the Bolshevik government in Moscow, were given orders to aid the "revolutionary forces" in Finland. As the *Small Soviet Encylopedia* presents it,

On the night of January 28, 1918, a worker's revolution began in Finland and soon achieved victory in the southern part of the country which led to the formation of a Revolutionary Government on January 28. On March 1, the R.S.F.S.R.

and the Finnish Socialist Worker's Republic signed a treaty of friendship. However, in May 1918 the revolution was crushed by the Finnish bourgeoisie with assistance from German troops. A reactionary regime was then installed. The Communist Party, which was established in August 1918, was forced to go underground. . . . The whole foreign policy of the Finnish government, up to the end of World War II, was oriented in a hostile way toward the Soviet government.[12]

The Finnish civil war was fought with a ferocity that was to be repeated 21 years later on a bigger scale in the "Winter War" (1939–1940) between Finland and the U.S.S.R. Casualties in the combat of 1918 have been estimated at around 50,000.[13] When the bourgeois government called in German troops, the radical Socialists and the Red Army forces were routed. Although some of its territory was taken away by the U.S.S.R. in the peace treaties concluding the Winter War and World War II (see next chapter), Finland has nevertheless managed to retain a large measure of national independence, enjoying the status of a quasi-satellite vis-à-vis its gigantic southern neighbor. Perhaps, as Lenin said, Finland could quite "naturally" exercise its right to independence.

The Ukraine

The fate that was to befall the Ukraine, a "fraternal Slavic nation," was quite different from that of Finland, the non-Slavic neighbor to the north. As in Finland and the other borderlands, the overthrow of the Tsar in March 1917 and the establishment of the Provisional Government under Prince Georgi Yevgenyevich Lvov lit the fires of national independence in the Ukraine. In Kiev the Ukranian Central Rada (Rada means council) was formed in March 1917 with the support of the Ukrainian National Congress. During the summer of 1917 and right up until the Bolshevik coup, the Ukrainians enjoyed a kind of spontaneous twilight independence as some of the Ukrainian Rada officials talked of some future loose federation or confederation with the Russians. Apparently "reading between the lines" of Bolshevik propaganda and statements by Soviet leaders after November 1917, the Ukrainians immediately became suspicious of the new government in Moscow and its promises of self-determination.* Therefore, on January 22, 1918, the Ukraine proclaimed its total independence from the empire, the Ukraine's right to self-determination having already been specifically recognized by the Soviet on December 17, 1917.

With the counterrevolutionary "White" forces closing ranks in the Don region of the Ukraine as the Russian Civil War got under way, Lenin presented the Ukrainian Central Rada with an ultimatum (drafted and signed by him) giving the Ukrainians 48 hours to assist the Red Army in its military

---

*These suspicions were extended to the Soviet decree on "The Rights of the Peoples of Russia to Self-determination," November 15, 1917. The key passages of this decree are reproduced in Mamatey, *op. cit.*, pp. 116–117 (note 11).

actions against the "Whites" led by Generals A. M. Kaledin and L. G. Kornilov. If the ultimatum were rejected, the Russians said, war would be declared against the Ukraine. Scarcely a week following Soviet recognition of Ukrainian independence, and upon rejection of the ultimatum by the Ukrainians, the Soviet forces launched an invasion.

At the same time, however, the Soviets were conducting peace negotiations—on the basis of Foreign Commissar Trotsky's "neither peace nor war" policy—with the Germans, who relished the opportunity of releasing forces from the Eastern Front for quick transfer to the West where the situation was worsening for the Central Powers. The Soviet-German talks were begun on December 22, 1917. They dragged on inconclusively until the Brest-Litovsk Treaty was signed on March 4, 1918. (The talks had however been preceded by a two-month armistice signed between the Soviet government and the Germans on December 15.)

As Red military forces began to sovietize the Ukraine in January 1918, the Brest-Litovsk negotiations were finally brought to a close. The two-month term of the armistice ran out on February 18, at the same time ending the Soviets' Satan's Holiday in the Ukraine. The Germans thereupon resumed their operations in the Ukrainian "breadbasket," and the Red Army began to retreat. By the time the Soviets had finally signed the humiliating Brest-Litovsk Treaty on March 4, the Soviet forces had been driven out of most of the Ukraine, including the capital of Kiev. This also brought to an end the *de facto* existence of the Ukrainian Soviet Republic, which had lasted for three weeks dating from only a few days after the Red Army's entrance into Kiev on February 8.

The German occupation of the Ukraine lasted until November 1918. But by that time, Polish and German onslaughts during the year had weakened the democratic Ukrainian forces. In the winter of 1919–1920, with the Ukraine cleared of Germans and the Red Army campaigns against Poland abandoned (see below, pp. 41–42), the Soviet government was able to dispatch forces throughout the Ukraine that succeeded in routing the remaining anti-Bolshevik forces. The Ukrainian Soviet Republic, whose *de facto* demise in March had never been recognized by Moscow, was thereby extended to the "liberated" areas.

The Rada's protests against Red Army interference contained some pungent language (protests from the Rada dated even as far back as November 1917 when there were already some intrusions made into the Ukraine by the Red troops):

On paper the Soviet of People's Commissars seemingly recognized the right of a nation to self-determination and even to separation—but only in words. In fact, the Government of Commissars is brutally attempting to interfere in the activities of the Ukrainian government. . . . What sort of self-determination is this? It is certain that the Commissars will permit self-determination only to their own party; all other groups and peoples they, like the Tsarist regime, desire to keep under their domination by force of arms.[14]

The Commissars, applying the arms of the Communist World Revolution, had thus forcibly incorporated into the new Russia their first major border-land nation.

Other Borderland Countries

A similar fate was to await one borderland country after the other in the years to come, their aspirations to national autonomy to the contrary. *Belorussia* became a Soviet Republic, by somewhat the same course of events as did the Ukraine, on January 1, 1919. *Georgia, Armenia,* and *Azerbaijan,* all of which had lashed out against Russian domination from 1917 to 1920, were subdued by the Red Army between 1920 and 1922. By February 1922, the "revolutionary army" had forcibly ejected democratic or anti-Bolshevik governments and set up puppet Soviet regimes in the *Crimea* (January 1918); *Bashkiria* (November 1919); *Turkestan* (February 1918); and, as already mentioned, in the three *Transcaucasion* nations (1920–1922).* Details of this process of invasion, occupation, and sovietization have been given previously in several objective studies and will not be recalled here.

The Special Cases of the Baltic States and Poland

Before turning to the successful empire-restoration campaigns of the Red Army in the Far East, we shall discuss the frustrated attempts to secure Poland and the Baltic States for the Soviet empire. These Soviet attempts are of particular interest to Americans because emigrants from these countries to the U.S. are numerous. These early frustrations may well have had a delaying influence on Stalin in 1939–1940, when the Red Army entered the three Baltic States *to stay* while Poland was severed in half by the Nazi-Soviet agreements of August 1939, then occupied and declared "non-existent" by the Soviet Foreign Commissar (see below, p. 50). When World War II ended, Poland, although not officially incorporated into the Soviet Union, had become one of Russia's most obedient satellites.

ESTONIA AND LATVIA. In both Estonia and Latvia, at the moment of the Bolshevik *coup d'état* in November 1917, Soviet regimes were proclaimed with the help of Red troops. But as the German armies swept into the area that winter, these regimes were destroyed and the nationalized properties returned to private owners. When the German capitulation came in late 1918, "bourgeois" national governments were established at Riga

*Engels had written in the 1850s: "Russian rule for all its nastiness, all its Slavic slovenliness, has a civilizing significance for the Black and Caspian Seas, for Central Asia, for the Bashkirs and the Tatars" (quoted in Carr, *op. cit.*, vol. I, p. 315).

(Latvia) and Tallinn (Estonia). But Red Army troops (composed of both native and Russian soldiers) crossed the frontiers of both these Baltic countries, and on November 29, 1918, the Estonian Soviet Republic was proclaimed at Narva while later, within three weeks, came a similar proclamation for Latvia.

A new phase began when the British navy steamed into the eastern Baltic, with the end of hostilities between the Allies and the Central Powers in the West. As the Allied intervention in Russia got under way, the British joined in the effort to de-sovietize the eastern Baltic and establish a base of operations for a "White" attack on Petrograd. The Estonian Soviet Republic collapsed in January 1919, while the Latvian Soviet Republic fell soon after. "Bourgeois" governments were thereupon reestablished.

When the Whites were cleared from the Baltic area by the counterattacking Red Army in 1919–1920, the Lenin government decided to follow the precedent it had established in the case of Finland. It permitted the Estonian and Latvian "bourgeois" regimes to exist, since, in any case, these governments had not assumed an unfriendly attitude toward the Soviets. Peace treaties were concluded between the R.S.F.S.R. and Estonia and Latvia on February 2 and August 11, 1920, respectively. As a result, these two countries were left alone by the Soviets until 1939.

LITHUANIA. The third Baltic country, Lithuania, presented a somewhat different case. There a "bourgeois" government was set up during the winter of 1917–1918. The proclamation of Lithuanian independence came, with German backing, on February 16, 1918. But once the Germans had left Lithuania in November 1918, a "Workers' and Peasants' Government" was proclaimed.

The next phase came as the Poles invaded Lithuania in the course of the Russo-Polish War of 1919–1920. Vilna was captured, and the Lithuanian Soviet was disbanded. However, when the Russians succeeded in driving the Poles back toward Warsaw in the spring and summer of 1920, the Red Army retook Vilna. But once again, as in the case of Finland, Estonia, and Latvia, the Lenin government refrained from outright sovietization of Lithuania. Instead, it concluded a treaty of friendship with the "bourgeois" government in Vilna on July 12, 1920. E. H. Carr comments as follows on Soviet tolerance of Lithuania's independence at this juncture:

Lithuania, though slightly larger and more populous than Latvia and Estonia, was an almost exclusively peasant country without a proletariat and with only a handful of intellectuals. Its claim to independence, whether under bourgeois or under Soviet auspices, rested on precarious foundations, drawing the major part of its support, moral and material, from a large Lithuanian population in the United States. The main interest of Lithuanian independence for Soviet Russia was negative. Were Lithuania not independent, it was likely to fall within the

Polish orbit; on the other hand, an independent Lithuania could be a thorn in the side of Poland. Here, therefore, it was of Soviet interest to give the widest possible scope to the principle of national self-determination.[15]

POLAND. As for Poland, the collapse of the three empires of Germany, Russia, and Austria-Hungary in World War I signified for it the rebirth of independence. Under Joseph Pilsudski, post-World War I Poland sought to weaken the Russian giant "through the creation of a series of independent states in the Western area of the former empire . . . isolating and weakening Russia to the point where she could no longer be a major menace to her neighbors."[16] Pilsudski was, of course, mistaken in thinking that *either* White or Red Russians would tolerate emasculation of the Russian empire which would reduce the Russian state approximately to its size before Peter the Great.

As the Whites swept through western European Russia in 1919, the Poles kept neutral, watching the course of events while at the same time opposing either White or Soviet control of these areas. As the Red Army retook territory from the Whites in the winter of 1919–1920, the undeclared war between Poland and Soviet Russia grew hotter as hostilities broke out between the Poles and the Reds, and in April 1920 the Polish legions launched their campaign against Russia without a formal declaration of war.

However, by the end of July the Red Army was successful in driving the Poles back to the ethnic Polish frontier. An alternative then confronted Lenin and his associates in Moscow: to stop at this point or to go on and invade ethnic Poland. They chose the more radical "revolutionary" course. The Red Army was thereupon sent into Poland under the leadership of Generals M. N. Tukhachevsky and S. M. Budyenny (the latter commanding the cavalry) amid propaganda cries of "Liberate Warsaw!" But Polish morale was high. Under Pilsudski's direction, a brilliant defense of the Polish capital of Warsaw held firm after terrible battles were fought outside the city and on the Nieman River. (Total casualties on both sides in the Russo-Polish War have been put at about 600,000.)

As the Red forces retreated back to home ground, and with the Soviet soldiers underfed, poorly equipped, and their supply lines overstretched, the Soviet government in a show of ostentatious audacity offered "peace conditions" to the Poles. They were indeed extreme: Polish armed forces were to be reduced to 50,000 men; any arms not required by this small force of some two divisions were to be handed over to the Russians, who in turn would create a "civil militia to be organized among the workers to maintain order and safeguard the security of the population"; Poland's foreign relations with all countries except the Soviet Union and Soviet Ukraine were to be specifically limited; certain directives were to be applied to Polish internal life. Meanwhile, Lenin spoke openly of Poland's becoming "Soviet."

But the grim realities of Soviet military defeat in Poland finally caught up with the heady political leaders in Moscow. On March 18, 1921, the Soviet government was obliged to sign the Treaty of Riga. By the treaty, which was by no means favorable to the Russians, Poland was granted Galicia and the western part of Belorussia, territories containing mostly non-Poles. This treaty, a "minor Brest-Litovsk," did, however, give the Russians a *peredyshka*, or breathing spell.[17] "The temporary sacrifices of a bad peace," Lenin was to say later, "seemed to me cheaper than prolongation of the war."[18] *But the treaty was annulled on September 17, 1939![19]* Less than twenty years later, the Soviets acquired what they had lost by the Treaty of Riga.

Soviet Expansion in the Far East

Prerevolutionary Russia sought expansion in the Far East, often at China's expense, for strategic as well as economic reasons. The following sample of this pre-1917 attitude provides a backdrop for the *Soviet* Russian expansionism in the Far East after 1917 (the quotation is from St. Petersburg's *Far Eastern Revue of 1910*):

Our border with China is irregular and hard to defend, nor does it correspond to geographic conditions. The natural borders of Russia are the deserts of Mongolia, the Gobi [which extends into Inner Mongolia] and Sinkiang. These dead seas of sand can be compared to oceans separating peoples and states. If we lose sight of this, the Chinese . . . will build roads through the deserts to the immediate neighborhood of the Russian border; they will become so strong that they will begin to push us Russians back toward . . . the Urals. There are many weak points on our side of the border. Lake Baikal, for instance. China could easily advance into Irkutsk Province and cut our communications with European Russia and the Amur region.

There is only one way of guaranteeing Russian security in Asia and it consists in rectifying the Russian-Chinese border. The natural border of Russia would be a straight line from the Sea of Japan to a point east of Lake Balkakh [in Kazakhstan].

Outer Mongolia

In the course of the reconsolidation of the empire to the west and south of the Bolshevik Great Russian center in Moscow, detachments of the Red Army were dispatched to the Far East to acquire territory there "for the Revolution." Outer Mongolia became a principal target for Soviet empire-building.

Outer Mongolia, with an area of 592,664 square miles, had been a Russian protectorate since 1916. In 1917–1918 all ties with Moscow were severed

---

*Quotation courtesy of Paul Wohl, who brought it to my attention in his study, "Peking Expects Soviet Attack in October," written for Equity Research Associates of New York, August 28, 1969.

as the Soviet Civil War commenced and as news of the Lenin government's declaration on national self-determination in November 1917 spread eastward. But as the Red Army became strengthened under the aegis of Trotsky, and the Civil War turned in the Bolsheviks' favor, the government in Moscow was able to send forces out to Siberia, to Outer Mongolia, which had meanwhile reverted to Chinese control, and stationed them there from 1920 to 1924. During this time Outer Mongolia became transformed into a Soviet satellite bearing the name Mongolian People's Republic, amid strong protests from China.* Soviet "advisors" were installed in every government agency and the Mongolian army was placed under Russian Bolshevik command. At the same time, the Mongolian economy was brought into the general Soviet economic scheme. Finally, with the backing of the Red Army and the Cheka, the Russian-dominated Communist Party was established within the government of Outer Mongolia as "the sole ruling party in the country."

Outer Mongolia affords an early example of Red Army coercion coupled with Fifth Column cooperation by native or Moscow-trained imported Communists, a practice that was to be followed later in the Baltic States, and in Eastern and Southeastern Europe. Forcible collectivization of private farms and meadowlands, purges of "bourgeois" officials, and one-party dictatorship—all part of the Mongolian scene by the late 1920s and early 1930s—became a precedent for what the Soviet armies were to accomplish in the Eastern half of Europe during and after World War II. Even the designation, "People's Democracy," used for Outer Mongolia, was to be applied to the Central, Eastern, and Southeastern European satellites twenty-five years later.

Tuva

Tuva, called Urankhai before 1921 and renamed Tannu-Tuva in 1921 (by which it was called until 1934), had at the time of Soviet incorporation a population equal to about one square mile of the City of New York—65,-000 in 1941 (today it is 150,000). Living on plains between Outer Mongolia and Russia, the Tuvinians are mostly nomads and hunters. However, Tuva is rich in minerals (including gold and uranium) and is therefore of economic "necessity" to the Russian center. Moreover, because it is located in the zone of Sino-Russian confrontation and is claimed by the Chinese as

*Peking's response was: "The Soviet government has suddenly gone back on its word and secretly and without any right concluded a treaty with Mongolia. Such action on the part of the Soviet government is similar to the policy the former Imperial Russian government assumed towards China."—From a note of the Chinese Foreign Office, May 1, 1922, quoted in Eliot R. Goodman, The Soviet Design for a World State (New York: Columbia University Press, 1957), p. 60. See discussion of Sino-Soviet cold war below, pp. 170–172 and 186–188.

their territory, it is of considerable strategic importance to the U.S.S.R. and to Soviet national security in the present post-1960 era of the Sino-Soviet cold war.

Under Tsar Nicholas II, Tuva became a Russian protectorate after 1912 and was controlled and exploited economically by the Tsarist government; it was incorporated into the empire in 1914. However, during the course of the Soviet Civil War, "White" Russian forces were driven out of the area by the Red Army (1920-1921). As in the case of the other regions brought into the Soviet sphere by military means, slogans were directed to the Tuvinians which promised them that Russian imperial hegemony would be abolished "forever." But as early as December 1921 an "All-People's Assembly" led by Communists declared Tuva a "People's State" and adopted a constitution. When a spontaneous anti-Bolshevik rebellion of Tuvinian natives broke out in the spring of 1924, it was forcefully quelled by the Red Army and by the local G.P.U (security police), which Moscow had established in Outer Mongolia under the leadership of the Communist Mongol A. Shoizelov. For twenty years a Soviet puppet state, Tuva was incorporated into the R.S.F.S.R. as an Autonomous Region on October 11, 1944.

The American Reaction

These conquests of the old Tsarist borderlands by the Bolsheviks were, of course, in clear violation of the Lenin government's pledge of self-determination for all nations issued in November 1917. But even before the Red Army began to fulfill its "revolutionary mission" of restoring the empire, U.S. reaction to the Leninist dictatorship had been far from favorable. Not only did the U.S. press and public opinion begin to display a Red scare soon after November 1917, but the Wilson Administration began to map out a policy designed to keep Russia in the war (which ran counter to the Lenin-Trotsky line) and to keep Allied arms from falling into the hands of the Bolsheviks. The result of all this was not only intervention and aid to the "Whites" (1918–1920), but prolongation and deepening of a distinctly unfavorable American reaction in general to the dictatorship of the proletariat in Russia, and vice versa. Soviet-American divergence thus ensued.

The first major contribution to this early expression of Soviet-American hostility in the U.S. was the Sisson mission to Bolshevik Russia in 1918. Edgar Sisson, a member of the American Committee on Public Information, had journeyed to Petrograd and returned to the U.S. in the autumn of 1918 in possession of documents which, he claimed, proved conclusively what had before been rumored throughout the Western world: that Lenin's "October Revolution" had actually been a German-Bolshevik conspiracy against the Western Allies.[20] Although these particular documents were later proved false, the fact was that Lenin *had* received money and other assistance from the Germans in order to make his return to Russia in April 1917. The reaction in the American press to the various misdeeds and would-be misdeeds of the Bolsheviks was loud and acrimonious:

Filthy pocket pickers and despicable degenerates of lucre—*Baltimore American.*[21]

Bolshevism means chaos, wholesale murder, the complete destruction of civilization—*The New York Times.*[22]

Some of the reaction rose to a hysterical pitch, the grand climax being the Red scare and the famous "raids" by the U.S. Attorney General A. Mitchell Palmer, and such press statements as these:

It is only a middling step from Petrograd to Seattle—*The Chicago Tribune.*[23]

The Russo-German movement . . . is now trying to dominate America—*The Saturday Evening Post.*[24]

The next milestone in this primordial U.S.-Soviet cold war came in 1919 when the Third International (Comintern) was established, and also the Communist Party (U.S.A.). Needless to say, the party line at the Comintern's foundation congress was radical. Worldwide revolt was loudly proclaimed, and the anger and fear it evoked in many Western countries was particularly high pitched when it spread to the U.S. News of the "Red terror" inside Russia (which need not take quotation marks, since the terror was very real indeed) also got a semihysterical press in the West. The Assistant Secretary of State Bainbridge Colby wrote to Senator William Wadsworth in November 1919:[25] "It is the declared purpose of the Bolsheviks in Russia to carry revolution throughout the world. They have availed themselves of every opportunity . . . to bring about the forcible overthrow of our present form of government." Ambassador David R. Francis, when he returned to the U.S. from his post in Moscow, declared that the 180 million Russian people should not be left helpless and hopeless under the tyrannical rule of a "ruthless, conscienceless, and bloodthirsty oligarchy, directed by a man with the brain of a sage and the heart of a monster."[26] The President himself, who had advocated a policy of neutrality toward Russia immediately after the Bolshevik *coup d'état*, now vigorously opposed the Soviet regime calling it "a little group of men just as selfish, just as ruthless, just as pitiless, as the agents of the Tsar himself"[27] (thus anticipating, for example, the Ukrainian reaction to the events of December 1917, as quoted on pp. 38–39, above, or the Chinese reaction to the events of March 1918).*

*Wilson went so far as to report that "they are about to brand the men under arms [in the Red Army], so that they will forever be marked as their servants and slaves," and one U.S. newspaper reported, also inaccurately, that Lenin was about to order the "nationalization of women"!

When the Red Army began to cross over into ethnic Polish territory in 1920, in the Russo-Polish War of that year, U.S. Ambassador to Russia Colby filed stern messages with the State Department back home. One of these was a letter in answer to a query presented to Ambassador Colby by the Italian ambassador to Washington. After answering the Italian query to the effect that U.S. policy toward the Russo-Polish War would be one of neutrality (the U.S. would neither recognize nor aid the White General Wrangel), Colby seized the occasion to sum up basic American policy toward Soviet Russia. The basic principles contained therein were to govern U.S. policy toward the Soviets for over a decade. The main points were:

1. Sympathy for the Russian and non-Russian peoples struggling to maintain their right of self-government and self-determination.
2. The right of the Soviet government to preserve its territorial integrity in European Russia.
3. Nonspecific affirmation by the American people and their faith in the Russian people's eventually finding a solution to the grave problems confronting them.
4. Assertion of the notion that the existing regime did not represent a majority of the Russian people (if it was based on the outcome of the elections to the Constituent Assembly held in December 1917, the notion was true).
5. Indictment of the Comintern for its subversive plans and practices.
6. Indictment of the Soviet government for failing to live up to proclaimed promises, such as, for example, the Declaration of the Rights of the People of Russia (to self-determination): "They sign agreements with no intention of keeping them," added Colby.

The Soviet reaction to this published statement by the American ambassador indicated that the Soviet-U.S. divergence was shared on the other side of the world:

The Russian Soviet government is convinced that not only the working masses but also farsighted businessmen in the United States of America will repudiate the policy expressed in Mr. Colby's note [to the Italian ambassador] and is harmful to American interests.[28]

Indeed, amid continued mutual animosity in the press and in public statements, U.S.-Soviet relations continued to remain poor until, and even after, the Roosevelt Administration in 1933 gave diplomatic recognition to the U.S.S.R. Although U.S. recognition of the Soviet Union gave legal foundation to the many business arrangements made between the two countries throughout the late 1920s and early 1930s (see Chapter V), no profound closing of the breach in U.S.-Soviet relations followed F.D.R.'s 1933 decision. Nor did any major change in the popular American attitude toward Communist Russia take place in the U.S., excluding, of course, the small radical

segment of American intellectuals who sympathized with Soviet policy.*
Neither did U.S.-Soviet diplomatic relations undergo any major improvement before or after 1933. In fact, with the coming of the Nazi-Soviet rapprochement, the joint German-Russian partition of Poland, and the Soviet
attack on Finland (all of which occurred late in 1939 or six years following
recognition), these relations took a distinctly downward turn from which
they did not recover—and then only partially—until the opening of the
"strange-alliance" era in American-Russian relàtions in 1941–1945.

NOTES

1. Aspaturian, *op. cit.*, p. 53 (see note 9, Chapter I).
2. Richard Pipes, *op. cit.*, p. 128 (see note 3, Chapter I). Lenin preferred, for
   tactical reasons, to delete "Russian" from the name of his worldwide republic.
3. Josef Stalin, *Marxism and the National Question* (New York: International
   Publishers, 1942), p. 76. From a 1920 article by Stalin entitled "Soviet Policy
   on the National Question" written in Stalin's third year as Soviet Commissar
   of Nationalities. For a comprehensive résumé of the evolution of Lenin's
   and Stalin's separate views on the subject of national self-determination, see
   Edward Hallett Carr, *The Bolshevik Revolution—1917–1923*, (New York:
   Macmillan, 1951), vol. 1, pp. 410–428.
4. V. I. Lenin, *Selected Works* (New York: International Publishers, 1943),
   vol. VI, p. 6.
5. Zinoviev in a speech before the Petrograd Soviet on September 17, 1920.
   Quoted in Merle Fainsod, *How Russia Is Ruled* (Cambridge, Mass.: Harvard University Press, 1963, pp. 361–362.
6. Hugh Seton-Watson, *The East European Revolution* (New York: Praeger,
   1950), p. 167–168, quoting Hungarian Worker's Party Leader Matyas
   Rakosi.
7. N. P. Farberov, *"Gosudarstvennoye pravo stran narodnoi demokratii"* ("Public Law in the Countries of People's Democracy"). A pamphlet published by
   the U.S.S.R. State Publisher, 1949, pp. 14–16.
8. From the Preamble of the first Constitution of Communist Hungary.
9. V. I. Lenin, *Collected Works* (New York: International Publishers, 1942),
   vol. 19, p. 255, from an essay entitled "Caricature of Marxism" written in
   October 1916.
10. Carr, *op. cit.*, vol. I, p. 286 (see note 3 above).

*Irving Howe and Lewis Coser, *The American Communist Party—A Critical History*
(New York: Praeger, 1962), mention Dreiser, Dos Passos, Caldwell, James Farrell, and
Hemingway among those writers contributing articles to a pro-Soviet publication; but,
with the exception of Dreiser, these men had no extended relations with the Communist
Party and were not members of the C.P. (U.S.A.). "It would be erroneous to assume,"
wrote the authors, "that because a writer contributed to a Communist literary magazine
he was necessarily a member of the CP" (p. 281).

11. *Ibid.*, p. 288. My account of the events in Finland follow closely the narratives found in Carr, and also in Jan Librach, *The Rise of the Soviet Empire —A Study of Soviet Foreign Policy* (New York: Praeger, 1964), pp. 43–45, and Victor S. Mamatey, *Soviet Russian Imperialism* (Princeton, N.J.: Van Nostrand, 1964), pp. 29–30.

12. *Malaya sovetskaya entsiklopediya (Small Soviet Encyclopedia)*, 3rd ed. (Moscow: State Scientific Publishers, 1960), p. 1018.

13. The estimate was made by Professor I. A. Kurganov in the newspaper *Novoye Russkoye Slovo* (Nov. 5, 1967). See Table 3 in Chapter I of the present book.

14. Clarence A. Manning, *Twentieth Century Ukraine* (New York: Bookman Associates, 1951), p. 46.

15. Carr, *op. cit.*, vol. I, p. 314.

16. Adam B. Ulam, *Expansion and Coexistence—The History of Soviet Foreign Policy 1917–1967* (New York: Praeger, 1968), p. 106.

17. Librach, *op. cit.*, p. 44.

18. Anatole G. Mazour, *Russia Past and Present* (Princeton, N.J.: Van Nostrand, 1951), p. 472.

19. From the *Small Soviet Encyclopedia* under "Riga Peace Treaty, 1921," p. 1097.

20. Foster Rhea Dulles, *The Road to Teheran—The Story of Russia and America, 1781–1943*, pp. 153–154. For a description of Lenin's involvement with the Kaiser's government in Berlin, see Alexander Kerensky, *Russia and History's Turning Point* (New York: Duell, Sloan & Pearce, 1965), Chapter 18, "The Path of Treason," pp. 301–323; or the briefer, more popularized account found in Robert K. Massie, *Nicholas and Alexandra* (New York: Atheneum, 1967), p. 442; or the longer exposition to be found in Adam B. Ulam, *The Bolsheviks—The Intellectual and Political History of the Triumph of Communism in Russia* (New York: Macmillan, 1965), pp. 325–329.

21. Dulles, *op. cit.*, p. 154.

22. Peter G. Filene, *Americans and the Soviet Experiment, 1917–1933* (Cambridge, Mass.: Harvard University Press, 1967), p. 59. This book reproduces several interesting cartoons from U.S. newspapers. See also my review of this book in *The Annals* of the American Academy of Political and Social Science, vol. 373, September 1967, pp. 244–245.

23. Filene, *op. cit.*, p. 63.

24. *Ibid.*

25. Dulles, *op. cit.*, p. 153.

26. Dulles, *op. cit.*, pp. 155–156.

27. *Ibid.*, p. 156.

28. *Ibid.*

CHAPTER III

Wartime and Postwar Soviet Expansion

The victorious proletariat of one country, in the event of necessity, even [comes out] with force against the exploiting classes and their governments.

— JOSEF STALIN

Soviet policy in the period immediately preceding the treacherous June 22, 1941, attack by the Germans on the cosigners of the Nazi-Soviet Nonaggression Pact (August 1939) sent U.S.-Soviet relations into a tailspin. Not only on the diplomatic level, but on the popular level as well, these relations underwent a freeze. The backlash even involved Communist Party members and sympathizers in the United States, who became disgusted and disillusioned, they said publicly, with the advent of a friendship pact concluded between the "democratic" Soviet power and the German Facists.[1] Even more disturbing, at least to the U.S. Department of State, and ultimately to the public at large, were the expansionistic policies launched by Stalin immediately after the signing of the Nazi-Soviet Pact, and continued during World War II and into the postwar period.

Expansion Under the Nazi-Soviet Pact of August 1939

The government of the U.S.S.R. in March 1939 took the initiative in reaching what seemed at the time to be a mutually profitable agreement with Nazi Germany. In his speech at the Eighteenth C.P.S.U.(b) Congress on March 10, 1939, Josef Stalin hinted at a rapprochement with Germany and evoked the following response from German Foreign Minister Joachim von Ribbentrop: "Marshal Stalin . . . expressed a desire to foster better relations with Germany."[2] Later, Stalin himself admitted that he had hoped for this response.[3]

Eastern Poland, Finland, the Baltic States, and the Balkans

Under the terms of the Nazi-Soviet Pact concluded at Moscow on August 23, 1939, Hitler guaranteed to Stalin eastern Poland along the rivers Narew, Vistula, and San, and consigned to the Soviet sphere of interest Finland, the three Baltic States—Estonia, Latvia, and Lithuania—and, tacitly, Bessarabia.

EASTERN POLAND. On September 17, 1939, Red Army troops invaded the area marked out in the Nazi-Soviet agreement for Soviet occupation of eastern Poland. Soviet Foreign Commissar V. M. Molotov attempted to justify the invasion in terms which, according to the 1933 Litvinov definition of aggression, were unwarranted. He said on September 17–18 that Red Army troops moved into Poland (1) to "extend a helping hand to our brother Ukrainians and brother White Russians who live in Poland"; (2) "to help the Polish population to reconstruct the conditions of its peaceful existence"; and, finally, (3) on the grounds that "the Polish state and its government have, in fact, ceased to exist" and therefore all Polish-Soviet agreements (including the nonaggression convention of July 3, 1933, concluded between Poland and the U.S.S.R. plus seven other states) had likewise ceased to be in force. (All such pretexts had been ruled out by the 1933 Litvinov definition of aggression. See footnote, p. 61.)

One should note in Molotov's three-point explanation that there is no reference to Russian national interest or national security. This obviously stemmed from the fact that no such admission probably could have been stressed in the atmosphere of the period 1939–1940, a period of supposedly ensuing German and Soviet amity, the Germans and Russians having just signed a friendship and nonaggression pact. The truth is, however, that national security was uppermost among the motivations for the Soviet push into Poland, if not for the nonaggression pact itself. The second motivation, of course, was traditional Russian expansion, a characteristic Russian form of service to the *national interest*.

Today, on the other hand, Soviet and Polish history books and commemorative articles noting the various Communist milestones in Poland do mention Soviet national security, failing to mention, however, Soviet national interest in general as a motivation for the Soviet invasion and occupation of eastern Poland in September 1939. For example, *Kommunist* (U.S.S.R.), No. 1 (January 1969), asserted:

> Under conditions of the open preparations for war in Europe, it was crucial for the U.S.S.R. to undertake whatever measures necessary to postpone the danger of an immediate military conflict—a postponement which was to prove later to be of invaluable assistance in routing the Hitlerite hordes. Namely in this military and political situation, the Non-Aggression Pact was signed by the U.S.S.R. and Germany. . . . Not a single Polish party-in-exile during the period of [Soviet and

German] occupation was able clearly to determine the road to Polish renascence . . . in fraternal, class solidarity with the U.S.S.R.[4]

Neither Polish nor Soviet publications for over 15 years have cited Molotov's imperial- and imperialistic-sounding statement in August 1939, that the "Polish state and its government have, in fact, ceased to exist." Rather, they stress the fact that history was eventually to bear out that it was crucial for the U.S.S.R. to make the various Soviet decisions at the time to "stall Hitler" by means of verbal and written assurances and grants of territory (nearly half of Poland), and later with mutually agreed-to spheres of influence to be exploited by Germany and the U.S.S.R. in perpetuity (discussed between the Germans and Russians in 1940).*

FINLAND. After Poland, the next Soviet target for Russian expansion was Finland. Demands were made by the Soviet government in October 1939, for cession to the U.S.S.R. of Finnish territory, partly on the grounds of the territory's importance to Russian national security. Negotiations ensued during the month, with the Finnish government agreeing to many concessions and compromises with the Soviet government. But when the Soviet government failed by diplomatic pressure alone to win as extensive an amount of Finnish territory as it demanded, it chose to resort to force "by which great historical questions are solved," to quote Lenin. A border incident was manufactured by the Soviets. And when the Finnish government proposed establishing a commission to investigate the incidents, the Soviet government refused. Instead, two days later (November 30, 1939) the Kremlin bombed Helsinki, and Red Army troops crossed the Finnish border, thus violating international law and the Soviet-Finnish Non-Aggression Treaty of January 21, 1932.

In the course of the Red invasion of Finnish territory, the Soviets resorted forcibly to installing a puppet government in the village of Terijoki, near the Soviet-Finnish border. The regime, headed by Otto V. Kunsinen and called the Democratic Republic of Finland (or the "People's Government of Finland"), immediately concluded a pact of assistance and friendship with the U.S.S.R. on December 2, 1939. Foreign Commissar Molotov informed the League of Nations that any other government in Finland was unrepresentative of the Finnish people. And he refused, in the name of the Soviet government, to allow the League to study the continuing war situation there or

---

*Currently, Soviet historiography, as directed on crucial matters of principle by the party, has begun to revise its treatment of Josef Stalin as a war and postwar leader and gradually to dismantle Khrushchev's dismantlement of Stalin as a war leader. In the January, No. 2 (1969) issue of *Kommunist* (U.S.S.R.), one reads the following: "There is a not a grain of truth in the erroneous assertions about his [Stalin's] military incompetence, about his leadership during the war by means of a 'globe,' which have been seized upon and disseminated by foreign falsifiers of history." *Kommunist* does not mention that the source for imputing incompetence in military matters to Stalin belongs to Khrushchev, who denounced Stalin at the Twentieth Party Congress in 1956 and who mentioned the "globe."

to mediate it, thereby leading to the expulsion of the U.S.S.R. from the League of Nations.[5] Instead, the Finnish Communist government in Red Army-conquered territory pledged itself to support any further "actions by the Red Army on the territory of Finland."

Thus, the war in Finland continued. But when the Red Army began piling up huge losses in men and matériel, and the U.S.S.R. was *in danger of embroiling itself in a large-scale war with the protesting anti-Axis Western powers*, the Soviet government sought in January 1940 to end hostilities and negotiate an advantageous peace. After 105 days of the "Winter War," a peace was arranged on March 12, 1940, by which Finland lost all of the Karelian Isthmus, including Vyborg (Viipuri) and the northern and western shores of Lake Ladoga; made other territorial cessions to the U.S.S.R., including Kuolajarvi; ceded part of the Rybachi and Sredni Peninsulas and some islands in the Gulf of Finland; and leased the cape of Hanko and surrounding waters to the U.S.S.R. for thirty years. In place of the People's Government of Finland, the Soviets substituted an enlarged Karelo-Finnish Soviet Socialist Republic.

By the armistice of September 19, 1944, and the peace treaty of February 10, 1947—in the latter of which the Western powers' foreign ministers had only a consultative voice—the U.S.S.R. gained still more Finnish territory. The Soviets acquired a 50-year lease of the Porkkala area and its peninsula (187 square miles) in the Gulf of Finland; the province of Petsamo became the "Petsamo Region" of the R.S.F.S.R.—its nickel mines and the warm water ports of Lunahamari and Petsamo—to be exploited in future by the Soviet state.

Soviet expansion at Finland's expense unleashed a ground swell of anti-Sovietism in the United States, much of it to the accompaniment of "Finlandia" composed by Sibelius. ("Finlandia," however, was *not* the Finnish national anthem. The anthem is entitled "Maamme" ["Our Land"] and was composed by the German-born composer Fredrik Pacius.) The small *official* U.S. loan to Finland of $20 million (approved by Congress) was scarcely a measure of the popular wrath of ordinary Americans (very few of whom, of course, are of Finnish extraction). Grassroots America showed an amazing concern for a small distant country through its generous contributions to the nationwide Finnish Relief Fund and the Fighting Funds for Finland.

The U.S. government, if somewhat niggardly about extending a loan to Finland, was lavish when it came to words of condemnation of the Soviets. President Roosevelt himself stated:

The Soviet Union, as everybody who has the courage to face the facts knows, is run by a dictatorship as absolute as any dictatorship in the world. It has allied itself with another dictatorship, and it has invaded a neighbor so infinitesimally small that it could do no conceivable harm to the Soviet Union.[6]

Soviet Foreign Commissar Molotov retaliated against the various official American statements, saying:

> I will not dwell upon our relations with the United States if only for the reason that there is nothing good that can be said about them. We have learned that there are certain people in the United States who are not pleased with the success of Soviet foreign policy in the Baltic countries. But, we must confess, we are little concerned over this fact, inasmuch as we are coping with our tasks without the assistance of these displeased gentlemen.[7]

Cries went up throughout America to withdraw the six-year-old recognition of the U.S.S.R. Writing in *Collier's* in April 1940, former President Herbert Hoover, for example, demanded the recall of the U.S. ambassador to Moscow and declared that American recognition of the Soviets had been "a gigantic political and moral mistake."[8]

Only when Hitler launched his armies into Western Europe—perhaps motivated in part by the fact that he was temporarily relieved of any danger from Russia on his eastern flank—did speculation begin to appear in America that some way, somehow, Russia should be enticed away from Germany. Some even went so far as to predict that goodwill might one day return to U.S.-Soviet relations, because continuing the quarrel on ideological grounds was too much of a luxury in the face of Hitler's aggression along the fringes of the North Atlantic world.

Meanwhile, until June 1941 and the invasion of Russia itself by the Germans, U.S.-Soviet relations remained at extremely low ebb, although some partial moves toward a new U.S.-Soviet rapprochement (despite the Nazi-Soviet Pact) were dimly visible in the late winter of 1940–1941 and spring of 1941.*

To continue the Finnish story. Early in the post-Stalin period, when a reappraisal of some of the worst features of Stalin's imperial policy was undertaken in the U.S.S.R., the Soviet government executed a minor retreat with respect to its Finnish acquisitions under the 1947 treaty. In 1956 the U.S.S.R. evacuated the naval base at Porkkala. (Even in 1945, however, the naval base had become obsolete, military technology having made new advances and Eastern Europe having become the new avenue for a Russian *Drang nach Westen*.)[9] Perhaps today, with renewed Soviet interest in the advantages of naval power on the part of the navalist party General-Secretary

---

*Russia's ambassador to the U.S. Oumansky informed U.S. Secretary of State Sumner Welles in the winter of 1940–1941 of the Soviet interest in increasing its purchases of military supplies from the U.S. Although the U.S. was fearful that such supplies would eventually fall into the hands of the Germans, Welles finally agreed to meet some of the Soviet requests, but only with Soviet assurances that the supplies, either military or nonmilitary, would not be transferred to Germany. Soon, increasing quantities of American wheat, cotton, copper, and petroleum products were to make their way across the Pacific to Vladivostok. Note that this bit of U.S.-Soviet rapprochement preceded the German attack on Russia in June 1941.

Brezhnev, the Soviets may regret having made the 1956 decision to relinquish Porkkala.

THE BALTIC STATES: ESTONIA, LATVIA, AND LITHUANIA. Formerly Tsarist colonies and newly become independent states after World War I, the three Baltic States were consigned to the Soviet sphere of influence by the Nazi-Soviet Pact of August 1939 and subsequent Nazi-Soviet secret agreements of September 1939. Within two months after the signing of the pact, Soviet pressure began to be applied to the Balts. Partial military occupation by over four Red Army divisions began in October, precisely at the time of the signing of "mutual assistance" treaties between the U.S.S.R. and the Baltic States,[10] a characteristic bit of Russian deception.

As early as 1936 the close associate of Stalin, Andrei A. Zhdanov, First Secretary of Leningrad Province and "architect of the Nazi-Soviet Pact," had issued a warning to Russia's smaller neighboring countries. The statement indicated that Russia would not stop short of using radical means—that is, its armed forces—to ensure its national security. It was, in fact, such a rare and frank admission of Soviet policy that it had to be retracted a few days later. What Zhdanov had said in the course of his speech to the U.S.S.R. Congress of Soviets, on November 29, 1936, was:

Round us are small countries which dream of great adventures or allow great adventurers to manipulate their territory. We are not afraid of these little countries, but if they do not mind their own business, we shall be compelled to use the Red Army on them.[11]

The Baltic States did "mind their own business," rejecting, for example, a Finnish offer in October 1936 to form an alliance between Finland and the Baltic States which was to have an anti-Comintern orientation.[12]

With the Germans looking on suspiciously, the Soviets began to hint openly in the spring of 1940—the Nazi-Soviet Pact to the contrary—that the U.S.S.R. would come to the aid of the Baltic States "in case of attack," as the Soviet newspaper Trud ominously phrased it on April 15, 1940.[13] This caused German officials to note on April 22, 1940, that the Soviet government intended to incorporate fully these border states into the Soviet Union. And, indeed, that was what was in the wind.

Lithuania was the first Baltic victim. An incident was manufactured, as it had been in Finland (see above, p. 51). The Soviets alleged that Red Army men were being kidnapped in Lithuania. Proposals by the Lithuanian government to undertake an impartial review of the situation failed. Instead, an ultimatum was issued by the Soviet government. In it, Moscow made the patently fabricated accusation that Lithuania was plotting with Estonia and Latvia to enter into an anti-Soviet military alliance. It demanded the arrest of certain Lithuanian government officials and the stationing of Soviet troops in all major centers of the country. Invasion and occupation by the

Red Army thence took place on May 28, 1940. Similar ultimatums were dispatched to Estonia and Latvia.

In all three countries, Red Army occupation forces and new puppet governments were established after forceful dissolution of native parliaments under the direction of the Kremlin through such "plenipotentiary representatives" and nefarious characters as V. G. Dekanozov, A. A. Zhdanov, and A. Y. Vyshinsky, all of whom were put in charge of sovietizing the area.

That something besides national security alone had motivated Soviet military occupation of these states was made quite explicit by the Moscow First Secretary Alexander S. Shcherbakov in his welcoming address to the new delegates from the Baltic States, July 31, 1940:

The capitalist world is shrinking constantly while the frontiers of Socialism are expanding under the sun of the Stalin Constitution.[14]

Foreign Commissar Molotov added his voice to the triumphant boasts about Soviet security-*cum*-expansionism:

It should be noted that . . . this population previously formed part of the population of Soviet [*sic*] Russia, but had been forcibly torn from her by Western imperialist powers at a time when Soviet Russia was militarily weak [during the Soviet Civil War]. Now this population has been re-united with the Soviet Union. . . . The fact that the frontier of the Soviet Union will now be shifted to the Baltic coast is of first-rate importance for our country. At the same time we shall now have ice-free ports on the Baltic of which we stand so much in need.[15]

This was Shcherbakov and Molotov apparently updating Stalin's assertion in 1934 (quoted above, p. 35) that a new world war would see "a revolution in a number of countries . . . and the overthrow of the bourgeois-landowner governments in these countries." The motif of Soviet expansionism rode on the crest of war alarms.

The Balkans

BESSARABIA. In the Balkans, a traditional area for Tsarist penetration, the Soviets assigned themselves "interests" in Bessarabia under the Nazi-Soviet agreements. Bessarabia, today a part of Soviet Moldavia and a potential bone of contention between present-day Rumania and the U.S.S.R., is a fertile area of some 17,600 square miles that had been a part of the ancient Roman province of Dacia. It was settled by Slavs in the seventh century and from the ninth to the eleventh century was part of the ancient Russian state of Kiev, a historic precedent lost neither to the Tsars nor to the Commissars. Upon the withdrawal of the Mongols from the area in the fourteenth century, Bessarabia became a part of the new principality of Moldavia. Bessarabia was conquered by the Turks, with the assistance of the Crimean Tatars, in the sixteenth century and remained under Turkish domination until the Russo-Turkish War of 1806–1812. By the Treaty of Bucharest (1812) ending this war, Russia acquired Bessarabia. But the Crimean War (1856) resulted in Russia's ceding southern Bessarabia to Moldavia. The Tsars regained this territory at the Congress of Berlin (1878), with a compensation paid to Rumania in the form of Northern Dobruja.

The year 1917, as it had meant to so many other former Tsarist lands, meant for the Bessarabians, too, assertion of their demand for independence. Under an anti-Soviet national council established in 1917, Bessarabia proclaimed itself an autonomous republic. In June 1918 it became an independent state, the Moldavian Republic; six months later it voted for union with Rumania which was recognized by the Treaty of Paris in 1920. On its part, the U.S.S.R. never recognized the merger of Moldavia with Rumania. It implied instead that the old Tsarist claim to the area dating back to Alexander I and the 1812 Treaty of Bucharest was still valid. Once again the specter of Russian irredentism stalked another area bordering on the Russian empire.

MOLDAVIA. In 1940, backed by the secret Nazi-Soviet agreements, the U.S.S.R. restaked its claim to Moldavia—with the help of the Red Army. By the summer several divisions of Russian troops under Marshal Semyon Timoshenko were brought up to the Soviet-Rumanian border, supplying the ingredients of tension and pressure as a prelude to invasion. Thereupon the Soviet government issued an ultimatum over the signature of Foreign Commissar Molotov stating that the U.S.S.R. had "never acquiesced in the separation of the Bessarabian territory from the U.S.S.R.,"[16] Thus implying Russian entitlement dating back to the time of the Tsars. When the Rumanian government proposed negotiating the question, a Soviet note sent on June 26, 1940, ignored the proposal and instead demanded that Rumanian troops vacate the area within four days beginning June 28. The Rumanian Crown Council voted 27 to 11 to bow to Soviet demands without an armed conflict. (The Czechoslovak government was similarly to bow to Soviet demands in August 1968—without a fight.) Soviet troops moved into the area on June 28 with paratroops and airborne tanks, which were followed on the ground by larger tanks, artillery, and infantry. Slightly over a month later (August 2), Bessarabia was formally incorporated into the newly created Moldavian Soviet Socialist Republic, one of the then 16 (now 15) Soviet Republics.*

NORTHERN BUKOVINA. Similarly, in August 1940 Northern Bukovina, an area of just over 2,000 square miles and rich in arable land and minerals, was incorporated into the U.S.S.R. (specifically, into the Ukrainian S.S.R.). Unlike the acquisition of Bessarabia, Soviet occupation of Northern Buko-

*It is undoubtedly not lost upon today's nationalistic Rumanian Communist regime headed by Nicolae Ceausecu that Soviet party General-Secretary Leonid Brezhnev spent an important part of his political career heading the Moldavian Soviet regime. Relations between Ceausescu and Brezhnev are known to be cold, and Rumanian demands for a review of the U.S.S.R.'s 1940 territorial acquisitions at Rumania's expense have been hinted at in recent issues of Rumanian historical journals.

vina had *not* been referred to in the Nazi-Soviet agreements of the year before. It was only by intensive diplomatic pressure that the Soviet government was able to induce the Germans to acquiesce.

Sovietization of both these former Rumanian areas was soon begun. All land, the banks, and trading enterprises were nationalized and, as in the case of the Balts, mass deportations of Rumanians to the U.S.S.R. were carried out.

As has already been mentioned (above, pp. 34–35 and 55), the Soviet occupation of the several countries of the Baltic and Southeastern Europe after 1939 was—and still is—described in Soviet histories as "liberation" of nations and "expansion of the frontiers of Socialism." In 1939–1940 and by the agreement alone with Hitler, Stalin had gained *over 172,000 square miles of territory and 20 million people of various nationalities.* Additionally, as revealed by Molotov's correspondence with the German Foreign Office in 1940, Stalin had sought partition of the British empire between the U.S.S.R. and Germany and control of other lands as well. Realization of these grandiose plans was, of course, arrested by Hitler's world-historical double-cross— the invasion of the U.S.S.R. on June 22, 1941.

However, Soviet territorial ambitions did not disappear on June 22, 1941. As Stalin had indicated in 1934, Russia expected that a new world war would serve as the midwife of Soviet expansion. Again, the means to be used for this expansion by the Russians were their armies. Again, too, the pattern of (1) *invasion and subjugation of parts of Russia by an enemy* followed by (2) *further expansion by the Russians* was revealed—in the case of (2)— from 1944 to 1948.

Soviet Expansion—1944–1948

With the Soviet armies stationed in Bulgaria, Poland, Czechoslovakia, East Germany, Hungary, Rumania, Manchuria in North China, and North Korea (but notably not in Yugoslavia and Albania), leverage was thereby acquired by which the Soviet government could apply pressure to control these areas and convert them into virtual duchies of the Soviet empire. The use of force for Russian imperial purposes ran counter to a number of protocols of the Yalta agreements (Crimean Conference) as well as other verbal or written agreements with the Western Allies, and treaties with the countries directly involved in the expansion. Here again, Soviet expansionism caused alarm within U.S. government circles, which eventually spread to the population at large, thus widening the divergence between the two countries.

Satellite-Building in Eastern and Central Europe

Perhaps the first East European country to be subjected to Soviet interference on a large scale after World War II was Poland. Soviet activities there, in fact, provided the first instance of Soviet violation of the Yalta agreements and thereby evoked alarm and disillusionment in President Franklin D. Roosevelt. President Roosevelt said of this behavior, as quoted by James F. Byrnes in *Speaking Frankly* from a message from F.D.R. to Generalissimo Stalin dated April 1, 1945, or just eleven days before the President's death:

the concern with which I view the development of events . . . the lack of progress made in the carrying out, which the world expects, of the political decisions which we reached at Yalta, particularly those relating to the Polish question . . . any such solution which would result in a thinly disguised continuation of the present government [the Communist Lublin government] would be entirely unacceptable, and would cause our people to regain the Yalta agreement as a failure.

In the same message, President Roosevelt expressed disappointment in the failure of Soviet occupation authorities to carry out the Yalta provisions in Rumania as well.

A pattern of seizure became apparent for Bulgaria, Czechoslovakia, East Germany, Hungary, and Rumania:

1. Red Army occupation in the course of the prosecution of the war against Nazi Germany
2. Infiltration of policy and army by Communists, installed in their positions by Soviet occupation plenipotentiaries
3. Seizure of power by the Communist Party followed by a short period of tenuous coalition government including Communists and non-Communists in the cabinet, but with the Communists holding key portfolios
4. Overthrow of coalition, setting up of outright Communist regime; purgings of Social Democrats, moderate and "nationalist" Communists, and others opposed to strict adherence to Moscow's direction in all major policy decisions, foreign and domestic
5. Sovietization of the country, the U.S.S.R. serving as the model

This pattern was followed to the accompaniment of promises by Stalin personally that non-Communist parties, within and without the East European countries' governments, would be allowed to function. For example, in his answer to Winston Churchill's Fulton, Missouri, "Iron Curtain" speech of March 5, 1946, Stalin referred to alleged East European "coalitions" consisting of "from four to six parties." "If the Opposition is more or less loyal," Stalin was quoted in *Pravda*, March 14, 1946, as saying, "it is given the right to participate in the government." "Loyal," however, was interpreted by the Communists to mean pro-Communist, supporting without question the policies laid down by the Soviet-led Communist Information Bureau (Cominform).

All promises to the contrary, however, Lenin's basic attitude toward multiparty parliamentary government expresses the essential Soviet view for carrying out the aforementioned five-point pattern: *

No parliament can in any circumstances be for Communists an arena of struggle for reforms for betterment of the situation of the working class. . . . The only question can be that of utilizing bourgeois state institutions for their destruction.

Rumania may be regarded as an example of this Leninist outlook and of carrying out phases one, two, and three of this pattern, in which the role of the Red Army was crucial. On April 2, 1944, Foreign Minister Molotov made a statement on the current Soviet policy toward Rumania in which he disclaimed any Soviet intention of interfering in Rumania's political or social system after World War II. The 1944 Soviet promise to Rumania was made suspect by the fact that in the 1939 Nazi-Soviet agreement and in secret Nazi-Soviet correspondence (until June 1941), not only Northern Bukovina but *all* of Bukovina had been unsuccessfully demanded by the Kremlin to be included in the Soviet "sphere of interest" along with Bessarabia.

In August 1944, King Michael of Rumania accomplished the defection of his country from the Axis camp by arresting the Nazi-sympathizing Rumanian Premier Ion Antonescu and sending in Rumanian troops against the Nazi forces. The king also proclaimed over Radio Bucharest that his country was no longer at war with the Allies. A government was then formed in which many political parties, including the Communists, participated. One of the first acts of the new government was to declare war on Nazi Germany.

But the anti-Fascist, representative government set up by the August 1944 coup was not permitted to last for long. By the Moscow Agreement of the Allied Foreign Ministers (Moscow, October 1943) the Soviet Union was allowed chairmanship of the Allied Control Commissions to be set up in the ex-Nazi satellite states of Eastern Europe and the Balkans after World War II. On those commissions, the U.S. and Great Britain were to have "consultative" representatives.** Two years later, at the Big Three Crimean Conference, in February 1945, the joint Declaration on Liberated Europe was issued. It stressed the *joint* responsibility of the U.S., Britain, and the U.S.S.R. for establishing democratic and representative interim governments in all occupied territories prior to fully democratic elections that were to set up permanent governments. These governments, the conferees pledged, were

*Lenin, *Selected Works*, Vol. XXV. Hitler said on July 18, 1930: "We National Socialists know that no election can conclusively decide the fate of a nation."

**Frequent complaints voiced to the Soviet Chairmen of these Commissions by the U.S. and the U.K. that the A.C.C.s in East Europe were not supplying the Western Allies with sufficient information nor were listening to their consultation were ignored by the Kremlin and its plenipotentiaries. On the other hand, in Italy, the Soviet representative to the Allied Advisory Council there was kept informed. Moreover, no interference in the democratic processes of Italy was carried out by the Anglo-American occupation. For example, the Political Section of the A.C.C. in Italy was abolished as early as January 1945 and in the following two years the remaining sections of this Commission fulfilled only advisory functions.

to be "broadly representative" on the basis of "free elections responsible to the will of the people"—elections that were to be carried out under Allied supervision.

However, even prior to the Yalta Declaration on Liberated Europe—that is, from August 1944 to February 1945—Red Army occupation authorities conducted or condoned attacks by local Rumanian Communists against the coalition regime under the successive premierships of Sanatescu and Radescu. Mobs led by Moscow-oriented Communists attacked public offices and led threatening street demonstrations. When protests were made to the Soviet High Command by the Rumanian government, General Vinogradov, Vice-Chairman of the Allied Control Commission, replied that the government was "suppressing the popular will" and "protecting Fascists." The Soviet occupation's censorship over press, radio, telegraph, and publishing houses (provided by the Soviet-Rumanian armistice agreement of August 24, 1944) ensured Moscow's access to these media for propagating only its own points of view.

In February 1945 omens of a forceful Communist *coup d'état* appeared in Moscow's *Pravda,* on Radio Moscow, and in the international Communist publication, *New Times.* Mob action intensified. The practically disbanded Rumanian Home Army (what was left of the Rumanian Army was in Transylvania fighting the Nazis) could not oppose the mobs backed by Soviet arms. Town halls, police stations, courthouses, newspaper offices, and factory offices were seized by the Communists. The "storm-the-throne" mass demonstration of February 24, 1945, led by the Communists resulted in bloodshed in the streets of Bucharest. Finally, on February 27 Deputy Foreign Affairs Commissar Andrei Y. Vyshinsky was dispatched to Rumania to deliver an ultimatum to the Radescu government. This, of course, was done without any consultation with Russia's two allies, the U.S. and Great Britain.

The ultimatum demanded a Communist-type "united front" ("National Democrat Front") government to be led by the Communist Party—the premiership going to Communist Dr. Petru Groza, and the Ministries of Interior, Justice, Propaganda, Public Works, and Communications to other leading Communists. When the young king at first refused to comply with the Soviet demand, new waves of Communist mobsters were unleashed to the accompaniment of threats in the Rumanian Communist press. Red Army tanks rolled through the streets of the capital in front of the Royal Palace. Several key buildings in the capital were surrounded or seized in a manner reminiscent of the Bolshevik *coup d'état* in Petrograd, Russia, November 7, 1917. With tension at the point of explosion, Vyshinsky again saw the king. After a stormy monologue, Vyshinsky emerged victorious.* The king thereupon dismissed the government on March 6; Premier Radescu fled the coun-

---

*Vyshinsky was awarded the Grand Cross of Carol for his "services" by the Groza regime. Molotov admitted that Vyshinsky "helped in the formation of the government" adding that the Soviet government had acted because "there was very serious danger

try. A Communist-led "National Democratic Front" government was installed with Red Army tanks standing by. Phase three of the pattern began (see above, p. 58).

This Communist-led "coalition government" agreed on January 8, 1946, to reintroduce democratic civil liberties, which the Communist regime and the Soviet occupation authorities had denied the Rumanians since 1944. But in spite of this and the Yalta pledges made to the Western Allies by the Groza and Soviet governments, no such liberties were introduced, nor were the elections held on November 19, 1946, either free or representative of the country's will. Within a year Rumania was declared a "People's Republic." All non-Communist parties, except those following the Communist line, were merged into the single Rumanian Workers' Party. Anti-Communist leaders, such as the popular anti-Fascist National Peasant Party leader Juliu Maniu, and Constantine Bratianu, head of the Rumanian National Liberal Party, and many other anti-Communist political leaders fled, were arrested, tried, and imprisoned or executed. Phase three was thus brought to a close.

The coalition governments were temporary, as Farberov's work admits (see above, p. 35). Communist parties predominated in the coalitions until the end of 1947 and early 1948 when the overt "Dictatorships of the People's Democracy" were proclaimed in the Soviet satellites of Eastern Europe and the Balkans. Then, phases four and five of the seizure pattern were put into effect.

The hypocrisy of the tenuous coalition governments of phase three of the Communist pattern of seizure was pointed out in the Fulton, Missouri, speech of Winston Churchill, March 5, 1946:

> From Stettin in the Baltic to Trieste in the Adriatic, an iron curtain has descended across the Continent. Behind that line lie all the capitals of the ancient states of Central and Eastern Europe. Warsaw, Berlin, Prague, Vienna, Budapest, Belgrade, Bucharest, and Sofia, all of these famous cities and the populations around them lie in the Soviet sphere and are all subject in one form or another, not only to Soviet influence, but to a very high and increasing measure of control from Moscow. . . . The Communist Parties, which were very small in these Eastern States of Europe, have been raised to preeminence and power far beyond their numbers and are seeking everywhere to obtain totalitarian control. Police governments are prevailing in nearly every case . . . there is no true democracy.[17]

The American Reaction

Stalin's satellite-building in Eastern and Central Europe unleashed another wave of alarm among the American people, equal in intensity to the anti-

---

of disorder and civil war." This "civil war" justification appears also in Farberov (Chapter II, note 7). But in the Litvinov definition of aggression in 1933 such a justification was declared to be an unwarranted pretext for interference and aggression. The Litvinov phrase read: "Justification for an attack may not be based . . . on the internal order of a given state, for example . . . on the political backwardness of a given country."

Sovietism of 1939 to June 1941. In fact, this expansionism was the principal cause of the opening of the U.S.-Soviet Cold War.

In their anti-Sovietism the American common man and most of his political leaders and representatives seemed oblivious of the fact that Eastern Europe was actually a remote part of the world, as far as the United States was concerned. It seemed to escape the popular American mind that these areas might, in an old-fashoined balance-of-power sense, belong to the Russian sphere of influence—as Churchill was to recognize freely in his wartime and postwar dealings with the Russians. What seemed to bother and irk many Americans was not only the fact that various homelands of a minority of its citizens were involved in the postwar Soviet expansion (particularly Poland), but also that an ally of America's should "behave," as it were, as slyly and as unfairly as Russia had behaved—for example, in its abandonment of the non-Communist underground in Warsaw in 1945 (the Soviets had refused permission for Allied airdrops to the anti-Nazi Polish guerrillas)* and its behind-the-scenes intrigues in Rumania (discussed a few pages earlier) and elsewhere revealed in numerous accounts in the U.S. press. The Americans were also worried that Soviet expansion would continue and eventually include Iran, Turkey, Greece, and even Western Europe.

Professor George F. Kennan has written of this period in terms critical of the wisdom of U.S. foreign policy and the way it coped with Soviet expansion:

> Let us remember, in particular, that a considerable portion of American Lend-Lease aid particularly industrial equipment, reached Russia [after 1944, or after the abortive Warsaw uprising]. It was after this date that both Yalta and the Potsdam conferences took place. It was after this date that we decided to associate ourselves with the Soviet armistice commissions in the Balkans . . . and exerted ourselves mightily to bring Russia into the United Nations. Would it not have been better to have paused at that time, to have had, then and there, the frank and unsparing political clarification with Stalin which the situation demanded? If that clarification did not give us real assurance of basic alteration of Soviet behavior, then we should have abandoned once and for all the dangerous dream of collaboration with Stalin's Russia in the postwar era and have taken every conceivable measure to rescue what could still be rescued. This might not have been much. It would scarcely have been Poland. It might have been Prague; and it might have been Berlin—Berlin in the sense that would at least have spared us the embarrassment in which we find ourselves today.[18]

Resistance to Further Soviet Expansion

The Cold War set in as Stalin consolidated his gains from the war period (see Table 4, p. 32) and appeared to have designs on other countries outside

---

*This reprehensible bit of Stalin trickery (about which native Poles still grumble even today) was preceded by another atrocious Soviet action, the Katyn Forest massacre of 15,000 Polish officers at the hands of the Russians. See George F. Kennan, *Russia and the West Under Lenin and Stalin* (Boston: Little, Brown, 1960), pp. 359–360.

the immediate East and Central European sphere of Soviet influence. If, indeed, he did have such designs, he was balked in a number of areas.

IN GREECE. The Truman Doctrine of 1947, giving military and other aid to Greece and Turkey, helped the legal government at Athens in defending itself against Communist-led guerrillas in northern Greece; rebel Greek Communist troops were trained and armed by the Soviet satellites Albania and Bulgaria. In the post-World War II period before 1947, British military forces in the eastern Mediterranean area also helped in preventing the Greek Communist guerrillas from seizing power.

IN TURKEY. Hitler-Molotov conversations throughout 1940 contained the Soviet insistence that unless Turkey joined the proposed four-power pact (between Italy, Germany, Japan and the U.S.S.R.), its territorial rights in the Straits and Anatolia (Anadolu) would fall to the Soviet government. Hitler refused such extensive conditions for the Kremlin's membership in the Axis. With World War II drawing to a close, the Soviet government renewed its attempts at gaining territory at Turkey's expense, although Turkey had been one of the Allies in the war. On March 20, 1945, the U.S.S.R. denounced its two treaties of neutrality and friendship with Turkey (December 17, 1925; March 24, 1941) and announced that the terms for a new mutual security pact would be cession to the U.S.S.R. of part of the Turkish Black Sea province of Anatolia, a new regime in the Straits, and satellite-type trade agreements favoring the U.S.S.R. In June 1945, the Soviet government notified Turkey of its interests in the Kars-Ardahan area along the border of the Armenian Soviet Socialist Republic. But Turkey remained adamant on preserving its territorial integrity and political independence. As in the case of Greece, the Truman Doctrine providing aid to Turkey buttressed the country in its successful effort to resist Soviet pressure, which continued to be applied throughout 1946 and 1947.

IN IRAN. Also among the Kremlin's stipulations as its price for joining the Axis Powers in the four-power pact was designation of the area "south of Baku and Batum in the general direction of the Persian Gulf . . . as the center of aspirations of the Soviet Union."[19] During the period of the wartime occupation of Iran to protect its territorial integrity from the Axis, Soviet occupying troops exceeded in number those of the U.S. and British combined. Interference in the administration of Iran and in its economic and political life by the Soviet government was repeatedly protested against by the government of Iran. When the U.S. had withdrawn its occupation forces, the Soviets had refused to withdraw theirs; Britain had retained its forces there for fear the U.S.S.R. would seize the oil fields. Iran appealed to the Security Council of the United Nations in January 1946. Subsequent to this, Britain agreed to withdraw its troops and did so by March 1, 1946. But the U.S.S.R. continued to maintain military units inside Iran, and even sent in reinforcements. When Iran again brought up its complaint before the Council (March 19, 1946), the Soviet delegation opposed putting the case on the Council's agenda, but in this effort the Soviet motion failed to win the support of a Council majority. The case was therefore discussed and the issue was thereby brought to the attention of the world. In the course of the discussion, it was revealed that the Soviets had demanded of Iran hegemony over Iranian Azerbaijan Province and a joint stock company for producing oil. No substantive action could be taken by the Council because of the unanimity rule and the Soviet veto. Iran thus remained in danger. Iran thereupon took military measures to end interference in the province of Azerbaijan, sending armed troops there on December 10, 1946. Thus, Soviet penetration had been balked, largely because of the Iranian appeal to the world tribune, and especially because of the Iranian show of force.

IN OTHER AREAS. Obvious attempts by Soviet army occupation authorities in *Berlin* in 1948, 1961, and 1962 to put an end to Allied occupation in West Berlin met with failure. The famous "Berlin Airlift" of 1948 and the refusal of the governments of the U.S., the U.K., and France to give in to Soviet pressure prevented a Communist seizure of the whole city. West Berlin German authorities also succeeded in frustrating German Communist attempts at seizing the city government. A strong Western occupation policy in *Austria* prevented a Communist coup there as well, although various attempts were apparently made to bring Austria into the Soviet sphere. When the North Korean "People's Republic" unleashed its invasion of the *Republic of Korea* in June 1950, this force was met with U.N. force, and the Soviet-armed northern invaders were repelled. Use of force in order to Sovietize *French Indo-China* was met with French counterforce against Communist guerrilla warfare similar to that employed earlier in Greece. Communist moves against *British Malaya, Burma, Indonesia* and other *Southeast Asian* areas have thus far been blocked.

All of these Soviet or Soviet-backed moves—in Greece, Turkey, Iran, Berlin, Korea, and so on—resulted in further aggravation of the Cold War divergence between the U.S. and the U.S.S.R. The "proxy war" in Vietnam has had the same result but with the addition of certain compensating factors which seem to portend not only an end to that costly "local war" but of eventual rapprochement between the two superpowers.*

The Soviet record of aggrandizement, security-*cum*-expansion, and unfulfilled pledges and broken treaties is surely not good. It is perhaps un-

---

*For the U.S., costly in the neighborhood of $30 billion per year with 39,000 American lives lost in combat to date. For the Soviets, no lives, but an estimated $1 billion to $3 billion per annum in military and nonmilitary aid to North Vietnam and the Vietcong. The Soviet G.N.P. is half that of America and may already be strained to provide Soviet citizens with an adequate standard of living.

derstandable that neither the U.S. government nor the American people have found any solid basis upon which to build lasting U.S.-Soviet cooperation beyond pro tem wartime collaboration, the World War II "strange alliance" lasting a mere four years. At times, however, the U.S. has appeared unduly alarmed at Soviet efforts to build an empire, or at least a bloc of friendly nations immediately adjacent to its borders. From a moral standpoint, Soviet methods were, of course, deplorable. But within a strictly balance-of-power frame of reference and taking into account Soviet hypersensitivity about its national security (which is not totally a pose), Soviet actions before, during, and after World War II are a logical expression of service to the national interest, although in often rather extreme form. We can perhaps agree with the following cool assessment:

Stalin has led what purported to be a world-wide revolution; but to those inured to modern Soviet pretensions his diplomacy seems curiously circumscribed. His arenas were Europe and the regions of the Far East adjacent to the Soviet frontiers and amenable to Soviet control.[20]

The primary question remains: Is this history of Soviet expansion from 1917 and on into the Cold War period irreparably damaging to the prospects of U.S.-Soviet rapprochement? Is Soviet expansionism to date so decidedly threatening to United States security and national interest as to preclude an effective overall U.S.-Soviet understanding or even cooperation in the foreseeable future?

The answers to these questions require not only an analysis of Soviet foreign policy *since the death of Stalin*, which will be taken up in Part Three, but also an examination of the foundations for *convergence* between the two nations, America and Russia, the subject of Part Two, which immediately follows.

N O T E S

1. *Trial of the Major German War Criminals: Proceedings of the International Military Tribunal* (Official Transcript), H. M. Stationery Office (London: 1946–1948), vol. X, p. 267.
2. A. Rossi, *The Russo-German Alliance—August 1939–June 1941* (Boston: Beacon Press, 1951), p. 9.
3. *Ibid.*
4. Zenon Kliszko, *"Kommunisticheskoi partii polshi—pyat desyat let"* ("Fifty Years of the Polish Communist Party"), *Kommunist* (U.S.S.R.), No. 1 (January 1969), p. 104. Kliszko, a member of the Polish Party Politburo and Secretariat, supervises ideology.
5. Commenting on Soviet breaking of treaties and nonaggression agreements made with countries which were later occupied by the U.S.S.R. (e.g., Finland and the Baltic countries, Estonia, Latvia, and Lithuania), A. Glenn

Mower, Jr., has written: "Treaties are instruments of foreign policy, agreements that embody arrangements that are to the mutual national interest of the parties to them *at the time they are contrived.* While an old principle of international law, *pacta sunt servanda*, expresses the idea that treaties are to be observed, another venerable principle, *rebus sic stantibus*, suggests that circumstances may so change as to render a treaty inoperative. In an essentially anarchic world, there is no one authority to pass with finality on the question of when circumstances have so altered as to release a treaty signatory from its obligation; and here, as throughout international law, *each sovereign state reserves to itself the right to decide.*" [italics mine] From A. Glenn Mower, Jr., "The International Morality of the Soviet Union," in Pentony (ed.), *op. cit.*, p. 184. Mr. Mower follows a generally plague-on-both-houses approach to violations of international law by both of the large nation-states, the U.S. and the Soviet Union. He sees no difference, either in degree or kind, between the many violations of international law by the U.S.S.R. and the obviously much less reprehensible transgressions by the U.S. which Mower singles out—for example, by its proclamation of neutrality in 1793, the U.S. violated its treaty with France in 1778 which required us to assist France in its struggle with England—and one or two other examples of similar antiquity or irrelevance.

6. Dulles, *op. cit.*, pp. 222–227.
7. Dulles, *ibid.*
8. Dulles, *ibid.*
9. Ulam, *Expansion and Coexistence*, p. 564.
10. Max Beloff, *The Foreign Policy of Soviet Russia—1929–1941* (London: Oxford University Press, 1955), vol. 2, p. 79; and A. Rossi, *op. cit.*, p. 122.
11. Beloff, *op. cit.*, vol. 2, p. 78.
12. *Ibid.*
13. *Ibid.*, p. 81.
14. *Pravda*, August 1, 1940.
15. Beloff, *op. cit.*, vol. 2, pp. 334–335.
16. David J. Dallin, *Soviet Russia's Foreign Policy—1939–1942* (New Haven, Conn.: Yale University Press, 1942), p. 201.
17. The key passages of the Churchill speech appear in Lawrence S. Kaplan, *Recent American Foreign Policy—Conflicting Interpretations* (Homewood, Ill.: Dorsey Press, 1968), pp. 27–29.
18. George F. Kennan, *Russia and the West Under Lenin and Stalin* (Boston: Little, Brown, 1960), p. 366.
19. Rossi, *op. cit.*, p. 259; a telegram from Molotov to the German Ambassador to the U.S.S.R. Schulenberg, November 25, 1940, marked "Very Urgent—Top Secret."
20. Edmund Stillman and William Pfaff, *The Politics of Hysteria—The Sources of Twentieth-Century Conflict* (New York: Harper & Row, 1941), p. 183.

PART TWO

CONVERGENCE

CHAPTER **IV**

Grounds for Convergence

Russia has a lively sympathy for the United States founded on sentiments of mutual friendship and on common interest.

— JOURNAL DE SAINT PETERSBOURG (1862)

• • •

Soviet-American friendship is related to the historical traditions of the two great peoples, who have common sympathies and respect for one another.

— PRAVDA (U.S.S.R.) editorial (1943)

Spurious as many of the comparisons between the U.S. and Russia may be (see Chapter I), does it follow necessarily that no grounds exist for a convergence of the *national interests* of the two countries? There must have been some basis for a degree of understanding between the two powers, otherwise those crucial world-historical moments, when they reached for and found each other, could never have occurred. Were the periods of alliance and cooperation—for example, in the American Civil War and in both world wars of this century—merely accidental or *ad hoc*? Or is there a real foundation for lasting Russian and American rapprochement?

Geography has played a curiously positive role in promoting cordiality in Russian and American relations. The very remoteness of the two countries from each other has precluded any direct confrontation or clash. They have never met as enemies on the field of battle, thus avoiding the Scriptural injunction against being "dipped in the blood of thine enemies." In fact, until the North Atlantic Treaty Organization (1949) and the Warsaw Pact

(1955), the two countries had never even been lasting members of opposing alliances.

If it had not been for America's physical remoteness from Europe (a gap that began to be closed only with the invention of the steamboat and the airplane), America and Russia would more than likely have contended with each other during the nineteenth century.* For in Europe, Russia under the Tsars and later under the Commissars played—and still plays—an important role in the traditionally competitive balance-of-power "Quadrille of Europe" consisting of itself, Britain, France, and Germany (before Germany, Austria). Strong and persistent Russian assertion of its expansionist aims in Balkan Europe and in the Black and Mediterranean seas was met with stern resistance on the part of the other members of the Quadrille. One major result of this unstable rectangle of forces was the Crimean War (1853–1856), during which America played a neutral role.

Fortunately for "traditional" Russian and American friendship, the United States remained largely aloof from the European machinations and conflicts of the nineteenth century. Geography and the essentially neutralist American foreign policy since the days of George Washington underlay Russian and American cordiality.

Early Phase of Russo-American Friendship

The United States and Russia stand at opposite poles in respect to cultural background, traditions, and political philosophy. Despite these differences, during a major part of the nineteenth century a peculiar relation of cordiality existed between these powers which gave rise to the 'historical tradition' of their friendship. Upon examination, it is found that this tradition has no basis other than the existence at given times of a common enemy and an absence of competing interest.[1]

Although the last of the European powers to recognize American independence, the Russia of Empress Catherine the Great saw in the American colonial rebellion an opportunity to weaken the power of its maritime competitor, Great Britain. Catherine refused, for example, to lend any of her Cossack soldiers to George III.

With the dispatch in 1780 of the first American envoy to the court of St. Petersburg, Francis Dana (representing the Continental Congress), it was expected that the American would be favorably received. Britain by this time appeared to be hopelessly bogged down in its futile war against the American colonists, and there seemed to be a basis for establishing a Rus-

*As Alexander Hertzen wrote in *Kolokol* (*The Bell*) in 1858, "Russia encounters America on opposite sides, because there is a whole ocean of salt water between them rather than a whole world of antiquated prejudices, petrified concepts, jealous preferences, and civilization in a stage of paralysis."

sian and American diplomatic and commercial relationship. But such was not the case. Dana, accompanied by the fourteen-year-old John Quincy Adams, who in several years was himself to become American minister to Russia, was not once granted an audience by the largely uninterested Russian ruler during the two years of Dana's sojourn in the Russian capital. At one point the American minister to Russia optimistically requested that Congress appropriate a sum of money equivalent to 6,000r, the Russian fee which had to be paid to each of the four Russian ministers empowered to sign a treaty. But the money was never sent. The Empress's delay, the end of the war in America, and the ensuing American policy of disengagement from Europe led the U.S. to table its efforts toward détente with Russia.

With the accession to the throne of the (initially) liberal Tsar Alexander I in 1801, a new upward turn in America's relations with Russia was in the offing. John Quincy Adams,* the new American envoy to the court of St. Petersburg, was now graciously received by the Tsar, an event that had been prepared by the friendly and rather sentimental correspondence that had previously taken place between Alexander and Thomas Jefferson. Sentiment aside, Russia had a no-nonsense reason for courting America's friendship. As indicated in the quotation above, there was a "common enemy," in this case Britain, and there was also a basis for bilateral commercial intercourse.

American merchant ships were appearing in increasing numbers in Russia's Baltic seaports.** The broad-beamed schooners carried such commodities as pepper, coffee, tea, cotton, tobacco, and especially sugar. These were traded for such Russian goods as hemp, flax, sailcloth, cordage, linen sheeting, iron, furs, and the inevitable caviar. Because the trade was valued in the millions of dollars, Russia was quite as interested in preserving it as the United States. Also, the threat of British interference with American and Russian ships hung over both countries. As for France, Alexander's stated willingness to comply to the terms of Napoleon's Continental System (refusing entry into Russian ports to all neutral as well as English ships engaged in trade from the British West Indies) was more honored in the breach than in the observance. These imports were too essential to Russia for Alexander permanently to respect a formal agreement; instead, he invoked the qualifying principle of *rebus sic stantibus* ("as long as things re-

---

*Succeeding ministers to Russia included some well-known Americans: besides Adams, William Pinckney; John Randolph; James Buchanan, later the 15th President; Cassius Marcellus Clay, the abolitionist and diplomat; Robert Sanderson McCormick, nephew of the inventor of the reaper; Ethan Allen Hitchcock, Theodore Roosevelt's vigorous secretary of the interior and conservationist; W. Averell Harriman, later to become governor of New York; George F. Kennan, the eminent scholar; and others.

**One of the first ships to enter a Russian seaport bearing the colors of the new American Republic was the *Light Horse*, a lumbering schooner of 300 tons which put in to the harbor at St. Petersburg from Boston in 1784.

main thus"). Russia therefore pursued its own interests, which ran counter to those of some of its European counterparts in the Quadrille but which happened to harmonize with those of the U.S. Russian and American amity and commercial intercourse thus continued unabated.

When Napoleon declared war on Russia in 1812 (opening the Fatherland War) and Alexander joined forces with England in a *marriage de convenance* directed against the dictator of France, America found itself in a war—the War of 1812—with England, Russia's new-found ally. However, there was no danger that America would become involved in Napoleon's adventure. This was not only because of the U.S. policy of neutrality, but because France, like Britain, had interfered with American shipping on the high seas. Nevertheless, Russia wished to make sure that America would not be drawn into Napoleon's orbit. Russia used the tactic of offering its good offices as mediator in the British-American War of 1812 (anticipating a similar American offer to be of service to Russia almost a century later when this country acted as mediator in the Russo-Japanese War of 1904–1905). President James Madison, eager to get off the hook of an untenable war, thereupon sent Secretary of State James Monroe and Secretary of the Treasury Albert Gallatin* to St. Petersburg in 1813 to join the U.S. minister to Russia John Quincy Adams and to act as a team of American troubleshooters to seek the help of Russia as mediator and at the same time conclude a trade treaty with her.

But international communications being what they were in 1813 (it took weeks for messages to be carried across the Atlantic by ship), the American envoys were surprised to learn upon their arrival in St. Petersburg that Britain had meanwhile let it be known that it had no intention of agreeing to Russia mediation. The war was going badly for its adversary, America, and the British were suspicious of the Tsar's motives—British-Russian rivalry on the seas, despite their alliance, had continued to be the *bête noire* in the relations between the two European powers.

Meanwhile, President Madison was being subjected to vehement antiwar criticism in the U.S. press. ("Madison's War" was an even more frequently used epithet than "McNamara's War" over 150 years later.) A contemporary journal, *Niles' Register*, attacked Madison from another angle: for having tried to do business, either diplomatic or commercial, with "Alexander the Deliverer" whose regime, said the influential journal, was a "government of horror," ruling over an empire composed of "*conquered* countries, *usurped* provinces, and *ravaged* territories."[2]

The eventual failure to win Russian mediation in the War of 1812 was not

---

*The confusing negotiations which ensued between the Tsarist government and the team of American envoys were further confounded by the fact that, meanwhile, the U.S. Senate had refused to confirm Gallatin's nomination as special envoy to Russia on the grounds that he still held the post of Secretary of the Treasury. But this news was relayed to Gallatin after he had taken up his duties in St. Petersburg!

the result, however, of these and similar anti-Russian attacks. Delays in communications, British obduracy, and the Tsar's absence from the Russian capital (he took personal command at the front where the Russians were driving the French westward) militated against it. Finally, the two belligerents, Britain and the U.S., agreed to a cease fire* and the war ended. Just before this occurred, however, and as the Tsar saw that his efforts to mediate were failing, Alexander offered to defray the expenses incurred by the American envoys during their stay in Russia. As a result of Alexander's show of good will during America's time of troubles, there ensued a friendly relationship, which was to remain intact for most of the rest of the century.

Russia in the American Northwest

The Monroe Doctrine of 1823, which was later to be applied in South America, was actually first inspired by a U.S.-Russian encounter in North America. (Likewise, in the Cuban missile showdown of October 1962, application of the Doctrine was again applied to Russia, in a dangerous confrontation of the two countries as the U.S.S.R. attempted a *coup de main* in this hemisphere.)

The Monroe Doctrine contained two basic ideas: (1) noncolonization of the Western Hemisphere by European powers, and (2) nonintervention by European powers in the affairs of nations of the New World, with the consequent threat to their newly won national independence. It was the first idea that was evoked by Russian actions along the northwest littoral of North America.

During the first two decades of the nineteenth century, both America and Russia had chartered companies and established settlements in the North Pacific area stretching from the rocky Aleutian Islands off Alaska (both the Russians and the Americans were also active in the Hawaiian Islands) to the then Spanish-ruled province of California. The Russians had established themselves in these areas as a consequence of the voyages of Vitus Jonassen Bering (1681–1741), Danish expatriate and an officer in the Tsarist navy. On his frigate *St. Petersburg* in the 1740s, Bering and his men sailed into the treacherous strait, now named for him, separating North America from Asia. Pursuant to these voyages, the Russian-American Company** was chartered under the authority of Tsar Paul I in 1799 as Siberian traders and

*The Americans acceded to the British request that the parleys be reopened in Sweden rather than continued in Russia. Eventually the treaty ending the War of 1812 was signed in Ghent, Belgium, where the envoys were transferred for a third time. They were apparently glad to get out of Russia, which they likened to a "prison" (Dulles, *op. cit.*, p. 26).

**A Russian version of the British East India Company, the British enterprise in colonial America. The hyphen usually employed in the name of the company does not, of course, denote joint American and Russian ownership. It was completely Russian owned.

fur hunters began to settle southward to what is now the area around San Francisco. Under a monopoly granted to it in a ukase issued by Tsar Alexander I in 1821, the company was given complete control over all Russian settlements from the Bering Straits to 51° north latitude. America was thus confronted with the possibility of a large Russian colony on the western littoral of North America an outpost of the Tsarist empire in the Western Hemisphere, with Sitka (then called Novy Archangel) in Alaska as its capital.

Although the Russians in "Russian America" endured every imaginable hardship, under a governor-general and units of Cossacks, to retain their tenuous hold upon the long strip of territory in the New World, it eventually became impossible to maintain liaison with the home country or to receive adequate assistance to defend the possessions.*

When the American minister to Russia Adams protested that the Tsar's ukase of 1821 had unwarrantedly designated the 51st rather than the 55th parallel north (as had been previously designated by Tsar Paul I in 1799) as the southern boundary of Russian America, Alexander yielded. The result: the signing on April 17, 1824, of the Convention as to the Pacific Ocean and Northwest Coast of North America. This was the first formal accord to be reached between the two countries, which the American press even then called the "two colossi." An American and Russian conflict over the continued expansion of the U.S. into the Far West was thus precluded. The southern boundary of Russian America was moved northward to 54° 40', now the southern border of Alaska. After "Seward's Folly" in 1867, the Russian presence in the Western Hemisphere was ended altogether, and the Monroe Doctrine was vindicated in its first practical application.

The Russians and the American Civil War

Some time before the Russian support for the Union in the American Civil War materialized, several events took place which were to solidify Russian and American friendship in the post-1824 period and pave the way for the anti-Confederacy policy of the Tsar.

John Randolph, following John Quincy Adams as the American minister to the court of Tsar Nicholas I, was to stay in the Russian capital for the shortest period of time for any American envoy to date. Although compelled to distract himself from his ill health with alcohol and drugs, the erratic envoy from Roanoke, Virginia, nevertheless proved to be an able diplomat

---

*Known as the "little Tsar," the Russian governor-general, Alexander Baranov, was described in Washington Irving's *Astoria* as a "rough, rugged, hard-drinking old Russian . . . with a strong cross of the bear" (Dulles, *op. cit.*, p. 30).

at the Tsar's court.* He succeeded in paving the way toward a new understanding on Russian and American commerce and neutral rights, both countries pursuing similar policies with regard to the protection of neutral commerce and free trade. For various reasons, however, the fruits of Randolph's efforts had to await the passage of various events which then occupied the attention of the Tsar (among them the revolts in Poland).

During the stay of America's next envoy, James Buchanan, the second important milestone marking the emergent tradition of Russian and American friendship was passed—the signing of the Russo-American Treaty of Commerce and Navigation on December 18, 1832, in St. Petersburg and ratified in Washington the next year.[3]

At about this time a major international crisis, eventually escalating into the Crimean War, was facing Russia—a crisis, however, that significantly left unaffected the tradition of Russian and American cordiality. By mid-century, the Ottoman empire and Turkey, "the sick man of Europe," became the objects of competing national interests between the members of the European Quadrille as well as various European "bystanders." It was largely the expansionist ambitions of Nicholas I in the Near East, however, which helped ignite the various rivalries into a major war. Leaving aside the details of the war, it is important here to note that the United States maintained the strictest neutrality in the conflict. An important document—the Convention as to the Rights of Neutrals on the Sea—was signed on July 22, 1854, as testimony of these U.S. intentions. It became the third major agreement between the two countries. By the time of the outbreak of the American Civil War, then, Russian and American relations were at a high point of friendliness.

On April 19, 1861, President Lincoln proclaimed the blockade of the southern U.S. seaports. This was a measure that immediately affected U.S. relations with foreign states. Great Britain and France thereupon offered their support to the Confederacy, an event which caused some observers, both in Europe and America, to predict the outbreak of war between America and the two European powers.

As for Russia, it had supported the Union from the very beginning. Its motives? Let us recall the following observation: "Upon examination, it is found that this tradition [of Russian and American friendship] has no other basis than the existence at given times of a common enemy and an absence of competing interests."[4] Russian motivation stemmed from Russia's own national interest (indeed, are not most nations so motivated?). Once again the Tsar sought to weaken Britain's domination of the seas. And, by a curious irony, Russia itself was faced with a similar threat to its own "Union." There was just at this time a danger of Russian "civil war" over Poland, the

*Washington Irving wrote that the proud Virginian had, after he departed Russia, "left behind the character of a rare bird" (Dulles, op. cit., p. 49).

key Western protectorate of the Russian empire. Serious uprisings took place in Russian Poland in 1830, 1846, 1848, and 1861–1864 under the banner of separatism. These events further aggravated relations between Russia on the one hand and Britain and France on the other, the two latter countries supporting the Polish rebellion. This weakness at home was another factor impelling the Russians to extend the hand of friendship toward America.

Early in the American Civil War, the Tsar's able foreign minister, Alexander Gorchakov, assured the U.S. minister in St. Petersburg, Cassius Marcellus Clay, that U.S. naval vessels would be permitted to bring "prizes" (captured British ships) into Russian ports. Russia, meanwhile, would display "unequivocal" support to the North. The Tsar made good on his pledges, amid a public fanfare of sentimental twaddle in both countries (see note 4). Russia's firm moral and diplomatic support undoubtedly deterred Great Britain from large-scale intervention in the American War Between the States.[5]

In 1863, at the climax of pro-Russian euphoria in the U.S. and the year of Union victories in the battles of Gettysburg, Chancellorsville, and Vicksburg in the East, two squadrons of the Russians' Pacific and Baltic fleets made surprise visits to San Francisco and New York.[6] These moves could not have been better timed. The Polish revolts were beginning to increase tensions between Russia and Britain and France. In case of a new war with the two West European powers, Russia would have found herself more "land-locked" than ever, as the British fleet would surely have been able to block her exits from the Baltic and the Black seas. Thus, Tsar Alexander II, on the advice of one of his admirals, decided to take the precaution of moving out the two squadrons to keep them from being bottled up by the British as well as to keep them ready to attack British shipping in the event of war. New York and San Francisco became the logical loci for setting out on any such anti-British action; and in any case, there were no other suitable friendly ports for the Russians to use.*

An emotional hoopla accompanied the presence of the Russian ships in the two American harbors. As Foster Rhea Dulles described it:

In New York delegates from every neighboring state came to the city to visit the Russian vessels lying at anchor in the bay; their officers were invited to cities throughout the East for memorial banquets. Secretary Seward [later to figure in the sale of Russian Alaska to the U.S.] received the Russian admiral at Washington and the Navy Department offered him the full facilities of the Brooklyn Navy Yard. On the West Coast too there were gala receptions for the officers.

*Dulles, op. cit., p. 59, points out that most newspapers in America overlooked the motives for dispatch of the Russian fleet to the two American ports. But Harper's Weekly succeeded partially, at least, in taking apart the Russian doll-puzzle. The journal recalled that the Russian fleet had almost been bottled up in the Baltic and Black seas during the Crimean War.

Everywhere the American people were drinking enthusiastic toasts to Lincoln the Emancipator and Alexander the Liberator. . . . The nation echoed Secretary of Navy Welles' heartfelt 'God bless the Russians.'[7]

One of the more ostentatious expressions of pro-Russian enthusiasm occurred when the Russian flagship *Alexander Nevsky* was treated to a 21-gun salute banged noisily in New York Harbor by no fewer than five U.S. frigates all firing simultaneously! The next day the *New York Herald Tribune* rhapsodized:

Hardly one but understands that while the great Protestant power of England, and the great Catholic power of France, had intrenched themselves behind the bristling abatis of diplomacy, ready to quarrel, to grumble, and to contend for the ninth part of a hair, Russia, far distant from us, but, in her turn, intent in an opposite quarter of the globe, upon the extension of popular civilization, has preserved those relations of friendship, which, when they become ancient, may also become indissoluble.[8]

Also in New York City, a grand ball was staged in the Academy of Music on (at that time) fashionable 14th Street. The gala event was attended by hundreds of couples, the ladies in their satin hoopskirts escorted by gentlemen sporting beards and long hair and sideburns (which would surely be the envy of today's American male escorts). The Russian naval officers, with their elaborate beards, St. George's crosses, gold buttons and epaulettes, and exotic animated dancing were, of course, the center of attention.

Under these euphoric conditions, needless to say, little or no thought was given in the press to the contrasting social, economic, and political systems of the two friendly countries. In Russia, pro-American feeling was running as high as pro-Russian feeling in New York and San Francisco. In both countries rather farfetched comparisons were made. The most common one was that the liberation of Russia's some 20 million serfs by Tsar Alexander's ukase of 1861 was the exact analogue, if not homologue, of Lincoln's Emancipation Proclamation of the year following which freed some 4 million black slaves. But, as Laserson correctly observed in *The American Impact on Russia*:

The social and juridical resemblance between Russia white serfdom and American Negro slavery, both of which were hindrances to a free capitalist society, did not lead the countries along similar lines. . . . For almost half a century more [the Russian landlord or *barin*] continued to exploit his former serfs, and they were obliged to pay him endless indemnification. . . . The Russian peasant had no chance to become anything like an American farmer. . . . In the United States the immense grants of land under the Homestead Act and other less spectacular confiscatory measures made slowly possible the creation of a farmer class whose dreams could be realized without revolution or rebellion. . . . The opposite is true for post-Emancipation Russia.[9]

This episode of nearly delirious pro-Russian sentiment in America during the Civil War is instructive—also prophetic. It illustrates the degree and the rapidity with which political and diplomatic decisions taken in two distant capitals, St. Petersburg and Washington, could unleash a spontaneous wave of popular feeling.* It occurred again in both countries less than a hundred years later during World War II. It could happen again.

"Seward's Folly"

In 1787, Thomas Jefferson met in Paris, where he was the American minister, with one John Ledyard, woodsman and explorer of the Lewis and Clark type, who was eager to return to America by way of Siberia, the Pacific Ocean, and the unexplored wilderness of the North American continent. The Virginian proposed to him that he "go by land to Kamchatka [on the Russian Pacific Coast], cross in some of the Russian vessels to Nootka Sound, fall down into the latitude of the Missouri [River], and penetrate to and through that to the United States." In the same year, Ledyard started out on his mission, having received permission of Empress Catherine the Great to traverse Siberia to reach the Russian Pacific northeast. However, after Ledyard had reached and wintered in Kamchatka and was preparing to resume his journey into the North Pacific waters in the spring of 1788, the Empress asserted her woman's prerogative and for some unknown reason changed her mind and retracted her permission for advancement of the American project. And there the matter rested until the U.S. was able to explore the North Pacific area by beginning from the American side.

With Russia's withdrawal from the California and Canadian Pacific coast (discussed earlier in this chapter), there followed a protracted period of Alaska's decline and a corresponding lack of interest in the area on the part of the Russians, the British, and the Americans. Following Russia's defeat in the Crimean War and with the sizable decrease in the population of fur-bearing sea otters in Alaskan waters, the Russians were finally persuaded to give up their last outpost in Russian America.

Before the end of the Crimean War, the U.S. initiated efforts to acquire Alaska. Secretary of State William L. Marcy (1853–1857) and Senator William M. Gwin of California had tried to interest the Russian envoy in Wash-

*Enthusiastic comparison-makers in St. Petersburg and Moscow eagerly alleged that there was a resemblance between John Wilkes Booth's assassination of Lincoln in 1865 and Dmitri Karakozov's attempt to assassinate the Tsar the next year. The U.S. Congress passed a resolution expressing its "deep regret" at the incident in Russia. Debate in the Senate revolved about the description of Karakozov in the bill as "an enemy of emancipation," thus establishing an analogy with Booth's motivation vis-à-vis Lincoln's Emancipation Proclamation. Although this was false (Karakozov *supported* emancipation of the serfs), the phrase was left in the final draft of the resolution. For the public reaction to the Tsar's eventual assassination and that of President Garfield, see below, p. 82.

ington, Baron Edward von Stoeckl, in making a deal on Alaska. In 1859 President James Buchanan (former minister to Russia) sanctioned Senator Gwin to approach von Stoeckl with the concrete offer of $5 million. But the Foreign Ministry in St. Petersburg delayed, despite von Stoeckl's enthusiastic support of the offer (von Stoeckl was a strong advocate of U.S.-Russian friendship; for his reasons see note 4). After a delay on the American side because of the Civil War, the question of selling Alaska was reopened with the Russians, who meantime had decided that the bankrupt Russian-American Company, which was barely hanging on in Alaska, was not worth continuing. In 1867, with the support of President Andrew Johnson, Secretary of State Seward once again proposed the price of $5 million. But this time the Russians doubled their selling price to $10 million. Finally, a compromise of $7.2 million was agreed upon, and on March 30, 1867, the treaty was signed, followed by Senate ratification only a week later. The deal had been "signed, sealed and delivered" so fast for the purchase of a territory that was practically unknown to most Americans that a public uproar broke out. Most famous among the epithets used to describe the new territory was "Seward's ice-box."

What were the Russian motives for the sale of Alaska and why did America buy it? The answer to the question finds considerable disagreement among American historians. Perhaps the consensus among them is that Russia feared that Britain might eventually lay hands on the territory; better that the friendly non-European power America acquire it than Great Britain, Russia's maritime adversary. As to the American motivation, perhaps an important factor was Secretary Seward's belief that it was the "manifest destiny" of the United States to expand into the Pacific Ocean.

In any case, at the time both governments showed satisfaction with the agreement.* The smoothly reached deal on Alaska served as one more milestone in the display of traditional friendship between Russia and America for most of the nineteenth century.

Discord in the Far East

With the irony that is characteristic of history, the American Civil War helped both to solidify American-Russian relations and to contribute, later, to a temporary divergence of their interests. The trend away from conver-

*In the age of strategic bombers and ICBMs, the importance of Alaska as a base for electronic detection devices, etc., can scarcely be exaggerated. Present-day Russian remorse over the sale of this vital Arctic territory is probably only slightly less bitter than when rich deposits of gold were found there near Klondike Creek and elsewhere in the 1890s and equally valuable oil fields discovered at North Slope in 1969. The newly-opened (1969) Northwest Passage connecting the American East Coast and European markets for Alaskan oil and minerals could boost the importance of Alaska even more.

gence was brought on by Russian and American disagreement over the balance-of-power relationship between the Great Powers in their encounters with each other in the Far East. One of the factors that impelled Russia to step up its eastward expansion into southern Siberia and beyond to the Pacific in the mid-nineteenth century was cotton. The Russian demand for American cotton was frustrated by the four-year Civil War, which had cut off its imports of this essential raw material.*

Despite their differences over the Far East, however, the overall pattern of convergence of Russian and American interests, right up until 1917, was never irrevocably disturbed.

American-Soviet Conflict of Interest in China

China was the location of first expression of the threat to U.S.-Russian friendship in the last century.

By the nineteenth century, the Ch'ing Dynasty of China had grown seriously weak. A phase of decline had set in in the traditional Chinese pattern of ebbs, and flows in the ability of the governing center at Peking to maintain control over the territorial extremities of the empire. Sun Yat-sen was referring to this Chinese phenomenon when he called his country even in the twentieth century a "table of sand"; the problem remains acute today and, as before, is still exploited by the rulers of Russia (see below, pp. 242–249, 275–276). Thus, the territories acquired in previous centuries by China, when its power was flowing and not ebbing, in Central Asia and north and east of the Amur now lay temptingly across the path of Russian expansion into Siberia.

Motivated partly by economic and partly by political factors, Russia found Central Asia to be a temptation it could not resist. Above all, the enormous cotton resources of the region, which lay partly in Chinese territory, attracted Russia as its supplies from the U.S. stopped. Moreover, the other European powers had become aware of Peking's weakness. They too had begun to seek out China as a semicolonial *ager publicum* for their own economic exploitation. Among the Great Powers, China's Eurasian neighbor, Russia, wanted to be the first to take advantage of the situation. And as for China's valuable Pacific littoral, that too was an enticement to the Europeans, and especially to Russia.

With the outbreak of the Opium War (1839–1842) between China and Great Britain and the anti-Ch'ing Taiping Rebellion (1850–1864), the European Great Powers stepped up their pressure on the Middle Kingdom. The Russians took the opportunity to send numerous settlers and troops down the Amur River inside Chinese territory. It was from this position of strength that Russia was able to force upon its neighbor the unequal Treaty of Aigun (1858), so often mentioned in the current Sino-Soviet cold war.

*The U.S. South supplied three-quarters of the world's demand for cotton.

Under its terms, Russia acquired territory north of the Amur and a joint Sino-Russian condominium east of the Ussuri in what was to become the Pacific Maritime Province of the Russian empire. Thus, Russia was brought to the very shores of the Pacific *below* the line of year-round solid Arctic block ice.[10] Soon after, the Treaty of Peking (1860) was signed, which confirmed the 1858 treaty and, moreover, ceded the area east of the Ussuri outright to Russia,* which is also a bone of contention in the Sino-Soviet debates of today.

With the rapid consolidation of its new Far Eastern possessions, Russia developed the ports of Vladivostok and Port Arthur into first-class naval bases and projected the building of the Trans-Siberian Railroad (begun in 1891 and completed in 1905). Russia also began to thrust outward into the Pacific basin, a policy that was, of course, to affect Japan and Korea. This trend of events in and about the northeastern Russian sector of the Eurasian Continent began to threaten the much-touted Russian and American tradition of cordiality. The United States itself was beginning to regard the Pacific Ocean as a partly "American lake." And, like the other Great Powers, the U.S. regarded the situation in China with close attention.

Until 1842 American trade with China was negligible and confined by law to Canton; moreover, the U.S., unlike the European naval powers, lacked naval bases in Far Eastern waters. But this did not prevent the U.S. from employing its own techniques in its relations with China, which included persuasion, tact, and a patronizing posture rather than application of armed force to establish an American presence in that country.

By the time of the Taiping Rebellion, the U.S. began to take serious note of Russia's ambitions in China. The American minister of Peking, Humphrey Marshall, voiced a degree of alarm in his message to Secretary of State Marcy in 1855:

Her [Russia's] assistance would probably end in passing China under a Russian protectorate, and in the extension of Russian limits to the Hoangho, or the mouth of the Yangtse. . . . I think almost any sacrifice should be made by the United States to keep Russia from spreading her Pacific boundary, and to avoid her coming directly to interference in Chinese domestic affairs.[11]

America had begun to realize that its own expansion into California (in the Gold Rush of 1849), the construction of a railroad across the Isthmus of Panama, and the introduction of clipper ships had put it squarely in the class of "Pacific maritime powers." "The Pacific Ocean, its shores, its islands and the vast region beyond," prophesied Secretary of State Seward, "will become the chief theater of events in the world's great hereafter."[12]

*This Far Eastern expansion caused Russian nationalist sentiment to run high—for example, Dostoyevsky's statement: "In Europe we were hangers-on and slaves. But we shall go to Asia as masters." This expansion and the two treaties accompanying it figure in the Sino-Soviet cold war of today.

The Assassination of Alexander II
Strikes a Discordant Note

Not only Russia's expansion to the Pacific and America's sense of its own "manifest destiny" began to threaten Russian-American amity. Another series of events introduced a new type of irritation into the relations of the two colossi. The discordance revolved about the assassination of Tsar Alexander II in 1881.

Recall the Congressional resolution of 1866 (see footnote above, p. 78): It had expressed America's "deep regret" over the attempted assassination of Tsar Alexander II, the comparison also being made between Lincoln and the Tsar. In 1881 another even more striking coincidence occurred. The Tsar this time was mortally wounded by assassins (March 13), and later the same year the American President James Garfield likewise died from an assassin's bullet (September 19) inflicted in July 1881. Once again messages of sympathy were exchanged by the two governments. However, this time, the populations of both countries became involved and the sympathies became confused. In liberal and radical circles on the Russian side, the assassination of the Tsar was deplored, not because of opprobrium attached to regicide per se, but because Alexander II's liberal reforms (including a project for promulgating a constitution) were extinguished. The new Tsar, Alexander III, was known to be opposed to his father's policies. Therefore, tension increased between the liberal/radical and conservative elements in Russia as the new Tsar unfolded his reactionary program.

Meanwhile, the message of sympathy addressed to the Russians by the New York State Assembly contained a loaded statement which was immediately pounced upon by the liberal and radical circles inside Russia. The passage implied that "the rule of the Empire, as in Russia" was different from "the government of the People, as in the Republic of America"—a contrast that had not been made in the 1866 Congressional resolution. Liberal and radical circles in Russia interpreted the New York Assembly statement to mean that America recognized a striking divergence in the political systems of the two countries. Conservative circles and their press became duly annoyed. Meanwhile, on the American side, the general public was becoming increasingly aware of the abhorrent features of Tsarist "rule by the knout" and rampant anti-Semitism. Stories were fed back to these shores by American tourists, shipowners, engineers, technicians, sea captains, and others, who told about the deplorable conditions existing in Russia. The flight of the famous anarchist-revolutionist Mikhail Bakunin from Siberia via America to Europe was another irritant. When the U.S. refused to extradite Bakunin to Tsarist authorities, the Russian ambassador to Washington von Stoeckl became irritated, remarking that the U.S. would never cease to "protect revolutionists."[13]

All this, plus the events in the Far East, contributed to a certain waning of American and Russian friendship in the years following the purchase of Alaska.

A Russian Expression of Cordiality Toward the U.S.

Before returning to the Far East, where conflict of interest acted as a divisive force working against Russian and American convergence, let us recall another incidence of the old cordiality. In the winter of 1871–1872 the third son of Tsar Alexander II, the Grand Duke Alexis, came to the United States on a much-publicized tour. He visited New York, Niagara Falls, Boston, San Francisco, Chicago, St. Louis, and so on, but the capstone of his stay was a buffalo hunt out West. Accompanied by General George A. Custer, Alexis and his party were the subjects of newspaper features and even cartoons (one of which showed Alexis being chased up a railroad telephone pole by a bull buffalo). As in the case of the visiting naval squadrons during the Civil War, the Grand Duke's visit, less than ten years later, was punctuated by a grand ball in each large city he visited, newspaper illustrations (news cameramen were then largely nonexistent), and speeches extolling Russian and American friendship over the past years.

The Grand Duke Alexis was the highest official of a Russian government ever to visit the United States until 1959 when Premier and First Secretary of the C.P.S.U. Nikita Khrushchev set a new record: the first head of any Russian government ever to visit this country. (No American head of state has visited Russia before or since 1917.

Soviet-American Rivalry in the Far East

To return to the Far East problem. By the end of the century, the Russians and Americans unexpectedly found themselves behaving like rivals. The U.S. reached East Asia via Guam, Hawaii, and the Philippines (acquired in the Spanish-American War of 1898) and the Russians by way of Siberia. And with the U.S. and Great Britain beginning to improve their relations, marked by the Hay-Pauncefote Treaty of 1901, the Russians on their part undertook a reappraisal of "traditional" Russian-American cordiality. The reappraisal, incidentally, was additionally sparked by the emergent trend toward Anglo-American support for and giving asylum to various anti-Tsarist Russian revolutionaries, a sore point with Russia's ruling circles.

Russia clearly perceived that America stood in its way as it contemplated further expansion on its side of the Pacific Ocean, as was indicated in the Russian ambassador's report.

It is quite evident to me [Count Arthur Cassini, Russian minister to the U.S.]* that the United States has firmly decided to break with the traditions of the past and to enter upon a new policy with wider horizons—a policy which if they follow it with the stubbornness characteristic of their race will not be without immediate and significant influence on the fate of the entire world. . . .

We should follow with undivided attention each small success in the rapprochement between the [two] Anglo-Saxon countries, not missing a single opportunity to point out to our American friends the disadvantages which confront them in the deceitful business into which they are being drawn.[14]

Rivalry Over China and Japan

Further Russian irritation was caused by the American promotion of its Open Door policy (made public by the U.S. in 1900). The American Open Door policy proposed that equal commercial and industrial rights obtain for the nationals of all countries. Russia, on the other hand, wished to "close the door," preserving China for its exclusive exploitation.

With regard to Japan, another target of Russian expansion, the U.S. supported this fast-expanding island nation in the defense of its national security, which was endangered by the extension of Russian control over territories near Japanese shores. The U.S. became concerned about the adventuristic Japanese (and Korean) policy of Nicholas II, who at this time was urged on the reckless course by such irresponsible counselors as Alexander Bezobrazov and Admiral Alexis Abaza.

In February 1904 came the retaliatory "sneak attack" by the Japanese on the Russian naval base of Port Arthur (Dalny). The American press and the public at first lent its sympathies to Japan, while the Roosevelt administration remained officially neutral but unofficially sympathetic toward Japan. As Theodore Roosevelt put it, "Japan is playing our game."[15] Addressing himself to friendship with Russia, Roosevelt further declared: "I should have liked to be friendly with her but she simply would not permit it, and those responsible for managing her foreign policy betrayed a brutality and shortsightedness, which are too often combined."[16] Despite the Russian minister Cassini's public attempts to revive the formerly exuberant pro-Russian feeling in the U.S., America remained pro-Japanese in the Russo-Japanese War. (Cassini even recalled the visits of the Russian naval squadrons during the Civil War, but to no avail.)

Finally, a shift of American public opinion took place—but not because of the minister's efforts from his ambassadorial post in Washington, D.C. The events in the war caused the veering of opinion. Russia was taking a terrible beating at the hands of the Japanese. To cite two examples: in 1905 Vice-Admiral Z. P. Rozhdestvensky's fleet at Tsushima in Chosen Strait

*The importance of Cassini's assignment to America was underlined by the fact that his previous ambassadorial post had been Peking.

was utterly destroyed and there were many casualties; the Russians were trounced in the battle about Mukden in Manchuria, where 90,000 soldiers perished or were imprisoned. Meanwhile, strong opposition to the war spread throughout Russia.

The reaction in the United States became one of surprise at Japan's show of military strength. But a degree of alarm was mixed with the surprise, and public sympathies began slowly to shift to the side of the underdog, Russia. As for the government in Washington, the attitude appeared also to be one of concern lest Japan tip the balance-of-power scales in the Far East too sharply in its favor.* American interests seemed to be best served by a Russian and Japanese standoff rather than an imbalance in one or the other's favor.

As has happened to belligerents bogged down in stalemated wars of the past, both sides in the Russo-Japanese War began to calculate the costs of continuing the conflict and found that they were too high. For example, the war is estimated to have cost the Japanese side alone $1 million per day! It was the Japanese, in fact, who sought out the U.S. to act as mediator at the peace table. Russia too was in a bad way. In 1905 Russia was confronted with a revolutionary situation at home in St. Petersburg and Moscow and was refused any further financial help from French bankers. Still, Tsar Nicholas II declined the Japanese offer to seek American mediation, even when the German Kaiser, his cousin, urged him to agree.

At this point, Roosevelt directed the U.S. ambassador to Russia George von Meyer to request an audience with the Tsar himself to persuade him personally to undertake peace talks. The interview took place, but the results of the meeting apparently left the American ambassador with an impression of (in his words) "the utterly loose way in which the Russian government works." Although the Russians agreed to enter into direct negotiations with the Japanese, a bit of unexpected jockeying intervened and delayed the opening of the talks for many weeks. Japan began to insist that the Russian plenipotentiaries to the peace conference have full powers to negotiate. But Russia refused. Then a dispute arose over the location of the peace talks (shades of a later hassle during the Vietnam negotiations in 1968). After various proposals that Washington, The Hague, or Paris should be the location, Washington, D.C., was mutually agreed to after the Russians agreed, reneged, and then agreed again; Russia also finally concurred that its plenipotentiaries should have full powers.

The peace talks opened in Portsmouth, New Hampshire, on August 10, 1905, the U.S. capital being rejected because it was in the throes of a stifling heat wave. After Russian threats to break off negotiations and after

---

*It would have been no surprise to Washington if the Japanese had been successful in driving Russia out of eastern Siberia all the way to Lake Baikal, as one authority reveals. See Tyler Dennet, *Roosevelt and the Russo-Japanese War* (New York: Doubleday, Page, 1925), p. 165.

much arguing and haggling, agreement was finally reached and the treaty was signed on September 5. The treaty was definitely favorable to Japan, but would have been even more so had not President Roosevelt brought pressure to bear on the Japanese negotiators during the month-long sessions. The Japanese were induced by the President's representatives to give up their demand that the Russians pay them reparations, that the Russian fleet be limited in its Far Eastern operations, and that the Russian ships seized and interned by the Japanese not be returned.

By the terms of the Portsmouth Treaty, Russia was obliged to recognize Korea as a Japanese sphere of influence; to cede the southern branch of the Chinese Eastern Railway to Japan; to give to Japan the Russian lease on the Liaotung Peninsula; to evacuate southern Manchuria; and to cede the southern half of Sakhalin Island to the Japanese.

Considering Russia's poor performance in the Russo-Japanese War (Soviet historians call it Britain's and America's "war by proxy") the treaty was not all that unfavorable to Russia, thanks to Roosevelt's efforts to prevent too great an advantage from falling to Japan. Although Roosevelt had saved Russia from an even worse fate at Portsmouth, this did not stop some voices in St. Petersburg from calling the President a "Nipponophile."[17] Likewise, Roosevelt's impressions of the Russians and Russian behavior at Portsmouth were distinctly negative, as the President's following letter to British historian Trevelyan indicates:

The Russians all pulled against one another, rarely knew their own minds, lied so to others that they finally got into the dangerous position of lying to themselves, and showed a most unhealthy and widespread corruption and selfishness. . . . I thought the Russian negotiator's [Sergius Witte's] bragging and bluster not only foolish but shockingly vulgar when compared with the gentlemanly self-respecting self-restraint [sic] of the Japanese.[18]

Despite T. R.'s policy of "balanced antagonisms" during the Russo-Japanese War and the Portsmouth negotiations, Japan emerged as a more formidable rival to U.S. interests in Manchuria than Russia. Judging from Russian Foreign Office and U.S. Department of State records, the Russians continued to fear new attacks by the Japanese even after the signing of the peace treaty. Also, there began to be a division of opinion at the Tsar's court on how to handle the United States in the postwar period. One group, an early species of "doves," favored U.S.-Russian rapprochement; a second, more hard-line group, on the other hand, favored a more flexible policy of alignment with Japan, and together with Japan, domination of East Asia. It was the second group that won. The joint Russian and Japanese exploitation of Manchuria which followed was supported by Britain and France, while the "dollar diplomacy" of President William Howard Taft and his Secretary of State Knox suffered a setback in its commercial and diplomatic application to the Far East.

Swinging Between Good and Poor Relations

Failure of both U.S. dollar diplomacy and the Open Door Policy (exploitation of China was neither equal nor "open" to all) coupled with declining American investments in Manchuria did have a useful by-product: partial restoration of the traditional friendship between America and Russia. This came about, first, because one of the two countries, the U.S., was becoming disengaged from Manchuria, the area of their former rivalry. Secondly, the "common enemy" motif was slowly reemerging after the Russo-Japanese War. In American and Russian eyes, Japan was now the powerful threat to balance-of-power equilibrium in the Far East, causing alarm both in St. Petersburg and Washington. But the old friendship, as we saw, was only *partially* restored. This stemmed from a number of non-*Realpolitik* considerations.

First, we have already referred to the ill-feeling provoked by the struggles between the conservative and liberal/radical circles in Russia over the assassination of Tsar Alexander II and the accession to the throne of Alexander III, and the way the anti-Tsarist sentiments of American visitors to Russia were disseminated in America. The continuation and deepening of anti-Tsarist feeling in the U.S. (the abortive revolution of 1905 being a contributing factor) was abetted by the anti-Semitic pogroms and victimization of Jews in Russia by the "Black Hundreds" and other groups. Thousands of Jews thus fled Russia to seek asylum in the United States. The stories they told revealed the scope of Tsarist oppression, not only of Jews, but of the entire worker and peasant classes of Russia.

With the outbreak of the First World War, America at first kept aloof, while remaining for the most part sympathetic to England and France, but not to Russia. Russia did, however, receive U.S. supplies, which were sent across the Pacific to Vladivostok. Although the shipments were considerable—in 1916 alone worth $500,000—they constituted a fraction of those sent across the Atlantic to the Western Allies. Russian bonds were sold in the U.S., and American loans by the U.S. government to Russia amounted to $86 million. But all this show of support was comparatively modest and was accompanied by very little editorial and public support for Russia in the war. By 1917, however, the whole military-diplomatic situation changed radically, once the actions by German U-boats in the Atlantic at the end of January 1917 led to America's entry into the war (in April 1917). Before March and April, however, a repugnance had been voiced at the prospects of America's joining forces with the autocratic and reactionary Tsarist regime.

American Reaction to Russia's Two Revolutions of 1917

In March came earth-shaking news from the Russian capital; it changed American sympathies overnight: the Tsar was overthrown (March 15, 1917). U.S. newspapers and public officials voiced satisfaction with the events taking place in Russia and hailed the advent of a new, democratic order in Russia:

A free people naturally wants all the other peoples of the world to be free. It is the American hope that Russia will hold its new freedom, develop it and through it work out a great national destiny.—*Washington Star*.[19]

Autocracy has received its death blow; democracy has triumphed. All of America rejoices to see the dawn of the new day for Russia.—*Zion's Herald*.[20]

American editors rejoice that instead of reluctantly taking the corrupt despotism of the Romanoffs as an ally, we may proudly join hands with the self-governing people of Russia in a war of peoples against kings.—*Literary Digest*.[21]

Even former President Theodore Roosevelt, a Russophobe of sorts, was moved to remark: "I rejoice from my soul that Russia, the hereditary friend of this country, has ranged herself on the side of orderly liberty, of enlightened freedom, and for the full performance of duty by free nations throughout the world."

The story of what happened in the Russian Revolution during 1917 and until November 7 and the Bolshevik *coup d'état* has been told many times, hence there is no need to retell it here. As for U.S.-Russian relations with the Lvov and Kerensky Provisional Governments, the central U.S. concern throughout the year was Russia's continued participation in World War I.

The commission headed by Elihu Root and sent to Russia by President Woodrow Wilson in mid-June 1917 was designed for the purpose of keeping Russia loyal to the Allied cause. At the same time, the actions of the Wilson government and the reports on the Russian domestic situation filed by Ambassador David R. Francis from Petrograd revealed a definite lack of understanding of the grim political realities of revolutionary Russia. Ambassador Francis was taken completely by surprise when the Bolsheviks seized power in late autumn, although the danger of such an event seemed more than likely to other observers in the country. The Provisional Government was so weak that it was unable in many instances to enforce discipline among the soldiers at the front or to maintain order in the streets at home.

We have reviewed (Chapter III) the American reaction to the Bolshevik seizure of power and the policies unfolded by Vladimir Ilyich Ulyanov (Lenin), Chairman of the Council of People's Commissars, the head of the

Bolshevik government, which as many have forgotten, was described in the founding decree establishing the regime as itself a "provisional" government. But this "provisional" regime certainly did not act as if it were a mere caretaker government! Its first measures and decrees revealed that under the Bolsheviks profound changes were to be made in Russia's domestic and foreign policy. Among the *domestic* developments were

—nationalization of the land
—suppression of "hostile" newspapers; establishment of Press Tribunals
—establishment of a "Workers' Militia," later to become the Cheka or Extraordinary Commission for Combatting Counterrevolution working in conjunction with "Revolutionary Tribunals" and often arbitrarily applying the death penalty
—nationalization of all banks
—state and party control over all publications
—separation of church and state and curtailment of the former
—"socialization of the national economy," including state monopoly of foreign trade
—abolition of military ranks and titles
—Declaration of the Rights of the Peoples of Russia (with foreign implications as well)
—dissolution of the freely elected Constituent Assembly in January 1918 by the Bolsheviks after a *one-day* convocation

Decrees and policies affecting the new regime's behavior in the *international* arena were

—Decree on Peace, including abolishment of secret diplomacy; publication of Tsarist secret treaties and agreements; calling upon belligerents in World War I to end hostilities; calling upon the "proletariat" in all countries participating in the war to "interfere in the question of war and peace"; encouragement of the creation of Soviet movements and regimes in other countries
—repudiation of all foreign debts
—decree establishing the Council of People's Commissars placing Leon D. Bronstein (Trotsky) at the head of the Commissariat of Foreign Affairs and J. V. Djugashvili (Stalin) Chairman of the Council on Affairs of Nationalities
—Lenin government's entering into direct contact with Germany resulting in armistice talks between Bolshevik Russia and Germany during which the Germans penetrated more deeply into Russian territory; eventual signing by Russia and Germany of the capitulationist Brest-Litovsk Treaty (March 3, 1918)
—the forcible spread of the Soviet system, with help of the Red Army, to nations which were formerly part of the Tsarist empire, despite Bolshevik promises of national autonomy and self-determination

Many of the policies of the Lenin-Trotsky regime fashioned in Petrograd from the Bolshevik seizure in November 1917 until the silencing of the guns of World War I in November 1918 seemed almost calculated to rupture

American and Russian relations. Foremost among the factors aggravating these relations was the Soviet Russian withdrawal from the war.

Lenin, who at this time was a revolutionary Jacobin first and a diplomat second, was hell bent on saving Bolshevism in Russia and spreading his brand of revolutionary socialism abroad. The Brest-Litovsk sellout to Germany was motivated mainly by the Bolsheviks' need for peace in order to spread and strengthen Soviet rule throughout Russia. It is possible that Lenin calculated that Germany, in any case, would be defeated by the Western powers. But his decision to withdraw from the war was scarcely welcomed in the Allied countries, especially not in America. Also, in Wilson's Fourteen Points issued in January 1918 and disseminated throughout Russia,* Article Six provided for Russia's territorial integrity—a war aim whose fulfillment Lenin may have counted upon when he surrendered over a quarter of Russia's population and the rich Ukraine to the Germans at Brest-Litovsk.

The intervention of the Allies in Russia from early 1918 to 1920 was at first motivated by the need to keep Russian military forces intact on the Eastern Front. Once the war ended, the Allied intervention acquired the tinge of a mission to aid the anti-Bolshevik forces of Russia in their effort to unseat the Bolsheviks in Moscow. (Lenin had moved the Soviet capital to Moscow in March 1918 as the Germans swept toward the former capital, Petrograd.) George F. Kennan has written the following about the Allied intervention:

If one were to sum up the whole story of the intervention, one might put it this way. For motives which initially consisted primarily of a desire to restore resistance to the Germans in the East, but which certainly also involved an active distaste for Soviet power and a strong desire to see it replaced by one more friendly to the Allied cause, the Allied governments involved themselves, in 1918, in a series of halfhearted efforts to give aid and support to anti-Bolshevik factions in Russia. . . . The allied efforts were unsuccessful and played, generally, into Communist hands.[22]

Although it may have been advantageous rather than baneful to the Bolsheviks, the Allied intervention continues to be cited in Soviet history books as a "concerted" attempt by the capitalists to destroy the Soviet regime.

The "Strange Alliance"

The term "strange alliance"[23] is an apt expression to describe Soviet-Allied collaboration during World War II. It was strange because of the contrast

*Copies of Wilson's address, containing the Fourteen Points, enjoyed wide distribution in Russia, thanks to the efforts of the Creel Committee on Public Information, which was established in Russia by the U.S. government during the era of the Provisional Government. Another American document to be translated into Russian and disseminated in Soviet Russia at this time was the American Declaration of Independence.

struck between this wartime cooperation and the era that immediately preceded it (see Chapters II and III). Strange also because the Soviet half of the alliance had declared an ideological war against its future allies which it suspended merely "for the duration"; it had predicted the eventual annihilation of the capitalist, liberal-democratic order in the West. But it was an alliance in a limited sense—"limited" for the reason that the Western Allies were never made privy to Soviet military planning within Stalin's Council for National Defense, and for other reasons. Still, the alliance provided another example of the mutual recognition of the convergence of the two countries' national interests. As in the previous instances of active cordiality, Russian and American friendship during what the Soviets call the *Great* Fatherland War (to distinguish it from the Fatherland War of 1812 against Napoleon*) was motivated by a "common enemy."

"I have today found," President Franklin D. Roosevelt declared on the 24th anniversary of the Bolshevik "October Revolution," November 7, 1941, "that the defense of the U.S.S.R. is vital to the defense of the United States." This date was just one month to the day prior to the Japanese sneak attack on Pearl Harbor and four months after the German sneak attack on Russia. Roosevelt's statement reflected a bridge-to-Russia policy, a new East-West détente that had already been largely prepared in London, since the U.K. had already been at war with the Axis for two years.

It had not been easy for the British to get a receptive audience with Stalin and his associates before the German invasion on June 22, 1941. British Ambassador Sir Stafford Cripps, a Fabian Socialist and well-known Labor Party figure, had tried more than once, following his assignment to Moscow by Churchill's coalition government in 1940. But at last he was granted a personal meeting with Stalin in the second week of July 1941, or three weeks after the Nazis' Operation Barbarossa (the conquest of Russia) went into effect. By July 12 an Anglo-Soviet mutual aid agreement was rapidly concluded and signed in Foreign Commissar Molotov's office, which was furnished with an ample supply of Soviet champagne and chocolate candy. Despite the refreshments, the occasion was markedly somber, according to a Western newspaper correspondent who was present.[24] During the remainder of the year, still more British visitors came to the Soviet capital, while Molotov made a trip to London. The most important of these British-Soviet get-togethers were headed on the British side by Lord William M. A. Beaverbrook, Churchill's minister for war production. It was Beaverbrook's mission to Moscow in September 1941 (the month that the U.S.S.R. grudgingly subscribed to the 1940 Atlantic Charter) that helped pave the way to the formal Anglo-Soviet alliance signed on May 26, 1942,

*Napoleon launched his invasion of Russia in June, as did Hitler 127 Junes after, only to find himself under siege later in the year by that master tactician of Russian defense, "Marshal Winter."

and to the broad cooperation between East and West during the Second World War.

This alliance was important not only as preparation for U.S.-Soviet collaboration during the war; it also may have served as the starting point for Allied recognition of the Soviets' territorial acquisitions that had been made immediately preceding and following the outbreak of World War II.

When British Foreign Secretary Anthony Eden went to Moscow in December 1941 to negotiate the twenty-year Anglo-Soviet treaty, the problem of Soviet territorial acquisitions was adroitly raised by Stalin and Molotov.[25] It appeared obvious that the Soviet leaders wanted explicit British recognition of the fact that their new territories were "legally" theirs; the Soviet leaders implied that this was the price for a treaty. But no such *formal* recognition was forthcoming from the British, at least not at this early juncture; it was to come in later conferences. For one thing, at this time there were strong objections from the United States (one reason being the existence of 5 million or more citizens of Polish extraction living in the U.S.). So the issue was tabled until it was brought up later at the Yalta and Potsdam Conferences. Still, the Soviets had broached the issue and had gotten what they considered tacit British support for these recent enlargements of the Soviet empire.

The story has often been told of how relations between America and Russia became closer at the very time America itself was drawn into the Second World War and as the Lend-Lease program (projected in 1940, not signed into law until March 1941) began to be applied to the U.S.S.R. after November 1941. The Nazi invasion of Russia and the ensuing shipments of American Lend-Lease supplies through Murmansk, U.S.S.R., were accompanied by a wave of pro-Soviet feeling in the U.S., which gradually escalated after Pearl Harbor, December 7, 1941.

Just after the Germans began carrying out Operation Barbarossa, the United States, as did England, began sounding out the Russians. At President Roosevelt's invitation Soviet ambassador to the U.S. Konstantin Oumansky accompanied by the Deputy Chief of the Soviet General Staff and chief of military intelligence. Lieutenant-General Filipp Golikov and his adjutant, came to the White House on July 31, 1941. Golikov told the press after his meeting with the President that it had been "easy" to talk to the President. It turned out that tentative arrangements for shipments of Lend-Lease aid to Russia were worked out with Golikov. Meantime in Moscow, the President's "roving Ambassador," Harry Hopkins, had a three-hour discussion with Marshal Stalin, preceded the night before by an equally lengthy conversation. In these talks, too, plans were laid for giving extensive American aid to the Russian war effort (see next chapter).

In these and succeeding negotiations, and in the eventual agreement on the nature and extent of the sizable American Lend-Lease shipments to the

U.S.S.R., no attempt at political bargaining with the Soviets was made by Roosevelt or his envoys. The negotiations might have provided an opportunity to demand a number of written pledges or clarifications from Stalin concerning the postwar boundaries and spheres of influence to be assigned the U.S.S.R. The breast-beating that accompanied the "great debates" of the early 1950s could have been avoided had the critics of U.S. foreign policy (some of whom were too busy looking for "Reds" and security risks in the Department of State) concentrated their fire on the obvious: failure by the U.S. to exploit its economic and military advantage vis-à-vis Russia when the latter was seized with a series of desperate military situations from 1941 through 1943.

By the time Stalin's armies had overswept half of Europe, it was clearly too late to clarify postwar territorial settlements or to exact a price from the Russians for restraining their territorial ambitions. Russian history should have taught Western diplomats that *a militarily assaulted Russia, once it is on the rebound, extends itself outwards beyond its original frontiers.* True, this tradition need not have "inevitably" repeated itself. But it is a persistent strain in Russian history and one of which Russian leaders themselves are undoubtedly perfectly cognizant.

American and Soviet Reactions

As another new period of pro-Soviet feeling opened in the United States, the "traditional" Russian and American friendship of bygone days began to be recalled—with the usual sentimentality. At times, the pro-Soviet euphoria went to ridiculous extremes: for example, the "similarity of the two countries consists in the essentially democratic structure of their basic socio-cultural institutions."[26] One need only examine, for example, the texts of various speeches and pamphlets issued under the auspices of the Congress of American-Soviet Friendship. Its Honorary Chairman was the former ambassador to Russia in the 1930s, the economist and diplomat-come-lately Joseph E. Davies, author of *Mission to Moscow,* which contained a strong plea for American understanding of Stalinist Russia.* From the Soviet side came *restrained* recognition of the tradition of Russian and American friendship. A few excerpts from articles or speeches illustrate this outbreak of Russian and American cordiality:[27]

Our alliance with Russia is no accident, but a natural result of common interests and aims in the sphere of democracy and national affairs. We must work together

*When a film version of Davies' book appeared during the war, it caused a great stir. The American Socialist leader, Norman Thomas, organized a protest petition, signed by 52 anti-Communist leftists, who objected that Davies had prettified and falsified Stalinist dictatorship and had made erroneous comparisons between Stalinism and Western democracy.

to build a secure and peaceful world.—Foreword to the report by the Congress of American-Soviet Friendship, 1942.

Friendship between the U.S.S.R. and the U.S.A., based upon complete mutual understanding, confidence, and respect, should occupy a conspicuous place in the system of United Nations cooperation—cooperation dictated by the common interest in bringing the war to a victorious end, and quite essential for the solution of the vast problems bound to arise after the war.—Soviet ambassador to the U.S., and preceding Molotov as U.S.S.R. Commissar of Foreign Affairs, Maxim M. Litvinov, 1943.

There is enough goodwill and wisdom in both countries to help build a bridge of permanent peace that will securely span the narrow waters that separate our mighty republics.—Harold L. Ickes, Secretary of the Interior, 1943.

There is no hedging, and no deviation from any commitment they make, no matter how inconvenient or difficult carrying out their word may seem to be when the time comes to deliver the goods.—Henry W. Morgenthau, Jr., Secretary of the Treasury, 1943.

The pro-Soviet euphoria, of course, had not captivated all minds in America. William C. Bullitt, the veteran diplomat and former U.S. ambassador to Moscow and Paris, warned against "Soviet imperialism" and predicted that one day an anti-Soviet alliance would have to be formed. In *America's Second Crusade*, William Henry Chamberlin, the well-known historian and writer on Russia, called the attitude toward Stalinist Russia in America during World War II "a depressing compound of profound factual ignorance, naiveté, wishful thinking and emotional hysteria."[28] Herbert Hoover remarked one week after the German attack on Russia that "joining in a war with Stalin to impose freedom is a travesty." Senator Harry S. Truman's alleged comment at the time of the Nazi invasion of Russia was reported in *The New York Times*. It was his hope, he was quoted as saying, that Russia and Germany would inflict as many fatalities on each other as possible.*

From these statements it was obvious that for some Americans it was not easy to forget a number of facts about the Soviet record, foreign and domestic: the purges, the forced labor camps, collectivization, the ideological warfare by the Comintern (not dissolved until 1943), the deal with Hitler, the invasion of Finland and the dismemberment of Poland in 1939, the occupation and sovietization of the three Baltic countries in 1940, and so on. Obviously, these black marks on the Soviet record did not affect—nor, perhaps, should they have affected—the policy-makers in London and Washington for whom U.S.–U.K.–U.S.S.R. military collaboration in World War II was more important than the moral question of helping out Stalin.

---

*In a recent letter to me, former President Truman disclaimed ever having heard he was so quoted, let alone having actually said what he was quoted as saying in *The New York Times*.

We have already mentioned that the Soviets were restrained in their handling of the historic-friendship line. On balance, there was far more favorable comment in the open societies of the Western world about this friendship—especially about alleged strong likenesses between "Soviet democracy and Western democracy"—than in the U.S.S.R., where no such similarities were drawn. Moreover, *what was said by the Soviets* was different in both quantity and quality from what was said in the West.

The Soviet presentation of its collaboration with the Western democracies proceeded somewhat as follows. Fascism (and later, "Japanese militarism," a term which was used by the Soviets only during and after their *one-week* war with Japan in August 1945) is the sworn enemy of *all* civilization. Fascism represents a bestial form of capitalist imperialism against which it is even in the interest of nonbestial capitalist imperialists themselves to struggle.

This line, of course, required the twisting of basic Marxist-Leninist-Stalinist ideology as does, indeed, today's anti-China line of the Kremlin, namely, that Maoist Communism is a threat to world civilization. But strictly according to the ideology, can there be *varying degrees* of imperialism—some bestial, some not? One would think not. In the Stalinist wartime party line, there was even the suggestion that World War II as a whole was a "liberating" struggle—liberating for whom and in what way became, of course, a sore point in the Cold War years after 1945 (see the preceding chapter).

Still, a precedent of sorts had been established during the four-year period of the war. Communist Russia could ally itself, as it surely had to under the circumstances of 1941–1945, with the "imperialist West" and still preserve its ideological virginity. Given the importance of ideology as the preservative and legitimizer of Soviet rule in Russia, it is a precedent worth remembering today and tomorrow as new titanic forces and trends of world-historical proportions are taking shape and as new alignments, loyalties, and strange alliances loom on the horizon.

The wartime experience of the alliance teaches perhaps another lesson. Ideology is, after all, fashioned from far more elastic fabric than is the national flag.

NOTES

1. Edward H. Zabriskie, *American-Russian Rivalry in the Far East 1895–1914 —A Study in Diplomacy and Power Politics* (Philadelphia: University of Pennsylvania Press, 1946), p. 1.
2. Dulles, *op. cit.*, p. 26. The *Niles' Register* (originally called the *Niles' Weekly Register*) was one of the most widely read and influential political journals of the day and is now of great interest to historians. The publication was

founded in 1811 by Hezekiah Niles (1777–1839), formerly editor-in-chief of the Baltimore *Evening Post*.

3. Zabriskie, *op. cit.*, p. 11.

4. *Ibid.*, p. 1. Foster Rhea Dulles observes, *op. cit.*, p. 54: "There was no question of the motive behind Russia's policy. Alexander II, who had succeeded the throne in 1855 [following Nicholas I], favored maintenance of the Union, as Catherine had in fact welcomed our independence and Alexander I upheld our rights during the Napoleonic Wars, because a powerful America offset the maritime supremacy of the British Empire. His policy was nationalistic, and realistic. It had little to do with sentiment." There was, nevertheless, considerable sentimentalizing on both sides. The one notable exception was the blunt statement by the Russian minister to Washington, Edward von Stoeckl, who said: "The best guarantee against the ambitious projects and political egotism of the Anglo-Saxon race" was the promotion of rivalry between the two Anglo-Saxon powers, the U.S. and Great Britain (Dulles, *op. cit.*, p. 54).

5. Zabriskie, *op. cit.*, p. 12; also Dulles, *op. cit.*, p. 54. Russia stoutly rejected offers by the Southern Confederacy to send a Confederate envoy to St. Petersburg.

6. See Max M. Laserson, *The American Impact on Russia—Diplomatic and Ideological* (New York: Macmillan, 1950), pp. 176–177, for a description.

7. Dulles, *op. cit.*, p. 59. See also Laserson, *op. cit.*, pp. 177–181.

8. Dulles, *op. cit.*, p. 61.

9. Laserson, *op. cit.*, pp. 242–243.

10. Dennis J. Doolin, *Territorial Claims in the Sino-Soviet Conflict—Documents and Analysis*. The Hoover Institution on War, Revolution, and Peace (Palo Alto, Calif.: Stanford University, 1965), pp. 13–14.

11. Zabriskie, *op. cit.*, pp. 21–22.

12. *Ibid.*, pp. 22–23.

13. Laserson, *op. cit.*, p. 171.

14. *Ibid.*, p. 49.

15. Dulles, *op. cit.*, p. 87.

16. Joseph Bucklin Bishop, *Theodore Roosevelt and His Time Shown in His Letters*, 2 vols. (New York: Scribner, 1920) vol. I, p. 418. The quotation is from a letter by Roosevelt to the British historian Sir George Trevelyan, September 12, 1905. Earlier, Roosevelt had remarked to Senator Henry Cabot Lodge: "Russia is so corrupt, so treacherous, so shifty, and so incompetent, that I am utterly unable to say whether or not it will make peace or break off the negotiations at any moment. Japan is, of course, utterly selfish, though with a veneer of courtesy . . . " (Zabriskie, *op. cit.*, p. 120).

17. Zabriskie, *op. cit.*, p. 129.

18. *Ibid.* Kennan, *op. cit.*, p. 393, recalls another bitterly anti-Russian statement made by T.R.: "Russia for a number of years has treated the United States as badly as she treated England. . . . Her diplomatists lied to us with brazen and contemptuous effrontery, and showed with cynical indifference their intention to organize China against our interests. . . . I should have liked to be friendly with her; but she simply would not permit it, and those respon-

sible for managing her foreign policy betrayed a brutality and ignorance, an arrogance and short-sightedness, which are not often combined."

19. Filene, *op. cit.*, p. 10.
20. *Ibid.*
21. Dulles, *op. cit.*, p. 98.
22. Kennan, *op. cit.*, p. 199.
23. From John R. Deane, *The Strange Alliance* (New York: Viking Press, 1946).
24. Alexander Werth, *Russia at War—1941–1945* (New York: Dutton, 1964), p. 179.
25. Werth, *op. cit.*, p. 383.
26. Sorokin, *op. cit.*, p. 63. See also Dr. Harry F. Ward, *The Story of American-Soviet Relations—1917–1959* (New York: National Council of American-Soviet Friendship, 1959). Ward was Professor Emeritus of Christian Ethics at Union Theological Seminary in New York at the time he wrote this book and an ardent proponent of what he termed "Soviet democracy."
27. Quoted in Ward, *op. cit.*, pp. 30–33.
28. *Ibid.*, p. 34.

CHAPTER V

Russian-American Economic Cooperation

Considering as necessary the future development of economic relations with capitalist countries . . . and the application of the technology of the foremost capitalist states for accelerating the industrialization of the U.S.S.R., the party congress stresses the great significance of Bolshevik tempos in Socialist industrialization of the country in order to provide economic self-sufficiency for the U.S.S.R.
—JOSEPH STALIN, to the Sixteenth C.P.S.U.(b) Congress, June 26, 1930

Reliance on capitalist know-how in order to attain economic self-sufficiency —this was Stalin's program in the area of foreign economic involvement. It was successful largely because the West—and especially the United States— was glad to do business with the Russians. An important economic link between East and West was thereby formed.

Under the Tsars, imports amounted to only a small part of total world trade, some 3 percent.[1] Thus the Bolsheviks had inherited a degree of Russian autarky from the previous regime even before they themselves deliberately set economic self-sufficiency as their goal. But the degree of industrialization in Russia lagged far behind that of the other great European powers. Thus, to achieve self-sufficiency in the modern world, it was first necessary to accelerate Russia's own industrialization. To accomplish this, however, partial *dependency* on foreign nations and foreign technologies became necessary for attaining *independence* from those same foreign states.[2]

One of the first feelers put out by the U.S.S.R. for financial help was in the direction of the United States. In the 1920s, the Chase Bank of New York extended a $20 million credit to the new Soviet Republic, an unusual action for a Western country in the early period of Soviet rule.[3] For dozens of years, no other Western bank was to make loans to the Soviets, although the Chase credit was dutifully repaid within a few months.

In speaking of the early period in the 1920s up to Stalin's First Five-Year Plan, the most outstanding case of U.S. economic assistance to Russia was the case of the emergency assistance under the American Relief Administration (ARA).

The ARA was of immense importance in saving untold millions of Russians from outright starvation during the years 1921–1923. The U.S. House of Representatives authorized an appropriation (which was approved by the Senate) of $20 million in food, medical, and other supplies, which, when added to other contributions from the U.S., amounted to a staggering (for that time) $66.3 million. Although the Soviet government eventually provided transportation and housing for ARA officials under Herbert Hoover, then Secretary of Commerce, negotiations for undertaking the mission were delayed because of Russian suspicions of the Hoover mission's motives. As part of the agreement, the U.S. promised no discrimination and no anti-Soviet activities. An auxiliary arrangement flowing from ARA was the Soviet payment of $10 million in Russian gold bullion for the purchase of seeds and additional foodstuffs.

The aid was received at the time with strongly but *unofficially* expressed gratitude on the part of the Russians, who pronounced the initials "ARA" as an acronym, "Ara." Officially, however, the aid has not been so received. The *Small Soviet Encyclopedia*, one of the most widely read Soviet reference books in the U.S.S.R., asserts:

'ARA,' headed by H. Hoover, claimed officially that its task was to give foodstuffs and all other types of aid to any European country suffering as a result of the First World War. In fact the principal aims of the 'ARA' was to conduct a struggle against revolutionary movements and strengthen the economic and political positions of American imperialism in the European countries. . . . In a number of instances, 'ARA' undertook espionage and underground activities and the support of counterrevolutionary elements.[4]

What is suspect here is not so much ARA's alleged motivations in 1921–1922, but the motivations of the party-directed editors of the Soviet encyclopedia in 1958 for painting a negative picture of the work of ARA. (The encyclopedia moreover omits any mention of the millions of Russians who received the aid.) In the next chapter of the present book the question of the C.P.S.U.'s "vested interest" in a generally anti-American line will be explored at length.

When the subject of U.S. economic aid to Russia is brought up, one immediately thinks not only of ARA, but especially of Lend-Lease aid during World War II. It is a relatively recent expression of American aid to Russia. And it was a very large contribution.

Total U.S. Lend-Lease aid is put at $11 billion (this figure does not include the contributions made to Russia by the other Allies). If the aid supplied by the three "Anglo-Saxon" Allies (the U.S., U.K., and Canada) is taken together, it amounts to this:

    10,000 tanks
    10,000 pieces of artillery
    14,500 airplanes
    100,000 tons of rubber
    500,000 tons of nonferrous metals
    Nearly 500,000 trucks (of crucial importance in the Soviet defense of Stalingrad)
    2.3 million tons of food provisions
    Hundreds of ships
    $3 billion worth of machinery, including whole factories
    Military cloth sufficient to clothe 3 million Red Army soldiers[5]

As impressive as this aid was—and the Soviet statements to this effect are testimony of its importance*—the Allied shipments of tanks and planes to Russia amounted to only four months of the Soviets' own production of tanks and planes during the last three years of the German-Russian phase of World War II. Moreover, a Russian general has claimed that Lend-Lease equalled only 6 percent of U.S.S.R. wartime production of tanks, guns, and planes. The American scholar and Russian specialist Ellsworth Raymond, who was on the scene in Russia working in the U.S. Embassy in Moscow during part of the war, has observed:

Most Lend-Lease reached Russia in the later years of war, when the Red Army was winning on its own. . . . Thus the Russian claim is probably true that the U.S.S.R. fought the war mostly with weapons made in Soviet factories from Soviet raw materials. On the other hand, Allied machinery and transportation supplies were very great. The most objective estimate is that Lend-Lease was marginal assistance, coming rather late in the war. Only the Kremlin knows whether or not this marginal aid was crucial for Soviet victory. But the grand 1,400 mile Russian offensive from Stalingrad [1943] to Berlin [1945] would certainly have been much slower had there been no Lend-Lease.[6]

As deserving in importance as Lend-Lease is on the historical record, another longer and broader American assistance to Russia is often ignored. It is of considerable importance for encouraging Russian and American convergence. It is doubtful, in fact, whether Russia could have been able to tool up for war in the late 1930s and in the 1940s as rapidly as it did had it not been for *the foundations laid by long-standing American technical assistance*. Doing-business-with-Russia not only predates U.S. recognition of the

*See this chapter below, pp. 112–113 and *passim.*

U.S.S.R. in 1933, it goes back to before 1917—in fact, to the beginning of the last century. Given below—for the first time in any comprehensive form —is an account of this assistance.

Early Period of U.S. Technical Assistance[7]

As far back as 1783 the U.S. Minister to Russia Francis Dana predicted that "in the nature of things" future relations between the United States and Russia would be commercial rather than political. Dating from the time when U.S. Army Major George Washington Whistler was called to St. Petersburg by Nicholas I in 1842 to serve as consulting engineer for the building of Russia's largest and best-equipped railroad to that date, every facet of the Russian economy has felt the influence of American technology, inventions, know-how, and assistance. This American role by no means diminished in the twentieth century with the establishment of the Soviet regime. Rather, it increased. The one-hundred-year experience of American involvement in the Russian economy laid in the nineteenth century served as the foundation upon which American assistance to the Soviets was undertaken in the late 1920s and early 1930s, despite nonrecognition of the Soviet regime by Washington.

Dependence of Russia upon the West generally for the development of its economy dates back to the reign of Peter the Great. Carpenters and blacksmiths from Holland visited the palace of the enterprising Tsar, the builder of the new city of "Sankt-Peterburg," named for his patron saint. Scientists, scholars and specialists of various kinds also were solicited by Tsar Peter I. The resultant great reforms in education and in the military and state structure of Russia reflected these direct Western influences. But until the West itself had begun to employ manufacture of goods at the end of the eighteenth century, Western Europe's influence upon Tsarist Russia earlier in the century had been intellectual and cultural, affecting mainly the small aristocratic élite or the court. The vast majority of the Russian population was left unaffected by the various Western influences: Peter's reforms only kept the Russian peasant more hopelessly subordinated to the landowning nobility.

However, during the reign of Nicholas I (1825–1855), Russia at last showed signs of becoming conscious of its incredible backwardness, compared to the Western standard of living. The Tsar's personal awareness of this fact was reflected, for example, in the law of 1840 which gave factory owners the option of liberating serfs bound specifically to their factories thereby opening the way for creation of a class of "free hired labor." This law meant little when the small size of both the middle-class entrepreneurs and their serfs is taken into account. Still, it signified the beginning of the Russian government's interest in laying the basis for industrialization of Russia, a country rich in natural resources and full of great potentiality.

"Some time in 1840," a U.S. engineer and traveler to Russia at that time, John S. Maxwell, tells us, the Emperor Nicholas assembled his counselors and requested their opinions as to the possibility of a railroad from St. Petersburg to Moscow. Everyone opposed it except Count Kleinmichel, the Minister of Ways and Communications. After due consideration it was concluded that railroads "as they are constructed in the United States" were the most suitable for the empire. Major George Washington Whistler, "an American gentleman of distinguished ability in his profession," was invited to visit Russia and superintend the making of the proposed road, subsequently called the Nicolayevsky Railroad. Neither money nor influence at court was of any importance, and all those who had built their hopes upon these two considerations were thrown aside for other foreigners who were known in Russia to possess the needed intelligence, energy, and perseverance. As soon as it was reported that the Americans had won the contract, reports Maxwell, "a prolonged growl was heard in the English quarter."

This early Russian dependence upon U.S. know-how in railroad building and maintenance was to lead to the journey of two Russian Army engineers, emissaries of Tsar Nicolas I, to the United States to acquaint themselves with American railroad techniques on-the-spot and to prepare themselves for application of this experience, with U.S. help, to Russia. The Russian engineers were especially impressed by Major Whistler's use of steep grades, sharp curves, machinery, and steam excavating devices—all these being applied by the Baltimore & Ohio Railroad, with whom Major Whistler had served as chief engineer. The Russians also admired the American system of bridge building. As a result, Major Whistler was invited to work for the Russian government for seven years on its ambitious railroad-building enterprise. It was on Whistler's advice, by the way, that the Russians adopted their well-known broad, five-foot wide gauge tracks which, as one version goes, resulted only accidentally from Russian misreading of Whistler's blueprints, by measuring track width from the outside edges of the rails instead of from the inside! (The wide gauge is still in use in the U.S.S.R.)

The actual railroad-building project was initiated with the construction in Russia of foundries and iron factories, together with the importation of those U.S.-made locomotives and machinery (steam pile drivers, earth excavators, machine tools, etc.) which had already been used so profitably in railroad construction in the United States.

"Human capital" was also lent to Russia by the U.S. at this time. American firms sent over to Russia numerous technicians, engineers, millwrights, bridge builders, and other specialists in fields relating to railroading. Maxwell reports that almost every steamer brought to Russia some "enterprising son of New England." Among them were Harmon and Eastwick of Philadelphia and, of course, Major Whistler himself, who received the Order of St. Anne from the Tsar before the American railroader's death in St. Petersburg in 1849.

One of the most outstanding achievements in this early Russian railroad building was the construction of one of the largest railroad foundries in the world at that time—the Alexander Foundry, sprawling over some 160 acres. It had been built by U.S. engineers and was staffed in the beginning with American technicians. It employed over 3,000 skilled workers. Hundreds of locomotives and thousands of railroad cars were built in this foundry. The Russian government was so pleased with it that it bestowed awards upon the U.S. technicians for the help they had given in its construction. Maxwell, who had become secretary of the U.S. legation in Russia at that time, predicted that a great economic future awaited Russia if it continued its railroad expansion. He added that U.S. engineers with experience in their own country could effect a regeneration of the economy of the Russian empire if they were invited to help and if their activities were not hampered by the barriers of passports and police. Such a regenerated economy, he said, would usher in extensive Russo-American trade. Perhaps if it had been a comprehensive program, it could have prevented revolution.

In addition to railroad construction, the U.S. played still another important role in the Russian economy in the early nineteenth century, in its most important sector—agriculture. Eleven times in the nineteenth century famine swept Russia, largely because of its inadequately plowed fields and the low level of agricultural science and technique. Even as late as 1905 the peasants, 80 percent of whom each held fewer than 18 acres of land as his share, "tickled" the soil with ancient, shallow wooden or iron plows and had in use a mere 138 tractors. What little agricultural innovation was made in the early as well as late nineteenth and early twentieth centuries most often bore a "Made in the U.S." stamp. Illustrative of this is the following story told by Maxwell:

One of the most amusing incidents attending our visit to this institution [an imperial farming institute near St. Petersburg] was to find there an American who had but lately arrived in the country. He spoke nothing but English and could hold no conversation whatever with those around him except through the medium of signs and gestures. He was a tall, thin man with a thoughtful countenance. He had brought with him a number of improved instruments of agriculture such as were never seen before in Russia. . . . He found the pupils of the farming institute reaping wheat with the old-fashioned sickle, mowing with a short scythe attached to a 10-foot pole, and plowing in every way but the right one. He perfectly astonished [the Russians] . . . with his long, straight furrows, his clean-cut sward, and his gigantic strides with the mysterious cradle. One blustering day he saw the scholar cleaning grain by throwing it up in the wind which carried off dust and chaff while the grain fell to the ground. One countryman did not like this antiquated process and constructed [on the spot] a winnowing mill out of such materials and such tools as happened to be on hand. . . . [He was] elected an honorary member of the Imperial Society for the Improvement of Agriculture.

Data are lacking on the quantity of U.S.-made farming equipment that found its way into Russia in the early period. By comparison with the amount imported at the *end of the nineteenth century* from the U.S.—when Russian foreign trade in general was coming enough into its own to start the country down the road to its first industrial revolution—it is of little significance.

U.S. Assistance in the Late Nineteenth Century and in the Twentieth

Although Russia and the United States differed considerably in their political customs and general outlook, various factors encouraged Americans after the American Civil War to visit Russia. The abolition of slavery in the United States and of serfdom in Russia was looked upon—somewhat mistakenly*— as a strong bond between both these countries. The visits of the Russian squadrons to the U.S. in 1864 and of the U.S. fleet to Russia in 1867, the assistance of the Russians to the North in the Civil War, and the purchase of Alaska—all contributed toward the travelers' sympathy and feeling of unity between the two developing countries. The economic growth of Russia, however, was sorely frustrated by various paradoxes in its national economy.

The Tsar levied high tariffs on imports (for example, 58 percent on pig iron) to protect the small amount of domestic industry, setting at the same time relatively low prices on grain, Russia's largest export. The result was that industrial goods were immeasurably higher priced than their foreign counterparts. Moreover, the purchasing power to buy them in Russia was severely restricted by the low income from grain sales and the general bankruptcy of both small peasant holders and the landowners themselves. Foreign imports of manufactured goods, once the tariff had been levied upon them, were also restrictive in price. In spite of the protests of the small, relatively powerless but rising industrial class, Tsarist legislation did little to release peasants from the village (the low agricultural technology required an abnormal amount of peasant labor in the fields) to become free labor in the urban areas. As a result, the country groaned on frustratedly until the significant financial reforms of N. K. Bunge, the brilliant Minister Finance under Alexander III, and of the talented Count Sergius Witte, Minister of Finance and influential in Russian finance after 1901. These able statesman started Russia up the road toward an industrial revolution.

*See footnote in Chapter IV above, p. 77.

Railroad Building

An official Soviet textbook on Russian economy, *History of the National Economy of Russia,* published 1947–1948, by Peter I. Lyashchenko, admits candidly that the period of the 1890s in Russia under Tsar Nicholas II witnessed "an industrial upsurge . . . one of the important stages in the history of the capitalist industry and national economy of Russia as a whole. . . . With respect to its tempo of development during these years, Russia outstripped nearly all countries." Quite a tribute to the Tsarists! The rate of expansion of industry—excluding its own perennial stimulus, railroad building—was indeed phenomenal. For example (according to Lyashchenko's figures), in the 1890s smelting of pig iron increased 190 percent (England, 18 percent); iron 116 percent (U.S., 63 percent); coal industry, 131 percent (Germany, 52 percent). The key industry of the railroads also showed huge advances and its influence over the rest of the economy was tremendous and crucial. A Russian government newspaper in 1897 assessed this influence as follows:

The building of railroad lines opened a new branch of industry for production of materials needed for them, the repercussions of which have not only been the building of large new factories and shops, but has caused large mining companies to busy themselves with one-extraction . . . materials necessary for building and use of railroads. Such influences of railroads upon the development of iron and steel and mechanical industries are immediate. Less direct influence, however, extends to all the other branches of industry, and also to trade.

Perry Collins, a U.S. businessman and explorer, predicted in the 1850s that if railroads could be strung across Siberia and industry developed there— a great possibility, he thought, after his explorations along the Amur River— Russia would enjoy the same upsurge of economic activity as did the United States when America began stretching itself westward, developing and lacing together new industries with railroad networks.

Figures given by the Tsarist government newspaper *Pravitelstvennii Vestnik* for the pace of railroad building in the 1880s and early 1900s are quite striking. For example:

1882–96	14,106 *versts* of track laid
1881–93	44% increase in number of passengers carried;
	43% increase in *versts* traveled
	108% increase in freight per *verst* (one verst = 1.067 km.; .6629 mi.)

The newspaper also listed industries that were stimulated because of their close connection with the maintenence of railroad transport and the production of fuel (domestic kerosene, coal, and gasoline industries).

The *financial* role of the United States was relatively small during this period (France's was much larger) as it had always been and continued to be. *But so far as its influence upon actual production know-how, equipping the railroads, and the setting up of construction facilities were concerned, the U.S. role was great and crucial.* The various forms that this American assistance took in railroad building—in the construction of the Chinese Eastern Railway and the Trans-Siberian Railway—were valued respectively at $286,260,000 and $172,525,000 (initial outlay), and can be categorized as follows:

> *U.S. inventions*
> *U.S. advanced technique made available to the Russian government*
> *U.S.-made machinery and equipment*

Moreover, certain basic inventions in the railroad field had their home in the United States. Among the important ones that have found their way into Russia have been the electric locomotive (invented by Page in 1851); diamond rock drill (Herman, 1854); sleeping car (Woodruff, 1856); air brake (Westinghouse, 1869); automatic coupler (Janney, 1873); and the development of any number of automatic railroad and signal devices, and so on, coming out of the rich railroading experience of manufacturing New England and Western U.S., with the largest rail networks in the world. Even more significant was the advanced American technique for producing and applying these and other non-American inventions in railroading.

Such American businessmen and travelers as Collins and Maxwell, Daniel Butterfield, Alexander Ford, and George F. Kennan were proved correct in their predictions that opening the Siberian lands for routes to the Pacific and the Far East for Russian trade, industrial expansion, and national defense would in turn open up trade with the United States, which itself had expanded to its own Pacific Coast. Not even the lack of a single U.S. banking house in Russia for conducting credit and foreign currency transactions prevented the U.S. from playing a large and varied role in Russia's eastward expansion, reflected in the construction and growing importance of the two Pacific ports of Vladivostok and Port Arthur.

Alexander Hume Ford, an American traveling engineer who was on hand at the time of the building of the Trans-Siberian railroad wrote at that time:

American activity was abroad in the land, and while Russian engineers at first laughed at the idea of American manufactures competing with Europe, they were induced to give a few orders [for goods]. To their astonishment the goods arrived in less than three months and proved the most durable and efficient tools up to that time. . . . The Russian officials suddenly realized that just across the Pacific pond, not 5,000 miles away, they [the Americans] could supply all the needs of the new railways and all hurry orders were promptly cabled [on the U.S.–British-made transatlantic cable] to America, whose markets were some 15,000 miles nearer eastern Siberia than those of Europe.

Realization of these facts of proximity of acquiring high-quality American goods and techniques resulted in the following events:

1. Visit of two Russian engineers in the 1890s as a committee empowered to make purchases of U.S. railroad equipment in the United States; they reported that three-quarters of the necessary equipment could be purchased in the U.S.;
2. The importation or construction in Siberia of U.S.-made steel bridges; track-laying tools; steel rails (production of steel rails instead of iron rails started on a small scale in Russia after 1874); air-brake system; automatic couplers; turning lathes; quartz mill; railroad machine shops; steamrollers and steam pile-driving machines; electric light plants; mogul machines for tearing up stumps, etc.; rolling stock of various types; telephone and telegraph wire; rock drills necessary for ripping through the Yablonoy, Baikal, and other high-lands; railroad-car wheel lathes; construction of the Saimova Railroad Works, and others.

Agricultural Machinery

In this field the U.S. role was also significant. What little agricultural machinery there was in Russia before Soviet importation of it and the Five-Year Plan production of agricultural implements and machinery (see below) almost always bore an American trademark. During Russia's boom periods of the 1890s and the early 1900s, when imports of machinery escalated along with domestic industry, huge amounts of U.S.-made farm equipment and almost every type of machinery were sent to Russia. While the U.S. "supplied the world" with agricultural machinery in the 1890s, *its biggest customer was Russia*. More than one-third of American agricultural machinery used outside the United States was found in Russia. Russian imports of American agricultural machinery quadrupled in five years during the 1890s. In 1901 alone, about $10 million was spent by Russia for U.S. agriculture machinery. It is hard to fix the figures for this accurately because of the fact that German shippers would sometimes fasten German labels over the U.S. labels during the machinery's transshipment.

In the 1890s the Russo-American Black Sea Steamship Line was established, thereby avoiding the expense of German or English transshipment. After these cargoes were unloaded, the machinery would then have to be transported by rail or river, which in turn stimulated construction of better land and river routes. Alexander Ford, an eyewitness at the wharves of Black Sea ports, particularly in Odessa at the time when these ships were arriving into port, related that he saw miles of American equipment lining the docks and trains. He also saw huge river barges on the Dnieper River, departing daily with loads of McCormick reapers, binders, movers, threshers, cleaners, and rakes—all of which were made in the United States. And where the railroads or rivers ended in trans-Urals Russia, camels took up the journey for the rest of the way into Siberia! In the spring of 1901 record shipments of agricultural machinery left New York bound for Russia: for example, 20,000 tons in 20 days.

Ford gives an account of the fading of the Russian peasant's initial suspiciousness of the machinery as "the inventions of the Devil":

After the man in the white blouse of the Russian soldier had been seen on the vast private estates of the Tsar, learning the use of the threshers and mowers, prejudice began to vanish, and village communes discussed the necessity of procuring harvesting that would enable the village *mir* [commune] to compete with the great overlords and pay taxes.

American business agents, completing orders for machinery personally with representatives of the village peasant communes, helped this peasant institution thrive and compete with both its Tsarist and landowner competitors. *Pravitelstvennii Vestnik* reported in 1896 (No. 224) on the creation of a fund for purchasing agricultural implements to the peasants. It was named Funds for Purchase of Implements and Agricultural Machinery to the Peasants, under the Administration of the Kiev Syndicate for Agriculture in the Counties (*uyezdy*). These banks were located in the cities and rich-soil provinces of Svenigorodsk, Kanevsk, Kiev, Bratislavl, and Mogilev-Podolsk. "The business is going well," the newspaper reported. Now the peasants, instead of relying on insufficient local industry, could "get the best foreign-made scythes, plows, harrows, machinery for cleaning grain, winnowing machines, sorting machines (*sortirovshchiki*), and others."

The arrival of U.S.-made agricultural machinery by river (to those thatched-roof Russian villages fortunate enough to receive it) was heralded with the ringing of the village churchbells. Led by the *Starosta* (head or elder) of the commune, the peasants would gather around the old Scottish-made river barges to watch the unloading of the valuable cargo. These barges were also employed for the "floating gardens" used to demonstrate and propagate the latest agronomical techniques, an idea employed by Russian government agronomists and well-suited to the river-oriented villages of the Ukraine.

In addition to the agricultural and other machinery purchased from U.S. concerns and sent to Russia, there were displays of American agricultural implements and machinery (and railroad equipment, locomotives, etc.) at Russia's famed Nizhni-Novgorod (now Gorky) fair of 1896. For the preceding nine years the fair had displayed an average of $89 million worth of goods and included some 4,000 booths for both the "outer" and "inner" fair grounds and the splendid palace built in 1890. A list of the American agricultural goods on display, many of which had already been ordered or purchased, included the following.

grain sorters (*sortirovshchiki*)

McCormick reapers

cotton-gins and presses (most often sent to Central Asian provinces and
   Vladivostok and elsewhere in Siberia)

rice-milling machines

threshers

cleaners

rakes

scythes

sulky plows

grain elevators

binders

mowers

dredging machinery (to deepen Russian rivers which in turn expedited transport of machinery to the villages)

lathes for turning axe handles and other wooden parts

Reports appeared daily in *Pravitelstvennii Vestnik* in the late 1890s on
the fair in the column headed "Around the Provinces." One such article (in
No. 136, 1896) cited the fact that in the "First Division" of the fair grounds
were displayed reapers (*zhneiki*) and reaper-binders (*zhneiki-sopovya-
zalki*) from "four famous American firms." The exhibit housing most of these
American samples was the "Second Exhibit of Agricultural Machines and
Equipment," set up by the Moscow Society of Agriculture on the Butyr *Khutor* (Farm) of the Moscow Agricultural School.

It was perhaps no exaggeration when Ford stated that the *regeneration
of Russian prairies was "left entirely" to American influence* and to the fact
that during the late 1890s "our shipments of mowers, reapers, and binders
doubled in one year." The importation of motor-driven equipment, such as
the tractor and bulldozer, came in the later Soviet period (see below).

The Short-lived U.S. Railroad Commission in Russia

The United States government sent the Root Commission to Russia in the
spring of 1917 "for the purpose of welcoming Russia to the sisterhood of
republics," but, more realistically, to ensure Russia's continued support of
the allies in World War I. Out of this commission, which toured throughout
most major parts of the country, came an economic recommendation: that a
commission of American railroad specialists be appointed to improve conditions on the Russian railroads to relieve both the military and civil bot-
tlenecks of supply during World War I.

The Allied Missions of England, France, and Italy by prior agreement
had assigned responsibility for all the transportation systems of the Russian
Provisional Government to the American ambassador—West European
recognition of America's stake in the railroad. At the suggestion of U.S.

Ambassador David R. Francis, a five-man advisory Commission of Railway Experts to Russia was appointed. The noted railroad engineer, John F. Stevens, was made chairman.

The commission arrived in Vladivostok in June 1917 and set about immediately to devise plans to alleviate congestion at Vladivostok and "to improve generally the transportation facilities of the Siberian railway." When the American Railroad commission went to Petrograd late in the summer, the experts reported to Ambassador Francis that they had inspected the Trans-Sib and had begun the erection of an assembly plant near Vladivostok. Soon, in October, at Ambassador Francis' suggestion and with the support of the Russian Ministry of Ways and Communications, the commission inspected the Donets system of railroads in the Ukraine. This inspection had just been completed when the Bolsheviks staged their coup in Moscow. Further work by the commission, and by Stevens in particular, was halted by disruption caused by the Bolshevik revolt. Ambassador Francis wrote of the frustration of any further helpful activity of this commission in Western Russia as follows: "The Bolshevik revolution prevented the consummation of the well-laid plans of these railroad experts." As a result, all the members of the commission returned to the United States, except Stevens. He remained in Russia, where he was established in the government's Ministry of Ways and Communications in the capacity of Special Adviser so that he could assist in the indeterminate future in carrying into effect the measures that the commission and Russian officials had agreed were vital for supplying the people of Russia with food and clothing.

Colonel Emerson's Group

Meanwhile, in Washington in September 1917, there had assembled, at the request of the Russian Provisional Government upon the recommendation of the Railway Advisory Commission, a party of 288 Americans consisting of railroad operating men, engineers, and interpreters, all under the command of Colonel George Emerson. This group, called the Russian Railway Service Corp, was organized by the U.S. War Department under the authority of President Wilson for the purpose of maintaining transportation between the Russian eastern front and the base of supplies at Valdivostok and of thus averting the threatened collapse of the Allies' eastern front. The Russian Railway Service Corp left the United States November 1, 1917, and arrived at the end of the month in Vladivostok. Because of the Bolshevik coup and widespread disorders in Russia, the "Corp," only after March 1918, managed to accomplish improvement of the Trans-Sib Railroad when it was able actually to direct the operation of the road, to maintain the road and equipment, and to supervise the movement of troops, of supplies and of ordnance of the Allied armies in the Allied intervention.

It was this U.S.-administered Russian Railway Service Corp which saved large numbers of the Czechoslovak Army in transit east through Siberia on their way to the United States and eventually to the West European front. But perhaps the Corp's chief accomplishment in its five years of existence was the feeding and supplying of the population of Siberia at the time of great civil upheaval. The population of west Siberia and the forces of Admiral Kolchak were entirely dependent on the Corp for assuring that supplies on the Trans-Siberian and other railways reached their destinations. The Kolchak anti-Bolshevik government arranged for the purchase of medical and other supplies under the Red Cross and was supplied transportation and protection for these shipments by Stevens' Corp and U.S. Army units under General William S. Graves stationed in Siberia.

Miscellaneous Technological Assistance

A list of other manufactured goods which came from the United States to Russia throughout the period 1894–1917 includes

tin plate
cast iron
oil well machinery
pipe-line tubing (supplied for the Odessa sewage system)
boilers (from the Ames Iron Works)
iron and steel railroad rails (Maryland Steel Co.)
piers
carriages and bicycles
railway cars, freight and passenger (Westinghouse)
rock drills (Ingersoll and Sergeant Co.)
gun lathes (Niles Co.)
machinery for turning out crankshafts for the Russian navy and shipbuilding
    tools including punching and sheering machines; pumps; plate-straightening and bending rolls (from Hilles and Jones Co., Wilmington, Delaware)
    —some of this machinery was located in the Nevsky Mechanics Works, St. Petersburg
machinery and ammunition (Bethlehem Steel Corp., and Remington Arms Co.)
Singer sewing machines
screw, universal-milling, surface-grinding, and universal-grinding machines
    (Brown and Sharpe Manufacturing Co., Providence, Rhode Island)
shingle-cutting machine (for the peasants' small-scale *artel* economy)
electric propelled, so-called American dredger (Linden W. Bates Engineer Works, Chicago)
locomotive boilers
locomotives (Baldwin Locomotive Co., Altoona, Pennsylvania)—
    Russian "Decapod" Locomotives first made here
office machines (International Business Machine Corp., New York)

Technical and material aid rendered Russia by U.S. firms in the field of dredging and ice-breaking was notable also. At the request of Tsar Nicholas II, Linden W. Bates, a famous dredging expert, visited some of Russia's frozen ports and drew up plans for both icebreakers and dredgers. Bates used his Chicago Company's experience in these activities on the Great Lakes. The result of Bates's Russian travels was the building of the world's largest dredger up to that time, the so-called electric-propelled "American Dredger." A contract for $7,000 was hence made with an American company to dredge the Pacific Ocean harbors of Russia. Among the completed projects was the important Alexander III Canal in St. Petersburg. Moreover, at least one committee of Russian engineers appointed by Tsar Nicholas II visited the United States in the 1890s to study the building of the Chicago Barge Canal. It had been constructed on land resembling Russia's flatland steppes. With the data on this American experience in their hands, the Russian engineers returned to their native country and set to work with U.S.-made dredgers, removing the shifting river and harbor shoals in various points of Russia.

Among the U.S firms doing business inside Russia at this time were the Walk-Over Shoe Co., the Singer Sewing Machine Co. (the building still stands in today's Leningrad), and the International Harvester Co., all with branch offices in Russia. Also, two U.S. bankers published reports on Russian economic problems. The banker, Wharton Barker, told how he had been invited to Russia in 1879 by the Grand Duke Constantine and Prince Sergius Dolgoruky to confer with them and other ministers on railroads and the coal, iron, and steel enterprises that were to be constructed or expanded in the south of Russia. In 1878 he had been appointed financial agent in the United States for the Russian government and had directed the building of four naval cruisers. Samuel McRoberts, vice-president of the National City Bank in New York, upon U.S. Ambassador David R. Francis' advice and with the support of the Tsar, investigated sources of Russia's wealth and its proposed plan for industrial development in 1916 preparatory to negotiating a loan to obtain the working capital necessary to finance several projects to aid Russia's war effort. A loan of $50 million was eventually negotiated through the Russian Foreign Minister Sazonov.

U.S. Technological Aid During the Soviet Period

The following quotations from Soviet sources illustrate the Russian's attitude toward American technical know-how:

Let the American capitalists leave us alone. We will not touch them. We are even ready to pay them with gold for machinery, tools, and so forth, useful for transport and production, and not only with gold but even with raw materials.— Quoted in *The Current Digest of the Soviet Press*, Vol. III, No. 1, p. 6, from Lenin's *Works*, Vol. XXXI (1920).

The Soviet people rate highly that American businesslike approach to things [*Amerikanskaya delovitost*] which, by Comrade Stalin's definition, is 'that indomitable strength which neither knows or accepts any impediments . . . , not letting a single thing come in the way of carrying an assigned task to the completion.'—From a *Pravda* editorial, June 11, 1943.

Is Russia prepared to enter into business relations with America? [Lenin]: 'Of course she is ready.'—From *The Current Digest of the Soviet Press* translation of an article from *Pravda* (April 22, 1950) and *Bolshevik* (No. 7, 1950) on publication of Vol. XXXI of Lenin's *Works* containing previously unpublished documents of Lenin. *C.D.S.P.* Vol. II, No. 17, 1950.

Another of the most powerful countries is the United States of America. Our relations with them, both as regards our agriculture by American agriculture which has been brought to a high technical level, develop apace. Not only has engineer Cooper [Colonel Hugh Cooper], to the great benefit of the concern, become the consulting engineer for the construction of the Dnieper Hydroelectric Station, but a large number of other important and skilled American engineers enable our skilled workers and engineers to become familiar with the industry and are being conducted with very big American firms with a view to concluding new agreements for technical assistance.—Report on foreign affairs by A. I. Rykov, President of the Council of Commissars, to the Fifth Congress of Soviets, May 1929.

Stalin to Gen. Dwight D. Eisenhower, August, 1945: There are many ways in which we need American help. It is our great task to raise the standard of living of all Russian people, which has been seriously damaged by the war. We must learn all about your scientific achievements in agriculture. Likewise, we must get your technicians to help us in our engineering and construction problems, and we want to know more about mass production methods in factories. We know that we are behind in these things and we know that you can help us.—From Eisenhower's *Crusade in Europe*, 1948.

Thanks to mass production, Americans have succeeded in raising their material standard of living. I think we can learn from the Americans on how quickly and well to produce shoes and pots and pans. . . . In a relatively short time America built up an amazing technology. I saw how fast she can build skyscrapers, how accurately and well she can produce automobiles in Detroit, and how many inventions she has which lighten the life of man.—Ilya Ehrenburg in *Izvestiya*, July 17, 1946, an article "In America" written on his return from a trip to the United States in 1946.

We observe the United States with interest, since this country ranks high as regards science and techniques. We should be glad to have American scientists and technicians as our teachers and in the technical field to be their pupils.— Stalin (in 1932), as quoted in Amtorg's *Economic Review of the Soviet Union*, No. 2, February 1934, p. 45, in an article entitled "Soviet Industry and U.S.," by Z. Sukhov.

The Soviet Union is indebted to Mr. [Henry] Ford. He helped build our tractor and automobile industries.—Stalin, quoted in Johnston's *We're All in It*, 1948.

Congratulations and greetings to the victorious workers and to the leading staff of the first gigantic tractor plant in the U.S.S.R., the 'Krasno-Znameni' [Stalingrad] plant. Our thanks to our technical teachers, the American specialists and technicians, who have helped us in the construction of the plant.—Stalin's telegram to the Albert Kahn engineers working on the Stalingrad Plant; reproduced in *Economic Review of the Soviet Union*, August 1, 1930, p. 314.

One could hardly find any other country which has such great possibilities of developing its exports to the U.S.S.R. as the United States.—Statement made by Commissar of Foreign Trade A. P. Rosengoltz in a speech on April 23, 1933, quoted in *Handbook of the Soviet Union*, published by the American-Russian Chamber of Commerce, 1936.

Like the United States, the U.S.S.R. is a country of great distances, of rich and multiform natural resources. . . . We have found, generally speaking, of all foreign technical men, Americans are best equipped to give advice on our development projects and American-type machinery is in most cases best adapted to our needs.—Statement to the press by U.S.S.R. Ambassador to the U.S. A. A. Troyanovsky, January 1934; quoted in *Handbook of the Soviet Union*, p. 380.

The Soviet period witnessed not only continuation of the Tsarist policy of the 1890–1917 period of borrowing technically and materially from the West, particularly from the United States, but a great increase in the volume of this assistance and a greater role played by the U.S. in helping the Russian people overcome backwardness. *In fact, the U.S. has sold and shipped more commodities of all types to the U.S.S.R. since the October Revolution of 1917 than any other country.* According to Soviet figures the U.S. supplied the U.S.S.R. with more exclusively industrial necessities in the period since the revolution than the U.S.S.R. was able to buy from *all* other countries in the ten-year period of the first two Five-Year Plans (1928–1937). Technical personnel from the U.S. numbered between 600 and 700 persons in 1930 alone, according to Peter Bogdanov, chairman of Amtorg, in a speech delivered in that year.

The United States did not formally recognize the Soviet government until November 16, 1933. Despite this fact, American businessmen, in many cases sympathetic to Soviet economic goals, although often deploring the methods of industrializing and advancing the country known as "backward Russia," sold or leased valuable machinery, equipment, or technical personnel to the Bolshevik government. All this was done despite unabating Soviet propaganda against "bourgeois imperialism." It was also done without full legal protection to U.S. businessmen, which could be provided only by stable diplomatic relations between the two countries. The enterprising businessmen seemed to echo the words of the U.S. Ambassador to St. Petersburg at the end of the eighteenth century, Francis Dana, who even then proposed establishing "a good understanding between both countries and intercourse to the mutual advantage of both nations," predicting that "in the nature of things" future relations between Russia and the U.S. would be *commercial rather than political.* That attribute of the U.S. businessman cited by the Soviet humorists Ilf and Petrov in "They and We" (from *Little Golden America*) and by Stalin (see quote above) of keeping his word was utilized by the Soviet government in its dealings with Americans. Dependence of the developing Soviet economy upon the advanced capitalist economy of the United States appeared in all the most basic sectors of the economy of the U.S.S.R.

An assessment of the U.S. contribution to the industrialization of the Soviet Union can be found in Elisha Friedman's *Russia in Transition: A Business Man's Appraisal.* The author was a traveling businessman to the U.S.S.R. in 1931 and formerly lecturer on finance at New York University and the New School for Social Research. Friedman's assessment reads as follows:

The Soviets lean strongly toward America for technical advice, because Russian and American conditions are so similar. Both countries are rich in natural resources, both constitute large free-trade areas with populations well over 100 millions, and neither has political designs against the other. America has advanced far along the road that Russia wishes to travel, namely of mechanization of industry, the emancipation of the worker from the heavy physical toil, the high productivity per man, and the resulting increase in the consuming capacity of the worker. For this reason the Soviets are looking toward American corporations to realize the Five-Year Plan. They are offering American engineers salaries far in excess of the maximum wages paid to Soviet engineers, and in addition give them numerous privileges and advantages.

The Russian engineering schools have not yet succeeded in turning out a sufficient number of trained men. Even though the courses in some of the schools were cut down to as little as six months, and the students worked day and night in order to finish their training . . . the number of graduates was found inadequate for the jobs. As a result the Soviet government planned to import approximately 13,000 additional foreigners, in order to keep up with the Five-Year Plan. These were to include about 3,000 engineers, 3,000 foremen, and 7,000 skilled laborers. About 5,000 were to be Americans. This is a large number in view of the fact that more than 4,000 foreign experts were already under contract with the Soviet government and 2,000 additional were employed by the 124 foreign corporations which have contracts for technical aid to the Soviets. The depression forces the Soviets to curtail this program.

According to official Soviet figures *the United States has been the chief supplier of commodities of all types of the U.S.S.R. for the period 1921–1947.* However, up to 1939, or the beginning of World War II, the United States ranked second among the top three suppliers of goods to the U.S.S.R. since 1921. The figures for the *pre*-World War II period are as follows.

Exports of All Types (1921–38)

Germany	$2,016,000,000
United States	$1,445,000,000
Great Britain	$ 907,000,000

During the war, shipments from Germany, of course, ceased while imports from Great Britain (excluding Lend-Lease) were insignificant. But with
the establishment of Lend-Lease, Soviet importation of U.S. goods received a
boost, sending the figure for U.S. imports to the U.S.S.R. during the whole
period 1921–1947 soaring high above that for any other country exporting
to the U.S.S.R.

U.S. Shipments to the U.S.S.R. (1939–47)

1939–40	$ 137,000,000
1941	$ 120,000,000
1941–45	$9,500,000,000
1946–47	$ 501,000,000

Breaking down the figures for U.S. exports in terms only of *metals* and *machinery*—the two major items in an industrialization program—the period
1921–1947 yields the following:

U.S. Shipments of Machinery and Metals
to the U.S.S.R.
(in millions of dollars)

	Machinery	Metals
1921–36	257	108
1937–41	204	78
1941–45	1,325	922
1946–47	278	39
	$2,064	$1,147

Meanwhile, during the period of the first two Five-Year Plans (1928–1937)
the U.S.S.R. imported from all other countries a total of only $1.8 billion
of machinery (*oborudovaniye*) and $981 million worth of metals: a total of
only about $2.8 billion. In other words *the total value of shipments of ma-
chinery and metals from the United States to the U.S.S.R. since the revolution (to 1947) is almost one billion dollars more than the total machinery-
metals shipments made to the U.S.S.R. by all other countries during the
period of the first two Five-Year Plans.*

Stalin himself acknowledged the overwhelming U.S. impact upon Soviet
industrialization. During a conversation with Eric Johnston in June 1944,
Marshal Stalin asserted that no less than *two-thirds of all the large industrial enterprises in the Soviet Union* had been built with United States material aid or technical assistance.

Agriculture

If the Soviet Union was to keep from becoming "a second China," as Stalin warned, its marketable grain (both in quantity and quality) would have to be considerably boosted if sale of grain abroad were to yield the necessary revenues vital, as Lenin said in 1920, for the purchase of machinery and tools applied to transport and production in the U.S.S.R. Mechanization of the country's agriculture was seen as the key to increasing the harvest. Toward this end factories were planned for production of tractors. But before this was begun, the Soviets had to import agricultural machinery from abroad, especially from the United States.

Amtorg's *Economic Review of the Soviet Union* reported on April 1, 1930, that "American agricultural implements are playing an important part in the spring sowing campaign now under way in the Soviet Union." In 1929 American farm machinery and tractor exports to the U.S.S.R. were valued at $20,121,429 (U.S. Department of Commerce figures*), representing an increase of 181 percent over the preceding year. The Soviet Union, which followed only Canada and Argentina as a market for farm machinery of American make, recorded the largest gain of any leading country, taking 17 percent of the total exports in 1929. Tractors made up 86 percent of the total Soviet imports from the U.S. in 1929, while combines increased from 134 machines in 1928 to 435 in 1929 at a value of $700,791.

With the onset of the First Five-Year Plan (1929), the Soviet Union launched its first major agricultural machinery construction projects. One of the first and largest of these was the Kharkov Tractor Plant, built in 1931. *The equipment and production-line setup of this factory were overwhelmingly American-made and influenced.* In *Machines and Men in Russia* (1932) Louis Fischer wrote of his visit to this plant in 1931: "During my visit to Kharkov the latest foreign machines were being mounted. At least 90 per-

*Economic Review of the Soviet Union, April 1, 1930, p. 128. Besides Amtorg (Soviet trading agency in the U.S.), the American-Russian Chamber of Commerce expedited commercial relations between the two countries. The organization was incorporated January 22, 1916, and reorganized June 11, 1926, with the purpose "to foster trade, encourage and generally promote the economic, commercial, and industrial relations between the United States of America and Russia." Its main office was in New York; it had a branch in Moscow. It furnished statistics and pertinent information to Soviet government officials regarding advice and supplies which came from American firms. Among the names of firms on the American-Russian Chamber of Commerce's roster of direction are some which turned up as active participants in the U.S.S.R.'s building and which appear in this report. Among these are Colonel Hugh Cooper's, Hugh L. Cooper and Co., Inc.; Baldwin Locomotive Co.; General Motors Corp.; International Business Machines; International General Electric Co.; Mr. Charles E. Stuart's, Stuart, James & Cooke, Inc. Above information is from *Handbook of the Soviet Union*, published by the American-Russian Chamber of Commerce, 1936.

cent of the equipment, including construction steel, is of foreign origin, mostly American."

Joseph E. Davies, appointed ambassador to the U.S.S.R. on November 16. 1936, asserted in his book *Mission to Moscow* that the Kharkov Plant had been designed in consultation with engineers of the United States, Britain, France, and Germany. The Soviet government, he wrote, had spent huge amounts of money on the plant in order to get the best foreign engineering, technical, and planning skill from the West that it could. However, he estimated the percentage of American-made machinery at 60 percent—lower than Fischer had.

Alcan Hirsch observed that another big Soviet agricultural machinery plant, the Rostov Agricultural Machinery Plant, was also put on the American conveyer-belt system.* The plant manufactured American-type combines (the Russian word is *kombain*) and farm machinery, including caterpillar tractors, harvesters, harrows, plows, and so forth. Likewise, Ambassador Davies noted that "in the mechanical section of the plant . . . most of the machinery was either of American or German make." The author of *Mission to Moscow* went on to tell a pertinent anecdote:

We were going through the woodworking shop where we found most of the machinery of American make. We were introduced to the manager of this section which employed 1,000 men. He was about 30 years of age. He said to me, "Mr. Ambassador, you come from Wisconsin, do you not?" . . . I said, "Yes, why?" His reply was, "I studied two years at the University of Wisconsin in Madison. What a great university it is and what a lovely city." He added that he had visited most of the large machinery-manufacturing plants of the United States after his technical education had been completed.

In 1931 Elisha Friedman, an advocate of opening diplomatic relations with the U.S.S.R., saw in the Leningrad Putilov Iron Works a tractor division in which "there is a large variety of American [U.S.] machines—in fact, the array looked like an exhibition of American machinery. Ten or fifteen American [U.S.] states are represented. One of the workmen, leading us through the plant, regarded the machines almost with affection, and put them through some stunts for us. It was evident that he looked upon them as a collection of grand toys."**

*From Hirsch's *Industrialized Russia* (1934). Mr. Hirsch, a chemical engineer, has been consultant to various industrial corporations in the U.S.; assisted the Japanese government in its chemical development (1916–1918); and was chief consultant to the Soviet government in the field of heavy chemical industry (1931–1933).

**Friedman states in *Russia in Transition* (1932) that around 1930 there were more than a thousand Russian engineers in the United States, according to Gosplan officials. One hundred were at the Ford Motor Plant at River Rouge, Michigan, considerable numbers in U.S. oil fields, in tractor factories, and at industrial construction projects. Fifteen Russian engineers were at the Schenectady plant of the General Electric Company.

Friedman reported as follows on his visit to another Soviet factory, the Stalingrad Tractor Plant, in 1931:

The Russians cite numerous advantages of American technical assistance in the construction of this plant [that is, the Stalingrad Tractor Plant]. The cooperation of American firms made it possible to complete the work in record time. The technological processes were improved by the application of American standards for machining, and of new methods in heat treating and in assembling. The preparation of the plans in the United States gave the Russian engineers who were to operate the plant an opportunity to study identical processes in American factories. As a result of American cooperation, the floor area of the machine shop was decreased 20%, the number of machines was diminished 25% and the capacity per machine was increased 28%. . . . They applied American methods of carrying on construction work during the winter. . . . In the opinion of the Russians, the utilization of foreign technical assistance in the construction of the Stalingrad Tractor Plant was considered very satisfactory.

Louis Fischer, in *Machines and Men in Russia* (1932), reported that the Kharkov Tractor Plant had a school on its premises which acted as an instructor and popularizer of this master tractor plant's U.S.-made machines and techniques. Soviet engineering graduates of this factory school would then apply their knowledge of U.S. industrial techniques to a whole industry in U.S.S.R.—tractor production—and the installation of that production. There were no fewer than 750 pupils taking two-and-a-half-year courses in tractor production at this school. Other such schools were located at other tractor plants—for example, at the Stalingrad Tractor Plant and the Leningrad Putilov Factory.

Axles for the tractors (and for automobiles) were produced with the technical production advice of representatives of the Timken-Detroit Axle Co., Detroit, Michigan. This assistance was rendered through the U.S.S.R. United Automobile and Tractor Industry.

A further unique form of technological aid was supplied Soviet Agriculture in the early 1920s and 1930s by the voluntary American Jewish Joint Distribution Committee (J.D.C.). This committee contributed $4,220,000 worth of aid from 1921 to 1924. During this preliminary period of dispensing aid, the committee established 250 pure-bred seed multiplication stations and 32 cheese manufacturing cooperatives, and distributed livestock. Agricultural machinery distributed as loans included 1,000 plows, 2,000 harrows, 1,400 cultivators, and much other agricultural machinery which was to be repaid in grain.

After the establishment in 1924 of the J.D.C.'s subsidiary organization, the American Jewish Joint Agricultural Corp. ("Agro-Joint"), the activities of the Jewish Distribution Committee were broadened: $16 million in aid was supplied from U.S. agencies and the Soviet government between 1924 and 1937. Among the items of technological and other aid supplied by the J.D.C. and Agro-Joint during this period were

1. Large-scale resettlement program establishing a total of 215 colonies providing for 20,000 families or approximately 100,000 Jews. These settlements were set up in the Crimea, Kherson, and Krivoi Rog regions and in the Ukraine;
2. These settlements of Jewish cooperative farmers were supplied by Agro-Joint with water supply system, tractor squad service, agricultural instruction, and the operation of necessary related agricultural and industrial enterprises.

Between 1924 and 1937, 10,000 houses were built, and 1,000 tractors, 700 tractor plows, 100 deep-well pumps, 36 combine harvesters, and a vast quantity of other equipment were provided. By 1938, however, these independent cooperative Jewish farms had been integrated into the Soviet collective farm system by the Stalin regime. The Soviets thereupon declared Agro-Joint activity to be at an end.

Hydroelectric Power Stations

Lenin told the Eighth All-Russian Communist Party Congress, December 1920, that "Communism equals electrification plus the Soviet power." The role played by U.S. industry in building the largest of these hydroelectric power projects, the Dnieprostroi Dam, was enormous, both in its material and personnel contributions. This totally U.S.-equipped, -designed, and -technically-developed dam served as a model for such future projects in the U.S.S.R.

Building of the Dnieprostroi Dam (today called Dnieproges Lenin Dam) with a capacity of 750,000 h.p. (558,000 kw.) was begun in 1927 and formally completed on October 10, 1932. The total project cost 200 million rubles, or approximately $44 million. It is located in the midst of an area rich in agricultural and mining resources and having many industries. At least two of these industries, aluminum and steel, were first introduced there into the U.S.S.R. or given a new boost due to the immense electric power made accessible by the dam. Many other plants in the area could thereby expedite more quickly their Five-Year Plan quotas as a result of the completion of the great dam.

The plant was erected under the direction of Colonel Hugh Cooper of the United States Corps of Engineers.* He had already become famous for his building of the Mississippi Power Company's dam at Keokuk, Iowa, the Muscle Shoals (Tennessee) plant, and other important projects. Cooper, who was assisted by Alcan Hirsch, had been called in by the Soviet gov-

---

*The *Small Soviet Encyclopedia* omits any mention of U.S. assistance or equipment, as do other Soviet reference books. The dam was almost totally destroyed by the Germans during World War II. The turbine room was completely demolished and more than half of the cement bulkheads of the dam and sluice mechanisms were destroyed.

ernment after many failures at building the Dnieprostroi Dam in the mid-twenties (Joseph E. Davies' statement) undertaken by the Soviet government without assistance by U.S. engineers. The five huge turbines, exceeding those of the U.S. Niagara turbines, had a capacity of 84,000 h.p., and more were built by the Newport News Engine Co. The large generators (and the parts for them assembled at Leningrad) were built by General Electric of the United States. The U.S. firm of Westvaco Chlorine Products, Inc., Charleston, West Virginia, supplied the famous Vorce electrolytic caustic and chlorine cells and the compressing equipment.

During the period of building, Colonel Cooper visited the project every six months. In his absence a staff of competent U.S. engineers lived on the project and executed his orders, contacting him for new information from time to time. So great was Cooper's contribution that the dam was called for some time "Cooper Dam." A new city, Zaporozhe, was created as a result of the dam project and increased navigability of the Dnieper River. Zaporozhe's streets were laid out in a rectangular American fashion. Experience gained from the building of Dnieprostroi has been applied to other large stations at Gorky, Yaroslavl on the Volga, and Molotov (now Perm) on the Kama River, and others.

Under Lend-Lease the U.S. supplied power installations to the U.S.S.R. capable of producing 1,457,000 kw. Included were stationary steam plants as well as mobile-train units designed for use in the reconstruction of devastated areas. This additional electric power-generating capacity amounted to about three times the prewar capacity of the Dnieprostroi Hydroelectric Station. During the fourth Five-Year Plan (1946–1950) 11.7 million kw. of generating capacity was scheduled to be installed. The 1.45 million kw. in the form of Lend-Lease aid was about 12 percent of the planned addition. It can be estimated that the total electric power capacity installed in the U.S.S.R. in 1945 was about 10.7 million kw. The Lend-Lease assistance therefore represents an additional 13½ percent of that year's total.

Mining, Metallurgical, and Chemical Industries

United States metallurgical industries and their branches have also contributed know-how to the Soviet Union in the form of specialists on plant construction, mining, ore-dressing, refining, and other processes. U.S.-made mining and other metallurgical machinery was as follows:

Nitric acid plant in Gorky (Chernorechensk Works) . . . designed and built in consultation with the E. I. duPont de Nemours & Co., Inc.

Apatite processing plant in Leningrad District for treating apatite from Kola Peninsula; put into operation in September 1931, and designed by General Engineering Co., Denver, Colorado; plant contained other U.S.-made equipment.

Aluminum plant at Volkhov, near Leningrad; started into operation May

1932; developed by consultation with Mr. Frank E. Dickie, an American aluminum specialist.

Synthetic ammonia plants: building of them under advisership of the President of the Nitrogen Engineering Corporation of New York (a subsidiary of the American Cyanamid Co.) for synthetizing ammonia from air, coal, and steam.

Coke-oven installations at Magnitogorsk by-product coke plant were designed and built in consultation with Koppers Engineering Co. of Pittsburgh, Pennsylvania.

Open-hearth blast furnaces, "first of their kind in the Soviet Union" (Hirsch, pp. 126–127) at Kuznetsk; each had 15-ton capacity.

New Soviet steel mills, built at Magnitogorsk and Kuznetsk, respectively, by Arthur G. McKee & Co. of Cleveland and Freyn Engineering Co. of Chicago; other plants built by these two firms.

Ferro-alloys imported mainly from U.S. and Germany, until early thirties when U.S.S.R. began to produce its own supplies.

Graphite electrodes; electrical equipment made by General Electric.*

Mining methods on Mt. Magnitnaya were U.S.-influenced; Magnitogorsk and and Kuznetsk are supplied by ore from these mines.

Manganese mining development in Chiaturi District in the Georgian Soviet Socialist Republic, Caucasus Mountains.

Planning, equipping, and rationalizing the coal industry: assistance in this field given by Stuart, James, and Cooke, Inc. at behest of Vice-Commissar Heavy Industry, G. L. Pyatakov.**

Technical information and exchange of patents in electronics field—Radio Corporation of America contract with Soviet Weak-Current Trust.

Design, construction, and operation of concentration plants (for treating by-products of ore-dressing) by Southwestern Engineering Corporation, Los Angeles, California; contract with U.S.S.R. United Non-ferrous Metals Industries.

"Large-scale American mining methods" were used in extracting ore from Mt. Magnitnaya. The story of the development of the Lena Gold Fields is one of great U.S. influence. Half of their output in the early thirties was from mechanical means employing American-designed electric dredges.

During the Lend-Lease period, a steel expansion program, (under U.S. guidance) was begun at a cost of $13,200,000. The program envisaged an

---

*A contract between the Soviet government and the International General Electric Company, effective for 10 years, was officially completed July 2, 1929. It provided for technical assistance in the field of electric power.

**Vice-Commissar Pyatakov wrote a letter of appreciation to Messrs. Stuart, James and Cooke in which he said that the American mining engineers were credited with "the removal of many difficulties in the development of the coal industry and with speeding up of coal production which in turn had a favorable effect on the steel industry." (Quoted in Friedman's *Russia in Transition* which in turn quoted a *New York Times* dispatch from Moscow, May 26, 1932.)

increase of Soviet production of carbon steel ingots by 2,500,000 a year. This project alone added about 20 to 25 percent to the U.S.S.R. wartime steel capacity. The steel expansion program was nearly completed by September 1945, except for a few remaining parts shipped under the agreement of October 15, 1945. Listed below are other U.S.-installed plants constructed under Lend-Lease:

Wall Board Plant	$ 662,000
Voltol Pilot Plant	46,000
Nitric Acid Plant	535,000
Hydrogen Gas Plant	531,000
Hydrogen and Catalyst Plant	2,626,000

Automobiles

Dr. D. B. Shimkin of Harvard University Russian Research Center published a special study, *Automotive Industries*, February 1, 1948, on the U.S.S.R. motor vehicle industry. He found that the U.S. influence on the Soviet motor vehicle industry *in the period of its formation and greatest foreign dependence*, 1928–1931, was crucial.* Shimkin wrote:

From the standpoint of automobile design, examination of the motor vehicle industry of the U.S.S.R. shows that, since its beginning, it has been overwhelmingly dependent upon foreign and especially American prototypes. However, in a few specialized fields—pre-heating devices and electrical systems for winter operation, gas-producer vehicles and alloy development—significant independent progress has been made. . . . Seven characteristics typify the motor-vehicle industry of the U.S.S.R. most sharply; extreme emphasis upon truck production, limited variety of models produced (coupled nevertheless with inadequate standardization); inefficiency of production with high overhead; low productivity per worker; great waste and low quality; short vehicle life and high operating costs; and very inferior gasoline and lubricants and appreciable gaps between announced plans and actual performance.

Dr. Shimkin produced in *Automotive Industries* (same date) a table showing U.S. influence upon specific Soviet models of vehicles (see Table 5). Mention should also be made of U.S. prototypes of various engine parts copied by the Soviets. Zenith, Marvel, and Solex carburetors were and may still be used in many models. Timken-Detroit and Clark rear axles, Spicer

Bolshaya sovetskaya entsiklopediya (Moscow, 1926) acknowledges the contribution made to the founding of the U.S.S.R.'s automobile industry by the Ford Motor Co., and many other U.S. firms (see Vol. 1, pp. 358–359). Soviet reference books have ignored this contribution ever since 1930.

TABLE 5. Reliance of Soviet Automobile Industry on Foreigners

Soviet Vehicle	Parts Borrowed	Foreign Model
Light-passenger - KIM–10 (and the postwar Moskvich)	Entire vehicles (1939)	British Ford 10 m.p. (1935)
Passenger - GAZ–A	Entire (1932)	Ford Model A (1928)
Passenger - GAZ–M1	Entire (1936)	Ford Model B (1933)
Passenger - GAZ–M11	Engine (1940)	Continental 16209 (1935)
Passenger - GAZ–M20	Engine (1947)	Continental 14140 (1938)
Passenger - GAZ–M20	Gearset (1947)	Ford Model B
Standard truck - GAZ–AA	Entire (1932)	Ford Model AA (1930)
Standard truck - GAZ–MM	Entire (1935)	Ford 1½-ton truck (1933)
Front wheel drive truck - GAZ–61	Chassis (1941)	Marmon-Harrington, LD 1–4 (1937)
Passenger - ZIS–101	Entire (1936)	Buick 33–90 (1933)
Passenger - ZIS–101A	Engine (1940)	Buick 36–90 (1936)
Passenger - ZIS–110	Entire (1945)	Packard Custom Super 8–1808 (1940)
Standard truck - AMO–2 & 3	Entire (1930)	Autocar SA–2 (1929)
Standard truck - ZIS–5	Engine (1933)	Hercules WKC (1928)
Standard truck - ZIS–5	Gearset (1933)	Brown-Lipe 314 (1930)
Standard truck - ZIS–150	Engine (ZIS–120) (1945)	Hercules WKC (1941)
Diesel truck - ZIS–253	Engine (1947)	GM Diesel 3–71 (1938)
Standard truck - Ya–5	Engine (1929)	Hercules YXC (1927)
Standard truck - Ya–5	Gearset (1929)	Brown-Lipe 314 (1930)
Standard truck - YaG–3	Engine (AMO–2) (1931)	Autocar SA–2 (1929)
Standard truck - YaG–6	Engine (ZIS–5) (1933?)	Hercules WXC (1928)
Standard truck - YaG–6	Gearset (1933?)	Brown-Lipe 314 (1930)
Standard truck - YA–10	Engine (1936)	Hercules YXC (1927)
Standard truck - YA–10	Gearset (1936)	Brown-Lipe 554 (1931)
7-ton diesel truck - YaAZ–200	Engine (YaAz–204) (1947)	GM Diesel 4–71 (1938)

SOURCE: D. B. Shimkin, *Automotive Industries* (February 1, 1948).

universals, Electric Auto-Lite electrical equipment,* Willard batteries, modifications of Purolator ("Timoshenko") and Cuno Auto-Klean oil filters, SKF

*Amtorg announced in March 1930 that the U.S.S.R. United Electrical Industries had signed a contract with the Electric Auto-Lite Co. of Toledo, Ohio, providing for technical assistance by this U.S. firm in the production of electrical equipment in the Soviet Union. The agreement provided for a detailed layout and working project for a plant to manufacture complete electrical units for automobiles and tractors. It also requested information and the assignment of a group of American engineers to work in the Soviet Union.

bearings, and Ross steering gears have all entered the design of motor vehicles in the U.S.S.R.

In the actual production of automobiles and trucks, the vast automotive practice of the United States was tapped by the Soviets. On May 31, 1929, the Henry Ford Motor Car Co. contracted with the Soviet Amtorg Trading Corp. for groups of 25 to 50 Soviet engineers, each to journey to Detroit in order to inspect production methods at the Ford River Rouge Plant. In the Soviet Union itself the "important motor-vehicle plants . . . were constructed with American aid during the period 1928–32," according to Shimkin. As Stalin said, "The Soviet Union is indebted to Mr. [Henry] Ford. He helped build our tractor and automobile industries."

A list of some of these constructions (at least 30 plants were built in Moscow, Gorky, Yaroslavl, Leningrad, Kuibyshev, Saratov, and Ufa), with the names of U.S. automobile companies participating, follows:

> GAZ plant at Gorky; largest single automobile factory: built under contract with W. J. Austin Co. and with technical assistance furnished by the Ford Motor Co. Construction completed January 1932.
>
> AMO (later ZIS) plant in Moscow; second largest factory: reconstructed and expanded with the help of the U.S. Autocar Co.; enlargement of its production capacity completed in 1937.
>
> Components and accessories to production factory: constructed by Brown-Lipe Gear Co., Electric Auto-Lite Co., Timken-Detroit Axle Co., and Seiberling Rubber Co., and others.

As a result of this initial construction, later acquisitions of machine tools and the building of new assembly plants at Moscow, Rostov, and Omak, native Soviet auto production rose sharply from 1928–1938. Whereas in 1928 only 474 vehicles were built in the U.S.S.R., in 1938, 212,000 vehicles were produced (Shimkin).

Railroads

D. Ye Sulimov,* Vice-Commissar for Transportation who was visiting the U.S., issued the following statement to Amtorg's *Economic Review of the Soviet Union*, May 1, 1939:

The plan for the reorganization of the Soviet railroad system includes the following points: introduction of more and powerful locomotives and larger freight cars; the equipment of the entire rolling stock with automatic brakes; introduction of automatic coupling and the increasing use of automatic blocking and signaling, etc.

In our attempts to solve these problems we expect to avail ourselves of the extensive experience of the powerful American railroad system. This is the reason

*Sulimov (his full Russian name was Daniil Yegorovich Sulimov) became Chairman of the R.S.F.S.R. Council of People's Commissars in 1930.

for the visit of the Soviet transport commission to the United States and it also explains the invitation by the Soviet Government to Ralph Budd, the President of the Great Northern Railroad. . . .

We are most interested in establishing connections with American industrial concerns serving railway transport . . . since the reconstruction of the Soviet transport system will be based largely on their experience.

And Budd of Great Northern Railroad left for the Soviet Union in June 1930 accompanied by Sulimov and the members of his staff, who had been visiting the U.S. and American railway firms and making purchases for over three months. Budd spent the whole summer in the U.S.S.R. as consultant to the Commissariat of Transportation and traveled some 10,000 miles over Soviet rails. In December 1930 he reported briefly in the *Economic Review of the Soviet Union* on his findings and recommendations concerning Soviet railroading. Although Soviet engineers also consulted and visited European countries and railroad industries, Budd felt that

the European system of railroading is possibly very well adapted to the conditions of the smaller European countries where length of freight movement is short and heavy tonnage trains are not desirable, but the same system is not economical where hauls are long and there is much bulk freight as in the United States and in the U.S.S.R. . . . As distinct from the European system, the American system of railroading is predicated upon the heavy use of heavy trains drawn by heavy and powerful locomotives. Large capacity freight cars are used, 3 or 4 times the size of those commonly used in the U.S.S.R. . . . This system has proved very satisfactory in the United States and should be found equally satisfactory in the U.S.S.R. where conditions are strikingly similar.

Amtorg's *Economic Review of the Soviet Union* in an article entitled "Railway Transport in the Soviet Union: A Statistical Review" stated:

The general reorganization of the railway system in the Soviet Union will be carried out to a considerable extent on the basis of American experience. Following the investigations of the Soviet railway commission, which visited the United States in the summer of 1930, D. Sulimov, Chairman of the Commission and former Vice-Commissar for Transportation, outlined the railway program on his return to the U.S.S.R. He pointed out that the significance of automatic coupling for Soviet railways is so great that for the next two years or three years it will occupy a dominant place in the reconstruction program. In his opinion the planned introduction of heavier locomotives and the general improvement of the railway system will be ineffective if not preceded by the introduction of automatic coupling.

As to future trips of Soviet railroad specialists abroad to the West, the *Economic Review of the Soviet Union* (December 1, 1930) reported:

Over two hundred Soviet experts and recent graduates of technical institutes are scheduled to go to Europe and America to specialize in specific branches of practical transport work. This group also includes railway engineers, executives, technicians and workers who will study new developments in Western countries for periods varying from three to seven months.

In an interview with *The New York Times*, May 3, 1939, the U.S.S.R. Transport Commissar Yan E. Rudzutak referred as follows to the aid Americans had given the Soviet government in the building of the Turkestan-Siberian Railway, officially opened April 28, 1930: "If the people of America would hear about some of the really big things we are doing here, I think they would have a far better understanding of the relations between the United States and Russia." The Turk-Sib Railway had been finished, he said, a year and a half ahead of time largely because of the use of American equipment such as excavators and the like. In this interview Rudzutak (like Pyatakov and Sulimov, a victim of the Stalin purges) also announced an intended contract to be made between the Soviet government and the J. G. White Engineer Company of Connecticut for the building of the Saratov-to-Milerovo, 430-mile railroad. Of that guidance which came from Budd and from the findings of the Soviet railroad experts who visited the United States, Rudzutak said: "In this [reorganization of Soviet railways] we look to the United States for guidance." This statement was reflected in what Budd said at a banquet held in his honor by the Soviet Commissariat for Transportation, July 27, 1930, on the conclusion of his 50-day sojourn in the U.S.S.R., that the Soviets should apply American railroading methods. *The New York Times* Russian correspondent Walter Duranty reported on this banquet, July 29, that "the Soviet Railway Commission, headed by Vice-Commissar Sulimov, which recently visited the United States, reports strongly for American methods as against European."

Later under Lend-Lease the United States gave considerable assistance to the Soviet Union in extension of its railroad block signal system. A project, valued at $10 million, provided equipment for about 3,000 kilometers of track. All of this equipment was exported from the U.S. by April 1945.

Airplanes

The Soviet Union also borrowed from the West in the field of airplane manufacture. Importation of engines from the United States, Great Britain, Germany, and France took place before World War II. In 1933 Curtiss-Wright concluded a foreign-licensing agreement with the Soviet Union for the manufacture of Wright airplane engines in the U.S.S.R. under the supervision of U.S. aeronautics specialists. Included in the agreement was provision for the training of Soviet aeronautical engineers.

As for civil aviation, the Soviet-made planes PS–84 and LI–2 were copies of the American Douglas DC–3, constructed under the Douglas license. These DC–3 type Soviet transport planes were used exclusively on the Moscow-London, Moscow-Berlin, and Moscow-Stockholm runs, as well as on domestic flights, until around September 1949. At that time a Reuters dispatch to *The New York Times* reported that a Soviet two-engined transport, the Ilyushin–12, was being used "to replace DC–3's previously operated by the

[Soviet] airline." John Steinbeck in his book *The Russian Journal* (1948) reports that he flew in a DC–3 type Soviet transport in his air travels from Stockholm to the U.S.S.R. and on other flights.

Although jet plane engines were sent the U.S.S.R. by Great Britain until January, 1948, mostly German and domestic aircraft research have been tapped in this field since World War II (according to Jane's *All the World's Aircraft* for 1950). As to medium bombers, it has been widely accepted by Western authorities on aviation that the Soviet TU–70 transport and its military counterpart, the TU–4, are copies of the U.S. B–29. This is obvious even to a layman's eye. Jane's *All the World's Aircraft* reported in 1950 that this Soviet airplane was copied from four B-29's "which landed in Russia during World War II" and "is probably becoming the standard Russian medium bomber." (*Komsomolskaya Pravda* on November 10, 1948, the thirty-first anniversary celebration of the Bolshevik revolution, ran a picture of this B–29-type TU–4 aircraft.)

During World War II, the United States added to Soviet military technology two crucial military inventions: the Norden automatic electric bombsight, and radar. The U.S. navy announced on September 26, 1946, that 100 of the 188 "Catalina"-type navy patrol airplanes sent to the U.S.S.R. in 1944 under a special $100 million agreement were equipped with radar and the Norden bombsight. To fly the planes to the U.S.S.R. and to receive training in the use of the new U.S. equipment, the Soviets sent 140 Soviet airmen under the command of Colonel V. Vasiliev to the U.S. These pilots received 80 hours of flight instruction and training in radar, aeronautics, and aerial navigation. Marshal Stalin said of U.S. assistance under Lend-Lease during World War II: "Without American machines the United Nations could never have won the war."*

Oil-Well Drilling and Oil Refining

In the important fields of oil-well drilling and oil refining U.S. assistance has taken various forms.** The reorganization of the twenties and early thirties of oil-drilling methods was directed toward the development of rotary drilling, to replace the old percussion method and with this, introduction into the U.S.S.R. for the first time of the now outmoded Perkins method of closing in the water with cement. During the years 1927–1929 more than $15 million was spent through Amtorg by the U.S.S.R. in the U.S. for equipment for developing the Soviet oil industry. This was facilitated for the U.S.S.R. by the willingness of leading U.S. oil firms to cooperate by extending long-term credits to the Soviet Union. In moderniz-

---

*In a toast to the United States at the Teheran Conference in 1943.

**Bolshaya sovetskaya entsiklopediya* states that the Soviet petroleum industry basically was patterned after the U.S. industry; that much U.S. equipment and many U.S. processes were used.

ing the refineries, liberal use was made of American engineering brains and of American equipment. The following U.S. firms played important roles in this area: Foster-Wheeler Corporation of New York; E. B. Badger & Sons Company of Boston; and Winkler-Koch Company of Wichita, Kansas. One consequence of this modernization was the production for the first time in the U.S.S.R. of paraffin wax, petroleum asphalt, and lampblack. Gasoline output was also raised considerably above the low prerevolutionary 1 percent of Russian refined-oil output. A high-octane gasoline plant for production of aviation gasoline was built in Ufa in 1940 with the help of U.S. engineers.

Izvestia reported as follows on Soviet adoption of U.S. oil-well drilling techniques:

The oil industry of Azerbaidzhan adopted American drilling and production methods in the year 1923. Since that time the fields have been rebuilt and the Five-Year Plan completed in half the time.

Reports by American engineers of Soviet pirating of U.S. developments in oil production have appeared since 1926. Included among these pirated developments were special rock-boring drills.

Among the oil-refining plants established under Lend-Lease were four basic plants and two subsidiary plants designed to produce high-test aviation gasoline and other gasoline and lubricating oils. These refineries are among the best in the world. Aviation gasoline from these refineries is made by the famous Houdry process and yields 100-octane gasoline, which the U.S.S.R. did not have previously. The lubricants that can be made by these refineries are designed for aviation use under most severe climatic conditions. The absence of such special purpose lubricants would place a definite operating ceiling on a country's manpower. The entire project (under Lend-Lease) was valued at $41 million. Fifteen U.S. engineers were sent to the U.S.S.R. to aid in the construction of these plants. They were built for operation in the Volga-Ural area.

Miscellaneous

An aluminum rolling mill valued at $6,367,000 and designed to supply aluminum sheet for the U.S.S.R. aircraft industry was shipped in September 1944. A merchant mill (for making iron and steel bars) valued at $3.5 million was procured in November 1942; most of this equipment had been shipped by the end of February 1945. Other mills shipped to the U.S.S.R. included two seamless pipe-fabricating mills, blooming, rail and structure, and railroad-tie and fishplate mills. Soaking pits were also sent.*

Very large quantities of other types of machinery and equipment were

*Another field in the U.S.S.R. influenced by the U.S. was the sugar industry. *Ekonnomicheskaya Zhizn* (June 26, 1930) credited U.S. techniques with increasing the efficiency of the Soviet sugar industry.

sent to the Soviet Union under Lend-Lease. These were unquestionably suited for peacetime as well as wartime use. Certain selected items are enumerated below:

A. $310 million worth of machine tools

$ 50 million worth of earth-boring, dredging, excavating, and construction machinery (Some of this machinery made possible the development of the Karaganda Coal Basin during the war, which made up, in part, for the destruction of the Donbass mines. This coal in turn made possible the production of steel and the operation of enlarged Soviet industry in the Urals.)

$2.8 million worth of locomotives and freight cars for industry and mining

B. 1,900 steam locomotives (This number should be compared with the highest quantity produced by the U.S.S.R. prior to the war: in 1935 the U.S.S.R. produced 1,518 locomotives.)

11,000 freight cars

C. 415,000 field telephones

7,056 tanks

14,795 planes

138 sea patrol bombers (some equipped with Norden bomb sight)

90 cargo vessels; 197 torpedo boats, etc.

To increase Soviet manufacture of tires, a whole tire plant was dismantled at the Ford Motor Car Company's River Rouge factory and the machinery and equipment shipped to the U.S.S.R. along with supplemental equipment, including a power plant.

With the acquisition of the East European sphere of influence and the imposition by Moscow of compulsory trade arrangements upon its satellites, Russia in turn acquired additional technical assistance. Reliable Western estimates state that the Soviet Union during 1944–1956 made a total profit of $20 to $25 billion from East Europe alone, without counting the acquisitions and profits from Manchuria and other Far Eastern areas during or after World War II. (The "profits," of course were not in money but in raw materials and equipment, even whole plants.) These imports or outright seizures were extremely important in Soviet postwar industrial recovery.*

*Professor Raymond, in *The Soviet State* (p. 425), notes that a Westerner visiting the U.S.S.R. cannot help noticing the variety of satellite contributions to the Soviet economy: a large tourist boat on the Volga-Don canal is of Hungarian make; the Volgograd Planetarium, the biggest in the U.S.S.R., is a gift from East Germany; pictorial magazines, far sprightlier that their Soviet counterparts, are Hungarian or Polish, while a supposedly Soviet album of rock 'n' roll music comes from Czechoslovakia. I, too, noticed similar phenomena on my trip to the U.S.S.R.: e.g., equipment in a textile thread factory of foreign make, ditto navigation equipment on a Soviet jet liner; a pirated Beatles' number which had been relabeled so as to suggest that it was a Soviet original—the tune is "Girl," the only Beatles' number currently circulating in Russia, perhaps because of its Russian-sounding melody.

United States assistance in various forms continued after World War II until the Berlin Blockade of 1948 and the American imposition of a partial embargo on "strategic" U.S. goods going to the U.S.S.R. Before the 1948 embargo, however, the U.S. had: (1) granted the Russians a U.S. credit of $250 million to purchase Lend-Lease equipment already manufactured by American industry but not delivered before the end of the war; (2) under U.N.R.R.A. (the United Nations Relief and Rehabilitation Administration) to which the United States contributed two-thirds of its total supplies, sent $200 million worth of food, clothing, seeds, and farm machinery to the U.S.S.R. (of this, $191 million was provided by the U.S.).[8] Moreover, in 1947 the United States invited the U.S.S.R. and its satellites to join in the Marshall Plan (European Recovery Program). The Soviets refused, having kept up a steady barrage of recriminations since 1946 against American "interference in Europe" (for example, in the statements by the Soviet envoy, Valerian Zorin, at meetings looking toward establishment of an Economic Commission for Europe [ECE] in 1946, Zorin accusing the Americans of trying to establish economic and political "hegemony" over Western Europe in the postwar period). When Czechoslovakia and perhaps other "satellite" countries indicated an interest in joining the Marshall Plan in 1949, the Soviets interceded. At the last minute the Czechoslovaks withdrew what appeared to be their initial acceptance. Some time after the Marshall Plan was under way, the Russians established their own "Molotov Plan" for the Soviet bloc.

With the ringing down of the Soviet Iron Curtain, the placing of the U.S. embargo restrictions on goods that the Soviets would be most interested in acquiring from America, and the imposition of Soviet economic and political controls over the Soviet bloc, the long history of wide-ranging American involvement in the Tsarist and Soviet economy came to an abrupt end. Within the single year of 1949, American exports to Russia decreased almost 90 percent, amounting to less than $100 million per annum.[9] With the establishment of N.A.T.O. (North Atlantic Treaty Organization) in 1949, all N.A.T.O members agreed to observe the embargo on "strategic goods"; the restrictions applied not only to the U.S.S.R. but to its satellites as well. Certain non-N.A.T.O. powers friendly to the West also observed the embargo—for example, Japan, Formosa, the Philippines, and others. The U.S.S.R. has attempted on several occasions to break the embargo, for example, by convoking an international economic conference in Moscow in 1952. Their attempts have failed, although a few goods do slip through to the Soviet East by resale from N.A.T.O. countries. Instead of relying on the West for important industrial commodities, the Soviets today turn mostly to their Warsaw Pact Allies in Eastern Europe.

The high degree (but not total, of course) self-sufficiency attained by the whole Soviet bloc has enormous political importance. The most obvious consequence of quasi-economic independence is the continuance of that remoteness of the "Soviet World" from the West. For if convergence were to be a persistent phenomenon in Russian and American relations, surely a high degree of economic interdependence would be an important contributing factor. But this factor is lacking. Therefore, until and unless the Soviets and their associated countries are hard pressed to meet domestic economic needs or face an overwhelming military adversary which would cause reappearance of *ad hoc* cooperation of the strange-alliance and Lend-Lease modes, it is doubtful that East-West trade in its present condition can serve significantly to bridge the gap that continues to separate these two worlds.

Meanwhile, coexistence, if it is to be active and cooperative, cannot in the foreseeable future be immediately based on economics. A number of changes must take place on the other side of coexistence—all of which are basically political.

NOTES

1. Raymond, *op. cit.*, p. 413.
2. *Ibid.*,
3. *Ibid.*, p. 414 .
4. *Malaya sovetskaya entsiklopediya (Small Soviet Encylopedia)*, 3rd ed. (1958), vol. I, p. 474. Professor Kennan notes in *Russia and the West under Lenin and Stalin* that, in his opinion, the principal motivation for ARA was "certainly to alleviate innocent human suffering, and the efforts of [Hoover's] organization were addressed strictly to this end." Kennan estimates that in the neighborhood of 10 million Russians were saved from starvation and disease by ARA supplies and maintains that it would have been nearly impossible for the Soviet regime to have overcome the food crises of 1921 and 1922 without ARA's help. The food made available to Soviet railroad personnel, Kennan further points out, kept the railways in operation and was thus of political importance to the Soviet regime in its effort to earn prestige and to survive in outlying areas away from Moscow and Petrograd.
5. Raymond, *op. cit.*, p. 129.
6. *Ibid.*, p. 130.
7. The sources used for the discussion which follows (pp. 101–129) are principally: David R. Francis, *Russia from the American Embassy* (New York: Scribner, 1921); Geroid T. Robinson, *Rural Russia Under the Old Regime* (New York: Macmillan, 1949); Anna M. Babey, *Americans in Russia (1776–1917)* (New York: Comet Press, 1938); John S. Maxwell, *The Czar, His Court and People* (New York: Baker and Scribner, 1848); Eric Allen Johnston, *We're All in It,* (New York: Dutton, 1948); Elisha Friedman, *Russia in Transition: A Businessman's Appraisal* (New York: Viking Press, 1932); Alcan Hirsch, *Industrialized Russia* (New York: The Chemical Catalogue Co., 1934); Louis Fischer, *Machines and Men in Russia,* (New York: H.

Smith, 1932); John Steinbeck, *The Russian Journal* (New York: Herald Tribune Syndicate, 1948); Joseph E. Davies, *op. cit.*; and various periodicals, series, etc. (exact numbers and dates in Bibliography): *Handbook of the Soviet Union* (1936); *Pravitelstvennii Vestnik* (Tsarist newspaper); *Economic Review of the Soviet Union* published by the American-Soviet trading organization, Amtorg; *Automotive Industries*; *Bolshaya sovetskaya entsiklopediya (Great Soviet Encyclopedia);* Jane's *All the World's Aircraft; Ekonomicheskaya Zhizn (Economic Life)* (a Soviet periodical); *The New York Times.*

8. Raymond, *op. cit.*, p. 424.
9. *Ibid.*, p. 425.
10. *Ibid.*, p. 426.

CHAPTER VI

Anti-Convergence Ideology

Dogmatisms . . . such as racism, Fascism, Stalinism, and Maoism . . . all bureaucratized dogmatism and the spreading of mass myths put entire nations and continents under the power of cruel and treacherous demagogues. . . . The preaching of the incompatibility of world ideologies and nations is madness and a crime.

— ANDREI D. SAKHAROV, Progress, Coexistence,
and Intellectual Freedom (1968)

•   •   •

Soviet insistence (derived from the conceptual elements of ideology . . .) that ultimate peace depends on the total victory of a particular social system led by a particular political party injects into international affairs an element of a fundamental struggle for survival not conducive to conflict resolution.

— ZBIGNIEW K. BRZEZINSKI, Ideology and
Power in Soviet Politics (1962)

There are plenty of rational arguments for why the two superpowers, the United States and the Soviet Union, should avoid conflict and encourage active coexistence.

Rationale for Russian and American Active Coexistence

First, their power to destroy each other and allied countries is so terrible that, for the first time in history, the potential destructiveness of the weapons

*This statement appears in the intensely idealistic and provocative essay by the Soviet physicist Andrei Dmitrievich Sakharov, who is known as the father of the Russian hydrogen bomb. The edition cited in the present book was published by W. W. Norton, New York, 1968, with an Introduction, Afterword, and Notes by Harrison E. Salisbury. Quotation may be found on p. 27. This work has circulated in typewritten copies from hand to hand in the U.S.S.R.

acts as a deterrent against war. One may cite the introduction of new terrifying weapons and inventions of bygone days—the crossbow, gunpowder,
the machine gun, the tank, poison gas, the airplane—to prove that fear
about new weapons has existed in the past as well. But as terrifying as these
innovations were at the time of their introduction into warfare, none has
had the impact on men's minds and on international diplomacy as have
atomic- and thermonuclear-tipped bombs, rockets, and satellites. Whether
from "kill" or "overkill," the toll in lives resulting from a thermonuclear Third
World War involving these two superpowers and their allies would reach
into the hundreds of millions. Fallout from first, second, and succeeding
strikes and exchanges of nuclear-armed ICBMs would infect and poison
countless additional millions of people, many of whom would reside in non-
combatant countries.

Despite the fear evoked by this equation of terror, however, it is important to remember that fear acts only as a *deterrent* and not an absolute
or even nearly absolute *preventive force* working "inevitably" against the
outbreak of such a world-historical *Götterdämmerung*. Still, the uniqueness
of the quantity and quality of the destructiveness of thermonuclear weapons
is of great importance and offers some hope of prolonged deterrence.

A second point raised by a rationalist argument in favor of Russian and
American active coexistence concerns the underdeveloped or "developing"
under half of the world dwelling on the continents of Asia, Africa, and
Latin America—the "Three A's." Lord C. P. Snow, to cite one of many who
have spoken out on the subject, has predicted that a "sea of famine" will
engulf the remaining rich "host" countries by the end of the century unless
a number of concrete steps are undertaken, principally by the two rich-
est countries, the United States and the U.S.S.R. To prevent untold millions from starvation, as much as 20 percent of the gross national product
of the two countries, according to Lord Snow, will have to be assigned to
help the underdeveloped regions of the world before the end of the century.[1] Sad to say, there appears to be the slimmest of prospects that the
two countries will invest such a sizable share of their G.N.P.'s for this purpose. Meanwhile, another prediction has been offered—unfortunately a somewhat likelier prospect than rational collaboration in behalf of the Three
A's. This was the projection of the famous "Lin Piao Manifesto," issued in
Peking in 1965. In it, Mao's heir-apparent predicted that the future will be
full of struggle between the Have and the Have-not Nations. Of course, many
of the assertions in the Lin Piao Manifesto are plainly grotesque—for example, that village-oriented peoples will engage in a life-and-death guerrilla
struggle with city-oriented peoples. Nevertheless, there appears to be the
very great danger that the population explosion and spreading agitation
for a better life *will* serve to ignite more violence in or between nation-
states (particularly between rich ones and poor ones). This in turn may

involve various combinations of by-standing host countries (including the United States and the U.S.S.R., who may find themselves on opposing sides). Thus, it is obvious, say the rationalists, that the two countries must pull together in an updated joint "Marshall-Molotov Plan" to keep the world from plunging into warring camps of poor versus rich countries.

A third argument is both rationalistic and optimistic. It maintains that the world is, in a sense, becoming more "educated," or so at least are the most influential, best-armed and most industrialized nations in it. The intelligentsias of the industrialized states of West Europe, East Europe, North America, and the Far Eastern state of Japan, and certain other countries, have attained a high level of social and political consciousness and responsibility, runs the argument, which almost automatically impels them in a rational direction. They have "learned" from the past, from two World Wars, from the excesses of Stalinism and Fascism, even from "local wars" of the 1960s that military solutions "do not pay." Moreover, because the ruling circles in these nations are falling increasingly under the influence of these enlightened intelligentsias, the prospects of equally enlightened and "scientifically based" political decisions, which will forestall war and ensure lasting peace, are good. The Soviet scientist and essayist Andrei D. Sakharov cannot necessarily be classed among the diehard optimists on this question. But he nonetheless displays a kind of indomitable rationalism and hope when he writes:

Modern technology and mass psychology constantly suggest new possibilities of managing the norms of behavior. . . . Today the key to a progressive restructuring of the system of government in the interests of mankind lies in intellectual freedom. . . . The facts suggest that on any other course except ever-increasing co-existence and collaboration between the two systems and the two superpowers, with a smoothing of contradictions and with mutual assistance, on any other course annihilation awaits mankind. There is no other way out.[2]

Sakharov notes with optimism that the "increasing complexity of structure and of industrial management [in the Soviet and the United States gives rise] in both countries to managerial groups that are similar in social character"[3] and predicts:

I believe that the leaders of the capitalist and socialist systems by the very nature of things will gradually be forced to adopt the point of view of the majority of mankind.[4]

Despite such rationalistic and convincing arguments as these, there are forces at work in the world which are blind to reason. For one thing, countervailing forces are active in certain countries on the other side of co-existence which counteract the potentially rational effects flowing from the spread of technology, modernization, and education, and which frustrate the development of rational policies.

The Aggravating Factor of Ideology in the Totalitarian State

Foremost among the potent countervailing forces working against rationalism in international politics is *ideology*. To understand how this happens it is necessary to canvass the function of ideology in the totalitarian state.

Ideology has been defined in various ways. First, there is the general sense in which the word "ideology" is made nearly synonymous with "credo" or set of beliefs, the underlying but unenforced political philosophy of a nation-state. In this use of the word, we might speak of "Jeffersonian liberalism" or even the Republican or Democratic party programs as ideologies of this type. In the stricter sense, however, ideology is most always construed to mean a set of political principles which are coercively implanted in the institutions of the state and propagated in the form of a secular religion in the schools, press, radio, and other media. That this is no easy process is admitted in the following statement about ideology made in the Soviet publication *Kommunist Vooruzhennykh Sil (Communist of the Armed Forces)*, No. 24, 1965 (pp. 16–18):

> Even in our society . . . negative elements and traits which are present in the psychology of some members of society are making acceptance of the ideas of Communism difficult. . . . Implanting an ideology in people's minds is a complex and contradictory process.

In the looser meaning of the word—for example, as applied to Jeffersonian liberalism—the elements of coercion and totalitarian indoctrination, of course, are missing. But in the second, narrower sense, coercion and indoctrination of the citizens in the orthodoxical state philosophy become one of the most important functions of the single ruling political party in the one-party state. The totalitarian states of Leninist and Stalinist Russia, Fascist Italy, and Nazi Germany provide modern examples of the application of ideology in its second and more commonly used signification.

It must be realized that ideology in totalitarian states does not function solely as "window-dressing" or as a sugar coating on the bitter pill of life in a police state. Nor is it simply a ritual performed by leaders and their subjects to release pent-up frustrations caused by unfulfilled dreams of world revolution or "communist abundance." If ideology were only these things —and it is *in part*—it would be utterly harmless so far as the international arena is concerned. But it is something more.

First, totalitarian ideology is rolled up in one ball of wax with *the legitimacy of one-party dictatorship*. This in turn has important international consequences.

Traditionally, theories of dictatorship presented by Western political philosophers were based on the assumption that for dictatorial rule to be legitimate, it must be *temporary*. To these philosophers, it had to be viewed as an *emergency* institution prompted by marginally critical circumstances. One may find this kind of legitimization of dictatorship in the classical works of Aristotle, Polybius, and Cicero, and in the post-Renaissance philosophies of Hobbes, Locke, and Rousseau. In the writings of Karl Marx in the nineteenth century, we likewise find the theory of a temporary "dictatorship of the proletariat." This concept is discussed at some length only once, in a single work by Marx, *The Critique of the Gotha Program.** But in his discussion, Marx has remained loyal to the classical tradition. He legitimizes dictatorship if it is in the interests of the workers and if it is pro tem. In fact, it undertakes measures the day after revolution, according to Marx, to eliminate itself as a dictatorship and to hasten the withering away of the state machine altogether.

With the coming of Lenin and Stalin, and Mussolini and Hitler, in the twentieth century, dictatorship began to be regarded as a *prolonged condition, a nearly permanent institution* made necessary by the extensive tasks set by the totalitarian state in the twentieth century. These tasks not only include economic and military construction and production, but "social engineering" and the indoctrination of the citizenry in the "new morality." Added to these tasks is the never-ending function of the totalitarian state and ruling party of providing "scientific guidance" of society and ensuring the "triumph of the new over the old."

In short, one-party dictatorship of the present century became institutionalized. To legitimize its permanent entrenchment in society, ideology functions as a continuously flowing fountain of youth (or, better, fountain of ideas) ever rejuvenating the ruling party's absolute right to rule absolutely. In fact, it is no exaggeration to say that the party could not get along without the ideology for a single day. (One can imagine the horror experienced by party functionaries [*apparatchiki*] should the day begin without the publication of any party-guided newspapers!** The present

---

*Thus, Marx in *The Critique of the Gotha Program*: "Between capitalist and communist society lies a period of the revolutionary transformation of one into the other. This period likewise corresponds to a political transition period, and the state in this period can be none other than a revolutionary dictatorship of the proletariat." In Marx's letter to Wedemeyer (1852), he wrote that the "class struggle necessarily leads to the dictatorship of the proletariat" and that "this dictatorship itself consists merely of a transition to the destruction of all classes and to a society without classes"—that is, to the disappearance of the state which, according to Marx, must always be class-based. The Austrian Marxist and Communist Ernst Fischer was taken to task in *Izvestiya* (April 10, 1969) because he considers Marx's dictatorship of the proletariat an "anachronism in contemporary industrial society." Fischer was expelled from the party in late 1969.

**This has never happened in the U.S.S.R. where no workers' strikes are permitted. However, *Izvestiya* failed to publish one day during the interregnum turmoil following Khrushchev's overthrow in October 1964, but all the other newspapers came out as

leadership in the Kremlin earns its right to rule from various hallowed phrases drawn from the official ideology. One of the most important of these is the notion that all post-Lenin leaders in the U.S.S.R. are a part of the Leninist Succession. For this reason the sanctity of the Lenin Cult is itself absolutely indispensable to the one-party oligarchy. Now to international implications.

It is clear from the preceding that *preservation of the ideology=preservation of the dictatorship*. For this reason, the totalitarian regime (for example, as found in most of the 14 Communist-ruled states today) guards its ideology from foreign infection as if its own life were at stake—which, in a sense, it is. Therefore, threats to ideological orthodoxy become threats to the oligarchs, and the threats more often than not come from abroad. This is the reason why large sums of money are allocated in certain totalitarian states for jamming equipment used to distort the incoming signal of foreign shortwave transmitters or why the Russians clamp down on the media of a neighboring Communist state, Czechoslovakia, to keep them from "polluting the air with revisionism."

With reference to U.S.-Soviet relations per se, ideological protection of the one-party oligarchy in the U.S.S.R. has a special meaning. The Soviet leadership perforce represents the United States, the *most powerful nation-state* and *most dangerous potential adversary* in the world, as likewise the most capitalist, the most imperialist, and therefore the most evil system in the world. Moreover, the American threat to Soviet ideological orthodoxy is composed of several special elements. One is the tremendous power of American media to carry the message abroad. Second is the widespread attention given American social, economic, and political developments in the foreign press of the world and the drawing in it of an often unfavorable contrast between the way of life in Communist states and that in Western states. Third is the intensity and persistence of what the Soviet press calls the "American campaign of anti-Communism." Often this "campaign" is backed up in the United States with a higher degree of scholarship and knowledge of Soviet affairs than in any other non-Communist country in the world—or so foreign specialists have conceded.[5]

There is a second consequence flowing from the function of ideology as political legitimizer of one-party dictatorship. This involves the basic concepts within the ideology itself.

It would not be enough for Marxism-Leninism to proclaim the mere need for totalitarian controls over the population or the legitimacy of absolute Communist Party rule omitting any supportive argumentation. Unlike

---

usual. Carrying *Pravda* and/or *Izvestiya* to work in the morning is S.O.P. in the U.S.S.R., perhaps partly as a show of loyalty, partly for the information that can be culled either in or between the lines, and also for exploitation as wrapping paper, or even as toilet tissue.

Nazism, there is no mystical *Führerprinzip* embedded in Marxism-Leninism. There is instead a mystique of a different sort: the notion that the dialectical development of history moves inevitably in the direction of totalitarian socialism but that its forward march is obstructed and delayed by an opposing, diabolical force called capitalist imperialism. To combat this evil force, Stalinist ideology develops the argument for a political priesthood composed of the most dedicated, talented, and "scientific"-minded elite. Their special function is not only to assist in ruling the country. They must lend to this rule those ingredients that are deemed necessary to prevent the recrudescence of the blighted Old Order or the invasion of the country by various forms of foreign heterodoxy. In a seldom-quoted, Platonic-sounding* exegesis by Stalin on the subject of the hierarchy of truth-cognition (political epistemology) in a Communist state, the *Vozhd* wrote:

The objective [economic] process is perceived first of all by the leaders of the Communist Party. They in turn derive from these economic processes political conclusions and point out the measures necessary for ensuring the victory of the new over the old. Then these new processes are perceived by basic membership of the Party—that is, by the vanguard of the toilers of the U.S.S.R. The next stage [in the process of cognition] is the work of the Party in convincing the broad masses of the toilers of the necessity of this or that change, this or that shift in policy or legislation. The Party influences the political and legal consciousness of the masses. . . . Only after the masses are politically prepared by a corresponding organ of state power may the necessary legislative act be promulgated. After this comes the realization of the act by the masses themselves. . . . Force is applied . . . to those parts of society who, because of remnants of capitalism or evil influences from the capitalist encirclement, show inertia and oppose the flourishing of what is new. . . . [Thus] on the one hand, the Party itself enlightens the masses and then, on the other hand, relies on the masses and proceeds from them.[6]

The quotation above represents, as far as Marxism-Leninism is concerned, the updating of the major concepts contained in Lenin's *What Is To Be Done?*, the 1901–1902 *chef d'oeuvre* of Lenin. For in *What Is To Be Done?*, which was based in part on reading the works of Peter Tkachev,** Lenin had ar-

*Plato's *Republic* contains a number of concepts which suggest certain totalitarian notions—i.e., a hierarchy of political knowledge; a political elite of philosopher-kings; the antidemocratic overtones of the pilot *vs.* crew allegory (the pilot has the necessary knowledge, the crew [the people] does not); political control and censorship of the arts (particularly in Plato's *Laws*); the "Royal Lie" establishing strata within society, etc. The British scholar K. R. Popper (in *The Open Society and Its Enemies*) perhaps finds too many quasi-totalitarian elements in the writings of Plato. But that the Greek aristocrat had many misgivings about democracy is perhaps an understatement, if Plato's *Republic* is an indication.

**The story in detail of Lenin's indebtedness to the Russian "Jacobin" of the 1870s, Peter N. Tkachev, is related in Albert L. Weeks, *The First Bolshevik: A Political Biography of Peter Tkachev* (New York: New York University Press, 1968). In speaking of Lenin's *What Is To Be Done?* Fidel Castro said on one occasion that this was the most important tract by Lenin that the Cuban leader had ever read.

gued for precisely the same kind of élite-to-masses relationship in his projected *pre*revolutionary political organization that was to bring about the
overthrow of Tsarism and the establishment of socialism in Russia. Stalin
merely applied Lenin's idea to the postrevolutionary period of one-party
"dictatorship *over* the proletariat."

The international consequences of this theory are similar to those which
flow from the function of ideology as the legitimizer of dictatorship. The
ideological argument for the existence of a hierarchy of "Philosopher-Kings"
(the Politburo), the "Guardians" (rank-and-file party membership), and
the "People" (the masses) stands or falls depending on whether the "Royal
Lie," as presented by Stalin in the quotation above, is accepted or rejected.
Various police-state instrumentalities are, of course, designed to *force* acceptance of the Stalinist hierarchy. But, obviously, force cannot be applied
to foreign countries in which no such hierarchy exists and where completely
opposite conceptions are propagated, both at home and abroad. Foremost
among such countries is the United States, which is especially critical of political élitism. America, in fact, constitutes the greatest threat abroad to the
acceptance of the Royal Lie at home in the U.S.S.R.

Another consequence stems from the Manichean good-versus-evil struggle ingrained in Marxism-Leninism. It is imperative that the ideology have
the *phantasm of evil* if the ideology is to have any reason for being. In this
context, the breach with America is useful to the Soviet regime, a *divorce
de convenance*.

Imagine if American capitalist imperialism overnight should (1) cease to
be "capitalist," in the evil connotation of the term, and become quasi-
socialist, and (2) ceased to be "imperialist." What need would there be for
the ideology? Indeed, what would be the purpose of having the one-party
dictatorship if there were no anticapitalist crusade for it to lead? The connection between this and U.S.-Soviet cooperation, or the lack of it, should
be quite obvious. If it is true that the Kremlin oligarchy has, as it were, a
vested interest in preserving its ideology, then it also must seek to preserve the foundation of *raison d'être* for the ideology. Communist media perform precisely this service for the regime. The propagandists conjure up
the worst—often fantasized—characteristics of "capitalist imperialism" allegedly found in the United States, West Germany, Britain, and so on.
Newspapers, press, radio, and TV in the U.S.S.R. monstrously distort events
and life in the "capitalist world" so that it appears to be a hell on earth
against which only the Communists effectively struggle.[7]

Incidentally, this fantasy-picture of the capitalist world may stem in
part from the lack of experience on the part of the leaders with the actual
conditions prevailing in capitalist countries. It may be no accident that the
most ideologically introverted among the top officials in Russia are most always persons who have either never traveled to the capitalist world or
who have very little direct knowledge of it. For example, the present

General-Secretary of the C.P.S.U., Leonid I. Brezhnev (age 63), is an experienced Communist leader in his own country; he was appointed by Stalin in 1952 to the highest party organ, the Presidium, in recognition of this experience. But "Ilyich" Brezhnev has never ventured outside the Soviet Bloc. Georgi M. Malenkov, Stalin's ruthless heir apparent and the First-Secretary and Premier of the U.S.S.R. immediately after Stalin's death in 1953, also used to be one of the least-traveled and most "reactionary" among the Kremlin leaders at the time of Stalin. But by the end of 1953 Malenkov had for political reasons divested himself of much of traditional domestic Stalinism and with striking flexibility had assumed the posture of a "liberalizer," even a strong advocate of peaceful coexistence. But Malenkov, whom foreign correspondents in 1954–1956 found to be an urbane, sophisticated individual, probably is an exception. (It is interesting to note that in 1955, when Malenkov's power was fading and Nikita Khrushchev's rising, Malenkov was the individual selected by the Presidium to go to England to smooth the way for the forthcoming visit by First Secretary Khrushchev and Premier Nikolai Bulganin. He was found by British journalists to be charming and quite without the terseness or withdrawn style of so many other Communist officials.)[8]

Mikhail A. Suslov is another nontraveling member of the Soviet ruling group. The Second Secretary of the C.P.S.U. and a paragon among the jealous keepers of the ideological convenant, Suslov (67) has never made a prolonged visit to a single Western capital or, except for trips to India and Japan, spent more than a day or two outside the Soviet bloc. Two other such officials, likewise reputed to be "hawks," are Politburo members Alexander N. Shelepin (51), head of the trade unions and former security chief, and Pyotr Ye. Shelest (61), head of the Ukrainian C.P. and who played a major role in the Soviet crackdown on Czechoslovakia in August 1968. Neither of these high officials has ever ventured for any length of time outside the Soviet bloc. While there is no guarantee that they would become liberals overnight if they did sojourn abroad, no doubt a personal encounter with the "evils of bourgeois life" in the West would at least serve as an eye-opener. Dmitri S. Polyansky (52), First Deputy Premier of the U.S.S.R. and member of the Politburo, on the other hand has spent some time in the West.* On tentative evidence Polyansky, a Ukrainian, is believed by Western Kremlinologists to be one of the members of the minority of moderates existing within the C.P.S.U. Politburo and Council of Ministers of the U.S.S.R. Alexei N. Kosygin (65), the Soviet Premier, and quite possibly his Foreign Minister, Andrei A. Gromyko (60), both of whom are

*It was Polyansky's singular good fortune to have been born on the very day of the October Revolution, November 7, 1917, a fact which, under Soviet conditions, lends a cubit to his stature. He led the Soviet delegation which attended the Expo-67 World's Fair in Montreal, Canada, in the summer of 1967.

well traveled, appear also to exert a moderating influence on the making of policy in the U.S.S.R.* However, as will be discussed later, it is evidently *not* the liberalizing or quasi-liberalizing elements of the C.P.S.U. Central Committee who presently wield the most power in the Kremlin. The intraparty alliance which was brought together with the overthrow of Khrushchev in October 1964 under Brezhnev introduced a hardening of Soviet policy at home and abroad, including especially the policy toward America. A number of liberal trends which were under way within the Soviet regime in the closing months of Khrushchev's rule were reversed or tabled after October 1964 (see Chapter IX).

Down with Convergence

"In recent years," reads a long *podval* in *Izvestiya* (September 22, 1967), "the anti-communists . . . have been speaking about a process of 'convergence,' a drawing together . . . of both systems, socialism and capitalism. . . . In actual fact, the basic social and economic differences between capitalism and socialism are not lessening, but in fact increasing." This is the way the Soviet government daily describes a theory which still enjoys widespread support among Western intellectual circles. Put simply, the American convergists believe that the United States is becoming more like the Soviet Union, and vice versa. (Incidentally, most Soviet specialists in the West disagree with this assessment.) Of more interest to us here is the Soviet reaction to the theory. As might be guessed from the quotation above, the Soviets give a resounding *nyet* to the theory of convergence.

Before discussing the Soviet interpretation of the concept, however, a word about my use of the term "convergence." Throughout Part Two of this book, we have described the various aspects and occurrences of *convergence of national interest* between the United States and the U.S.S.R. A synonym for "convergence" in this sense of the word might be "coincidence," or the coming together of the interests of the two countries. In Part One (Chapter I), dealing with *divergence*, we noted the several instances of grounds for disagreement existing between the two: differences in their social and political systems and so on. It is in this sense and this context that *Izvestiya* rejects convergence—that is, the allegedly increasing similarity or "convergence" between the social, economic, and political systems of the U.S. and the Soviet Union. In other words, neither convergence nor divergence of *national interest* is involved in this discussion, but rather the *similarities in their systems*.

What has led certain people in the West to find a process of convergence

*See discussion of Gromyko's July 10, 1969, address to the U.S.S.R. Supreme Soviet below, pp. 270–271.

taking place between the two systems? Are there phenomena in the two countries which warrant a convergence theory? Are the two systems becoming more alike and thereby will their foreign policies also coincide harmoniously?

By following the convergence argumentation step by step, we can analyze its several pitfalls. As the theory has been presented to this author in various conversations on American university campuses and in various readings, it runs somewhat as follows. The Soviet economy is becoming steadily more "consumerist." The Soviet people are growing ever more accustomed to a higher standard of living and ever more covetous of the types of consumer goods found in the West—the abundance of packaged foods, TV sets, cosmetics, fashionable clothes, automobiles, and so on. Accordingly, the regime is becoming more willing to satisfy the demands of the Soviet consumer. Result? Not, as Dickens' Micawber said, "Misery!", but rather the pursuit of happiness, a whetted desire for more consumer goods and a general state of mind which is totally unreceptive and ill suited to warmongering and warmaking and instead is conducive to peaceful policies. Presumably, too, a regime dispensing such goods and luxuries could ill afford simultaneously to pursue a war policy. Thus, as the society becomes more consumerist, so also does the regime begin to reflect this and to become more consumer-oriented and less inclined to pour money into arms. Economically, therefore, the U.S.S.R. gradually grows to resemble the United States and to share its standard of living until alas! one fine day, runs the chiliastic projection, the two countries meet on a millennial Elbe River for a world-historical handshake. At which time both sides agree that they have grown so much alike that there is no longer any reason for them to fight.

The convergists also make a number of observations about the two political systems. They find that, like their economies, the Soviet and American political systems are growing more similar too. You see, they point out, capitalism in America is in essence big business; a few dozen corporations dominate the economy while big finance supplies the money capital. Moreover, the federal government is becoming ever more involved in the economy. Which means the United States is developing into a system of "state capitalism." Moreover, as the importance of *ownership* of business and property steadily decreases, and *management* becomes a crucial factor, the government, which is today assuming more and more regulatory functions vis-à-vis the American economy, eventually takes over the management of "private" business. Result? State socialism—and perhaps also Micawber's "Misery!"

Meanwhile "back in the U.S.S.R." (apologies to the Beatles*) the Rus-

*The lyric to the Beatles' tune "Back in the U.S.S.R." possibly provides a rock 'n' roll interpretation of the convergence theory by suggesting that the U.S. and U.S.S.R. are really quite similar *already*—e.g., the line "back in the U.S., back in the U.S., back in the U.S.S.R. . . ."

sians are dismantling some of their overcentralized institutions for managing their economy, note the convergists. Moreover, the profit motive is being encouraged. Even some branches of *heavy* industry have undergone a measure of decentralization and are operating in part on the profit motive. This will eventually involve dismantlement of the overly centralized and totalitarian party control over society. The three countries, the U.S., Yugoslavia, and the Soviet Union, plus any others who might move in this direction, will all tend eventually to resemble one another, say the convergists. Their economies will become more market-oriented while retaining some state planning and their governments more representative and technocratic, less absolute and totalitarian. (This is precisely the projection made by the Czechoslovak reformers in their New Model Socialism program in post-January 1968 Czechoslovakia, before Soviet troops invaded the country to stop the drift toward "democracy-within-communism.") The Soviet scientist whom we quoted above, Andrei Sakharov, foresees, or at least hopes for, such a convergence when he writes:

Both capitalism and socialism are capable of long-term development, borrowing positive elements from each other, and actually coming closer to each other in a number of essential aspects.[9]

And of the Czechoslovak experiments, before they were snuffed out by the August invasion, Sakharov wrote:

Today the key to a progressive restructuring of the system of government in the interests of mankind lies in intellectual freedom. This has been understood, in particular, by the Czechoslovaks, and there can be no doubt that we should support their bold initiative, which is so valuable for the future of socialism and all mankind.[10]

The convergists draw a number of conclusions from all this which relate to international politics. One is that they expect the domestic economic and political-structural changes to bring about in turn changes in foreign policy. As the systems of the two nations (not to mention others) converge, their foreign policies begin to converge too. Particular national interests become common international interests, in other words, the general welfare on an international scale. What begins to emerge is a World Welfare State, or a system of welfare states, whose main interest is to ensure the progress and welfare of their societies.

All well and good. A rationalist's and idealist's dream. Unfortunately, however, the theory is untenable in several respects. Based essentially as it is on a Marxist or neo-Marxist determinist assumption that the economic system controls or affects the political order, the convergence theory blithely ignores the independent status of politics and the force of *political motivation*. In actual fact, as the experiences of both the Soviet and American systems prove, it is *political* decisions—or indecision—that effect economics and the whole society, and not the other way around. For example, Stalin's decision in the early 1930s to collectivize the Russian peasants was only one of several alternative measures for establishing *political* control over farm production and ensuring a supply of peasant labor to be transferred to the urban centers mushrooming under industrialization. Other alternative programs—for example, *free* cooperatives based on the family-sized *khutor*, or individual farm—were arbitrarily ruled out by Stalin as punishable heresy. But the decision to collectivize, one of the most far-ranging and also grotesque of all Stalin's decisions, was political, not economic.* The same could be said of most of the major policy decisions taken during the fifty years of Communist rule in Russia. They were not basically motivated or activated by economics or "economic laws." The political decisions were made by political leaders for largely political reasons.

Returning to the alleged convergence of the two systems: the convergists suggest that changes in the economic and social order (perhaps including "psycho-social" changes) from below will have lasting effects as they filter up to the political order above. But this follows from the assumption that this is the way that changes in society are brought about—from the grass roots upwards. In liberal democracies perhaps this may be the way changes are sometimes effected. But even in them, this *ascending mode* of political power is not always in evidence. Prohibition in America in the 1920s, for example, was surely not based on plebiscitary democracy! And in any case, its repeal in 1933 was obviously far more popular with the grass roots than was the Eighteenth Amendment in 1919, which prohibited the manufacture and sale of alcoholic beverages of all types.** The New Deal, the Marshall Plan, the decisions to intervene in Korea and Vietnam—all were major post-World War II *political* decisions which resulted in social and economic effects. The decisions came from the top down, not from below.

In totalitarian societies the *descending mode* of political power is even more strikingly evident—as Stalin said, collectivization was a "reform from above." Absent from Soviet political life are any *substantively* representative institutions for conveying the wills of the people from the bottom upwards. Even the decision of whom to vote for is conveyed from the top down via the single-list ballot. I had the opportunity to observe the process of "consent from the top" during an all-Union election day in the

---

*When Churchill broached the subject of collectivization with Stalin in one of their postwar encounters and inquired as to how "difficult" collectivization had been for the Russian people, Stalin indicated the price in lives which this "reform from above," as Stalin termed it, had exacted. Stalin held up ten fingers which Churchill correctly interpreted to mean not ten people or even ten thousand people, but ten million victims—of starvation, forced labor camps, "liquidation-of-kulaks" pogroms, etc., confirming an estimate of the victims which had already been made in West.

**The fact that an amendment could be an unpopular measure in America stems from the fact that the *amending process* involves more indirect than direct democracy.

U.S.S.R. In the polling place, I saw voters walking up to the sign-in-desk, registering, then picking up their ballots with the singly listed names printed on them and simply dropping them into the "urn" or box. There was no need even to mark them, and neither pencils nor curtained booths were available to the "secret" voters for scratching out names or writing in others. It should be added that this particular polling place in Moscow functions as a show-place for Western tourists and would therefore surely have been equipped with curtained booths if the regime found any purpose in displaying or utilizing them. It does not.

So the question comes back to the convergists: What difference does it make if Soviet consumers *do* have capitalist-shaped ideas about the good life and the pursuit of happiness? Can they really effect any changes in their *political* system through viable institutions that will reflect their wills? Is the Communist regime inclined to permit "bourgeois-democratic" inroads? The obvious answer to both questions is No.

There is another objection to the convergists' argument. It is based on their too light-headed assumption about the two systems, capitalist and "Socialist." In the first place, it is by no means clear that the Soviet leadership would ever knowingly permit their economic system to "degenerate" into a capitalist one—at least not short of a complete turn-around in the Kremlin, a palace revolt, or a widespread popular rebellion. (None of these seems even remotely possible, as things stand today.) Furthermore, as the *Izvestiya* article explains:

Scientific and technical progress and strengthening state and political tendencies *deepen the objective dissimilarities between the two systems* and the objective base is widened for the historically necessary social reforms to occur in the capitalist countries. . . . The ideologues of 'convergence' are attempting to link up the real perspectives of socialism with the development of capitalism. If in actual fact, thirty to forty years ago bourgeois sociologists had dared state that capitalism and socialism were proceeding along 'converging' lines, they would have been excoriated. . . . Today, the authors of the doctrine—W. W. Rostow for example—have had dizzying success, going from being modest and little known professors to presidential advisers. . . .

The basic social and economic differences between capitalism and socialism at the present state in the development of society *are not lessening but in fact increasing* [italics mine].

In other words, *Izvestiya* says, as the capitalist system "matures," the state will become stronger and stronger. This is the old Stalinist formulation that as capitalism reaches its dotage, the political "superstructure" becomes more oppressive and reactionary, and the class warfare more violent. This is the meaning behind the phrase "the objective base is widened for historically necessary social reforms." In other words, the chances for proletarian revolution increase. The "contradictions" of capitalism increase, misery increases, coercion by the state increases, and the downfall of capitalism thereby is hastened. Eventually, to use Khrushchev's term borrowed from Marx, the capitalists will "bury themselves."

Finally, it is important to note the *countervailing action* that is unleashed in the totalitarian state by an increased threat to the one-party oligarchy. Suppose that "consumerism" *should* become a political force in the U.S.S.R., although there is no indication that it will. Suppose moreover that the Soviet citizens' "pursuit of happiness" should begin to clash with the regime's pursuit of security and expansionism in the international arena. Could we necessarily expect that the regime would yield to this popular pressure and begin to liberalize itself? Indeed, not. Much more likely is the political version of Newton's third law: For every action there is an equal and opposite or contrary reaction. The oligarchy would obviously strike back for its own protection. Which is exactly what happened in October 1964. At that time, the relatively liberal Khrushchev period was brought to an abrupt close by a more conservative-minded regime under Brezhnev, Kosygin, Suslov, and Podgorny.

Unfortunate it is that as grass-roots liberalism gains momentum in Soviet society—as it has during the post-Stalin period—it unleashes an opposing reaction within the ruling *verkhushka* (summit). Under police-state conditions, this reaction from the ruling summit tends to stifle grass-roots liberalism. The result: an unequal stalemate. The majority of the citizens grumble about their leaders, but go about their daily business in a more or less disciplined way, while the authoritarian regime wields the carrot and the stick, at the same time only gradually edging up the Soviet standard of living. The locked-in stalemate consists in the fact that neither the citizens nor their leaders get the social and economic situation each side desires; each settles for half a loaf. Although force is on the side of the rulers, it is employed overtly only in marginal situations. Nonetheless, the stalemate is unequal, in the regime's favor.

As far as foreign policy is concerned, this state of affairs still permits the Soviet leaders almost complete latitude in the making of policy. This in turn considerably strengthens the Soviet hand when dealing with the Western powers. In the latter, the electorates and the free press can and do exert pressure on the elected officials. At election time, especially, the voters possess the power of "firing" their leaders. This "weakness," if it can be so termed, in the Western liberal democracies is, of course, well known to the Soviets and their Communist allies. The Vietnam impasse, which we shall discuss later, provides a striking example of how the North Vietnamese and Soviet leaders exploit this difference between the two systems—Communist and liberal-democratic.

Nationalism, National Interest, and Convergence

One might well ask at this point, What are the chances of ideology giving way in priority to national interests, when the two are in conflict? Is it not true that when the chips are down, national interests, not ideology, determine policy? And, do not one nation's interests sometimes converge with another's? Answers to these questions have great relevance in testing the possibilities for convergence between the United States and the Soviet Union.

As we saw from the historical survey in Chapter IV, above, there have been several instances when Russian and American (meaning also Soviet and American) convergence of national interests has resulted in Russian and American cooperation. During these times, ideology and the systemic differences between the two countries have been conveniently laid aside or forgotten, or have been reshaped to fit the new foreign policy design.

During the American Civil War, for example, Russia was no less autocratic and oppressive than before it, and yet America eagerly welcomed Russian support for the Union. In World War II, Stalinist Russia welcomed Lend-Lease aid from "capitalist-imperialist" U.S.A. and partially, at least, tabled anti-U.S. propaganda, thereby wrenching ideology to fit U.S.-Soviet collaboration during the war. Can the regime afford to revise or forget ideology in this way and still maintain the underpinning for one-party rule?

The determining factor in the regime's ability or readiness to make the "ideological sacrifice" is *a threat to the national survival and along with it the very survival of the regime.* If a policy of protecting the state from invading foreign enemies should for some reason clash with ideology, the latter would logically have to give way to the former.

"A good friend is better than a hundred relatives," runs an old Russian proverb. The Communist parties associated with the Soviets in the pre-1943 Comintern were "relatives" of the U.S.S.R., but hardly the elements Stalin wished to rely upon when the U.S.S.R. was under siege by invading German armies. Thus, Stalin dissolved the cantankerous Comintern in 1943. The "friend" became the United States, and also Britain, although neither was a Communist relative. But another Russian proverb warns that if you "lie down with dogs, you'll get up with fleas." And imperialist "dogs" do have "fleas," according to Soviet history books. They were flea-ridden even during the heyday of wartime collaboration—for example, the Soviet texts assert that the Western Allies intentionally delayed opening of the second front in Western Europe in 1943.* After the war, Stalin hastened to

*This plainly ridiculous and deliberately "paranoid" fantasy is repeated in Marshal Vasili Chuikov's memoirs, *The Fall of Berlin* (New York: Ballantine, 1969), p. 9. Chuikov also revives the bogey of a joint U.S.-British effort to conclude a separate peace with the Germans (p. 183). And yet Chuikov, with typical Soviet ambiguity put ideology back in the forefront. Two of his closest assistants, the late Andrei A. Zhdanov and G. M. Malenkov, were assigned the task of restoring, as it were, the demonology of Marxism-Leninism. Stalin himself became the keynote spokesman for this new postwar era when he said in his famous February 1946 preelection speech:

It would be wrong to think that the Second World War was an accidental occurrence. . . . Actually the war was the inevitable result of the development of world economic and political forces on the basis of modern monopoly capitalism. . . . The capitalist system of world economy harbors elements of general crises and armed conflicts.[11]

Stalin then asserted that until the world economy is planned from a "single center" wars will continue to be inevitable. The *Vozhd* also told Milovan Djilas in 1944-1945 (at the time Djilas was second in importance to Tito in the Communist Party in Yugoslavia) that "the war will soon be over. . . . We shall recover in fifteen or twenty years, and then we'll have another go at it."[12]

Thus, ideology was again restored to prominence in 1945–1946 and the Comintern-like Communist Information Bureau (Cominform) was established in 1947. East-versus-West demonology became central in the editorial line of the press, in textbooks, and in Soviet diplomacy. Having routed the German enemy—with the help of their Western Allies—the Soviets under Stalin returned to their pre-June 1941 anti-imperialist stance.

The postwar resurgence of ideology had several purposes. First, it was designed to serve Soviet *imperial* interests with respect to the territories in Eastern and Central Europe occupied by the Soviet armies. The imposition of Moscow's imperial controls could only be justified in terms of ideology; the anticapitalist activities of the Communists in these countries also needed the underpinning of authoritative ideological pronouncements. Second, the Communist movements in Western countries experienced an "upturn" (*podyom*, as the Russians say) as the result of the war. Underground guerrilla or "partisan" movements were often led or their leadership was shared with Communists, and the postwar radicalism of the Communists had appeal for segments of the war-weary and reform-minded populations in the Western countries. The Communists played upon the people's critical attitude toward the "old order," presenting the people with socialist

---

with respect to the Western Allies, asserts the following (p. 255): "Between the military Allies, between the soldiers of the anti-Hitler coalition, there were no contradictions. We had one common aim, one common enemy, and did our best to finish off that enemy as quickly as possible. The closer the contact became between Soviet soldiers and those of the Allies, the stronger their union grew, and the more their mutual respect for one another increased."

panaceas. Of course, Western C.P.s got much moral, political, and financial support in these efforts from the U.S.S.R. But whether Stalin was determined actually to capture power in certain of the West European or Balkan countries (for example, France, Italy, Greece, Turkey) is a moot question. At the very least, he sought to gain a Soviet foothold in the ruling apparatuses of these "bourgeois" countries; seizing power would be the best guarantee that this influence would be preserved. It is also quite possible that Stalin—and his successors, for that matter—seriously pursued the old Leninist goal of world revolution leading to the creation of a worldwide political and economic hegemony and administration for managing the world economy from a "single center," as Stalin said in his February 1946 preelection address. That the goal of world revolution is in the minds of Soviet leaders even today, is illustrated by this recent definition of "proletarian internationalism" (*Kommunist* [U.S.S.R.] No. 5, March 1969).

Proletarian internationalism . . . is the weapon used for an offensive struggle of the international working class against imperialism and for a fundamental reconstruction of the world along socialist lines.[13]

(One can imagine the problems the Soviets would face in "running the world," when managing affairs in the Soviet bloc is complicated enough!)

As was suggested earlier in this book, part of the function of ideology *is* ceremonial, or as Erich Fromm puts it, "ritualistic" and therefore quite harmless. But it must also be remembered that ideology *by no means need always clash with Soviet national interests* as the leaders view those interests. Quite the contrary. When Maurice Thorez said, "A *Communist* Cabinet in France will be the last," he also implied that Moscow would have acquired a regime which could be counted upon *permanently* to serve its interests better than the preceding non-Communist regime, and that no future non-Communist government would ever be permitted to come into office. (No ruling Communist Party in a nation-state has ever permitted its own removal or been removed from power.)

In the U.S.S.R. (see Gromyko quote below, p. 154), ideology frequently— and ideally—works hand in glove with foreign policy, as shown in Table 6. Table 6 illustrates how ideology and diplomacy can be wedded in such a way as to produce policies that serve *both* ideology and the Soviet national interest (*raison d'état*).

Now, it is not necessarily true that the Communist ideology that underpins the diplomacy of one Communist state may necessarily harmonize with either the ideology or the diplomacy of another Communist state. Ever since the Yugoslav defection from the Cominform in 1948, it is clear to Communist and non-Communist observers alike that a Communist regime in a given country does not necessarily ensure 100 percent loyalty to the

TABLE 6. Ideology in Relation to Diplomacy

Ideological Position	Diplomatic Action	Desired Result in Both Ideology and Diplomacy
Peaceful coexistence between unlike social and political systems; avoidance of World War III; war no longer fatally inevitable.	"De-ideologized"[a] East-West contacts, trade negotiations, and retaining World War II links with Western powers; preventing spread of nuclear weapons; etc.	*Ideology*: Peace campaign as bait for support by leftists and fellow travelers in capitalist countries. *Diplomacy*: Extending Soviet contacts and influence in foreign countries; new allies or retaining old allies for future reference.
Incompatibility of Soviet and "capitalist-imperialist" ideology.	Buttressing adversary principle which defines clearly the basis of alliance between the U.S.S.R. and its bloc plus addition of neutral states leaning to Soviet direction (Finland, India, etc.); establishing a position of power— as, for example, in Southeast Asia as a result of Soviet involvement in the Vietnam War.	*Ideology*: Dichotomy between Good and Evil useful in Communist movements abroad; a "rallying point." *Diplomacy*: Helps discipline Warsaw Pact Alliance by pointing up dangers of capitalist imperialism; polarizes Communist powers into either Chinese or Soviet camp, Soviets hope the latter.

[a]For an interesting analysis of this phenomenon by the author who coined the expression "de-ideologize" when applied to Soviet foreign policy in 1955 and after, see Vernon Aspaturian, "Foreign Policy Perspectives in the Sixties," in Alexander Dallin and Thomas B. Larson (eds.), *Soviet Politics Since Khrushchev* (Englewood Cliffs, N.J.: Prentice-Hall, 1968), pp. 130–133. My use of quotation marks indicates that ideological considerations have not been discarded by the Soviets, but only suspended or "tabled" in diplomatic intercourse.

policies worked out in Moscow. This has been made increasingly clear in the 1950s and 1960s. The Rumanians and Chinese have gone their own ways, and the Yugoslavs and Albanians theirs. Ditto several nonruling West European C.P.s.

In speaking of the U.S.S.R. itself, the Soviet Communist ideal is, of course, for ideology *and* diplomacy (and national interest) to work together. In his address to the Supreme Soviet on June 27, 1968, Soviet Foreign Minister Gromyko discussed the connection between diplomacy and ideology in the context of Soviet-American relations:

As far as the Soviet side is concerned, we want good relations with the U.S.A. and are in favor of negotiating outstanding international problems. And we consider at present that there are no bases for conflict between our two countries if the American side will show the necessary respect for our security and the security of our friends, and if the U.S.A. does not encroach on the security and independence of other peoples.

Our country will never make any deals with anybody to the detriment of the interests of any people. It depends on the government of the U.S.A. to what degree existing possibilities of agreement between the U.S.S.R. and the U.S.A. may be exploited.

In international life, acts are encountered which are difficult to classify as being either purely diplomatic or purely ideological. *More often they are one and the same.* It could not be any other way since no foreign policy has existed or exists which does not include in itself and reflect the interests of certain classes and their ideologies. Conflict between ideologies, the struggle for recognition by the masses and for their sympathy accompanies the foreign policy activity of governments and is organically intertwined with that activity. [italics mine][14]

The first thing to notice in this excerpt from Gromyko's address is the sentence, *"More often* they are one and the same." The interesting words here are "more often." For in the two sentences that follow this, the Foreign Minister more or less mechanically reverts to traditional Marxism-Leninism in suggesting that foreign policy is logically the reflection of class interests and therefore must be "ideological." However, he has already qualified the connection between ideology and diplomacy with his "more often." He thus implies, but unfortunately gives no examples, of occasions when Soviet ideology and foreign policy do *not* harmonize. Indeed, they sometimes do not.

When the Soviets court the friendship of Arab countries, an anomaly is immediately presented. In most of these countries, the Communist Party is outlawed! In Egypt, for example, where the Communists function as an illegal underground group, the party seeks the overthrow of the Nasser regime. And yet Soviet diplomacy vis-à-vis the U.A.R. is bent upon upholding Nasser and ensuring his continuance in office. This is because Nasser's foreign policy presumably serves Soviet national interests. In Latin America, too, Moscow has alienated a number of radical Communist apparatuses because the Russians place trade and orderly diplomatic intercourse between themselves and certain Latin American countries at a higher level of priority than ideological considerations. This causes the Communist movements in these countries to feel abandoned by the "Socialist Citadel." Some have splintered and have become Peking-oriented. The Cuban Communist leader, Fidel Castro, has reminded the Soviet comrades more than once of his disagreement with them on this score. Castro, until perhaps very recently, has favored much more militant tactics and strategy for South America than Moscow, including even the application of guerrilla warfare to overturn the "bourgeois" governments.

To continue with Gromyko. The second interesting element in the excerpt from his address is the link between the discussion in paragraph three with the discussion of Soviet policy toward America in paragraphs one and two. The implication is, supposedly, that the U.S.-Soviet relationship presents a special case. But in the paragraphs immediately following these three, Gromyko proceeds to make several points about the *merging* of foreign policy and ideology. Above all, Vietnam is stressed as an example of how the two may be coordinated:

Those who are responsible for the unleashing of this war and for its escalation frankly state that the American aim in the war is to preserve the prevailing order in South Vietnam—e.g., to protect the reactionary puppet regime which right and left trafficks in the interests of the country to the profit of foreigners. . . . All this must be taken and is taken into account in our foreign policy *as well as in our ideological activity insofar as it bears upon international affairs.* Our foreign policy and our ideology make a striking contrast to the grim future anticipated by many officials in the capitalist world. They are haunted by nightmares when they contemplate that system, the representatives of whose policy and ideology they are. [italics mine]

The point here is: When or wherever possible, Soviet diplomacy *should* merge with the ideological struggle between the two systems, Vietnam being an example. Thus, Vietnam is useful to the overall purposes of the Soviet regime—including especially the spread of Communism throughout the world—by pointing up dramatically, the Soviets hope, the "bankruptcy" of American policy in retaining an outworn puppet regime in a foreign country.

Needless to say, the Soviet government has devoted prime attention in its media to Vietnam since the overthrow of Khrushchev, as will be detailed later. It has used Vietnam as a magnet to attract world attention to the failures of "world imperialism" and the success and rectitude of the Communist "offensive against the positions of imperialism."[15] And, also, Vietnam has acted as a rallying point for rejuvenating slackening Communist unity. It is noteworthy that despite partial or complete defection from the Warsaw Alliance by Yugoslavia, Rumania, and Albania, all three of these Balkan Communist countries give support to the North Vietnamese and their allies in the war and reiterate the North Vietnamese goal of "liberating the South."

To conclude, Gromyko's address leaves one with several impressions: (1) The ideal is for Soviet ideology and diplomacy to work together; (2) but this does not always happen; (3) lodging the subject of U.S.-Soviet relations within this section of the speech could suggest either (a) Soviet policy toward America *often* (but *not always*) displays a marriage of Soviet ideology and foreign policy or (b) here is where the two *should be* brought together (for example, as in Vietnam). Perhaps both (a) and (b) are operative in Gromyko's mind. In any case, the Supreme Soviet address provides a rare treatment by a Soviet foreign minister of the relationship between ideology and foreign policy.

If ideology is ever sacrificed, as we mentioned before, it is because national security is of overriding importance. This subject needs to be explored further if the behavior on the other side of coexistence is to be understood.

Gromyko himself, in the same interesting speech, gave a definition of Soviet national security which he spelled out as follows:

> Our foreign policy shows and will continue to show firmness in defending the state interests of the Soviet people, in providing for the inviolability of our land borders, coastlines, air space, the honor of our flag, and the rights and safety of Soviet citizens.
>
> A likewise organically basic element in our foreign policy is loyalty to our duties as an ally and to international obligations which we have assumed.[16]

In reading the last section of Gromyko's speech (from where this excerpt was taken), one is struck by the Foreign Minister's nationalistic overtones. Indeed, some observers, who have attempted to sum up or epitomize post-Khrushchev foreign policy, detect a strong note of *nationalism* in Soviet policy.[17] As a result, "internationalism" (and along with it, ideology) has often had to take a back seat in the scheme of Soviet priorities.

What is meant by "nationalism" when applied to Soviet policies? In what way may it clash with ideological considerations? How is it related to the problem of U.S. and Soviet convergence?

Nationalism is a frequently distorted concept in both Western and Soviet books on international affairs. More often than not, the writers who use it, and abuse it, have in their minds, apparently, the species of *extreme* nationalism generally associated with Mussolini's fascism or Hitler's national socialism. However, this is a very narrow and one-sided view of this important phenomenon in the modern world.

It would be better to try to define the term "nationalism" in this way: Imagine two extremes, in Aristotelian fashion.* At one end is a distorted form of nationalism known as *chauvinism, jingoism,* or *imperialism.* This form of nationalism is accompanied by a fanatical ideology which says, in essence, "My country's political program, its way of life, and so forth, are so superior that we are going to impose it on the rest of the world." Mean-

---

*In describing the various ethical attributes in his *Nichomachean Ethics,* Aristotle uses the methodology of extremes to find the Golden Mean for optimum ethical behavior. For example, "lavishness" is at one extreme while "penuriousness" is at the other of an ethical attribute whose mean is "charity." While the Stagirite is recommending a *via media* of ethical behavior by this methodology, the method is suggestive for clarifying definitions of other types of behavior as well.

time, at the other extreme end, we find another species of distorted nationalism: *isolationism*. This equally fanatical ideology says, essentially, "My country is so righteous and pure that it refuses to sully itself with binding commitments and relations with other countries."

Obviously, the two extremes do not exhaust the definition of "nationalism," although for too many people it does suffice. What is missing are the elements of the following "mean" definition: *Consciousness, even love, for the national character and contributions of a nation to the world by the people of that nation as expressed in its foreign policy; a corresponding policy which reflects a fervent desire to preserve the nation, refrain from undertaking reckless foreign adventures, and protect it from military attack or the surrender of its national sovereignty or sovereign interests to a foreign power or to any presently conceivable "World State."*

By the definition of moderate or "mean" nationalism given above, certain exaggerated forms of nationalism are relegated to the two extremes of *chauvinism* and *isolationism*. India in the years following its independence in 1946 and the U.S. after the war of 1812 provided examples of median nationalism. And there are several contemporary manifestations of it.

Thus, today the Soviets have begun to restore churches and monasteries, to make increasing use of the term "Rossiya" as opposed to "Soviet," to print letters to the editor recommending that church bells be permitted to ring once again (which Stalin had permitted only during World War II, after which they were again silenced), and to give more attention than before to prerevolutionary Tsarist military heroes. What do we term these phenomena? Are they not a renascence of national consciousness to which Communist ideology is supposedly indifferent or even hostile? Resurgent national consciousness—the above examples are taken from the contemporary Soviet scene—could just as well be termed evidences of "nationalism," without implying a resemblance to the program found in *Mein Kampf*. True, Soviet nationalism in its current expression in the post-Khrushchev period *does* occasionally express itself in distorted form. An example of this was the invasion of Czechoslovakia in August 1968. Even certain well-known Communists and several writers in Yugoslav Communist publications have stated implicitly or explicitly that this Soviet action was plainly intemperate and even "imperialistic."

However, the partial sacrifice of ideology evident in Soviet policy since 1955 and the tradition of ideological suspension when the national interest and national security so dictate are highly suggestive. They indicate that Soviet policy-makers retain sufficient flexibility and consciousness of *Russian raison d'état* to make ideological sacrifices for the sake of higher goals —namely national survival. A recasting of priorities appears to be under

*Patriotism might be defined as nationalism "writ small," in the hearts and minds of individual citizens.

way at present in the Kremlin. It could especially affect Russian and American relations (despite their entanglement in ideology), the Sino-Russian cold war, and the entire global picture of opposing alliances and contending forces. The world-historical potentialities of the ideology-versus-diplomacy juxtaposition and in particular, its meaning for Russian-American relations, will be explored at the conclusion of this book.

N O T E S

1. *The New York Times*, November 13, 1968, publishing excerpts from a lecture delivered by C. P. Snow at Westminster College in Fulton, Missouri, on November 12.
2. Sakharov, *op. cit.*, p. 60.
3. *Ibid.*, p. 76.
4. *Ibid.*, p. 80.
5. See, for example, Walter Laqueur, "In Search of Russia," *Survey* (U.K.), No. 50 (January 1964), pp. 41–52.
6. Stalin quoted in *Voprosy Filosofii (Problems of Philosophy)*, vol. VIII, No. 5, 1952, p. 60.
7. For three excellent books which describe comprehensively and with many examples how the Communist press make distortions of Western life see: Frederick C. Barghoorn, *The Soviet Image of the United States* (New York: Harcourt, Brace & World, 1950); Antony Buzek, *How the Communist Press Works* (New York: Praeger, 1964); and Donald Dunham, *Kremlin Target: U.S.A.—Conquest by Propaganda* (New York: Ives Washburn, 1961).
8. One newsman who interviewed Malenkov on his trip to Britain in the early summer of 1956 (after his deposition from the premiership) was Edward Crankshaw, who describes Malenkov in his book *Khrushchev—A Career* (New York: Viking Press, 1966), pp. 204–205. Anastas Mikoyan, a frequent visitor to Western capitals, was one of the most outstanding liberalizers during reign of Khrushchev; he was often the Kremlin's spokesman for a soft line on America. Mikoyan was the Kremlin official delegated to prepare the way for Khrushchev's trip to the U.S. in 1959; he was demoted soon after Khrushchev's fall from power.
9. Sakharov, *op. cit.*, p. 74.
10. *Ibid.*, p. 67.
11. *Pravda*, February 10, 1946, p. 1.
12. Milovan Djilas, *Conversations with Stalin* (New York: Harcourt, Brace & World, 1962), pp. 114–115.
13. B. Ponomarev, "*Istoricheskoye znacheniye Kominterna*" ("The Historical Importance of the Comintern"), *Kommunist*, No. 5 (March 1969), p. 26. Ponomarev is a top Soviet official, a full member of the C.P.S.U. Secretariat and serves as the Secretary in charge of C.P.S.U. relations with nonruling foreign Communist parties.
14. *Pravda*, June 28, 1968, p. 4.

15. From the "Manifesto on International Communist Solidarity" issued by the C.P.S.U. in November 1965. Discussion in Albert L. Weeks, "The Other Side of Coexistence," *The Reporter* (April 4, 1968), p. 14.

16. *Pravda*, June 28, 1968, p. 4.

17. Several specialists have suggested that the Soviets, sooner or later, will have to cope with (1) playing the game of international politics in an essentially traditional setting *vs.* (2) according to the book of Marxism-Leninism, the latter of which may clash with the former. See Samuel L. Sharp, "National Interest: Key to Soviet Politics," in Pentony (ed.), *op. cit.*, pp. 115–126; Harold R. Isaacs, "Nationalism Revisited—Group Identity and Political Change," *Survey* (U.K.) (October 1968), pp. 76–78; Richard Lowenthal, "The Logic of One-Party Rule," Pentony (ed.), *op. cit.*, pp. 127–144. Although there are occasional references to the possibility of a rebirth of Russian nationalism in the U.S.S.R. today, the subject has been somewhat neglected in the literature up to now.

PART THREE

THE BIPOLAR STANDOFF

CHAPTER VII

Khrushchev's Big-Bang Diplomacy

The task is to erect insurmountable obstacles to the unleashing of wars by the imperialists. . . . The imperialists can unleash a war, but they are obliged to consider its consequences.

—N. S. KHRUSHCHEV, January 6, 1961

A small imperialist [local] war . . . might develop into a world thermonuclear, rocket war. Therefore, we must wage a struggle both against world wars and against local wars.

—IBID.

The year 1955 was a crucial one in the post-Stalin era. In foreign policy, the year saw several momentous developments. They were either directly or indirectly related to the problem of the bipolar division of the world into two spheres of influence—one sphere inclining toward the United States, the other toward the Soviet Union. The third "uncommitted" world was also profoundly affected.

The year 1955 marked the culmination of a number of trends which had been triggered by the death of Stalin in 1953 and his departure from the helm in the Kremlin. First, Stalin's global strategy was based largely on pre-Atomic Age calculations. True, the Soviets had developed and tested their first bomb in 1949, four years before Stalin left the scene. But development and testing are one thing; stockpiling bombs, producing bombers to carry them, and readjusting policy are another. During the five-year period of reconstruction after World War II, Stalin apparently saw no reason to alter significantly the basic lines of his postwar foreign policy, either with respect

161

to the world as a whole or to the United States in particular. Instead, his policy remained that of a traditionally Stalinist mixture consisting of (1) probing for weakness in the Western armor and Western resolve (for example, Berlin in 1948, Korea in 1950–1953); (2) the indissoluble marriage of ideology and foreign policy (for example, the *ideological* depiction of the Korean War as a "just" war and a war of "national liberation," coupled to Stalin's *diplomatic* goal of acquiring a larger sphere of influence in the Western Pacific, possibly as the first stage of a Soviet endeavor to fence in Red China); (3) the campaign to upset military and political planning within N.A.T.O. (established, ironically, in the same year as the successful testing of a Soviet A-bomb); (4) the ideological formulation, updating the Leninist-Stalinist projection, that the next world war would break out *between the imperialist powers alone*, excluding the Communist world, formulated in Stalin's last major work, *The Economic Problems of Socialism in the U.S.S.R.* (1952); (5) consolidation of the Soviet empire in Balkan, Central, and Eastern Europe; (6) strengthening of the Soviet hold on East Germany (the German Democratic Republic was established in 1949) coupled to an adroit policy of retaining as a safeguard a measure of joint four-power control over all of "Germany,"* but especially in Berlin, as stipulated in the Potsdam Agreement of 1945; (7) stepping up of the ideological war against the "capitalist imperialist" states (whose proletariats would allegedly arise in anger and disgust over defense appropriations for N.A.T.O.) by means of what Stalin ominously called in his last major speech to the Nineteenth Party Congress in October 1952 international "shock brigades."

By 1955, two years after Stalin's death, some of the above-mentioned seven policy positions appeared to be too risky once two other great events in the technology of superweapons had occurred: American test-firing of a thermonuclear bomb in 1952; Soviet test-firing of the same in 1954.

With the death of Stalin in March 1953, the new team of Soviet leaders, faced with a host of domestic problems including a near crisis of national disunity, began to modify a number of Stalin's adventuristic and overly ideological international policies.** First, Moscow's control over the East European satellites began to show signs of relaxation. For example, when the workers of East Berlin revolted in June 1953, the Soviets responded by ordering lower consumer goods prices and raising wages. Satellite Commu-

---

*As Adam B. Ulam points out in *Expansion and Coexistence—The History of Soviet Foreign Policy 1917–1967*, p. 442: "[Germany] was to be treated as a single political unit," despite Germany's division into four occupation zones. The Soviets, even as late as 1969, have referred to this ghostly Four-Power control over *all* of Germany as being still in force. See discussion of the point, below, pp. 197–200 and 253–258.

**The late Boris I. Nicolaevsky, the astute observer of the Russian scene living in America, developed a well-argued thesis that Stalin had planned to initiate a Third World War shortly before his death, which was to be accompanied by a massive purge at home. It was moreover Nicolaevsky's guess that Stalin had been forcibly removed from the scene by his colleagues precisely because of his adventuristic plans.

nist leaders purged by Stalin (when they remained alive) began to creep back into power. When in 1953–1954 the Hungarian Communists began to de-collective many of their *kolkhoz*-type farms, which had been modeled after the *kolkhozes* and *sovkhozes* in the U.S.S.R., the Russians merely looked the other way. Finally, partial liberalization of various types and in varying degrees swept over the whole Soviet empire. But Moscow did not retaliate.

Second, Stalin's radical "shock brigade" idea was discarded. In its place came a new form of peace campaign coupled to popular-front cooperation between non-Communist socialists (in most countries called Social Democrats) and the Communists, both in capitalist countries and "colonial" countries seeking "liberation." This modification of the "international line" for the world Communist movement stemmed largely from the development of the hydrogen bomb.

The development of the hydrogen bomb by the bipolar giants, the U.S. and the Soviet Union, "cooled" the policies of both powers considerably. It led eventually to the realization of the principle of *mutual deterrence*. Mutual deterrence, or the "balance of terror" as it is sometimes termed, was linked in several respects to Soviet foreign policy, from both ideological and *raison d'état* points of view. The consequences that deterrence was to have for the Soviet formula of world revolution is epitomized by this statement by First Secretary Nikita S. Khrushchev:

You cannot drive people to paradise with a club, or drive them to communism by means of war. When people realize that communism alone will give them a truly free and happy life, they will come running of their own free will.[1]

Earlier, under Stalin, *war as a means for spreading Soviet-type revolution* was never ruled out. In fact, until the Twentieth Party Congress in February 1956, Stalin's old formula that "war is inevitable as long as capitalism exists" stood at the core of the Soviet General Line on foreign policy. (Both Stalin and Lenin had predicted that a cataclysmic war would finally decide which system, capitalist or Soviet, would rule the earth.) Given weapons as lethal and *self*-destructive as H-bombs, however, and with the development of rocket carriers to boot (these were already on the drawing boards), "exportation of revolution" on the tips of nuclear bombs became foolhardy. Thus, under the leadership of Khrushchev—who knows with how much profound philosophical reflection—the Russians rediscovered the "Leninist" concept of "*communism-by-example.*"*

*Khrushchev's conception, which was alleged to conform to Lenin's, was that the achievements in the Soviet economy and Soviet society would set an attractive example for socialist and semisocialist countries abroad to follow. It was particularly designed to attract "bourgeois-nationalist" groups in colonial and ex-colonial lands and in the "uncommitted" Third World.

Nonmilitary Communism-by-Example

Communism-by-example took two forms, ideological and diplomatic. It reflected a very important change which began to emerge in 1955–1956 in Soviet doctrine. First, thermonuclear world war should be avoided; in any case, it was certainly not "inevitable." Second, for the purposes of those foreign peace campaigns financed and inspired by the Soviets, preaching of the line that "war is inevitable" would only cause the peace workers to become dispirited. Instead, the line was changed (in 1956) to "war is not *fatally* inevitable." It has remained thus until today.

In 1955, just a few months before these and other doctrinal changes were to be made public and handed down to the party at the Twentieth Party Congress, Soviet foreign policy had already taken a definitive turn in the direction of "peaceful coexistence." The changes not only reflected Soviet awakening to the dangers of living in a world of thermonuclear weapons. It was based on other considerations as well.

With the Soviet Foreign Ministry "purged," reconstructed, and modernized,[2] Soviet foreign policy was ready to make some bold new starts in 1954–1955. New embassies were opened in states where they had never before existed. India began to be the target of a campaign of Soviet wooing. Nehru and even Gandhi, earlier depicted in Soviet publications as reactionaries, were now called champions of the welfare of the Indian people. Extensive traveling throughout the world—for example, by the team of "B & K" (Bulganin and Khrushchev)—began to be used as a means of acquainting the Soviet leaders personally with the ruling "summits" in foreign lands and, for that matter, with the actual situations prevailing in a number of key foreign countries.* Soviet foreign trade took a sharp upturn, while hotels in Moscow began to burst at the seams with foreign visitors, a result of attempts to "win friends and influence people."

Three other major events in Soviet foreign policy took place during 1955 and deserve special mention. On May 15, 1955, the Soviets signed a peace treaty with Austria and thus backtracked on their earlier position that an Austrian treaty would have to await the signing of a general peace treaty with Germany (which until today has not yet been drafted). As a result, Austria became a disarmed, largely agricultural neutral country which had been the fortunate and somewhat surprised recipient of Soviet largesse. Apparently, the Kremlin had calculated that the creation of a neutral state out of a formerly belligerent one might set an example for handling other states (such as Germany, for example); Finland had been treated in this

*Like so many other momentous Soviet developments, this opening of a window *on the world* (Peter the Great had opened his only on Europe!) was hinted at ever so delicately early in 1953 when the post-Stalin collectivirs opened the Kremlin for the first time in over twenty years.

way before Austria. It also may have been in preparation or anticipation of the "Rapacki Plan" for creating a belt of denuclearized states in the heart of Europe.

Then on May 26, 1955, B & K made their famous pilgrimage to Tito's Yugoslavia. This "journey to Canossa" amounted to a public apology for Stalin's hostile policy toward Yugoslavia after 1948. The visit lasted a week and went a long way—but not all the way, as it turned out later—toward repairing the damage done during the preceding seven years. By 1967, however, much of the old hostility had begun to return.

From July 18 to 23, the famous Geneva "summit" meeting took place in Switzerland and with it unleashing of the "Geneva Spirit." It was a jolly affair, with Marshal Georgi K. Zhukov meeting and chatting amiably with General, also President, Dwight D. Eisenhower, while the two heads of the Soviet delegation, Bulganin and Khrushchev, comported themselves as if to show that a whole new attitude toward America was about to be adopted. It even appeared at the time that Soviet disarmament and arms control proposals were only in part motivated by propaganda. Unfortunately, however, the Geneva Spirit soon evaporated, leaving only a little tangible evidence that it had ever existed.

What had motivated the Soviets in this new policy of what one specialist has called "imprecise friendliness"?[3] Why were such ideological handles as the "American instigators of the Third World War" and "American imperialists" soft-pedaled in Soviet propaganda for the duration of the Geneva Spirit? Several possible explanations suggest themselves. The evident Soviet intention was to "soften up" the United States. President Eisenhower, former leader of the Western Alliance, symbol of Russian and American wartime cooperation, and an essentially "nonpolitical" type, was the obvious target for this Soviet effort, but it didn't work. What the Soviets expected to gain and what sparked their effort can be summarized as follows:

1. Building Soviet respectability in the world; U.S. acceptance of the *status quo* in Eastern Europe.
2. Reduction of Western fears of "Stalinist Russia" resulting in eventual withdrawal of American forces from Europe and subsequent neutralization of Germany.*
3. "Relaxation of tension" for Soviet domestic consumption as the post-Stalin regime undertook measures to improve the Soviet standard of living so neglected under Stalin.
4. A stalling tactic of mollifying the U.S. and its allies in order to decelerate their military construction, so that the Soviets could catch up to and eventually surpass America's military advantage by Russian development of rockets (already in the planning stage), which were later to be armed with thermonuclear

---

*Although the Soviets talked much of "German unification" at this time, they appear never to have taken their own diplomatic line seriously.

warheads; this tactic aimed also at slowing efforts at West German rearmament.

5. A feeling of security and confidence in the Kremlin as the post-Stalin interregnum crisis eased and the Soviets were able to build their own "N.A.T.O." in the form of the Warsaw Treaty; while lagging far behind the U.S. in overall military strength, and especially with respect to sophisticated weaponry and nuclear strength, the Soviets ironically almost made up for it by the imposing strength of their *conventional* forces added to that of their Warsaw Pact allies.

6. In the Far East,* the Soviet softness-toward-the-West policy, the Communism-by-example line, and the B & K travels in Asia were all intended to offset China's growing influence and prestige in the region, which had developed apace since Mao and his forces secured mainland China in October 1949.

Clearly, Soviet behavior in 1954–1955 was aimed in part at securing a "breathing space" during which the Soviets would be free to develop their own position of strength. In so doing, and by adding rockets to their arsenal, the Soviets might then be able to stand up to the West and wield more power and influence in the world than before. First, however, it was necessary to walk softly while fashioning a big stick.

Military-Diplomatic Policy in the Khrushchev Era

We have already indicated that the existence of such a lethal, destructive and self-destructive weapon as the H-bomb in the hands of the two superpowers was a key factor leading to various changes in Soviet policy. As a consequence, from the mid-1950s until the overthrow of Khrushchev in October 1964, a number of changes in Soviet military-diplomatic strategy took place. In no sense did these changes occur in some "automatic" or linear fashion; the policy changes were subject to a great deal of discussion in the Soviet military press and in speeches by the civilian leaders, including Khrushchev himself. The Kremlin global military-diplomatic strategy, together with its various shifts, has, of course, direct relevance to American and Soviet relations and for understanding the other side of coexistence.

The Biggest-Bang-per-Ruble Policy

Until the overthrow of Khrushchev, Soviet military doctrine and policy hinged on the concept of the "biggest bang for the smallest number of rubles invested." In 1955 the United States had a clear military lead over the Soviets in several respects. First, the Soviet economy was no match for the American, even when the whole Soviet bloc was added to the totals—the West being about a third to half again as economically productive as the

---

*An important event in this area in 1955 was the Bandung Conference of Asians in Indonesia, April 18–27, to which the U.S.S.R., a *half*-Asian power, was *not even invited*.

East. Second, the superiority of the U.S. in heavy bombers of the B-36 and B-52 types and B-47 medium bombers meant that the Americans could deliver heavy nuclear payloads over Soviet targets at long range and at high speed. By contrast the Soviet heavy bomber, the obsolete TU-4 of B-29 vintage, was a piston job representing only a minimum threat to the U.S. (It is interesting to note, in retrospect, that in the "bomber-parity" debates in Washington in the mid-1950s, Soviet strength in the air was greatly exaggerated, there being no grounds for the suspicion that a "bomber gap" to American disadvantage then existed.[4]) However, the Soviets got busy improving their air arm. In fact, they rushed through a program that may well have been planned in Stalin's time. In the air shows staged on Soviet Air Force Day (in the summers of 1955 and 1956), the Russians displayed more advanced heavy and medium bombers than earlier—the M-4, TU-16 ("Badger"), and TU-20 or TU-95 ("Bear").[5] But apparently these aircraft were never mass produced. The reason was that the Soviet *rocket-building program* was receiving top priority. The Soviets may well have calculated that the advent of Intercontinental Ballistic Missiles would make heavy bombers largely obsolete.[6]

With the successful orbiting of Sputnik I in October 1957, the biggest-bang-per-ruble policy was given a shot in the arm. Sputnik I had been sent on its glorious beep-beep course around the earth, the fruit of the sharp annual increase (23 percent) in 1956–1957 in budgetary expenditures on military research and development. Overt defense expenditures per se, however, were *not* affected significantly by this program. The Soviet leaders, with Khrushchev at the helm, apparently calculated that within a few years following Sputnik I and the inauguration of the Soviet ICBM crash program, the U.S.S.R. *would tilt the strategic balance between itself and the United States in its own favor.* The Russians probably also counted on a political spin-off from their awesome rocket weapons: a new and heightened threat of force to be used against any wayward members of their empire.

In addition to their big-bang buildup at home, which was aimed directly at American prestige and military superiority, the Soviets began in 1956 to show a desire to export conventional arms, some of them obsolete, for various "revolutionary" and diplomatic purposes abroad, for the purpose of sapping the "rear of imperialism," one of Lenin's tactics. Trade was also involved in this effort.

The Capital *vs.* Colonies Policy

The post-Stalin Kremlin leaders had discarded the Stalin thesis (in Stalin's *The Economic Problems of Socialism in the U.S.S.R.*) of "capital *vs.* capital." This notion was based on Stalin's assumption that a revived Germany and Japan would lead the *capitalist* nations into having "another go at it," as

Stalin told Djilas. In its place, the new rulers developed the thesis of "capital *vs.* colonies and "capital *vs.* ex-colonies." This policy had two prongs.

First, it consisted of *foreign aid* to underdeveloped countries, a new phenomenon in Soviet foreign policy. The program was begun with considerable propaganda fanfare in 1954 with the Soviet offer to build an Indian steel mill. By 1958 and 1959 the Soviets had a foreign-aid program amounting to about $1 billion per year.[7] By April 1960, $3.8 billion in credits and grants for economic and military assistance had been extended by Soviet Bloc countries to 20 underdeveloped countries on all "Four-A" continents. Most of Soviet and European satellite assistance was—and is—in the form of interest-bearing credits for the purpose of financing specific projects.[8]

By its trade with underdeveloped nations after 1954, the U.S.S.R. gave a further indication of its changed global policy. It clearly wished to capture a large share of the trade which had formerly gone to Western countries, particularly in Africa (north and sub-Sahara) and Latin America. From 1954 to 1958, total Soviet bloc trade turnover with less developed countries increased from $871 million in 1954 to $2.1 billion in 1958, or by an increase of more than 143 percent!

The second prong of this thesis of capital *vs.* colonies and capital *vs.* ex-colonies was the Soviet endeavor to weaken the "imperialists" at such key points as the Suez Canal, Southeast Asia (standing at the crucial water passage of the Strait of Malacca), the Mediterranean basin, and in sub-Sahara Africa where the rival was not only "capitalist," but Red Chinese.

Thus, in the mid-1950s the Soviets began to restore to prominence a revolutionary theorist whom Stalin had neglected: Sultan-Galiev.[9] Galiev favored for colonies and ex-colonies a policy of "revolution from above," with outside Soviet help. The Soviets, he taught, should penetrate nationalist-minded "bourgeois" governments by making friends with the bourgeois-nationalist leaders. In certain areas where penetration of the ruling summits was impossible (for example, in South Vietnam), guerrilla warfare, armed seizure of power, even civil war (all of which are subsumed in the Soviet political lexicon under the category of "national-liberation struggle"), were the means recommended to spread Communism in the thermonuclear-ICBM age, according to the updated version of the teachings of Galiev.

This policy of wooing the "imperialist rear" with trade and aid on the one hand and supplying arms to insurgents on the other dovetailed nicely with the Soviets' diplomatic tactic of "cold peace" with the West, the policy of imprecise détente, or *subdued* cold war. The ICBM standoff, the by-product of Khrushchev's big-bang military strategy, ensured that the capitalist West, meaning above all the United States, would react cautiously to Soviet-backed national-liberation struggle. The threat of a Third World War fought with nuclear-tipped ICBMs would presumably cool heads within the National Security Council in Washington as well as in the councils of N.A.T.O. The thermonuclear standoff, in other words, *opened possibilities for a field of revolutionary action, even local wars "by proxy,"* as the two bipolar giants peered frustratedly at each other, both fearing a worldwide conflict if they dared retaliate on the level of strategic weapons.

Khrushchev, however, stopped short of exploiting this standoff to the hilt. And this undoubtedly was one reason why a more militant group was finally successful in unseating him in October 1964 (see below, pp. 177–179). True, the First Secretary, who was increasingly (but not totally) in control of major foreign policy decisions by 1958 and in the following six years, made a number of bold and even reckless moves. The Berlin Crisis of 1961, the Cuban Crisis of 1962, both took the two superpowers "to the brink." But on balance, and especially after the Soviets' Cuban backdown, Khrushchev's foreign policy was characterized more by inflated talk than risky actions. His military-diplomatic strategy as a whole could be summed up as follows:

1. Enhancing the balance-of-terror factor to the utmost by making impressive strides in ICBM development and thermonuclear testing, and by noisily advertising both (for example, "Our rockets can shoot down a fly in the sky"—Khrushchev)
2. Continuing the 1955–1956 tactic of winning and influencing friends in the Third World
3. Keeping Germany safe (the Allied Watch on the Reich), if not disarmed at least denuclearized
4. Maintaining a "cold peace" with the West, with the possibility of full-fledged détente as an ace in the hole
5. Settling for something less than parity with the U.S. in numbers of missiles, while advertising the accuracy and threat of the current Soviet stockpile; relative deemphasis on the development of conventional armament (for example, the surface navy) and on-the-ground forces*

The Policy of Peaceful Coexistence

Coupled with these Khrushchev positions in military strategy and foreign policy was his manipulation of the slogan of *"peaceful coexistence."*

As mentioned earlier, the Leninist-Stalinist traditional formula that "war is inevitable as long as capitalism exists" was recast after the Twentieth Party Congress in 1956 to read: "War is not *fatally* inevitable." It was a clever, perhaps *too* clever wording. On close analysis, nothing much changed. If war is not fatally inevitable, is it *somewhat* inevitable? Why insert "fatally" or retain the word "inevitable" at all? It was as if the "internationalists" within the Kremlin—the Suslovs, the Ponomarevs, the Kuusinens, and the

---

*In 1958, troop strength was cut back to 3,623,000; in 1960 came a law for a further reduction of 1,200,000 men. The latter reduction was broken off, however, on account of the Berlin crisis of 1961. However, the Khrushchevism trend toward diminishing the role of conventional forces continued into his ouster in October 1964. At one point in the early 1960s, Khrushchev went so far as to say that warships had become obsolete.

other ideologues and keepers of the ideological covenant had decided that they wanted to have their cake and eat it too. Under the former war-is-inevitable rubric, the whole peace movement was undercut by a kind of grim and dogmatic hopelessness conveyed by the word "inevitable." If war is inevitable *in any case*, why, then, struggle for peace? Not wishing to de-Leninize the ideology altogether or strip it of its demonological treatment of "capitalist imperialism," Khrushchev, undoubtedly upon the advice of Suslov and Kuusinen, and the "philosophers" of Agitprop, now retained the word "inevitable" in the new 1956 formulation: "War is not fatally inevitable." In other words he was saying, "Go ahead, peace workers, and fight for peace and Socialism. You *may* be able to keep war from being inevitable." "Ingenious," the *apparatchiki* must have thought.

Just to make sure that the peace workers associated with the Soviet-led World Peace Council understood the meaning of peaceful coexistence *within the context of world revolution*, the C.P.S.U. was at pains to explain its revolutionary significance from time to time—for example:

> Peaceful coexistence is *a specific form of class struggle between socialism and capitalism*. . . . There is no contradiction between the policy of peaceful coexistence and the Marxist-Leninist position on the inevitable victory of Communism in the entire world [italics mine].[10]

Today, Soviet media make the same connection by asserting that the peace campaign and Communist attacks on the capitalist system must be linked together—as for example, when foreign Communists and their fellow travelers, in their agitation for Communism tie in the costly American war effort in Vietnam to alleged neglect of the citizens back home, implying that only a "Socialist America" would preclude repetition of "anti-people's policies."*

Khrushchev's Policy Toward Red China

Khrushchev's policy toward Red China and his condemnation of Maoism (especially for its advocacy of war as a means of attaining Communism) also dovetailed with peaceful coexistence and several other elements in his foreign policy.

First, the Russians as early as 1957 were aware of the potential dangers of a nuclearized mainland China, their next-door neighbor and historical enemy. They had agreed to help Mao build a nuclear capability, but only if Russian civilians and the military would be permitted to administer the program and man the sites. China's response was: We will not permit "Russian occupation" of our country. (The Soviet missiles implanted on Cuba in 1962 were so manned by the Soviets, to the Cubans' displeasure.) The Chinese considered these demands to be strings that the Soviets attached to their offer and that could only result in diminution of Chinese national sover-

*The Program of the C.P. (U.S.A.), adopted in 1967, makes this argument.

eignty. The Sino-Soviet disagreement over China's joining the world nuclear club marked the beginning of the current Sino-Soviet cold war, which has been going on for the past ten years.

By insisting on a Soviet presence in China as the price for assistance in building China's A- and H-bomb installations, the Soviets were clearly seeking to preserve a position of strength in the Far East. Moreover, they appear to have been aware *immediately after Stalin's death* of the possibility of an outbreak of Maoist territorial irredentism.

In the early post-Stalin years, several attempts had been made at placating the Chinese. An amusing example of this occurred just a few days after the announcement of Stalin's death. The C.P.S.U. daily *Pravda* published a faked photograph showing Mao, Stalin, and Malenkov (then Premier and First Secretary) grouped together in an allegedly friendly show of international solidarity. The trouble was that in the original photograph, made in 1950, Malenkov was some twenty feet away from the other two leaders! Now in 1953 he was depicted as standing at their very elbows, facing Mao in an ingratiating manner, while intervening personages were clipped out. Another episode concerned the May Day and October Revolution slogans customarily published in the Soviet press in, respectively, mid-April and mid-October every year. In the slogans, numbering over a hundred, Communist China—during the early 1950s—was always listed first among the "fraternal Socialist states." Moreover, the extremely flattering Russian adjective *velikii* ("great") was always appended to "Chinese people" ("the *great* Chinese people"). The Albanian, Bulgarian, Hungarian, and the other fraternal peoples had to do without *velikii*. Moreover, during the 1950s, on successive anniversaries (October 30) of the establishment of the Chinese People's Republic in 1949, the Russians loyally demanded the return of Taiwan to mainland China.

More important than these pictorial and verbal gestures of respect was the momentous Soviet decision in 1955* to return some Soviet-controlled Chinese real estate to the Chinese. The Changchun Railroad in Manchuria and the ports and naval bases of Dalny (Dairen) and Port Arthur (Liushun) were returned to the Chinese. Moreover, the "joint-stock companies," run mostly by the Russians in the western Chinese province of Sinkiang and in Manchuria, were disbanded, their assets and plants devolving to the Chinese. As had been the case with the Austrian peace treaty of the same year, a Sino-Soviet peace treaty settling the disposition of Port Arthur and other territory originally was supposed to await the signing of a larger peace treaty, in this case with Japan. But it was never signed. Instead, the Soviets went ahead with their concession to the Chinese.

Only in August 1964 was it revealed by Mao Tse-tung himself that the

---

*The 1955 decision was, however, based on two earlier agreements concluded between the U.S.S.R. and Red China, in 1950 and 1952. (See *Malaya sovetskaya entsiklopediya* [*Small Soviet Encyclopedia*], 3rd ed., vol. 5, under "Liushun," p. 759.)

question of Soviet extraterritorial rights in China had been put to Khrushchev and Bulganin during their brief stay in the same year, 1954, in Peking.
Chairman Mao on August 11, 1964, described their discussions of ten
years earlier: "In 1954, when Khrushchev and Bulganin came to
China, we took up this (territorial) question, but they refused to talk to
us."[11] Thus, the 1954 Soviet "concession" may have been something less than
gratuitous. In any case, Khrushchev's policy toward China after 1958 became something quite different. There were neither concessions nor flattery.
Instead, came the opening of a campaign of polemics against both the domestic and foreign policies of Mao. Meanwhile, the Soviets indicated they
would surely maintain their right to the nearly 600,000 square miles of
former Chinese territory now part of the U.S.S.R.

The second aspect of Khrushchev's post-1958 policy toward China concerned the international policy (both in its ideological and diplomatic settings) of communism-by-example. On this question, the Maoists reverted to
what they considered to be essential Leninism. War *is* the "midwife" of revolution, the Maoists said, no matter how catastrophic. Moreover, the sacrifice
of millions of civilians who would die in a cataclysmic world-historical
war involving thermonuclear weapons with capitalist imperialism would
be worth it for the attainment of communism.

To this, the Russians under Khrushchev responded (in exhaustive documents in 1964) that the Chinese ideology was "adventuristic" and fiercely
misanthropic. If the *proletariats* of warring countries perished in a Third
World War, the Soviets said, such a conflict, even if capitalism were destroyed (*as it surely would be,* the Soviets significantly added), would not
be worth it. Instead, the world should come around to communism by a
number of other possible routes, either peaceful or nonpeaceful. The "nonpeaceful" route meant, in Soviet parlance, that the class struggle and Communist seizure of power in a given country *might* be accompanied by violence. This was the meaning imparted to the agreements signed at the two
full-fledged meetings of the world's Communist parties convening in Moscow
in 1957 and 1960.[12]

The more the Chinese challenged the Soviet policy of cold peace with
the West and Khrushchev's nonmilitary communism-by-example, the more
the Soviet ideologists condemned Maoism for adventurism and misanthropy.
And there the matter stood in the Sino-Soviet cold war until October 1964
and the ouster of Khrushchev.

Soviet Policy in Vietnam

A word about Vietnam, this area of "national-liberation struggle" assigned
by the Kremlin for a degree of military assistance and diplomatic and ideo-

logical support in the 1960s. Even as early as 1955, when the Soviets were vigorously promoting disarmament within the framework of the "Geneva Spirit," Soviet- and Czech-made arms were on their way to Nasser in Cairo. Arms likewise were sent to other "liberation forces" in the world. However, the year before, another important meeting had taken place in Geneva, the Geneva Conference on Southeast Asia. Among other things, the conference partitioned Vietnam at the 17th parallel. During and immediately after the meeting, the Russians displayed a degree of indifference to the fate of Vietnam. When, for example, no national elections were held in 1956, as specified by the Geneva accords of 1954, the Soviet protest in the United Nations was muffled.[13] As a matter of fact, in 1957 the Soviets were proposing that *both* North and South Vietnam be admitted into the U.N.! They thereby recognized that the partitioned country had, like Korea, become the unavoidable and hapless victim of the global struggle between "capitalist imperialism" and Communism. As a result of this Russian indifference, the North Vietnamese under Ho Chi Minh's leadership *turned increasingly to Red China for support.*

During the late 1950s and 1960s, Khrushchev's policy in Southeast Asia and Vietnam in particular displayed a degree of indecision. In 1960 Russia intervened in Laos and gave its support to the "neutralist" Vietminh-dominated Pathet Lao forces of Kong Le. Meanwhile, the U.S. lent its support to the central-government forces of General Phoumi Nosavan, which alarmed and restrained Moscow. Also in 1960 Khrushchev's government offered North Vietnam credits to finance industrialization. But despite this aid and the support shown Hanoi in Soviet propaganda, Ho continued to turn to his northern neighbor, Red China, for shipments of arms.

So far as Vietnam was concerned, the year 1964 marked a turning point in what one U.S. specialist calls the "Vietnam triangle" of Russia, China, and Vietnam.[14] First, shipments of arms and supplies sent from the North to the Vietcong fifth column in South Vietnam had begun to show results. Large areas below the 17th parallel had fallen under the control of the Vietcong by the summer of 1964. There was the danger that the whole country would soon fall to the Communist insurgents. Second, as Ho turned northward for support, the Khrushchev regime showed increasingly *less* interest in lending its support to Ho or the Vietcong, although there was a trickle of token military aid coming from the U.S.S.R.

Then came the Gulf of Tonkin Incident of August 1964. This momentous event had been preceded by a number of other events in the same year which, when ticked off, illustrate the status of the Khrushchev policy with respect to Vietnam just before his fall from power:

—North Vietnam and the Vietcong sharply intensify the war; *North Vietnamese regulars appear south of the 17th parallel in at least regimental strength (summer 1964).*

—Communist China opens a press campaign warning that it may intervene directly in Vietnam, and in any case will broaden its military assistance to the Communists in Vietnam; simultaneously, two Vietcong delegations go to Peking and are received by Chairman Mao (*July 1964*).

—North Vietnam begins constructing defense installations against possible aerial bombing attacks (*July 1964*).

—The Soviets reverse their previous policy and call for a permanent peace-keeping force *excluding* the participation of the five permanent members of the Security Council (*July 1964*).

—The Laotian central government reports new North Vietnamese troop movements en route to South Vietnam (*August 1964*).

Finally, August 1964 saw the Gulf of Tonkin Incident. The U.S. Department reported that North Vietnamese PT boats attacked two U.S. destroyers in international waters off the North Vietnamese coast. The U.S. then retaliated with air strikes against the North Vietnamese coastal installations from which the PT boats had originated.

The Soviet reaction to the U.S. air raids displayed a striking mildness and restraint, a reaction which was evident from the end of August into September. When the U.N. Security Council was called into emergency session, the Soviet representative Platon Morozov supported the Council's taking up discussion of the incident. But Hanoi refused to participate or to discuss it at the U.N., charging that the U.N. had no authority in the matter. This was a strong rebuff to the Soviets. Meantime, Communist China's reaction to the incident was, of course, to heap abuse on the U.S. imperialists. But Peking also condemned the Soviets for their relatively soft reaction to Tonkin and for their support of the U.S. position in the U.N. Security Council. While *Renmin Ribao* (the Peking *People's Daily*) railed against "Khrushchev revisionism," the Soviet press lashed out with an unprecedented accusation against a "fraternal" Communist state: the Chinese "adventurists" were trying *to push the Soviets into major war with the U.S.* in Vietnam, while the Chinese hoped to stand by and enjoy the spectacle.

Consumerism vs. Military Buildup

At this point a number of *domestic* Soviet political developments occurred which bear directly on Soviet policy in Vietnam. In the final months of his regime, Khrushchev, disagreeing with a number of his more militantly inclined colleagues and especially with many of his marshals, generals and admirals, asserted outright that the Soviet defense capacity was *"presently at a satisfactory level."* On his own, the ebullient First Secretary then proceeded to convene (in September 1964) a sort of latter-day "Council of the Boyars," a rump conference made up of influential provincial party First Secretaries plus a small group of hand-picked central bureaucrats. In so doing, Khrushchev had recklessly bypassed his powerful colleagues on the party Presidium (since 1966 renamed the Politburo) and in the party Central Committee, although he had used this tactic on more than one previous occasion.

The gist of the September rump meeting in the Kremlin, with Khrushchev as the main speaker, was summarized in a delayed and strangely worded, paraphrased report, which was published belatedly days later in the Soviet press. The important paragraph of this report was:

If in the period of the first Five-year Plans and in the postwar years we placed the main emphasis [on the development of heavy industry as the basis for the development] of the national economy and the *strengthening of the nation's defense capability, now that we have a powerful industry, when the defense of the country is at a satisfactory level,* the party sets the task for a more rapid advance of the branches of industry producing consumer goods [italics mine].[15]

In other words, the First Secretary was informing the heavy industry/defense industry/military complex of "vested interests" in the Kremlin that *a major shift in expenditures and allocation of natural resources was about to take place under his leadership.* A new Five-Year Plan was due and it would be based, Khrushchev asserted, on the fact that the "defense of the country is [now] at a satisfactory level." In Khrushchev's mind, the big-bang diplomacy and the investment in ICBMs and thermonuclear bombs had paid off; no one would dare lay a hand on the Soviet Union. Moreover, the Soviets should refrain from foreign adventures and "proxy wars." The Soviets should now turn primarily to their domestic needs.

This infuriated the military and the defense-military bloc, which had become a much more powerful group than even Khrushchev himself realized. Months earlier this group of "metal-eating" (Khrushchev's term) and expenditure-hungry officials had made their views known through the military press. Their ideas appeared in articles in such publications as *Krasnaya Zvezda* (*Red Star,* daily of the Soviet Defense Ministry), *Voennaya Mysl* (*Military Thought,* another organ of the military), and so on, which supported their views. In these writings, as well as in the second (1963) edition of the 1962 book *Voennaya strategiya* (*Military Strategy*), edited by Marshal V. D. Sokolovsky, the publicists, with the backing of some of the Soviet defense-industry bureaucracy (whom Brezhnev was to rely upon heavily for his coup, and who were promoted after October 1964), made a number of points. Given the thermonuclear standoff between the bipolar superpowers, they said, "wars of national liberation" need not necessarily escalate into general world wars. In the second edition of *Military Strategy,* a significant correction was made concerning "local wars" (*lokalniye voiny*): these wars were *not* as potentially dangerous as some observers made them out to be; they might occur without a world war or without the two super-powers employing strategic weapons. It was quite possible for a local war to be fought with *conventional weapons alone* and for that war to be limited to a given small theater of operations, other writers argued in 1964. Meanwhile, a few military writers, of course, disagreed with the riskier position of their colleagues. For example, it was argued by the moderates that whether "local" or not, these "limited wars" would as likely as not escalate into large ones. The major powers were therefore liable to get involved in a major world war.

Who, one might well ask, condoned the revival of discussion of a more reckless military strategy in 1964? After all, Khrushchev and some of his associates (who were later to defect to the Brezhnev-Kosygin faction which overthrew him) were taking Soviet policy down a more cautious road. Was not the openness of the discussion symptomatic of Khrushchev's waning authority among influential circles in the Soviet hierarchy?

The essence of Sokolovsky's argument, as revived in the summer of 1964, was this:

1. Soviet armed forces are *not* at a satisfactory level.
2. The Soviet Union must develop an up-to-date *flexible-response* strategy with its correspondingly varied military hardware, which would necessitate large expenditures on all branches of the service (including the navy) and not merely on glamorous big-bang missiles alone.
3. Local wars need not necessarily grow into a world war.
4. Wars of national liberation are certainly *not* excluded by the concept of peaceful coexistence.

Undoubtedly, there was a considerable amount of pent-up vengeance existing in a large segment of the Soviet military which was provoked by Khrushchev's recent policies—his cuts in defense expenditures, his retirement of officers from the army and navy, the projected further cuts in accordance with his speech to the rump meeting in the Kremlin, and so on. All of this was a bitter pill, not only for the military per se, but for all those elements—and their roots are deep in Soviet society and politics—who stood to lose from a major swing toward "consumerism."

It should not be forgotten that this group of officials controlling heavy industry, the armed forces, and the defense industry command in turn *the largest share of investments, plant, and equipment within the whole Soviet economy.* This is a Soviet version of what Eisenhower, upon leaving the Presidency in 1960, called in America the powerful "defense-industrial complex." Under *Soviet* conditions, however, this complex is far more powerful than its American counterpart, if indeed "counterpart" is the appropriate word. For in the U.S.S.R., the major decisions on allocation of resources and the dividing of the budgetary pie are in the hands of a very small group of officials consisting of some fifty men at the utmost among whom there is a high degree of pulling and tugging over shares of the pie. Moreover, under Soviet conditions the pie is bigger. A much larger portion of the total G.N.P. is carried on the central national budget than in the U.S.; the U.S.S.R. is, after all, a "Socialist" state, with state planning, nationalized property, and police-state conditions for controlling wages and salaries, production norms, and in general the volume and type of inputs and outputs of industry. And heavy industry (making producers' goods) and the defense industry together monopolize the "commanding heights" of the Soviet economy. Accordingly, the power of the bureaucrats who manage the "trusts," ministries, and State Committees within this system likewise possess enormous power. Khrushchev himself acknowledged this fact of life on several occasions.*

Political Demise of Khrushchev

It became abundantly clear within weeks after Khrushchev was overthrown (in devious Byzantine fashion) that it was precisely this group of defense- and military-minded bureaucrats and a majority of the military brass plus the ideology-conscious party hierarchy and the security apparatus who gained from the coup on October 14, 1964. It was this group of bureaucrats and *apparatchiki* who improved their status almost immediately within the party Presidium and the Central Committee, as was revealed later at the Twenty-third Party Congress in 1966, the occasion on which the names of the Central Committee were listed in full. Many new ministerial posts were assigned these officials and a special defense-industry administrative authority was established within the U.S.S.R. Council of Ministers. Even the new First Secretary, later renaming himself pompously the "General-Secretary" (Stalin's former title), Leonid Ilyich Brezhnev, himself qualified as a "metal-eater"; moreover, he stood close to the military. A graduate of a metallurgical institute, Brezhnev served in various Army political posts and later as Deputy Chief of the Main Political Administration of the Soviet armed forces and political commissar for the Soviet navy. His links with the party *apparatchiki* were strong, too, for he had served for a time as First Secretary of the party apparatus for the whole Moldavian Soviet Socialist Republic (part of which once belonged to Rumania, incidentally), and also as First Secretary of the Kazakh S.S.R.; before that he had been an important functionary in one of the most important heavy industrial cities of the Ukrainian S.S.R., Dnepropetrovsk. Many of Brezhnev's former colleagues in the Ukraine were promoted after October 1964.

Khrushchev was overthrown at the instigation of this aforementioned power bloc in the Kremlin. Besides certain members of the Party Presidium, the group had the cooperation of the crucial security police apparatus as

*The First Secretary spoke at times as if he were not in complete control of the situation. One can examine Khrushchev's speeches as far back as 1960 and find traces of this insecurity. Two of his favorite epithets leveled at the defense industry-military complex were "metal-eaters" and "certain comrades" suffering from "bureaucratic inertia."

well. It was they who were the instruments for executing the overthrow of October 13–14. Supervised at the time by the ambitious Alexander N. Shelepin,* the security forces had even taken the precaution of changing the official Kremlin telephone extension numbers so that in case Khrushchev tried a last-minute retaliation, he would be frustrated in his attempt. The coup was engineered smoothly. Khrushchev was telephoned at his vacation spa on the Black Sea on October 13 and was asked to return to the capital for a meeting of the Presidium. A plane was sent to Sochi to fetch him. But what the hapless Khrushchev did not realize was that the plane was commanded by K.G.B. agents under Shelepin's and Semichastny's orders. When Khrushchev arrived in Moscow, he was driven "under protective custody" to the Kremlin and there confronted with the *fait accompli* of his "retirement"—as the official account put it—"on grounds of old age and health." Ironically, on his 70th birthday just six months before the coup, his colleagues under Brezhnev's emceeship had toasted him and given him, as the birthday boy put it in his own expression of thanks, "an advance" on many more years of fruitful work! The First Secretary's demand on October 14 that his Presidium colleagues call the Central Committee into emergency session was granted. But the Central Committee, apparently meeting in something less than a quorum, voted Khrushchev down after hearing speeches by Suslov, Polyansky, and a bombastic self-defense by Khrushchev.[16]

We have gone into the coup in some detail because the policies inaugurated soon after Khrushchev's fall reflected the mentality and outlook of the group of conspirators who had engineered the ouster and stood to gain from it. Not only did the defense-industry bureaucracy, the military, and the ideological "hawks" profit from the coup, so also did the security apparatus, a notoriously reactionary group. This fact too had enormous importance for the shaping of post-Khrushchev foreign policy in the years to follow. Soviet and American relations in particular stood at the center of the shift in foreign policy.

Right up to the present, Soviet foreign policy has never returned to the relatively moderate posture it had assumed from late 1963 to the autumn of 1964 when Khrushchev's personal authority was great—but also isolated. The post-1964 changes have affected every aspect of Soviet policy, do-

---

*Although V. Ye. Semichastny had been in charge of the K.G.B. since 1961, Shelepin, his predecessor in this post and former boss in the Secretariat of the Komsomol, continued for a time to exercise top-level supervision over internal security. The present head of the K.G.B. is Yuri V. Andropov. Andropov replaced Semichastny in May 1967 and was promoted a month later to Candidate Member of the C.P.S.U. Politburo. Semichastny, an ex-Komsomol official of the Shelepin stripe, was demoted to First Deputy Chairman of the Council of Ministers of the Ukrainian S.S.R. Shelepin too soon lost his position in the party Secretariat after he was made head of Soviet trade unions. He remains a full member of the Politburo despite his removal from security affairs.

mestic and foreign. In the foreign field, which is our major concern, Soviet policy soon underwent noticeable changes vis-à-vis Vietnam, West Germany, the United States, Communist China, foreign (nonruling) Communist parties, ruling Communist parties in the fourteen Communist countries (but especially in the East European Soviet bloc), and in other areas (see next chapter).

The pensioned Nikita Khrushchev, meanwhile, lit bonfires in the backyard of his suburban-Moscow *dacha* only to emerge in the center of the capital every two years to cast his ballot in local Soviet elections, and every four years to do the same in the national Supreme Soviet elections.

The last published words of Khrushchev to be read by the Soviet people were part of a dialogue with three orbiting cosmonauts Yegorov, Feoktistov, and the late Komarov. According to *Pravda* (October 13, 1964) the ironic exchange went like this:

N. S. KHRUSHCHEV: Good-bye, Comrades. I await you on earth. Good-bye!

V. M. KOMAROV: Good-bye, dear Nikita Sergeyevich and Anastas Ivanovich [Mikoyan]. We understand you—you're waiting for us back on earth. We will meet you. We will fulfill our assigned tasks.

N. S. KHRUSHCHEV: *Do svidaniya!* [Good-bye!]

It was "good-bye," indeed. And not only for Khrushchev, but soon after for Anastas Mikoyan as well.

NOTES

1. Quoted in Michael P. Gehlen, *The Politics of Coexistence—Soviet Methods and Motives* (Bloomington: Indiana University Press, 1967), p. 65.
2. See Raymond, *op. cit.*, chapter 22, for the best discussion currently in print of the administration of Soviet foreign affairs in the U.S.S.R. The author gives several examples of the important changes which took place within the ministry in the 1950s and 1960s.
3. Ulam, *Expansion and Coexistence*, p. 569.
4. Lincoln P. Bloomfield, Walter C. Clemens, Jr., and Franklyn Griffiths, *Khrushchev and the Arms Race—Soviet Interest in Arms Control and Disarmament 1954–1964* (Cambridge, Mass.: M.I.T. Press, 1966), p. 45.
5. *Jane's All the World's Aircraft* (New York: McGraw-Hill, 1966 and 1968), edition for 1965–1966, pp. 334–335; for 1967–1968, pp. 396–397.
6. Bloomfield, Clemens, and Griffiths, *op. cit.*, p. 41.
7. *Communist Economic Policy in the Less Developed Areas*, U.S. Department of State Publication 7020, July 1960, in Pentony (ed.), *op. cit.*, p. 199.
8. *Ibid.*, p. 201.
9. Raymond, *op. cit.*, p. 376.

10. "Peaceful Coexistence," *Diplomatic Dictionary* (Moscow: State Printing House for Political Literature, 1961), pp. 297–299.

11. Doolin, *op. cit.*, Document 14, "Mao's Statement to the Japanese Socialist Delegation, August 11, 1964," p. 43.

12. Edited texts of these two conferences may be found in Robert H. McNeal (ed.), *International Relations Among Communists* (Englewood Cliffs, N.J.: Prentice-Hall, 1967). Document 18, "Declaration of the Conference of Representatives of Communist and Workers' Parties of Socialist Countries," Moscow (November 22, 1957), pp. 98–101; Document 22, "Statement of Representatives of Communist and Workers' Parties," Moscow (December 6, 1960), pp. 108–112.

13. Donald S. Zagoria, *Vietnam Triangle—Moscow/Peking/Hanoi* (New York: Western Publishing, 1967), p. 42.

14. *Ibid.*

15. *Pravda*, October 2, 1964. The report was published in all Soviet newspapers on the same day. For an excellent short account of Khrushchev's last weeks in power, see William Hyland and Richard W. Shryock, *The Fall of Khrushchev* (New York: Funk & Wagnalls, 1968). Especially detailed and incisive is Michel Tatu's book, *Power in the Kremlin from Khrushchev to Kosygin* (New York: Viking Press, 1969). Tatu writes on Soviet affairs for French publications and was *Le Monde's* Moscow correspondent from 1957–1964.

16. For a discussion of how the voting procedure may have been carried out, see my article "Struggle at the Top," *The New Leader* (October 26, 1964).

CHAPTER VIII

New Beginnings After Khrushchev

The forces of Socialism are waging an active offensive against the positions held by imperialism.

—"International Communist Duty Manifesto,"
PRAVDA, November 28, 1965

•   •   •

It is necessary to state with complete firmness that the borders of the Soviet Union and of the other fraternal countries are sacred and inviolable in any region or in any sector, in the West or in the East. And those who try to violate these borders will suffer bitter defeat.

— D. S. POLYANSKY, U.S.S.R. First Deputy
Premier, March 21, 1969

In 1963, and until October 1964 and the years following Khrushchev's ouster, American and Soviet relations and Soviet foreign policy in general displayed signs of reasonableness and East-West détente.

By early 1963 "Hot Line" teleprinters had been installed in the capitals of both the United States and the Soviet Union for the purpose of carrying out instant summitry. In the same year, the partial nuclear test-ban treaty was signed in Moscow, amid exchanges of friendly statements and *tête-à-têtes* between highly placed representatives of the two superpowers. Moreover, the Soviet press and Soviet leaders in their speeches began to make distinctions between different types of "capitalist officials." On the one hand, they said, there were the "hotheads" (*besheniye*), who fortunately were still

181

a minority; on the other hand there were the "realists" (*realisty* or *razum-niye*), who were in control. As for the White House itself, the Soviets referred specifically to "President Kennedy's realism."[1]

As has already been mentioned in connection with Vietnam, the U.S.S.R. under Khrushchev's leadership displayed a definite reluctance to become involved in a local war in Southeast Asia. Peaceful coexistence with the capitalists, as interpreted by Moscow under Khrushchev in 1963–1964, evidently extended far from the shores of both the U.S. and the Soviet Union. Otherwise, there was always the danger, said the pro-Khrushchev military writers, that local wars could escalate into big ones.

In his German policy too, Khrushchev was quite obviously ready to undertake some dramatic new moves.[2] In the spring of 1964, as the American and Russian détente appeared to be in full swing, West German Chancellor Ludwig Erhard suggested publicly that he and Khrushchev get together for some bilateral Russian-German summitry. (Just twenty-five years befor this it had been the Soviets who had first hinted that a rapprochement with the Germans was possible.) Khrushchev appeared more than willing to take up the suggestion. He saw that the Sino-Soviet conflict had reached such a furious pitch that the Chinese were now demanding return of all 600,000 square miles of territory which they claimed (in Mao's statement of August 11, 1964) the Russians—Tsarist and Soviet—had appropriated from them. Thus, Khrushchev may have reasoned that Russia once again faced a potentially dangerous two-front predicament with enemies to the east and west. His favorable response to Erhard's bid took several forms.*

First, Khrushchev invited the prestigious and arrogant East German Communist chief, Walter Ulbricht, to come to Moscow for discussions. Presumably, the Russian First Secretary would reassure the German First Secretary that the budding Soviet romance with Bonn should not degenerate into a love triangle between the U.S.S.R., West Germany, and East Germany. The ostensible reason for Ulbricht's June 1964 trip had been to sign a new mutual assistance and friendship pact with the U.S.S.R. Although the treaty was signed, it was not immediately ratified by the East Germans; neither for that matter, by the Russians. Moreover, Article 9 of the unratified treaty stated that the Soviets adhered to the Potsdam Agreements of 1945, another rebuff to Ulbricht. Was there not obvious tension between the two Communist regimes?

---

*Khrushchev had approached Erhard's predecessor, Konrad Adenauer, as well on the question of German-Soviet rapprochement. During Adenauer's visit to the U.S.S.R. in the mid-1950s Khrushchev said to the German leader: "Just imagine! China has already more than 600 million people. And every year there are 12 million more. . . . What will come of it? We can deal with this problem, but it is difficult. Therefore, I ask you to help us. Help us to deal with China!" Then, Adenauer notes in his memoirs, Khrushchev added after this: " . . . and with the Americans." From *Konrad Adenauer: Errinerungen 1953–1955* (Stuttgart: Deutsche Verlags Anstalt, 1966), p. 528.

Then in July came a startling announcement. Khrushchev's son-in-law, the editor of *Izvestiya* and a rising star among the Kremlin's foreign policy-makers, Alexei Adzhubei, was to go on a friendly visit to West Germany, the first of its kind to a "bourgeois" Germany since 1939. Chancellor Erhard, sensing what was in the wind, thereupon graciously received Adzhubei, whose principal mission was to smooth the way for a forthcoming visit by his father-in-law, the First Secretary of the C.P.S.U. and Chairman of the U.S.S.R. Council of Ministers. (Incidentally, one of the offhand remarks allegedly made by Adzhubei while he was in Germany was that Ulbricht had only a short time to live and would probably soon die of cancer—hardly a flattering thing to say in West Germany about the East German comrade!)* Although a tentative date was set for Khrushchev's unprecedented trip to West Germany, the visit never materialized. Khrushchev was overthrown before it could be carried out.

Another Khrushchev policy appeared aimed at calming "hotheads" that might exist within the Communist camp itself. Since 1962, the Soviets had, for example, turned a deaf ear to the militant entreaties of North Korea for more aid, especially in military hardware. To Moscow, it appeared that the regime in Pyongyang had much in common with that of Ho Chi Minh in Hanoi. First, the North Koreans had been led for almost twenty years by the veteran Communist figure, Kim Il Sung, around whom a cult had been developed which rivaled in its pathological dimensions only that of Mao in Red China.[3] Kim has permitted himself to be described as a "great leader in the *international Communist and workers' movement* and an outstanding Marxist-Leninist" (italics mine). With a firmly entrenched and obviously radical Communist leader at the helm in Pyongyang and one who pushes relentlessly for forcible unification of north and south, the Kremlin must have seen the resemblance between Kim and his policies and those of the other two radical Far Eastern demigods, Mao and Ho. And Khrushchev would have little or nothing to do with any of these ambitious extremists.

On his part, Kim seemed to be aware of the trend of events in Moscow. After having been rebuffed on military aid by the Soviets in November 1962 (when a North Korean delegation including a top military expert came to Moscow), Pyongyang consequently moved steadily closer to Peking. By 1964 North Korean media were going down the line with those of Peking. "U.S. imperialism" and "Soviet revisionism" appeared nearly as often in the pages of the North Korean daily *Nodong Sinmun* (*Workers' News*) as in *Renminh Ribao* (*People's Daily*) of Peking.

*The Chinese gleefully exploited the possibility of a Soviet-West German get-together. The Peking *People's Daily* spoke of the Soviets' "abandoning" the East Germans and tried to prove the existence of disagreement between Pankow and Moscow. In an angry frame of mind, the East German newspaper *Neues Deutschland* snarled back a denial.

Looking back at 1963–1964, therefore, it is clear that in the wake of the Soviets' Cuban gamble and fiasco, Khrushchev had begun taking the U.S.S.R. down new untrod paths of coexistence and relaxation of tension. Germany, as we said earlier, was a key factor in this nascent policy.

What if Khrushchev's trip to Bonn *had* materialized? What might have resulted? First, it now appears more than likely that soon after the trip had been consummated, Alexei Adzhubei would have acquired the portfolio of U.S.S.R. Minister of Foreign Affairs. Several Soviet specialists in the West predicted as much. This would have placed Khrushchev in complete charge of Soviet foreign policy, which, of course, meant adhering to the new "soft" posture toward the West. Even the Vatican was included in this program of normalization, and once again Adzhubei, who had had an audience with Pope John XXIII, figured in the détente policy.

Second, a real West German-Soviet bridge might have eventually been constructed. This in turn might have brought about certain other events in its train: the political demise of the hard-liner Ulbricht; a succession of bridge-building operations by Bonn to other Soviet bloc states (which, for some East European states, followed Khrushchev's overthrow in any case); and perhaps sooner West German agreement to forego nuclear weapons than what may be expected today with the many irritating and militant post-Khrushchev policies emanating from Moscow.

These and the other emergent policies in the closing months of 1964 clearly must have alarmed the heavy industry/defense industry/military group—the H–D–M group—in the Kremlin. The "internationalists," of the Suslov stripe, must also have been upset. To all of these officials and satraps, Khrushchev's new departures signified (1) general relaxation of tension, which for the most part was being promoted by Moscow in 1963–1964 both in word and deed, and with it, tabling of a new program for military construction and modernization of the armed forces in the U.S.S.R. which the marshals were pushing; (2) undercutting of the line on the "incompatibility" of the two ideologies, capitalist-imperialist and Communist—if détente with the Western capitalist states, above all, the U.S., the bastion of capitalism, were broadened and carried forward, what would be left of the Marxist-Leninist demonology on "warmongering" imperialism?; (3) encouragement of East European rapprochement (in diplomacy and trade) with Western Europe encouraging further centrifugality of the Soviet bloc satellites away from the mother-planet Russia; (4) undercutting of the Czechoslovakian (under Novotny) and Polish (under Gomulka) domestic fearmongering campaign against the "danger of West German revanchism," one of the props for the regimes of these two countries; (5) loss of "revolutionary face" in the competition with China for the loyalties of the world's Communists.

*Several contingencies abetted the plans of the anti-Khrushchev forces. The first was the assassination of President Kennedy in November 1963, thus knocking out from under

One can imagine the consternation felt and undoubtedly expressed in secret in the summer and fall of 1964 by the militant H–D–M lobby in the Kremlin. They now proceeded to group themselves around their fellow conspirator and working-chairman, Leonid Brezhnev.*

No sooner had the team of Brezhnev and Kosygin (heading the party and government apparatuses, respectively) and their associates gotten into office, than some new blips began to appear on the political radars of West European and American observers of the Soviet scene. Immediately, the new group posted a list of twenty-nine grievances against the former regime of Khrushchev; for their bitterness, acrimony, and reformation-like zeal, they surely rivaled Martin Luther's Ninety-five Theses posted on the church door at Wittenberg. These "Twenty-nine Points" were circulated among the Communist Party *apparats* of the world.[4] As far as foreign affairs were concerned, the indictments included the following attacks on Khrushchev's policies:

1. The Cuban missile buildup in late 1962 was carried out blunderingly.
2. Adzhubei had been sent to West Germany without prior approval by the party Presidium, "nepotism" being a factor.
3. Consumer goods were overemphasized to the detriment of heavy industry and defense-building.
4. Khrushchev's "false policies" led to increasing estrangement between independence-minded Rumania and the U.S.S.R.
5. Khrushchev's unfavorable personal remarks against V. A. Molotov and N. A. Bulganin (both of whom Khrushchev deposed in 1957 on grounds of "conservatism" in domestic and foreign policy) during the First Secretary's swing through Scandinavia in June and July 1964 were uncalled for.*
6. Khrushchev caused "disruption" of COMECON (Council for Mutual Economic Assistance), economic and trade administrative organ of the Warsaw Pact countries.
7. There was too much "one-man leadership" by Khrushchev, smacking of the cult of Stalin, and the making of too many important decisions, foreign and domestic, on his own.

Second, in the *immediate* post-Khrushchev period, a number of straws in the wind were quite visible to close watchers of the Soviet and East Euro-

---

Khrushchev a major prop in his efforts toward bilateral détente with the U.S. after the Cuban Crisis in the fall of 1962, heads-of-government summitry having been one of Khrushchev's trademarks. Another contingency was the publication of the essentially anti-Khrushchev "Togliatti Memorandum" in August 1964, the month in which he died; the Italian Communist leader warned of "serious danger from the United States" in the aftermath of Kennedy's death; he also predicted that an upswing in revolutionism existed throughout the world. A third piece of luck for the anti-Khrushchevites was the death of a strong Khrushchev ally on the C.P.S.U. Presidium, Otto V. Kuusinen, in May 1964.

*This was a particularly revealing indictment, hinting as it did that the new leaders shared some of the views of Messrs. Molotov and Bulganin. Molotov especially was known for his conservative views with respect to both domestic and foreign policy.

pean press. The militant *podzhigateli voiny* ("warmongers") epithet reappeared in the Soviet press for the first time in years, in application to the Western powers, just days after the coup. Nikolai Gribachev, the most notorious of the literary "hawks," had an anti-Western piece published under his byline in the daily press the very day after Khrushchev's fall; the implications of this for both domestic and foreign policy were obvious to anyone adept at reading the "Aesopian language" of the Soviet press or between the lines. Moreover, the chairman of the Soviet State Bank published a long *podval* in *Pravda* commending the advocates of centralization in economic management and hinting that the voice of the defense-industry lobby had been strengthened, that decentralization and steps in the direction of Yugoslav-type Communism would not now be taken, as had been hinted during the last months of Khrushchev's reign.

The New Soviet Foreign Policy

Finally, there came a number of developments which were directly related to foreign affairs. Anti-U.S. propaganda began to be stepped up in Soviet media (we have already mentioned the reappearance of the "warmonger" handle). Changes in Soviet attitudes toward Vietnam, Communist China, Japan, North Korea, Eastern Europe, and Western Europe also surfaced.

Change in Soviet Policy in Vietnam

The subject of Vietnam underwent a very noticeable change of treatment. *This change, took place before the U.S. bombing runs on North Vietnamese cities were undertaken* in February 1965 in retaliation for the Vietcong sneak attacks on Pleiku and Qui Nhon. There is also evidence that in late October or early November 1964 the Soviets took the initiative in approaching Ho Chi Minh with offers of stepped-up Soviet military assistance. This "wrinkle" appeared in the form of the opening of the National Liberation Front's first mission in the U.S.S.R., on January 23, 1965—again, *before* Pleiku and Qui Nhon and the retaliatory U.S. bombing raids.

Relations with China

Another early hint had come with the surprise visit of Chinese Communist Premier Chou En-lai to Moscow for the November 7, 1964, "October Revolution" celebrations.* (Chou had the good sense this time not to attempt to lay a wreath at Stalin's grave, as the Chinese had done in 1962, when they came with a good-sized delegation to Moscow to attend the

---

*The Chinese had just made a coup of their own: On October 16, 1964, in the same week as the overthrow of Khrushchev in Moscow, the Chinese successfully tested their first A-bomb device in Sinkiang Province bordering on the U.S.S.R.

Twenty-second Congress of the C.P.S.U.) In November 1964, the Soviet press revealed that high-level talks had taken place between the new First Secretary Brezhnev and his associates and Chou En-lai and his delegation. The discussions ended within a week after the October Revolution holiday. The final communique on the talks contained the telltale phrase "*frank* and comradely," "frank" being Sovietese for disagreement. Indeed, the Chinese press soon—but not immediately—took up its anti-Soviet line where it had left off in mid-October. Thereafter, the polemics showed a steadily escalating ferocity.

What had the new leaders discussed with the Chinese? What had prompted such a high-level visit—the first in several years—on the very heels of Khrushchev's political demise? The answer to these questions (like many of the reports given by Brezhnev to the C.P.S.U. since 1964) is shrouded in Byzantine secrecy. Not even the garrulous Chinese have revealed what all the discussion was about in November 1964. But a few "guesstimates" can be made.

It is quite possible that the Soviets informed their Chinese guests, after the passage of almost a month since the overthrow of the errant Khrushchev, that during this interregnum they had worked out a number of new policies which might be of interest to Mao and his associates. Henceforth, the Russians probably told Chou, a pipeline would be established for funneling significant amounts of Soviet bloc military and nonmilitary aid to North Vietnam. No less a personage than the new Soviet Premier Alexei Kosygin, traveled to Hanoi, to Pyongyang (North Korea), and to Peking just two months later to work out the details of the new, "escalated" Soviet Far Eastern policy with the leaders of the three principal Far Eastern Communist states.* The Russians probably told the Chinese and others that they would henceforth fulfill their "international duty" so neglected in the last years of Khrushchev's reign. And for a brief spell after Khrushchev's

---

*Four and a half years later, in September 1969, Premier Kosygin again met with the North Vietnamese and North Koreans (in Hanoi) and with the Chinese in Peking). The occasion was the funeral of Ho Chi Minh. The topic: very likely Vietnam, although speculation ran that Kosygin and Chou Enlai had spoken about the dangerous Sino-Soviet border skirmishes of March, May, June, and August. I suspect that, as in February 1965, the Soviet leader wished to inform the Asian comrades of future Soviet plans with respect to the war in Vietnam in the aftermath of Ho's death. Quite likely, Soviet aid to the North was to be continued. To do so, transshipment of Russian military hardware and foodstuffs across mainland China would be made necessary by the fact that the Suez Canal would remain closed for the foreseeable future. Thus, the Soviet supply route through Suez, the Indian Ocean, the Strait of Malacca, and on up to Haiphong would be blocked necessitating transshipment overland via China and out of the Soviet Pacific seaport of Vladivostok. Kosygin may well have informed the Chinese of this necessity thereby putting the onus on them if cargoes should be interfered with by the Chinese.

overthrow, the Red Chinese press granted a reprieve to the Soviets during the interregnum honeymoon.

To the Chinese, this new policy revealed to them in November 1964 signified a bold challenge to their more-Catholic-than-the-Pope line: that their Maoist brand of Marxism-Leninism was the most "revolutionary." After October 1964, it would not be so easy for the Chinese to claim that the leaders in Moscow were tainted with the brush of revisionism or that they neglected the peoples struggling for national liberation, and so on.

More than these ideological considerations alone must have bothered the Chinese after Chou returned to Peking in mid-November with a report of his talks with the Russians. For now it must have dawned on the Chinese that the new Kremlin leaders were embarking on *a more forthright diplomatic-military strategy in general in the Far East* (not to mention the whole world) as, indeed, it turned out they were. Moreover, this could eventually involve China's old enemy Japan, the linchpin in the whole Western Pacific area.

Relations with Japan

Even during the Khrushchev era, there had been several hints that a Soviet diplomatic bridge-building effort respecting Japan was under way. For example, in 1963 a major trade accord was concluded between Japan and the U.S.S.R. It included a three-year exchange of commodities under which the Soviets exported to Japan pig iron, coking coal, machinery, and other raw materials and finished products. Meanwhile, Japan exported to the U.S.S.R. oil tankers, pipe, electron microscopes, floating cranes, and other hoisting and transport instruments.[5]

Khrushchev's policy toward Japan (in the formulation of which the then First Deputy Premier Anastas Mikoyan played an important role) was continued and broadened after his overthrow. Japanese-Soviet trade advanced by leaps. In 1968 this trade was double the value of 1967 reaching the unprecedented figure for trade between the two countries of $610 million.[6] In addition to trade, the Soviets and the Japanese worked out other unique (for them) cooperative arrangements in the economic area. In 1968 it was agreed, for example, that Japanese banks would extend a five-year loan of $133 million at 5.8 percent interest to enable the Russians to develop their Siberian timber cutting industry. In addition, a consortium of 13 Japanese companies, including the former armaments-making concerns of Mitsui and Mitsubishi, would sell $30 million worth of consumer goods to Russian settlers in Siberia (an interesting admission, by the way, that European Russia could not cope adequately with the problems of supplying the new Siberian settlements with consumer goods). As recompensation for the Japanese loan and to cover the interest, the Russians agreed to ship 8,020,000 cubic feet of timber to Japan over a five-year period. And there are presently other joint Japanese-Russian economic projects afoot—for example, a loan to construct an oil pipeline leading from Siberian oil fields to the Pacific and a joint enterprise for developing the copper mines in the Lake Baikal area. On its part, Japan, which has a paucity of raw materials and has heretofore been obliged to get them (especially high-cost oil*) from faraway countries on other continents, evidently relishes the business opportunities now opened between itself and its Russian neighbor in Asia.

Despite the burgeoning commercial intercourse, however, the Soviet Union and Japan have several diplomatic knots to untie before their political relations can be described as cordial enough to alarm the Chinese. One problem concerns four of the Kurile Islands, which the Russians acquired by virtue of their one-week war against Japan in August 1945. Moscow has agreed to vacate two of these islands, Habomai and Shikotan, upon conclusion of a formal peace treaty with the Japanese. Japan, meanwhile, demands the other two islands, Etorofu and Kunashiri, as well. And there are other disagreements concerning fishing rights off Japanese coasts, detained Japanese fishermen, and so on. But the improved economic relations between the two countries could eventually rise to the political and diplomatic level. A hint that this may be in the cards are two recent developments: a consular treaty signed between the two countries and an agreement to hold regular consultations on the foreign ministers' level. There are also plans afoot to step up cultural contacts.

Communist China regards these developments with great bitterness. The Chinese press points to Russian-Japanese cooperation as evidence of plans for "encirclement" of mainland China which, it says, is a joint policy of the U.S.S.R., Japan, and the United States. The post-Khrushchev Kremlin policy toward Japan must seem to the Chinese to be just as injurious to China's plan of becoming the dominating factor on mainland East Asia (obvious since 1955) as was the Soviet decision to become more deeply involved in Vietnam after October 1964.

New Soviet Policy Toward North Korea

Not only Soviet actions in Vietnam and Japan confirm Chinese fears, but the new Soviet policy toward North Korea has the same effect as well. Kim

*The fact that Russia sold Japan crude oil in 1966 at a lower price and in larger amounts than she did to Castro's Cuba and Kim Il Sung's North Korea angered the latter two Communist states, which complained of a Soviet "oil squeeze" upon them. Japan appears to have been given higher priority in this trade than the Communist puppet state of the Mongolian People's Republic—a measure of the importance which has been assigned to Japan by the Kremlin leaders.

Il Sung's bailiwick has become, in fact, one of the focal points for detecting the change in the Soviets' Far Eastern policy.

Almost immediately after the Brezhnev-Kosygin regime* was installed in the Kremlin, overtures began to be made to Kim's regime in Pyongyang. Tangible results soon followed. A new era of escalated political, diplomatic, and military intercourse opened between the two countries. The regime in the Kremlin was obviously bent upon wooing friends in the West Pacific perimeter circling Red China; North Korea, like North Vietnam, falls into this category. From 1965 to the present, therefore, the North Koreans have responded by giving solid support to each and every policy initiated in the Kremlin, including the August 1968 invasion of Czechoslovakia.** And their loyalty has been reciprocated by Moscow, which supported Pyongyang in the *Pueblo* "spy ship" and EC–121 "spy plane" episodes of 1968 and 1969. Moreover, there have been Soviet hints of late that it intends to give more support than heretofore to North Korea's efforts at forcible unification of North and South Korea. For example, at the time of the celebration of North Korea's twentieth anniversary in September 1968, the Kremlin sent a top Kremlin figure, Dmitri S. Polyansky, a Politburo member and the First Deputy Premier of the U.S.S.R., to Pyongyang to join in the festivities and speechmaking. Among the remarks conveyed by Polyansky from the Soviet Politburo were:

Today the Korean People's Democratic Republic is the true focal point of Socialism in the Far East. . . . The Soviet people show deep understanding toward the struggle of the Korean people for unification of the country on a democratic basis. The Soviet Union warmly supports the just demands of the Korean People's Democratic Republic for the withdrawal of American troops from South Korea and supports the struggle of the Korean people for the right to solve itself the problem of its national unity. The Americans must get out of South Korea. We wish in this connection to state that any attempts by enemies to violate the peaceful creative labor of the Korean people will suffer bitter defeat. People's Korea has treaty agreements with the Soviet Union for mutual defense of our Socialist order, and enemies must not forget this.[7]

*One is tempted on good grounds to call the post-Khrushchev regime a *quadrumvirate* consisting of Brezhnev, Kosygin, Suslov, and Podgorny. Suslov became Second Secretary of the C.P.S.U. after Khrushchev's fall while Podgorny acts primarily as a figurehead (he is the Soviet "President"). All four are members of the party Politburo, while only Brezhnev and Suslov among these four are members of *both* the Politburo and the Secretariat. The Western press often abbreviates the regime into a "Brezhnev-Kosygin" duumvirate, which is at least space saving. There can be no doubt that Suslov's role in the post-Khrushchev regime is sufficiently important to warrant his inclusion among the top four collectivirs.

**This was Kim's policy despite his many pleas for independence of Communist parties and regimes (see B. C. Koh's article in *Problems of Communism* cited in note 3). Kim, like Ho Chi Minh of North Vietnam, has been careful at the same time not to alienate the Chinese. Shrewdly, both Kim and Ho walk a tightrope and display double loyalty to both Peking and Moscow.

On this occasion the only other major representation in Pyongyang from the rest of the European Soviet bloc was by East Germany, in the person of George Ewald, a member of the East German Politburo.*

The friendly reorientation of Soviet policy toward North Korea was a major departure from the frigid attitude of 1961–1964—part and parcel, as we have suggested, of the overall stepped-up Soviet involvement in the Far East as a whole, especially as relates to the periphery about Maoist China. Also, the power represented by North Korea is an important factor, as is its strategic location: it borders on Red China in the north along the Yalu River; its extreme northeast corner borders on the U.S.S.R., and is situated a mere 150 air miles from Vladivostok, the Soviets' most important Pacific naval outpost, near the scene of the March 1969 bloody Sino-Soviet border clashes. Moreover, North Korea possesses armed forces numbering 420,000 men not counting a 1.3 million-man backup militia.[8] Its air force too is large: 680 planes including almost 100 MIG–21s with Sidewinder-type air-to-air missiles slung under their bellies. North Korea is known also to have several SAM-type ground-to-air missile sites, 900 Soviet-built tanks, and a small navy including over 60 high-speed torpedo boats. This represents a considerable military establishment for a country that is only slightly larger than the State of New York and has a population of about 13 million.**

The recent incidents involving North Korea and the United States (the *Pueblo* and EC–121 episodes of 1968 and 1969) suggest Soviet collusion. This cannot be proved, of course, but it appears probable that the decision in the case of the EC–121 reconnaissance plane in April 1969 to dispatch MIG–21s to take by surprise and shoot down the *American* plane (of a type which had made during the previous three months some 190 runs off the North Korean coast outside the 12-mile territorial limit) could surely not have been made in Pyongyang alone; any attacks on the other super power, the U.S., surely must be cleared with Moscow. The same may be true in the *Pueblo* case of 1968. It is noteworthy, moreover, that both incidents involved

---

*In June 1969, the Soviet President Nikolai Podgorny embarked on a five-day tour to North Korea. This was the highest Soviet personage ever to visit Kim in Pyongyang. It should raise eyebrows in Peking, and perhaps in the West too, if this visit should presage more EC–121 and *Pueblo*-type incidents or indicate new escalation in the Soviets' participation in The Vietnam War.

**Were it not for the fact that South Korea too is well equipped militarily, Kim Il Sung, with Soviet backing, might well have attempted forcible unification of the country before now. The South has over one-half million under arms, 300 of the most modern types of fighter planes (F–86s and F–5's) not counting planes at U.S. bases in the country. South Korea is the third most militarily powerful country in the whole non-Communist world. Moreover, its rapid economic progress since 1966 is the "success story" of the Far East; next to Japan, it is the most prosperous Far Eastern country. It falls, of course, within a defense perimeter defended by the U.S., and its relations with Japan are on an unprecedentedly strong basis.

naval or naval-support units. The Soviet navy has been increasingly active in the Sea of Japan since 1965; one or two "brush" incidents involving American and Soviet naval vessels have taken place in these waters over the past three years. Moreover, what appears to be General-Secretary Brezhnev's personal interest in boosting the Soviet naval arm (Brezhnev served as political commissar of the Soviet navy for a time after Stalin's death) and making the U.S.S.R. a formidable sea power may be factors as well. Finally, it should be noted that since the *Pueblo* and the EC–121 were both on "listening-in" missions relating above all to *Soviet* communications athwart the Soviet merchant shipping route to Haiphong, North Vietnam, it stands to reason that armed retaliation by North Korea against these "American spies" would more than likely originate in Moscow than in Pyongyang. Also, the Soviet press made out a sternly worded case in support of the two North Korean actions against the U.S. ignored the fact—treated so optimistically in the American press—that a Soviet destroyer had picked up debris from the EC–121. In any event, the supposition concerning Soviet collusion is worth serious consideration. If true, it affords an illustration of the way in which the post-Khrushchev Soviet leadership regards in certain circumstances its "cold peace" or "limited coexistence" with the United States. If untrue and if the EC–121 incident resulted from unilateral North Korean adventurism, the inference is that the Soviets wield considerably less influence in Pyongyang than they would wish.

Discord in the East European Soviet Bloc

In Eastern Europe, the post-Khrushchev collectivirs undertook a number of moves calculated to bolster Soviet relations with their western duchies and to strengthen Soviet influence over their policies to a greater degree than was possible under Khrushchev.

In the closing Khrushchev years, the countries of the East European Soviet bloc were fast becoming *ex*-satellites, with the word accent on the *"ex-."* One of the contributing factors in this process of de-satellization—and a phenomenon that was increasingly to plague the Kremlin during and after the "liberal" or "New Course" years—was *renascent nationalism*. The feeling was rampant throughout the whole region from Tirana (Albania) to Belgrade (Yugoslavia) to Bucharest (Rumania) and to Prague (Czechoslovakia). This "romantic" feeling, as one author has called it,[9] sometimes has territorial overtones. Transylvania, which was detached from Hungary and given to Rummania after World War II, was a sore point with the Hungarians. and the issue began to be treated not too delicately in Hungarian publications; it boded ill for "comradely" Hungarian-Rumanian relations within the Warsaw Alliance. Rumanian publications began to refer obliquely to a

bête noir of their own: the Soviet appropriation of Bessarabia and Bukovina in 1940 in the deal with Hitler. The Poles were unhappy at Czechoslovakia's acquisition of the southern Cieszyn (Teschen) area, which had been
taken from them by force by the Czechs in 1919 while Poland was at war
with the young Soviet Republic, then seized by Poland during the Munich
crisis of 1938, and finally returned to Czechoslovakia in 1945.

Furthermore, there was even talk, especially in Yugoslav publications, of a
new-style Balkan Union. This idea had helped poison relations between
Stalin and Tito after 1948, the Russians by that time having become suspicious of attempts at regionalism within their East European empire. Regionalism, moreover, ran counter to Moscow's efforts after 1957 at *coordinating*
the economic plans of the Soviet bloc countries and creating a "Communist
Market" within the bloc. Autarky on the part of individual countries or
regions within the bloc merely added to the forces of centrifugality pulling
the satellites out of orbit and away from the Russian mother-planet.

In foreign policy, too, some of the East European countries began to fall
out of step with Moscow. Rumania, although before and after 1964 supporting the North Vietnamese-Vietcong effort to forcibly unify all of Vietnam
under Communist leadership, chose not to follow the Soviet course in
alienating Red China. Instead, Bucharest's relations with Peking remained
almost as close as those of Albania's, another recalcitrant ex-satellite of the
U.S.S.R. Unlike Albania, however, the Rumanians did not clearly align
themselves with China in the Sino-Soviet dispute.

Albania, Peking's Pawn

As for Albania, this small, mountainous and largely sheepherding country
availed itself of its lucky geographical separation from and its many political
differences with the U.S.S.R. and went its own way. The Soviet effort from
1949–1960 to hold onto Albania with all kinds of aid and inducements—not
to mention infiltration of Albania's security and military forces—failed in
the last analysis. Albania had become pro-Chinese and anti-Russian by 1961;
so obviously, in fact, that the Russians refused to help it out in that year
when Albania suffered from a shortage of grain. This was, in fact, the
start of overt aid coming to Albania from Communist China, taking the
form in 1961 of grain cargoes in the bottoms of Canadian ships which had
been originally bound for Communist China but which Peking now directed to Albanian ports in the Adriatic. Albania was thereby saved from
famine.[10] There followed a period of bitter recrimination between the two
countries, Albania and the U.S.S.R., with the prize for acrimoniousness going to Tirana. Among Albania's complaints was Khrushchev's demand for
"slavish obedience from all Communist countries, encouraging hero worship of himself while disparaging past hero worship of Stalin; subordinat-
ing Communist world revolution to disarmament; and betraying Albania

by courting Yugoslavia," and so forth.[11] It was probably doubly painful to Moscow to find others in its East European camp continuing to trade with Albania. Moscow was simply unable to enforce any longer a boycott of a recalcitrant ex-satellite, as it had been able to do in the case of Yugoslavia after 1948 and until the death of Stalin. In 1969, the Red Chinese press began to hint that Peking was eager to develop Albania into an anti-Soviet East European guerrilla base.

Soviet-Rumanian Differences on Economic Policy

Rumania's grievances against the U.S.S.R. went beyond the territorial matter of Bessarabia and Bukovina, or differences with Russia over relations with Red China. By 1964 she was overtly balking at Khrushchev's attempts to knit COMECON into a tightly coordinated pan-bloc economic administration or "ruble bloc." Even as early as 1962, signs of Rumanian defection had appeared at a meeting of COMECON held in the summer of that year. The Rumanians claimed that COMECON, under Russian leadership, was forcing the Rumanians to abandon or postpone their plans for developing their own heavy industry. Moscow undoubtedly sensed that an independent Rumanian policy under Gheorghiu-Dej's skillful leadership would surely increase that country's opportunities for trade with Western Europe, perhaps leading to eventual economic detachment of the country from the Soviet bloc. Pressure was then evidently applied by the Russians under Khrushchev's leadership and was, in fact, one of the grievances in the Twenty-nine Points against Khrushchev circulated after his ouster—namely that he had unnecessarily alienated the Rumanians. In a COMECON meeting in December of the same year, Rumanian recalcitrance led to the shelving of the whole scheme.[12] In his book *Expansion and Coexistence*, Adam B. Ulam makes the following observation about Rumania on the eve of Khrushchev's fall:

Rumania was the only state in the world that could boast of the following combination of achievements in foreign relations: she was an ally to the Soviet Union, friend of China, and the one Communist state whose diplomatic and commercial relations with the West had grown better and more extensive over the past few years. . . . The prestige of the Rumanian Communist Party and the self-confidence of its leaders was bound to get a tremendous boost.[13]

The Three Northern Tier Countries

The only area in Eastern Europe, with the exception of Bulgaria, where Soviet influence was still very strong was in the so-called Northern Tier, consisting of Poland, East Germany, and Czechoslovakia.* But even here, there were potentially upsetting, centrifugal elements.

*Hungary under Kadar was only a lukewarm satellite.

The regimes of Antonin Novotny in Czechoslovakia, Walter Ulbricht in East Germany, and Wladyslaw Gomulka in Poland kept themselves propped up largely on the basis of a strong anti-West German policy. Their line went somewhat as follows. A clear threat of "German revanchism" exists in the form of the German Federal Republic. In order to protect the three Northern Tier countries from resurgent German expansionism and irredentism, a Communist regime is necessary, with its policy of encouraging heavy (and defense) industry and maintaining a high degree of vigilance against the threat posed by "capitalist-imperialist Germany."

Meanwhile, on the other hand, Khrushchev was hinting strongly at a new German policy and a Moscow-Bonn rapprochement. We have already mentioned the grounds for and the partial evidence of discord between the Soviets and the East German regime on this very point. Likewise, the regimes of Novotny and Gomulka appeared to be threatened, not only by the undercutting of the ideological props for their regimes (their anti-Germanism), but also for the reason that elements within their societies and ruling circles would be encouraged by the atmosphere of détente and relaxation of tension to pressure the existing regimes for bold changes in both domestic and foreign policy. Obviously, the two most developed East European countries of the Soviet bloc, East Germany and Czechoslovakia, and also, of all the countries in the Soviet bloc, the two with the longest experience with democracy during the interwar period 1918–1939, obviously stood in the greatest danger of having their totalitarian control sapped from within by "liberalism," "revisionism," and "holdovers from the bourgeois past." The Russians surely must have been aware of this too. But under Khrushchev, the policy of détente appeared to take precedence over imperial considerations. This in turn helped to bring about an anti-Khrushchev coalition, which formed secretly in the Kremlin in the closing months of 1964. And not only in the Kremlin.

As might have been expected from the foregoing, at least two of the leaders of the three Northern Tier countries, Gomulka and Ulbricht, appear to have been instrumental in supporting, if not helping to instigate, the conspiratorial plan to overthrow Khrushchev. (Novotny apparently wavered, his good personal relations with "Nikita Sergeyevich" perhaps being a factor.)*

On the very eve of the coup, there was an extraordinary amount of telltale activity between the Kremlin and the East Germans.[14] From October 1 to 3, 1964, Willi Stoph, the East German Premier, was in Moscow, ostensibly to open an exhibition there. On October 5, a week before the conspiracy was put into effect, Brezhnev flew to East Germany with a delegation including

---

*In a rare unalphabetical listing of the countries of the Soviet bloc, Gromyko (July 10, 1969) placed Poland, Czechoslovakia, and East Germany at the top in that order. See *Pravda*, July 11, 1969, p. 2.

two other reputed "hawks," K. T. Mazurov and A. Ya. Pelshe (both of whom were duly promoted after Khrushchev's fall), ostensibly to celebrate the tenth anniversary of the establishment of the Pankow regime. These two visits—the East Germans in Moscow and the Russians in Pankow— were suitable occasions for various expressions of East German-Soviet "fraternal relations." But there were noticeable differences in the manner in which expressions were made. In Suslov's speech at a Moscow rally in honor of the establishment of East Germany, the Kremlin "internationalist" and defender of ideological purity took a far more definite stand in East Germany's favor than was taken in an analogous speech by the then First Deputy Premier Kosygin. Party Secretary Suslov assured and reassured the East German comrades that the "possibility of a deal [with West Germany] at the expense of the G.D.R. is a foolish illusion. . . . The fraternal amity and Socialist solidarity which link the U.S.S.R. and the G.D.R. are not to be bought and sold, even for all the gold in the world."[15] This reassurance was quite obviously aimed at placating Ulbricht in the face of Khrushchev's nascent policy of rapprochement with West Germany.

Brezhnev's speech in East Berlin on October 5 was also quite revealing, as this author pointed out in a letter published in *The New York Times* on October 20, or a week after Khrushchev's ouster.* Hints of events to come suggested that Brezhnev might have gone to East Germany to inform Ulbricht of the details of the conspiracy. One tip-off that something was in the wind was Brezhnev's mention of Khrushchev's name only once, and then *without* either the customary *Tovarishch* ("Comrade") or his first name and patronymic, Nikita Sergeyevich. Nor did Brezhnev say he had brought greetings "personally" from Khrushchev, as was the usual custom, but merely from the C.P.S.U. Central Committee. Instead of references to "dear Nikita Sergeyevich," I noticed that Brezhnev conspicuously employed the first-person singular several times in his speech, suggesting to me a note of new-found authority and prestige in Brezhnev's use of *Ya* ("I").

Another bit of confirmation for the suspicion that Ulbricht and Gomulka may have given support to the coup was the fact that the first leaders with whom the new leaders conferred after October 14 were Gomulka and Ulbricht, in that order. In fact, the first trip made by the new leaders outside

---

*One of the main points of my letter was to contend a suggestion by the *Times* writer Harrison Salisbury that the new leaders would now attempt to *heal the breach with China.* I argued back: "On the contrary, the Chinese challenge to the Soviet right to parts of its contemporary territory could only drive the Soviet leaders together in their common Russian contempt for this Chinese *revanchism* and territorial jealousy. The differences within the Kremlin are of a different sort" (*The New York Times*, October 20, 1964). See also my article in *The New Leader*, October 26, 1964, entitled "Struggle at the Top," in which I deal with the various policy differences that marked Khrushchev's downfall, and what could be expected from the Kremlin under the new leaders.

the U.S.S.R. was to an unnamed location near Warsaw, to where the "triumvirate" of Brezhnev, Kosygin, and Podgorny journeyed for talks with Gomulka only a few days after Khrushchev had been removed.

A Double-Encirclement Strategy?

No sooner had the new group installed itself in the Kremlin than a series of new trends in policy began to emerge. By their new moves in foreign policy and in their presentation of it in the party press, the Soviets revealed that they were fashioning a new worldwide strategy. The three countries most directly affected were West Germany, Communist China, and the United States. Other countries, such as North Vietnam, North Korea, Egypt, India, France, Japan, also figured in the new policy, but largely as instruments or pawns within the context of a larger strategy affecting the much more powerful three countries.

New Soviet Stance Toward West Germany and Gaullist France

On October 15, two days after Khrushchev's ouster, *Pravda* published this item under the by-line V. Mikhailov, a name which was to be associated in the post-Khrushchev years with vitriolic ideological sabre-rattling:[16]

Bonn, Oct. 14. (Special Correspondent for *Pravda*). Admiration for the new accomplishment by the Soviet Union in the cosmos [the flight of Komarov, Feoktistov, and Yegorov] is everywhere. It paralyzes adversaries, opens the eyes of persons who have been blinded by anti-Communist slanders, and swells the ranks of our friends.

The news from Moscow throws into the shadows everything that West Germany has been fuming about up to now.

Soon the cartooning talents of Abramov, Fomichev, and the "Kukryniksy Boys,"* with assists from Polish and East German cartoonists, began to be put to use depicting political figures in Bonn as successors to the Nazis (a pictorial device being the depiction of skeletons of Hitler, Goering, and others wearing jackboots and Nazi-style helmets and, from the grave, approving of the actions of the Bonn government).

Soviet actions on the diplomatic front pointed in the same direction of a Soviet version of *Drang nacht Westen*. First, the slated trip of Khrushchev to West Germany was quietly forgotten and scrapped. Instead, the Soviets

---

*An acronym formed from a trio of cartoonists named Kupriyanov, Krylov, and Sokolov, who have worked as a team since 1924. It should be added that the editors of the two leading Soviet dailies, *Pravda* and *Izvestiya*, changed editors immediately after Khrushchev's dismissal: Satyukov leaving Pravda, Adzhubei *Izvestiya*. This was, in fact, the first major step in the process of de-Khrushchevizing the central party *apparat*.

began diligently to fashion a "bridge to France," an effort which was soon to emerge as part of a policy of *encircling Germany to the West*, a scheme of what one Western specialist on Soviet foreign policy has called "preventive containment" of West Germany.[17]

The Russians undoubtedly saw in their courting of de Gaulle (evident already in late October 1964 in a major speech by the Soviet "President" at that time, Anastas Mikoyan) an opportunity to isolate Germany. Among other things, Mikoyan described with optimism future relations between the U.S.S.R. and France, pointing out that such a development would be an "important contribution to the attainment of European security and peace throughout the world."[18] A process set in whereby as Soviet friendship with France grew, Soviet policy with respect to West Germany hardened, almost in direct proportion. As early as March 19, 1965,[19] for example, U.S.S.R. Foreign Minister Gromyko (whom the *détentiste* Adzhubei very likely would have replaced had Khrushchev not been overthrown) made a significant statement on Germany at a press conference in London: Gromyko expressed for the first time the Soviet view that the reunification of Germany was altogether impossible. Moreover, Gromyko alleged, it was the West German government that was responsible for the growing differences between the "two German states," as he put it significantly. The Soviet government also hardened on the question of Germany's eastern borders. On the occasion of signing the Polish-Soviet friendship treaty, April 8, 1965, First Secretary Brezhnev spoke of the eastern border and Berlin problems as follows:

> The question of the borders of the Polish People's Republic, together with all the postwar boundaries in Europe, was decided long ago in 1945 by the Potsdam Agreement of the powers comprising the anti-Hitlerite coalition. It was decided finally and irrevocably.[20]

Even before this statement was made, however, the Soviet government had provoked a test of strength over the issue of West Berlin's being a part of the German Federal Republic. The Soviets had refused to accept West Germany's ratification of the Moscow partial test-ban treaty of 1963 on the grounds that the German Federal Republic had no right to include in the treaty West Berlin, which, they declared, was not a part of West Germany either geographically or politically. This refusal was followed up by a new East German interference with travel into West Berlin early in 1965. Members of the East German Bundestag were prevented from entering Berlin by train, and normal railroad and automobile and water traffic into the city was disrupted. The pretext given was that the Soviet army was conducting maneuvers in the area, a harbinger of pretexts to come in future years! Similarly, West Germany's proposed participation in a multilateral nuclear force within N.A.T.O. and the suggestion to lay a belt of atomic mines along the border with East Germany met with violent opposition from the Soviets.[21]

Besides these actions and the vitriolic press campaign against West Germany, the Soviets attempted to needle the Germans in various ways. For example, the old issue of German war crimes was brought up in January 1965 by the new Soviet Premier, Alexei Kosygin, who accused Bonn of dragging its feet on bringing war criminals to trial. The Soviets also indicated that they, the Russians, would decide when they wished to bring to West German attention or to expose neglected war criminals residing in West Germany. Presumably, it would be the Soviets who would henceforth spring surprises on Bonn and take the credit for unearthing notorious war criminals whom Bonn overlooked or sought to ignore.

French-Soviet relations continued apace, and the new Soviet "President," Nikolai V. Podgorny, appeared to be in charge of it. Gromyko visited France in the spring of 1965 and the campaign to build a bridge to Paris was well under way. What motivated it?

One hint came in *Pravda's* version on May 3, 1965, of the German reaction to an imminent Franco-Russian rapprochement: "Bonn is prepared to resort to any means and to stab in the back those who only yesterday were held in 'eternal friendship.' " In other words, deterioration of Franco-German relations, which was in evidence at the time, was blamed not on de Gaulle but on the West German government.* Another hint of the post-Khrushchev Soviet motivations for cultivating Franco-Russian amity (amid great hoopla about "traditional Franco-Russian friendship") could be found in the C.P.S.U. journal, *Kommunist. Kommunist* (No. 8, 1965) asserted that Franco-Soviet cooperation was a guarantee against "German militarism."[22] In her informative article for the *Bulletin* of the Institute for the Study of the U.S.S.R. (in Munich), Albertine Aubery cogently wrote in late 1965:

The present trend of Soviet policy toward West Germany is dictated by a number of considerations. In the first place the Soviets need at least the semblance of a tense situation in Europe in order to justify their failure to provide adequate aid to North Vietnam. In the second place—and this is a new consideration reflected in the close [Soviet] relations with de Gaulle—the aggravation of relations with West Germany represents an attempt by the Soviet leaders to test the seriousness of the conflicts between various N.A.T.O. countries and especially test the behavior of de Gaulle himself.

What was not readily apparent, understandably, to Miss Aubery and most

Pravda's position did not jive at all with a suspicion that had been voiced in *1963* concerning Franco-German relations. At that time, the Soviet press said that "de Gaulle had ulterior motives for entering into a bargain [with Germany] . . . de Gaulle is dreaming of the creation of a strong continental Europe in which he assigns the role of an armored robot to West Germany and to himself the role of enlightened ruler. . . . He needs support in order to settle accounts with the Americans and drive them back across the ocean" (*Pravda*, January 24, 1963).

other observers at that time were several other factors that were also motivating the Soviets' new stance toward West Germany.

1. Using the "German menace" as a whipping boy or rallying point for girding up the Warsaw Alliance
2. Working, thereby, through the *military* organs of the Warsaw Pact toward restoring greater unity in the camp—an effort that had been stymied whenever the Soviets attempted to accomplish this through the *economic* arm of the Alliance, COMECON
3. Lumping together of "American aggression in Vietnam," "German revanchism," and slackening discipline within the bloc in the face of these two threats—the ultimate aim of this mix being to mount a campaign against "revisionism" within the Communist parties (for example, in Czechoslovakia) or East European societies and to outflank attempts by the Rumanians, Yugoslavs, and others to work out policies entirely independently from the Soviet bloc
4. Moscow's close relations with Ulbricht and Gomulka, culminating in a three-way squeeze on Czechoslovakia, forcing it into line with its two other allies in the Northern Tier
5. An attempt by the Soviets to frustrate the plans of the German military and the conservatives to have West Germany acquire a measure of control over tactical atomic weapons and eventually to create atomic installations on West German soil—apparently through isolating Germany via the Soviets' links to France, thus leaving Germany dependent on the United States, a non-European power, which the Soviets increasingly attacked in their press as an abettor of German rearmament and "nuclearization"*

The Triangle of Russia, China, and Vietnam

With respect to Red China, we have already indicated the lines along which the Kremlin's attitude toward the Maoists of Peking was to develop (see above, pp. 186–188). First, the Khrushchev policy of diplomatically and ideologically isolating China and reviling it for "adventurism" was stepped up and carried out much more forthrightly by the new leaders than it had been under the First Secretary, for all his bombast and obvious Sinophobia.

At the head of the list in this effort stood Vietnam. Whereas under Khrushchev in late 1964, the Soviet press complained that China was trying to push the Soviet Union into a war with the United States over Vietnam, after Khrushchev's fall from power the new leaders in the Kremlin actively and immediately set about (a) *increasing their involvement in Vietnam* dozens of times over what it had been earlier; (b) *drawing the U.S. more deeply into the struggle* by a shrewd diplomatic game.

As to escalated Soviet aid to North Vietnam, in 1965 alone Soviet arms

*In Chapter X (below, pp. 253–258), we shall consider another possible motivation for the Soviet posture toward France and Germany as it relates to the U.S.

and military equipment was worth half a billion rubles ($555 million) and included rocket installations and conventional antiaircraft guns, MIGs and other planes, tanks, coastal artillery, small warships, and other items as well.[23] (In preceding years, this aid, mostly nonmilitary, had been a mere trickle.) In 1966, the value of these shipments nearly doubled as the Soviets added more sophisticated hardware to the mixture, some of which came to North Vietnam via rail across Communist China, others by ship from the Black Sea port of Odessa through the Suez Canal and thence to the Indian Ocean, through the Strait of Malacca, and around the Indochinese Peninsula to Haiphong, North Vietnam. When obstructions were put up by the Chinese at various rail hubs in 1966–1967, and with the blocking of the Suez Canal during and since the Arab-Israeli six-day war of June 1967, a large quantity of this Soviet aid has come from Vladivostok—another factor that contributes to the strategic importance of this vital Soviet Pacific seaport and to the surrounding waters, particularly the Sea of Japan and the Korean [Chosen] Strait.

By late 1965, Suslov and his band of Kremlin "internationalists" had begun to fit the new Soviet Vietnam policy into an ideological context. The November 1965 International Communist Duty Manifesto,* from where the epigraph at the beginning of this chapter was taken, was published ostentatiously on the front page of all Soviet newspapers on November 28, 1965. It contained the key phrase "waging an *active offensive* (*aktivnoye nastupleniye*) against the positions held by imperialism." This reference to taking the "offensive" had a clear implication to comrades reading the Soviet press, especially those in foreign ruling and nonruling Communist parties. The U.S.S.R. was now stepping up its ideological war against "American imperialism." At the same time, the claim by the Maoists that the Russians were notorious revisionists would have no basis in fact. For from now on, the Soviets were going to *prove* that their offensive was tangible by lending tangible military aid to the North Vietnamese and the Vietcong.

This reference to an "offensive" also had several diplomatic overtones. For the Sino-Soviet cold war, it meant that Peking's allegations of U.S.-Soviet collusion would no longer be credible. Also, with a stronger Soviet presence in Hanoi, with more sophisticated weapons in the hands of the N.V.A. and the Cong, and with an extremely adventuristic military strategy being applied by the North Vietnamese military chief, General Vo Nguyen Giap, in which the North and the Cong were willing to suffer

---

*The Lin Piao Manifesto, published in Peking on *September 3, 1965*, may well have spurred on the Soviets to get out their own manifesto! This Chinese *Mein Kampf* captured worldwide attention and must have upset the internationalists in Moscow who had banked on the new "revolutionariness" (*revolyutsionnost*) of their own policies as being sufficient unto itself to prove that the Russian Communists were at least as orthodox as the "Pope in Peking."

losses sometimes at the rate of 5 to 1, sometimes 10 to 1 that of the enemy, in vicious surprise attacks, and so forth, only one thing could result: *increased American military presence in Vietnam and in Southeast Asia generally*. This in turn constituted (and still constitutes) a *brake on Maoist expansion* in Southeast Asia—into Cambodia, Laos, Thailand, and Burma, for example. This, needless to say, suits Soviet designs as well.*

Windfalls from Soviet Policy in Vietnam

Thus, with deliberate irony, Moscow worked for and got a large American military commitment to defend South Vietnam, and in fact, other areas of Southeast Asia as well, while at the same time increasing its own influence at the court of Ho Chi Minh in Hanoi.** All the time, of course, the Soviets increased the bitterness of their anti-American line in the Soviet press—a phenomenon that emerged, as we have already noted, shortly after Khrushchev's "retirement." Working together in the Soviet interest, then, were *ideology* ("aggressive American imperialism, as in Vietnam") and *diplomacy* (outflanking the Chinese). And there were a few other windfalls stemming from this policy too.

The American public became increasingly bothered and upset by the turn of events in Vietnam which indicated that American forces had become "bogged down in a hopeless war." Moreover, the frustration of full American prosecution of the war (which would include, for example, bombing of North Vietnam's vital sources of water during the dry season, its ample aqueducts and dikes) was an added irritant and insult to the tragic loss of life incurred by the U.S. and its allies in the steaming tropics of South Vietnam. Self-inhibition of the staggering military power of the United States was undoubtedly quite a spectacle to behold from the vantage point of the Kremlin. The Kremlin internationalists were obviously jubilant over the opportunities for leftist political actionism afforded by the American public's agonizing over the war. The Soviet press gave—and still gives—wide coverage to political unrest and debates about Vietnam in the

---

*An interesting example of where the Soviets find it necessary to curb ideology and place the flag above Marxism-Leninism, or "revolution," is Cambodia. Here the Soviets are willing to give, and have given, considerable military aid to Prince Sihanouk. The Prince has in turn used this Soviet aid to combat insurgent forces in the northern and eastern parts of his country, some of whom are supported by Red China, some by Hanoi. The Soviets evidently reason that an independent Cambodia better suits their policy with respect to both North Vietnam and China than a "revolutionary" Cambodia.

**I first developed this concept in print in a letter published in *The New Leader* in 1965—to my knowledge, the first time such a theory was advanced. Somewhat later, or more likely simultaneously (I do not wish to develop a "cult" about myself!), a few specialists began toying with the same idea. Finally, there is the excellent piece containing this theory, by Dr. Vernon V. Aspaturian, which I have cited above and which is cited again below in this chapter.

United States, particularly among the youth and in American colleges and universities. *"Raskolotaya Amerika"*—"America Is Split Asunder"—is a headline that has appeared more than once in the Soviet press since the beginning of 1965.

In conclusion, post-Khrushchev policy toward China—as viewed through the Soviets' Vietnam policy after October 1964—appears to be one of encirclement. When Japanese-Soviet relations and Soviet policy toward North Korea are added into the mix of Soviet Far Eastern policy, this becomes even clearer. Moscow is clearly surrounding Communist China with strong Soviet allies. Indeed, the Chinese often point this out in their own press.

With respect to Germany, or more particularly West Germany, an encirclement policy also appears to be in effect. However, there is room here for considerable qualification, which an examination and analysis of post-Khrushchev policy specifically toward the United States, discussed in the next chapter, reveals. Courting of Gaullist France also fits into this pattern, as we discussed above. So also does Soviet protection of the pro-Soviet regimes of Gomulka and Ulbricht in Eastern and Central Europe. The Soviet invasion of post-Novotny Czechoslovakia in August 1968 is likewise part of the same scheme.

Thus it seems clear that the Soviet policy is one of "double encirclement" of China and West Germany. The specialist who apparently coined this expression explains this phenomenon as follows:

Moscow perceives of the German threat as real but *potential* or latent, and Soviet policy is designed to prevent its development, whereas the Chinese threat is viewed as much more immediate and ominous.

In the Far East, the Soviet Union has envisaged the United States as a partner in the encirclement and containment of China and thus, with some reservations, desires a United States presence in that area. On the other hand, in Europe the United States is viewed as the chief bulwark of West Germany and the main source of her power and influence.[24]

Except for the last sentence of this quotation, this specialist's observation is, in my opinion, quite accurate. But the current Soviet attitude toward U.S. involvement in Europe needs exploring from the Kremlin's standpoint. So also does the notion that Moscow wishes the U.S. "out of Europe" or that it views America as the "chief bulwark of West Germany" and of possible West German "nuclearization" needs to be more closely scrutinized. Surely, Soviet propaganda alone, even some of the Soviet diplomacy in Europe since 1964, would suggest this hypothesis. On closer examination, however, these and other elements in the post-Khrushchev policy toward West Germany and the United States suggest a *more complex attitude* on the part of the Kremlin than is generally assumed in the West.

NOTES

1. Gehlen, *op. cit.*, p. 148. In keeping with the détente atmosphere of 1963–1964, Khrushchev's New Year's message to all heads of state of the world in 1964 called for a renunciation of the use of force in settling territorial disputes. No such Soviet message has ever been sent before, or since.

2. Khrushchev and his supporters among the military made a distinction between local wars and "wars of national liberation." Identified with the latter were the Algerian revolution and Castro's Cuban revolution. On one occasion, the Khrushchevite Chief of the General Staff, Marshal Sergei Biryuzov (who died in a mysterious air crash just hours after Khrushchev's ouster) significantly avoided making any specific pledge of military support for national-liberation wars (*Izvestiya*, December 11, 1963). For a discussion of this problem, see Thomas W. Wolfe, *Soviet Strategy at the Crossroads* (Cambridge, Mass.: Harvard University Press, 1965), pp. 124–129. The anti-Khrushchev military spokesmen, on the other hand, *did* indicate that military aid should be given "revolutionary forces" in national-liberation wars (Wolfe, *op. cit.*, p. 126, gives examples). Moreover, this latter group of spokesmen saw no danger of local wars (which they lumped in with national-liberation wars), escalating into world wars; one of these writers (in an interesting article in the Ministry of Defense daily *Krasnaya Zvezda [Red Star]*, November 2, 1963) cited some 70 different limited conflicts since World War II which did not escalate as proof that escalation was not inevitable.

3. B. C. Koh, "North Korea: Profile of a Garrison State," *Problems of Communism* (January–February, 1969), p. 19. This article is highly informative as a brief recapitulation of North Korean political history over the twenty years since the establishment of the Democratic People's Republic of Korea in 1948.

4. Edited text of the Twenty-nine Points may be found in *Today's Vital World Problems on Record*, vol. 2, no. 8 (1965), pp. 38–39 (published by Keynote Publications, Inc., New York).

5. *Time*, September 13, 1968; *Far Eastern Economic Review*, Hong Kong, reproduced in *Atlas* (July 1968). Data in this paragraph are from these two publications.

6. *Izvestiya*, September 13, 1968.

7. *The New York Times*, April 18, 1969.

8. *Ibid.* For an article containing much useful information on South Korea, see Emerson Chapin, "Success Story in South Korea," *Foreign Affairs* (April 1969), pp. 560–574.

9. Zbigniew K. Brzezinski, *The Soviet Bloc—Unity and Conflict* (New York: Praeger, 1960), p. 53.

10. Raymond, *op. cit.*, p. 448.

11. *Ibid.*

12. Ulam, *Expansion and Coexistence*, p. 712.

13. *Ibid.*
14. I am indebted to Michel Tatu, whose excellent account of this activity may be found in his *Power in the Kremlin from Khrushchev to Kosygin*, pp. 401–403.
15. *Ibid.*, p. 402.
16. *Pravda*, October 15, 1964.
17. Aspaturian, "Foreign Policy Perspectives in the Sixties," in Dallin and Larson, *op. cit.*, p. 154. I am indebted to Aspaturian for the excellent description of post-Khrushchev strategy as one of "double encirclement," although I do not entirely agree that this is the Soviet strategy on the western flank.
18. See the *Bulletin* of the Institute for the Study of the U.S.S.R. (September 1965), pp. 22–27, for an interesting and informative discussion of the new Soviet policy toward Germany after October 1964. The article is by Albertine Aubery and is entitled "The Change in Soviet Policy Toward Germany." Mikoyan's speech is found in *Pravda*, October 28, 1964.
19. *Pravda*, March 20, 1965.
20. *Pravda*, April 9, 1965.
21. Aubery, "The Change in Soviet Policy Toward Germany," *op. cit.*, p. 23.
22. Quoted in Aubery, *op. cit.*, p. 26.
23. Albert Perry, "Soviet Aid to Vietnam," *The Reporter* (January 12, 1967), p. 29.
24. Aspaturian, in Dallin and Larson, *op. cit.*, p. 149.

CHAPTER IX

U. S.-Soviet "Limited Coexistence" Since Khrushchev

History has imposed on our two peoples a great responsibility for the destiny of the world. . . . Our interests do not clash directly anywhere, either territorially or economically.

—N. S. KHRUSHCHEV, December 30, 1961

•   •   •

The government of the United States is in essence pursuing . . . an aggressive foreign policy directed against the Socialist countries, against the states that have liberated themselves from colonial domination, and against the revolutionary movement of the peoples.

—A. N. KOSYGIN, June 18, 1965

With the overthrow of Khrushchev and of Khrushchev's policy in his last months in office of working toward U.S.-Soviet détente, the new leaders began to reorient Soviet foreign policy, and also Soviet military strategy. Some of these post-Khrushchev departures were evident almost immediately after the coup; others surfaced only later in 1965. However, by the end of 1965, the reorientation of Soviet policy had "matured" sufficiently as to be discernible to open-eyed—and open-minded—observers in the West.

Reorientation of Soviet Policy

By setting the new policies in a condensed juxtaposition to the old ones, we can see the contrasts (see Table 7).

Several of the statements on foreign policy made by the new leaders in the immediate aftermath of the coup did not appear to suggest a worsening in U.S.-Soviet relations. The Kremlin apparently had not abandoned the principle of peaceful coexistence with the United States. Nor did the Russians appear to be plotting another "proxy war" (such as Korea, 1950–1953), least of all a major war fought with strategic weapons. This "Khrushchevism without Khrushchev" appeared to be the policy, despite the fact that the newly installed Chief of the Soviet General Staff, Marshal Matvei V. Zakharov,* was surely not known for a "dovish" position on military strategy and defense-production allocation.

On October 16, 1964, messages were widely circulated by the Kremlin to a number of Western and other governments throughout the world via the Soviet embassies in these countries, including the one in Washington, D.C. The gist of the missives from Moscow was that the Soviet Union would "continue the policy of coexistence and collaboration in the efforts to reduce tension."[1]

It is quite possible that a good deal of this Soviet reassurance that the policies of the preceding regime would be continued was a blind for what was to follow. For example, the new regime made much use of Mikoyan as the spokesman for continuation of Khrushchev's policies. It was he who met with foreign dignitaries, signed reassuring diplomatic notes, and so forth, in his capacity of Soviet "President" (Chairman of the Presidium of the U.S.S.R. Supreme Soviet, not to be confused with the Presidium of the C.P.S.U.). But as we have noted earlier, soon after the interregnum period, Mikoyan was dropped.

Reactions to Khrushchev's Ouster

Reassurances also had to be extended to the East European allies of Moscow, as well as to foreign Communist parties. Many of these regimes and

*Ironically, just a few days after Khrushchev was purged by his colleagues, the new leaders were handed a piece of luck, assuming that it was an accident: A plane carrying top officials—including Khrushchev's Chief of Staff Marshal Sergei S. Biryuzov and the shadowy figure Nikolai R. Mironov, chief of the Central Committee's Administrative Organs Department, with connections with civilian and military intelligence and security—crashed as it was approaching an airfield in Yugoslavia. It was doubly ironic that this occurred in Yugoslavia, scene of the downfall of another military figure, Marshal Georgi K. Zhukov, who was ousted from the party Presidium in October 1957— to his great surprise—while he was in Tito's homeland. Upon his death Khrushchevite Biryuzov was replaced by Marshal Zakharov, whom Khrushchev had previously removed as Chief of Staff in the spring of 1963. After his reinstallation in this important post, the reputedly "hawkish" Marshal immediately set about repudiating Khrushchev's "anti-military" policies and hinted that, under Zakharov, the military would get a much larger slice of the budgetary pie and increase their political influence.

TABLE 7.   Contrasts Between Khrushchev and Post-Khrushchev Policies

Khrushchev	Post-Khrushchev
Distinction between "wars of national liberation" and "local wars" and condemnation of the latter.	Military-political intervention in wars, uprisings and revolutionisms, with no distinction made between national-liberation and local wars (for example, in Vietnam and the Near East).
Leveling-off, perhaps even cutting of military expenditures; continuation of "big-bang" strategy of maintaining adequate stockpile of H-bombs while not necessarily reaching for parity with the United States.	Increase in military expenditures (similar development in East European Soviet bloc); program of modernization of the armed forces begun; launching of a concerted effort to attain parity with the U.S. in thermonuclear bomb stockpile and ICBMs.
Playing-*down* of "imperialist" and "aggressive" nature of American capitalism.	Playing-*up* of the "aggressive" nature of "American imperialism."
Using an emotional press campaign against Maoist China; imputing to Peking that it wants to drag U.S.S.R. into war with the U.S., for example, in Vietnam; Soviet "withdrawal" from Southeast Asia; concentration on close Soviet-Indian relationship.	Making penetrating and "sober" analyses of the domestic situation in Maoist China; suggesting that the U.S. and Red China are in collusion against U.S.S.R.; establishing positions of strength in Western Pacific and Southeast Asia "encircling" China—for example, in Vietnam and North Korea; closer relations with both India and Pakistan; stepping up Japanese-Soviet commercial intercourse.
Opening of Moscow-Bonn dialogue leading to German-Russian *rapprochement*—a policy of "killing German revanchism with friendship," possibly also a policy of revived Rapalloism.	Escalating anti-West German press campaign using alleged threat of German revanchism for tightening discipline and strengthening the Soviet *diktat* over the East European bloc; "icing" Moscow-Bonn relations.
"Peaceful coexistence" between U.S. and U.S.S.R. leading toward tangible reduction of tension, for example, partial test-ban treaty, Hot Line, U.S.-Soviet summitry, and so on.	"Peaceful coexistence" (without specific reference to American-Soviet relations) as a phase or tactic for waging "uncompromising" class struggle between "incompatible ideologies, Socialist and imperialist"; interpreting *positive* or *constructive* peaceful coexistence to mean closer relations between U.S.S.R. and new "ex-colonial" non-Communist states and the Third World generally.

TABLE 7. *(Continued)*

Khrushchev	Post-Khrushchev
"Many roads to socialism" and equal status for all parties within a loose or "parleying" world Communist relationship, falling far short of a revived Comintern or Cominform; playing down of Soviet party hegemony over the movement.[a]	Stepping up aid to world Communist movement and making allusions to "world-revolutionary process," reactivating class struggle in capitalist countries, strengthening relations between Communist parties, employing Vietnam War to "struggle against U.S. imperialism"; Soviet effort toward *organizational* expression of worldwide Communist movement and reassertion of Moscow's entitlement to a dominant role in such an organization.
Improving party and government relations between liberalized Yugoslavia and the U.S.S.R. (late 1963 to mid-October 1964).	Worsening of party and government relations between "revisionist" Yugoslavia and the U.S.S.R.—for example, as revealed in Yugoslav refusal to allow any more than partial use of its seaports by the Soviet navy and in the anti-Yugoslav Communist League Soviet press campaign, stepped up after Soviet invasion of Czechoslovakia.
Attractiveness of Soviet Socialism ("communism-by-example") as principal means of spreading Communism throughout the world; deemphasizing world revolution.	Shifting of emphasis from passive "communism in one country" and communism-by-example to that of waging an *"offensive against the positions held by imperialism"*[b] and *"activating"* the world-revolutionary movement.
Concept that a thermonuclear war *can* be avoided, that "no one wins" a thermonuclear war fought with ICBMs, and that mutual deterrence is good insurance against its outbreak, even when the "balance of terror" is not entirely equal.	Thermonuclear war can be avoided but also *can be won* if it did break out; mutual deterrence is not enough, since steady and continuous technological advances in defensive and offensive rocketry significantly tip the balance in one or another's favor; Soviet effort toward acquiring superiority and a balance in their favor.
Concept of a short push-button war involving ICBMs, should one break out between the superpowers, viewed as highly unlikely.	Concept of a *long war*, and one that would include several phases and a *wide range* of weapons, both "sophisticated" and conventional; such a war not so unlikely, given "increased tensions" in the world.

[a]Subject as brief recapitulations are to be oversimplification, this one concerning Soviet

party *apparats* had formed close links with the Khrushchev regime or with the purged First Secretary personally. The sudden overthrow of Khrushchev, after ten years as C.P.S.U. First Secretary, obviously shocked the foreign comrades. For a few days after the coup, some of the foreign Communist parties, including ruling ones in Eastern Europe, issued statements hinting that they did not altogether approve of Khrushchev's ouster. For example, the First Secretary of the Hungarian Worker's Party, Janos Kadar, made this statement on October 19, 1964:

I think that Comrade Khrushchev had acquired great merits in the struggle against the Stalinist personality cult and in the preservation of peace. The hundreds of thousands of Hungarians who greeted Khrushchev in the recent past and also this year in Hungary—and they did it from their hearts—as the representative of the great Soviet Party, state, and people and as an unrelenting fighter for peace, did well to do so. They need have no afterthoughts about this.[2]

This statement by the Communist leader of a Soviet bloc country was extremely unusual for the way it departed from the line laid down in Moscow. Particularly since the Soviet press, through front-page editorials (October 17), had already asserted authoritatively that Khrushchev had been guilty of profound errors, of "hare-brained schemes" and "subjectivism," and so on.

Some of the "satellite" press even went so far as to suggest that the post-Khrushchev leaders *should* continue the policies of their predecessor. The Czechoslovaks, the Hungarians, even the East Germans and Poles, all made pleas for the "continuation and realization of the Leninist General Line as determined . . . by the Twentieth and Twenty-second Party Congress," a bloc euphemism for continuation of Khrushchev-style foreign and domestic policies.

When it came to the Yugoslav reaction to Khrushchev's precipitous downfall, a certain pessimism was manifest. On October 19 the Moscow correspondent for the *Zagreb Vjesnik* was obviously dismayed at the coup in Moscow.[3] With an expertise reserved only to Communist correspondents in Communist countries, the Moscow stringer, Bilic, adroitly compared the

---

imperial control under Khrushchev needs an added explanation. For one thing, Khrushchev was anything but opposed to closing ranks in the bloc. But he chose mostly political persuasion and economic coordination as a means toward attaining this rather than military occupation, as in the case of Czechoslovakia, August 1968.

[b]The most recent expression of the post-Khrushchev "offensive against imperialism" idea may be found in Ivan V. Kapitonov's address on Lenin's 99th birthday, *Pravda*, April 23, 1969. To wit: "New perspectives have been opened for an offensive against imperialism and for seriously moving forward the cause of social and national liberation of the peoples." Kapitonov is one of the newer secretaries of the C.P.S.U. appointed by Brezhnev and appears to be in charge of party cadres, the position he held when he was dismissed by his former boss, Khrushchev.

October Revolution slogans for 1964 (published after Khrushchev's fall) with the quite different slogans for 1963 and of May Day 1964. Bilic found that the 1963 and pre-coup 1964 slogans were based on the Khrushchev-oriented Twenty-second Party Congress of 1961, whereas the *post*-Khrushchev October Revolution slogans were "anti-revisionist" and "anti-Yugoslav" in character.

Bilic's suspicions were justified. The policy toward Yugoslavia did steadily chill during the post-Khrushchev years. Meantime, Soviet references to the "anti-Yugoslav" Twenty-*first* Party Congress of the C.P.S.U. (1959), an "Extraordinary" Congress—which was indeed extraordinary in several respects and particularly for its anti-Tito line—began to appear in Russian media. A minor cold war eventually set in between Yugoslav publications and those of the Soviet Union in 1967 and 1968. After the Soviet invasion of Czechoslovakia in August 1968, party relations between the Yugoslav Communist League and the C.P.S.U. were so poor that they were openly accusing each other of deviation—the Yugoslavs calling the post-Khrushchev leaders "neo-Stalinist," the Russians calling the Yugoslav Communists "revisionists."

The nonruling C.P.s were similarly jolted by the coup. Some of the Western Communist party leaders were not content merely to request "clarification" from the Kremlin for what had occurred in the early part of the second week in October (October 11–14). They began to draw "concrete conclusions" from the coup—and they were not favorable. For example, the Belgian Communist Party leader, Ernest Burnelle, described the events in Moscow as "astonishing." He went on to demand more autonomy for individual Communist Parties. Relations between the Belgian party and the C.P.S.U., Burnelle asserted, were in a process of "complete evolution." Several other West European parties likewise hinted that their displeasure with the coup would spur them on to greater independence from Moscow. The Swedish Communists even went so far as to state that Khrushchev had been removed without due regard for Soviet laws and the C.P.S.U. Party Statute: "The manner in which Khrushchev resigned or was forced to resign leaves a bitter taste in one's mouth."[4]

These reactions in the immediate aftermath of the overthrow of Khrushchev are significant in several respects as pertains to foreign policy. First, the mostly unfavorable reaction and the attributions to Khrushchev's peace line suggest that the foreign comrades were not sure that the new leaders would follow, as they had stated they would, Khrushchev's General Line. On the contrary. Many ruling and nonruling foreign party *apparats* displayed a certain anxiety about the consequences that Khrushchev's overthrow would have for relations between the Soviets and other Communist countries and between the C.P.S.U. and foreign C.P.s, if not for Soviet foreign policy generally.

Hints of Changes to Come

On October 19, the new First Secretary, Leonid I. Brezhnev, gave assurances more or less similar to those that had been circulated from Moscow to the world's Soviet embassies a few days·earlier. But in this first major address by the Kremlin leader, there were one or two hints of new things to come.[5] Brezhnev laid rather unusual stress, for example, upon "strengthening the unity of the great Commonwealth of fraternal Socialist nations." This was in striking contrast to the intimations of new-found autonomy and free- dom-of-action voiced by various foreign Communist leaders in the days immediately preceding—or for that matter following—the new First Secre- tary's address. The new First Secretary also indicated that efforts would be undertaken to "overcome the difficulties" within the ranks of the world Com- munist movement—meaning especially "polycentrism." The C.P.S.U., said Brezhnev, would "rally together all fraternal parties on the basis of Marx- ism-Leninism." Even more significantly, Brezhnev explicitly altered the Khrushchev line on the "satisfactory level" of Soviet defense capabilities. Instead, he asserted that the new leadership would "take measures to *strengthen the country's defense capabilities*," since the "imperialist forces" (meaning especially the U.S.) constitute a threat to world peace.

Soviet "Hawks" Ascendant in the New Regime

While these and other straws in the wind in the weeks following the coup eluded most of the correspondents· and columnists writing in the Western press, the policies and deeds of the new regime did begin to assume a rec- ognizable shape during the next six months, at least to close observers of Soviet affairs.[6]

First came the *reshuffling of the hierarchy*—always a harbinger of things to come in the Kremlin, for good or ill. The initial major personnel changes to take place in Moscow, once the leaders of the Soviet media (editors of *Pravda* and *Izvestiya* and the director of Soviet radio and TV) had been jettisoned, obviously reflected a reorientation of policy, foreign and domestic. *Dmitri F. Ustinov*, the "defense tsar," whom Khrushchev had kicked up- stairs with the reorganization of the C.P.S.U. in late 1962, was put back at the center of power, being appointed by Brezhnev and his associates to the position of candidate member of the Presidium of the party, the highest party organ in the country. The chief of the K.G.B., *Vladimir Ye. Semi- chastny*, was promoted to full member of the C.P.S.U. Central Committee; two "hard-liners," *Pyotr Ye. Shelest*, head of the Ukrainian C.P., and *Alexan- der N. Shelepin*, supervising security and whose relations with the Marshals are close, were appointed to full membership on the party Presidium; *Alexei A. Yepishev*, Chief of the Main Political Administration of the Soviet Army and Navy and a reputed hard-liner,* was promoted to full membership in the C.P.S.U. Central Committee.

Meanwhile, several of those known as *moderating* influences in the Kremlin began noticeably to weaken in authority. Foremost among these was *Anastas I. Mikoyan*. It was he who had launched the de-Stalinization campaign at the Twentieth Party Congress in 1956 and who often acted as spokesman for "reasonableness" toward the United States. Although merely Soviet "President" since July 1964 (when he acquired the post vacated by Brezhnev when Brezhnev was propitiously shifted to the party Secretariat), a ceremonial post in many respects, Mikoyan nonetheless remained a venerable and influential member of the Khrushchev "kitchen cabinet." (Mikoyan and Khrushchev were the only current members of the Presidium to have sojourned in the United States.) He was also a close friend of the First Secretary's, the two often vacationing together. Incidentally, he was the sole party Presidium member to accompany Khrushchev on his ill-fated vacation to Sochi on the Black Sea coast in October 1964 at the very time the plot to overthrow Khrushchev was being engineered back in Moscow. Thus, it appears that Mikoyan was not one of the conspirators, a fact that may have contributed to his steady eclipse during the post-Khrushchev period and to his alienation from his colleagues in the Kremlin. Accordingly, after the overthrow of Khrushchev, Mikoyan's role in the hierarchy became increasingly "titular" and less and less effective. Compared to his other colleagues' attendance at conferences, their meetings with party delegations from abroad, and their travels to the capitals of Soviet bloc countries, Mikoyan's strictly *state* (that is not party or government) business was routine and ceremonial. Finally, in a few months, Mikoyan was demoted. He became a "member," not Chairman as he had been previously, of the numerous Presidium of the Supreme Soviet of the U.S.S.R. Stepping down as Chairman (or Soviet "President"), Mikoyan, the Armenian, gave way to the Ukrainian, Nikolai V. Podgorny, the new member of the official Soviet triumvirate.

The steady decline of this formerly prestigious spokesman for Soviet consumerism, for détente with the West, and for curbing the military appetite— Anastas I. Mikoyan—took place in inverse proportion to the rise of the "internationalist" and ideological forces headed by *Mikhail A. Suslov*, an old enemy of Mikoyan's.

From his vantage point of Second Secretary of the C.P.S.U., which he acquired as a result of the purge of Khrushchev, and also as a full member of the party Presidium, the veteran Suslov was in an extremely strong po-

*Should there be any doubt on this score, see Yepishev's article in *Kommunist*, No. 6, 1969, parts of which were quoted by Anatole Shub in *The Washington Post*, April 27, 1969, p. 1, headlined "Russia Says West Plots War, Warns It Would Be Loser."

sition. And he used it. Although it took several months to accomplish, Suslov (assisted by the *apparatchik* Sergei P. Trapeznikov) had sufficiently cleansed the media, books, academic institutes, editorial boards of most of the scholarly *tolstiye* ("fat" journals), *et al.*, so that rarely if ever by late 1965 did an article appear which smacked even remotely of the doctrines on foreign and military strategy current during the last months of Khrushchev. Since this restoration of the "correct party line" on international affairs reflected the changed attitude toward America after October 1964 and had to precede and accompany any change in those relations to protect the sanctity of the party line, it is important to examine it.

As was already mentioned, Khrushchev's position on U.S.-Soviet relations after the Cuban missile showdown of October 1962 was one of live-and-let-live and is probably best summed up by the following:

> History has imposed on our two peoples a great responsibility for the destiny of the world. . . . Our interests do not clash directly anywhere, either territorially or economically.[7]

Khrushchev was an advocate of U.S.-Soviet mutual deterrence and scorned those (whom he called "metal-eaters") who would pour rubles and resources into arms or into modernization of the conventional branches of the armed forces. A below-parity stockpile of nuclear weapons, he thought, would suffice nicely to "frighten the capitalists."

As might be expected, Khrushchev's position on these matters from mid-1963 to October 1964 got support from various circles *outside* the immediate C.P.S.U. *apparat; in* the party *apparat* there was only lukewarm support or none at all, as it turned out. For one thing, not all of the military writers took the pro-local war or pro-long war position, as we have already indicated. Moreover, some academicians elaborating on problems in international affairs seemed to greet the emerging Khrushchev policies in the summer and early fall with enthusiasm, while not necessarily relishing the sometimes "crude" First Secretary personally.[*] One theoretic problem concerned the ideological treatment of the office of the Presidency of the United States.

Traditional or "Suslovist" Marxism-Leninism (-Stalinism) views the office of the President—indeed, the whole political "superstructure" in America—as the tool of "big monopoly capitalism," or, in abbreviated form, "Wall Street." Marx, after all, had taught that economics is the base, politics the superstructure, of society. So, the Congress, the Supreme Court, and even the President himself all function as the captains of industry say they should or as the forces and laws of "monopoly capitalism" dictate.

However, during the post-Cuban Crisis period (1963–1964) when the par-

---

[*]Khrushchev's boastfulness and his occasional rough treatment of intellectuals (although it was Khrushchev who approved publication of Solzhenitsyn's candid *A Day in the Life of Ivan Denisovich*) did not win friends among Russia's intellectuals. Even criticism of the shoe-banging incident at the U.N. in 1960 died hard among Soviet intellectuals, who regarded their leader's behavior with disgust.

tial test-ban treaty was signed (over the objections of several spokesmen for the Soviet military) and a closer relationship to America was emerging, not to mention other developments in the direction of relaxation of tension, the traditional approach had begun to lose ground to a kind of "revisionism." Articles and books began to take the line that the American President *might well act powerfully in his own right.* The Soviet view at that time of the American decision-making power thus tended to be non-Marxist, non-Leninist, and non-Stalinist.[8] Surely, it fit neatly into Khrushchev's scheme of "summit diplomacy," that is, settling problems directly with the powerful political heads of state or heads of government, and with the head-of-government/head-of-state President of the United States.

Another development in the Soviet treatment of America toward the end of the Khrushchev era concerned the distinction between "hotheads" (*besheniye*) and "reasonables" (*razumniye*), which has already been explained in the preceding chapter. *Razumniye* began to disappear.

In the important area of "class struggle" in the United States, the line in the journals in 1963–1964, and with a certain "political lag" extending midway into 1965, was that

1. The U.S. economy was in better shape than had been previously conceded in Soviet writings, and the chances of revolution therefore slight; to expect another American depression in the near future was foolhardy, Keynesian policies having been effective.
2. It was highly unlikely that the hotheads would get control of things in Washington.
3. There were many elements in American society—yes, even in Wall Street—who would, by their influence and reasonableness, help keep American imperialism tame and sufficiently sensitive to the threat of mutual annihilation in a Third World War should it involve the U.S. and the U.S.S.R. on opposing sides, thus ensuring a protracted period of lasting peace.

In short, the Soviet academic community, joined by professional diplomat-memoirists, diplomatic service institutes, and instructors and "generalists" of various sorts began to discuss openly the consequences that the nascent policies being initiated by Khrushchev in 1963–1964 would have for the overall philosophy of Soviet foreign policy. It was a generally optimistic assessment. But it was also in many respects strictly *non*-ideological in the traditional sense of "ideology," as were several of Khrushchev's "de-ideologized" foreign policies.* And because it undercut or ignored ideology, it aroused the ire of the ideologues.

*As mentioned earlier, Professor Vernon A. Asbaturian terms this phenomenon under Khrushchev the "de-ideologization of Soviet foreign policy goals" and the resort to "traditional operational norms and assumptions of interest, security, survival, economic and material well-being, national pride and prestige" which were more characteristic of Soviet foreign policy in the years 1962–1964 than earlier when world revolution and world communism were central in Soviet foreign policy behavior (see Asbaturian, "Foreign Policy Perspectives in the Sixties," in Dallin and Larson [eds.], *op. cit.*, p. 132).

As was suggested, Suslov's campaign in 1965–1966 to cleanse the schools and journals of this expression of Khrushchevism and pro-Americanism ("The only country the leaders of the C.P.S.U. look up to is the United States," cried Peking[9]) was not immediately successful in stopping de-ideologization. For example, take a book published by the Institute of International Economy and International Relations attached to the U.S.S.R. Academy of Sciences entitled *Motive Forces in the Foreign Policy of the U.S.A.* and published in 1965.[10]

In *Motive Forces* we find the *razumniye* ("reasonable men") characterization applied not only to Lyndon B. Johnson, but to his two predecessors, John F. Kennedy and Dwight D. Eisenhower (the latter's implication in the U–2 "spy plane" episode of May 1960 being conveniently forgotten). In the book, too, the White House was appraised as a strong institution in its own right which, far from being influenced by "Wall Street" alone, had to listen and respond to *public opinion!* American newspaper columnists were cited in such a way as to indicate to a reasonably well-informed Soviet reader that American politics was strongly affected by such *non*-class factors as differences of opinion within the "ruling circles" or the establishment and within the public generally. *Motive Forces* even went so far as to say that American use of force in its relations with the U.S.S.R. and the Soviet bloc was *less likely to characterize Washington's behavior in the future.* Suprisingly, the book spoke of a "community of national interest" existing between the two superpowers. Echoing Khrushchev's statement quoted above, *Motive Forces* further asserted:

At the present time there exist no territorial [or] economic disputes and conflicts between [the United States and the Soviet Union]; their national intrerests do not collide either globally or regionally.

And there were a few other books and articles. In most cases, they originated with the aforementioned Institute of International Economy and International Relations (IMEMO is the Soviet acronym), attached to the Soviet Academy of Sciences, or in other nonparty-*apparat* circles.

While Suslov and Trapeznikov* were taking action against these and other Khrushchevist hangovers, several important "wrinkles" became evident within the Agitation and Propaganda and Ideological Departments and other ideological subdivisions of the C.P.S.U. Central Committee from late 1964 and well into 1965. This is not the place to go into various Kremlinological nuances beyond noting the excessive shuffling and reshuffling of personnel

---

*The "little Zhdanov," Sergei P. Trapeznikov, chief of the C.P.S.U. Central Committee Department of Sciences and Educational Institutions, was appointed to his post in early 1965 and was described by Dr. Andrei Sakharov, the Soviet scientist (see p. 134 above), as a "shrewd and highly consistent man [whose views] are basically Stalinist" (Sakharov, *op. cit.*, p. 56).

that took place within these several Central Committee departments, as well as on the various editorial boards of academic and literary journals and other publications from October 1964 through 1965. Clearly, this jockeying was of high order importance, revealed by the fact that many of the new appointees had excellent connections with certain old and new members of the post-Khrushchev Secretariat and Presidium. There were even some very evident "national" tugs-of-war going on with respect to these positions—sometimes a Great Russian getting the job, sometimes a Belorussian, and sometimes a Ukrainian, thus reflecting the national backgrounds of the top-most leaders—for example, Brezhnev and Suslov (Russian), Podgorny and Polyansky (Ukrainian), Mazurov and Masherov (Belorussian), and so forth.

So bitter and indecisive was this in-fighting over ideological control within the *apparat* in late 1964 and into 1965 that the Twenty-third Party Congress, which should have met in 1965, could not meet until 1966. A C.P.S.U. party congress involves a great deal of ideological decision-making and preparation *before* it can be held. By the time the delayed Twenty-third Party Congress was convened, March 29-April 8, 1966, ideological reorganization of the party and purging of Khrushchevism in foreign policy and military doctrine had been largely completed, although there is no sure guarantee that they were free of all impurities even after 1966.

Before turning to the watershed party congress of 1966, it is important to know what the military strategists and their spokesmen were saying in the weeks and months *immediately* following the overthrow of the "hare-brained" Khrushchev. This bears upon U.S.-Soviet relations.

It became quite obvious, even within two months after the coup, that the military had at last come into its own. Articles began to appear in *Red Star*, the Ministry of Defense daily, which followed *in toto* the line laid down in Marshal V. D. Sokolovsky's book *Military Strategy* (see above, pp. 175–176). The same trend was observed in other military publications. Sometimes these spokesmen for the military openly accused the purged First Secretary of having frustrated the strengthening of the military capabilities of the U.S.S.R. (Khrushchev, you recall, had said a few weeks before his downfall that "the defense of the country is at a satisfactory level" [*Pravda*, October 2, 1964].) The accusation was never made by name—Khrushchev was soon to become a *1984*-like "un-person"—but rather by mentioning the Central Committee plenum of October 1964, which sanctified the coup, as a turning point in a new party policy respecting the military.

New Policy on Military Strategy

Military strategy, too, figured in the *post*-Khrushchev writings of military publicists. The names in the by-lines over some of these articles were to figure in events later in the post-Khrushchev period. One of these, Colonel-

General Sergei M. Shtemenko* (appointed Chief of Staff of the Warsaw Pact Forces in August 1968 and a key figure in the execution of the invasion of Czechoslovakia) took up the cudgels within two months after the coup for a more radical military-strategy line. General Shtemenko strongly attacked the "big-bang" or strategic-weapon strategy of Khrushchev and his military advisors, including, of course, the late Chief of Staff, Marshal Biryuzov. The ICBM may be the "queen of battle," conceded Shtemenko, but the ground forces, air and naval forces, and combined operations by all types of forces had not therefore lessened in importance "to achieve full victory" in a modern war.[12] Far from it. What the Soviet armed forces needed now, said the general, was a *broader-based* military establishment than what the Soviets presently had. Moreover, as to the issue of the long versus the short war, there was no doubt that the next major (and nuclear) war would not end quickly. It would be a *long war* and would involve the application of many types of weapons.

Shtemenko was joined in these points of view by other military commanders and publicists who were known for their writings attacking the Khrushchev strategy *before* the coup. Among these spokesmen were Marshal Sokolovsky and Major-General M. I. Cherednichenko, the latter also playing an important part in planning the invasion of Czechoslovakia in 1968. Even the new Chief of Staff, Marshal M. V. Zakharov, found time to get his views into print during the very first months of the Brezhnev-Kosygin-*et al.* regime.[13]

From all of these writings and speeches (for example, Defense Minister Marshal Malinovsky's address atop Lenin's Tomb at the October Revolution ceremony in Red Square on November 7, 1964[14]), it was obvious that the official line during the last year of Khrushchev's reign had been changed once the First Secretary was ousted. The changes were along the lines of the position taken by the generals and marshals and military writers who had obliquely attacked the First Secretary and his immediate circle of military brass and advisers in the closing months before October 14, 1964. Summing up this post-Khrushchev discussion in the military press and the changes that took place, the following new positions on military strategy emerged, some of them overtly, some of them covertly:

1. Tensions and the danger of a new war have increased.
2. The "capitalist imperialists" could be counted on to launch local wars, which would not necessarily escalate into big ones and which, if joined in by any

*General Shtemenko (age 62) was Stalin's Chief of Staff at the bitter end of Stalin's regime. Just before Stalin was officially reported to have had a stroke, Shtemenko was replaced by Marshal V. D. Sokolovsky (February 1953). The late Boris Nicolaevsky, well-known Western Soviet analyst, speculated that it was Shtemenko who was to be Stalin's aide in a new military adventure that the dictator was planning just before he died. Shtemenko's star has been rising steadily ever since Khrushchev's overthrow.

Communist powers on the side opposite to that of the "imperialists," would be *just* (that is legitimate)* national-liberation wars.
3. Should a worldwide conflict break out, and whether or not the "surprise-attack" tactic were used at the beginning, the war would not be a short one, but would pass through many phases and involve many types of weapons.
4. Less-than-parity in ICBMs was an unsafe strategy; the Soviets must continue to work toward superiority in this and other strategic respects over the "imperialists."**
5. A Third World War is by no means unlikely and *could be won*, should the imperialists be so foolish as to launch it; moreover, a Communist victory in such a war would spell the end of capitalism in the world.†

In conjunction with the changed line on military strategy, there were corresponding changes in personnel within the Soviet General Staff after Khrushchev's ouster. Table 8 shows the composition of the General Staff as it looked after the coup and through 1969. The date on which the position was assumed by the given general or marshal is shown together with the date of birth, where it has been determined.

*In Russian, *spravedlivaya voina*, a "just war."

**The Soviet effort, launched after Khrushchev's fall, to attain ICBM parity with the United States had become so nearly successful by spring 1969 that President Nixon's Secretary of Defense Melvin R. Laird began to warn of the Soviets' attaining parity in numbers of ICBMs. Secretary of the Air Force Robert C. Seamans, Jr. told Congress early in 1969 that the Soviets are fast approaching a 1-to-1 relationship with the U.S. in ICBMs. At present, said Laird on April 24, 1969, the U.S. has 1,054 long-range missiles to the Soviets' present 1,000. According to the prestigious London Institute of Strategic Studies, September 11, 1969, the Soviets have nearly reached parity and deploy 1,050 ICBMs. The U.S.S.R. deploys at the rate of 250 new missiles a year, Laird said (*The New York Times*, April 26 and September 12, 1969).

†The line introduced by the former Soviet Premier Georgi M. Malenkov in the autumn of 1953, after Stalin's death, that a new world war would mean the "destruction of world civilization" was occasionally reiterated in the last years of Khrushchev's reign. In attacking the Chinese, Khrushchev once pointed out that the imperialist "paper tiger" had "nuclear teeth" and was therefore very dangerous. In a Third World War, the First Secretary said, the proletariat would suffer terrible and unnecessary hardships. Such a war should therefore be avoided since, in a sense, no one could "win" it. For a recent reiteration of the line that the Communists *can* win a Third World War and that *capitalism would be destroyed in it*, see the *Kommunist* statement by Soviet General A. A. Yepishev, quoted in *The Washington Post*, April 27, 1969: "A Third World War, if imperialism should start one, would be the decisive class conflict between the two antagonistic systems. From the side of the imperialist states, this war would be a continuation of the criminal, reactionary, and aggressive policies of imperialism. From the side of the Soviet Union and the countries of the Socialist commonwealth, it would be the continuation of the revolutionary policies of freedom and independence of the Socialist state, a guarantee of the construction of socialism and communism, and a legal and justified counteraction to aggression," in *Kommunist*, No. 6 (April 1969), p. 69. The same statement was made by Marshal N. I. Krylov in *Sovetskaya Rossiya*, August 30, 1969.

TABLE 8.   U.S.S.R. Ministry of Defense (1969)

Minister
Marshal A. A. Grechko (b. 1903), 1967

First Deputy Ministers
Army General S. L. Sokolov (b. 1911), April 1967
Marshal I. I. Yakubovsky (b. 1912), April 1967
Marshal M. V. Zakharov (b. 1898), November 1964

Deputy Ministers
Army General P. F. Batitsky (b. 1910), October 1966
Admiral S. G. Gorshkov (b. 1910), February 1962ᵃ
Colonel General A. N. Komarovsky (b. 1906), 1954
Air Marshal P. S. Kutakhov (b. 1920), 1969
Marshal N. I. Krylov (b. 1903), May 1963
General of the Army S. S. Maryakhin (b. 1911), 1968
Marshal K. A. Moskalenko (b. 1902), October 1960
Army General V. A. Penkovsky (b. 1904), July 1964
Army General I. G. Pavlovsky (b. 1909), April 1967
Air Chief Marshal K. A. Vershinin (b. 1900), February 1957

GENERAL STAFF (1969)
Chief
Marshal M. V. Zakharovᵃ (b. 1898), November 1964

First Deputy Chiefs
Army General M. I. Kazakov (b. 1901), early 1965
Colonel-General N. V. Ogarkov (b. 1917), 1968

Deputy Chiefs
Colonel-General M. I. Povaly, November 1964
Colonel-General P. I. Ivashutin (b. 1909), 1966
Colonel-General A. V. Gerasimov, 1965

Party Committee Secretary
Colonel-General P. A. Lapkin, late 1964

ᵃFirst Deputy Minister of Defense from 1956 to 1962.
ᵇUpon his appointment as Chief of the Soviet General Staff, Zakharov (who had been Chief of Staff from 1960–1963) also assumed the post of First Deputy Minister of Defense. Of the four First Deputy Ministers, all are post-Khrushchev appointees. The Minister at the time of Khrushchev's ouster was Marshal Rodion Y. Malinovsky, the military mastermind of the Soviet-backed North Korean effort in the Korean War (1950–1953), and who is believed to have played a role in Khrushchev's overthrow. Malinovsky died in 1967. A debate thereupon ensued between the party and the military over whether Marshal Malinovsky's replacement should be a military man or a civilian. The civilian contender was Dmitri F. Ustinov, chief of the whole defense-industry bureaucracy. The party obviously lost the argument, because it was the military candidate, Marshal A. A. Grechko, who was finally appointed, after weeks of delay. It had been Marshal G. K. Zhukov who had set the post-Stalin precedent for filling

As an extremely well-qualified Soviet specialist has observed, the post-Khrushchev leadership, by altering the strategy line of its predecessor regime, has reverted to the "Stalin line of 1948–1952." Anatole Shub of *The Washington Post* further explains:

The Stalin line of 1948–1952 . . . also charged that the West was preparing a third world war. In September 1953, Georgi Malenkov . . . made the first attempted break away from that view. . . . However, it was not until the Soviet 20th Party Congress in February, 1956, that Nikita Khrushchev and other Kremlin leaders began seriously preaching 'coexistence' and acknowledging that nuclear war was a horror far exceeding in importance the East-West political conflict.

Only during Khrushchev's conflict with the Chinese, starting in 1958, did the Kremlin become explicit in recognizing that even a bad peace was preferable to a 'just' nuclear war.

The post-Khrushchev administration has steadily, although undramatically, retreated from the 'coexistence' line, ceased stressing the dangers of nuclear holocaust and accelerated offensive and defensive rocket development. Emphasis on negotiations between the great powers has given way to stress on strengthening Soviet military potential in the 'struggle for peace.' . . . Whatever has remained of the coexistence line has been largely for export.[15]

Foreign Policy Pronouncements at the 1966 Party Congress

Examination of the major speeches made by the top leaders at the Twenty-third Party Congress yields a great deal of information concerning the new departures in Soviet foreign policy after October 1964. A degree of theoretical entrenchment had taken place by that time. The revised ideological foundations for the Soviet foreign policy had been firmly established by March 1966, so that the Kremlin's new posture toward the United States could also be discerned.

Before we analyze what transpired at the most recent party congress, it would be helpful to set forth a number of actual Soviet developments in Soviet foreign relations and other developments which immediately preceded the March-April 1966 party conclave. Listing them briefly:

1. Moves in the military and defense-industry complex in the direction of creating an up-to-date flexible-response military establishment, including Soviet

---

this position with a *professional* military man; before Stalin's death the holder of the position of Minister of Defense often went to "political marshals" of the type of N. A. Bulganin or K. A. Voroshilov.

SOURCE: *Bulletin* of the Institute for the Study of the U.S.S.R., Vol. XIV, No. 7, July 1967, p. 42.

"Black Beret" commandos of a refurbished marine corps, aircraft carriers, MIRVs, FOBs, ABMs, SS-9s, etc.*

2. Opening of the first Vietcong Mission on Soviet soil, in January 1965.

3. Various high-level visits to or from Hanoi, North Vietnam, involving top Soviet military and civilian officials and culminating in February 1965 (*before* retaliatory U.S. air raids on North Vietnam for the bloody Communist sneak attacks against Pleiku and Qui Nhon had begun) in the round-robin visits by the new Premier, Alexei N. Kosygin, to Hanoi (North Vietnam), Pyongyang (North Korea), and Peking (China), where undoubtedly the important message to the three East Asian capitals was that the new rulers in the Kremlin *would fulfill their "revolutionary duty" in Vietnam***

4. The revealing scuffles in front of the American Embassy in the late winter of 1965 between Cossack-like Soviet mounted police on the one hand and frantic and fanatical Chinese (and possibly some North Vietnamese, too), who spattered the American Embassy building at 19/13 Tchaikovsky Street

---

*This modernization program was not immediately evident in the *published* version of the Soviet national budget containing expenditures on defense. In fact, some 500 million rubles were supposedly *cut* from defense for 1965, while increased expenditures for the modernization program were concealed within other budgetary categories—namely for "scientific research" or "other expenditures not shown." On this point, see Timothy Sosnovy, "The Soviet Military Budget," *Foreign Affairs* (July 1965), pp. 490–91. See also Thomas W. Wolfe, "Problems of Soviet Defense Policy Under the New Regime," Rand Corporation, Document P–3098 (March 1965), p. 4. Wolfe observes: "Given the fact that the single published line-term for defense expenditure in the annual Soviet budget has been a notoriously poor guide in the past to actual allocation of resources for military purposes, there was room for reasonable doubt that the new budget necessarily told the whole story." Development of new weapons, escalated Soviet aid to Vietnam, and others eventually surfaced in the form of greatly increased defense expenditures overtly listed in the published budgetary expenditures for 1966 through 1969. Cf. J. G. Godaire, "The Claim of the Soviet Military Establishment," in *Dimensions of Soviet Economic Power*, hearings of the Joint Economic Committee, Congress of the United States (Washington: U.S. Government Printing Office, 1962), pp. 36–46.

**It should have been obvious from the aforementioned developments respecting Vietnam and the other post-Khrushchev developments that the U.S. bombing attacks on North Vietnam, while Kosygin was in the Far East, had nothing to do with the *prior* decision in Moscow to send the Premier to Hanoi. Nevertheless, some persons in the West complained of "poor timing" by the Johnson Administration in launching the attacks. Kosygin was accompanied on his trip to Hanoi by three experts, whose specialties revealed at least part of the intent of the new Premier's mission: Air Chief Marshal K. A. Vershinin, an expert on *fighter defense*; Marshal of Aviation Ye. F. Loginov, Minister of Civil Aviation and specialist on *helicopters and airlift operations*; and G. S. Sidorovich, Deputy Chairman of the State Committee for Foreign Economic Relations, an expert on *military aid* (*Pravda*, February 6, 1965). In retrospect, it appears that the Soviet military specialists brought their particular brands of knowledge to Hanoi in expectation of what U.S. military strategy would be in the months to come and to prepare the North Vietnamese for an escalated Soviet presence in this "proxy war" against "imperialism." It is possible that Kosygin's talks with North Vietnamese and North Korean leaders four and a half years later on the occasion of Ho Chi Minh's funeral in Hanoi and his discussion with Chou En-lai in Peking at the same time in September 1969 concerned Soviet Vietnam policy.

with ink and broke windows—an example of Maoist taunting of the Kremlin staged directly in front of an *American* "imperialist" installation in the Soviet capital (the Soviets, incidentally, merely confined the demonstration and did little to stop the demonstrators or to prevent considerable damage to the building)

5. Strong personal condemnation of President Johnson, in speeches by top Soviet officials, including Brezhnev, and in the Soviet press

6. Solidifying relations with North Korea, including greatly increased military aid

7. Soviet warning of a spread of the Vietnam War to neighboring countries in Southeast Asia coupled with Soviet courting of Prince Sihanouk of Cambodia, India, and Burma

8. Calming the stormy relations between Russia's two southern neighbors, India and Pakistan, when the Soviets, represented by Premier Kosygin, acted as a go-between in helping the two countries reach a settlement at Tashkent in January 1966; this was followed by Soviet military aid to both

9. "Building bridges" to Gaullist France, one of the purposes being to solidify relations with a power lying to the west of the German Federal Republic and which had all but detached itself from N.A.T.O.

10. Moves aimed at tightening discipline within the Warsaw Pact countries of the Soviet bloc, and exercising "vigilance" against encouragement from within or without these countries of a drift toward Yugoslav-style liberalization and revisionism

11. Activization of the foreign "Communist *armies*"—the term "armies" used in the Soviet Union for the first time in many years as a metaphor for Communist Party movements in capitalist, non-Communist, or ex-colonial countries

12. Moves toward achieving closer relations with the more militant anti-Israeli elements and ruling circles in Moslem North Africa—for example, in Algeria, the U.A.R., and Syria

These developments, when added to American foreign policy initiatives and responses and to a number of *domestic* policy changes and events within the Soviet Union, all pointed in the direction of *de-Khrushchevization of Soviet policy* by many of the very colleagues whose careers Khrushchev had helped to advance when he was in power. By the time the Twenty-third Party Congress had opened at the end of March 1966, a number of the pronouncements made at the Congress were not quite as earthshaking as they otherwise might have been. But it was perhaps too often remarked in the West—even by certain "Kremlinologists," during and after this congress—that the new leaders had behaved like mere "clerks" in grey-flannel suits and felt homburgs; they had lost their "revolutionary fervor," some said.*

---

*I. V. Kapitonov, a Secretary of the C.P.S.U., said on a related point (April 22, 1969 [*Pravda*, April 23, 1969]): "The sharpness of [recent] class struggles has completely repudiated the fantasies of bourgeois and revisionist ideologues that the proletariat in capitalist countries has lost its revolutionary fervor [*revolyutsionnost*]." The post-Khrushchev leadership claims that its own *revolyutsionnost* has matched that of the proletariat in capitalist countries.

A "dull party congress, no excitement as in the days of Khrushchev," said others. This was a congress, they said, which only reflected the lackluster and quietistic conservativism of the leaders who had staged it.

Dull or not, and despite the sartorial sameness of the present Soviet collectivirs, the Twenty-third Party Congress of the C.P.S.U. in Moscow was most certainly not crustaceous or tired. From March 29 to April 8, in fact, the Palace of Congresses inside the Kremlin walls rang with the strains of the "Internationale" and with the loud voices that unprecedentedly sang *all* (!) the verses to it. The speeches bristled and crackled with militancy. Suslov's concluding report on the congress's special resolution on Vietnam was not only un-clerk-like; it was enough to curl one's hair. The brittle, tenor voice of this *éminence grise* almost screeched as it echoed in the gigantic Rockefeller Muisc Hall-like setting of the congress.

The main address was given by First Secretary Leonid I. Brezhnev, who was given the Stalinist title of "General-Secretary" by the end of the congress. Brezhnev spoke in a low, somber voice, intoning a leonine snarl when the topic was "capitalists" or "imperialists." His speech was in striking contrast to the one given by Khrushchev at the preceding party congress, the Twenty-second, held five years previously. Much of the international part of Brezhnev's long address sounded like the Stalin of *The Economic Problems of Socialism in the U.S.S.R.* (1952). "The class contradictions within the capitalist system are deepening," said Brezhnev—this was Stalin's point in his last exegetical work of 1952.[16] "The working class in capitalist countries faces serious difficulties and will have to wage severe [*tyazheliye*] battles. Many of these battles lie ahead of them." Further, the First Secretary described American capitalism in these bitter terms: "plundering, predatory, in every way the hateful strangler of the peoples."

Turning to the international Communist movement, Brezhnev asserted that Communist ranks must be closed, that the *"armies"* of Communism must step up their activities (Stalin's term in 1952 was "shock brigades," and also "armies"). The movement would encounter the "terror of reaction" and a "gigantic police machine for exacting violence." A new conference of the world's parties, predicted Brezhnev, would help the international movement carry on the "offensive" against the positions of imperialism. The "revolutionary process" would thereby develop more successfully, Brezhnev predicted.

With regard to Soviet policy toward the United States, the General-Secretary took a most pessimistic position at the 1966 congress. American imperialism, he warned, was becoming more dangerous, with international tensions increasing as a consequence. He pointed to "American intervention" in the Dominican Republic, "military interference into the affairs of the Latin American countries," and America's "piratical" escalation in

Vietnam as examples, among others, of American imperialism's desire to protect "exploitation of peoples by new, even more despicable means." In all its "foul enterprises," American imperialism "revealed its true face. By its aggression in Vietnam," Brezhnev continued, "the U.S.A. brings shame upon itself which will never be forgotten. . . . Our relations with the United States have worsened as the result of American aggression in Vietnam and the other aggressive activities of American imperialism. The fault for this lies with the ruling circles of the U.S.A." Brezhnev then offered these conditions for improving relations:

As concerns the U.S.S.R., it is ready to live in peace with all countries. But it will not approve of arbitrariness on the part of the imperialists in their relations with other peoples. We have stated more than once that we are prepared to improve our relations with the U.S.A. and we now still hold to this position. But for this to happen, it will be necessary for the U.S.A. to stop its policy of aggression. . . . *Our party and our state categorically renounce the absurd notion that the Great Powers can improve their relations at the expense of the interests of other countries* [italics mine].

In the section of his speech devoted to America, Brezhnev said nothing about the principle of peaceful coexistence, which had supposedly been embedded in the philosophy of Soviet foreign policy since Khrushchev's address at the Twentieth Party Congress in 1956.* Instead, as we saw, Brezhnev revived an almost ancient Stalinist idea (again, found in Stalin's *Economic Problems of Socialism in the U.S.S.R.*) that "the contradictions *between the capitalist states* were growing deeper."

Concerning West Germany, the First Secretary-*cum*-General-Secretary had this to say:

Comrades! The Soviet Union is with heart and soul committed to strengthening European security. Today's principal ally of America in Europe for increasing international tension is West German imperialism. West Germany is increasingly becoming the hotbed of military danger in which passions for revenge are whetted. . . . The policy of the G.F.R. is more and more being determined by the same monopolistic circles who had earlier brought Hitler to power. American and West German imperialism are one and the same partners.

At the same time—and we shall return to this point later—in his congress report Brezhnev did make a characteristic reference to the four-power agreements on Germany made at the Potsdam Conference in 1945. The Potsdam agreements *will never lose their force*, said Brezhnev. "No one has

---

*Three years later, however, General-Secretary Brezhnev *was* to link up peaceful coexistence with U.S.–Soviet relations. See discussion below in Chapter X, p. 270.

the right to forget that the participants in the anti-Hitler coalition*—the Soviet Union, the U.S.A., England, and France—after routing the Hitlerite aggressors took upon themselves via the Potsdam agreements a monumental responsibility in the face of the peoples—to do everything necessary to prevent Germany from threatening its neighbors and to preserve peace throughout the world. The Soviet Union will remain true to this obligation."

Several other speakers at the congress addressed themselves to various aspects of Soviet foreign policy in "co-reports," as the Soviets call them, to the main speech by the First Secretary. It was extremely revealing that among the few top leaders who did *not* say a word to the congress was Anastas I. Mikoyan. In the previous congresses—the Twenty-second (1961), the Twenty-first (1959), and the Twentieth (1956)—Mikoyan's reports were characteristically original and trail-blazing. In them, it almost seemed that Mikoyan had been exempted from prior Presidium clearance for what he was going to tell the delegates to the congress. But in 1966, if Mikoyan had any such report ready for the Twenty-third or if it was rejected by the Brezhnev-controlled Presidium, we cannot know for certain. (It is my suspicion, however, that Mikoyan either deliberately chose not to speak or was frustrated in an attempt to do so by the Brezhnev-Suslov group.)

The role played at the Twenty-third Party Congress by Mikhail A. Suslov was a key one.[17] It fell to Suslov to act as chairman of the proceedings on certain auspicious occasions. It was Suslov who presided on opening day and who introduced Brezhnev to the nearly 5,000 delegates seated in the Palace of Congresses, plus delegations from workers' and Communist Parties from 86 countries.[18] Suslov also read the text of the important congress resolution on Vietnam—the occasion for bitter anti-U.S. statements—which he had undoubtedly drafted. His tenor voive pitched almost to shouting,** Suslov exclaimed:

*It is noteworthy that at the 1966 congress, when Brezhnev referred to the wartime alliance with the Western powers, he did *not* use the term "Allies." Instead, the customary term "anti-Hitlerite coalition" was used, which has the merit of preserving ideological purity. For how could Communist Russia form an *alliance* with the imperialists? However, shortly after the Sino-Soviet border conflicts of March 1969, the "Allied" responsibility for containing Germany began to creep back into Soviet media. This could be a harbinger of things to come if the Soviets should find it necessary to restore the old alliance with the West in the face of the Chinese menace to the east. It is much too early to predict this eventuality, however. The Ussuri River incidents of March 1969 and the Kazakhstan-Sinkiang incident of August 13, 1969, did *not* unleash a wave of friendliness toward the West. On the contrary. Soviet media after March 1969 began to talk about Russia's becoming encircled on *both* west and east by West Germany and Maoist China, respectively. America, the press said, supported this encirclement and was plotting a détente with Red China (quoting unfavorably Senator Edward Kennedy's recommendations in March 1969 for opening relations with Peking).

**I heard tapes of the original broadcasts, carried on Soviet radio direct from the Kremlin Palace of Congresses, with the leaders' own voices.

The American military has broken the elementary norms of international law and are employing the bestial and totally inhuman means. American aircraft make raids on North Vietnamese cities and villages, destroying industrial enterprises, homes, schools, and hospitals, and spread death among a peaceful population.

. . . The ruling circles of the U.S.A. try to cover the true nature of their activities with hypocritical phrases about defending 'freedom' against 'Communist expansion,' and so on. However, no one believes these lies. By its aggression in Vietnam, the U.S.A. has brought shame upon itself which will never be erased. . . . *Voices of protest are rising in the United States itself.* The moral and political isolation of the aggressors is becoming all the more obvious. . . .

The National Liberation Front of South Vietnam must be recognized as the sole legal representative of the South Vietnamese population. . . .

The Twenty-third Congress of the C.P.S.U. proudly proclaims its fraternal solidarity with the heroic Vietnamese people, with the Workers' Party of Vietnam, the National Liberation Front, and appeals to all workers' and Communist parties to *increase their unity of action* in the struggle against American aggression in Vietnam and to show effective aid and support to the struggling Vietnamese people. . . .

Hands off Vietnam!

The just cause of the Vietnamese people will be victorious! [italics mine]

Following Suslov's emotional reading of this statement, the delegates stood and sang all the verses of the "Internationale" as General-Secretary Brezhnev closed the congress.

In the Vietnam resolution, Suslov made reference to the N.L.F.'s being the "only legitimate representative of the South Vietnamese people." This line was never changed in Soviet media during the various bomb pauses, Tet Holiday observances, and so forth. Even during the current "rectangular" peace talks in Paris between the U.S., South Vietnam, the Front, and North Vietnam, Soviet bloc media and those of Hanoi have not ceased repeating the following three positions (among others) for a Vietnam settlement, as they have been repeating them since 1965.

1. The N.L.F. is the *"sole,* genuine representative of the South Vietnamese people."
2. The *"North will liberate the South"* (with quotations to this effect from Ho Chi Minh).*

*The "North-liberating-the-South" line not only appeared in *Nhan Dan*, Communist daily in Hanoi, but was reproduced in the Soviet press *after* the Paris peace talks got under way. Thus, *Izvestiya*, November 3, 1968, reported: "The whole Vietnamese people have shown resoluteness . . . in defeating the enemy so that the South may be liberated and the North defended, which will lead to the peaceful reunification of the country and support of peace in Asia and the whole world." The line has been repeated subsequent to Ho Chi Minh's death in September 1969.

3. All U.S. troops must be withdrawn "unconditionally" from Vietnam and all bombing raids on North Vietnam stopped unconditionally.

It is worthwhile, too, to look at the final Resolution adopted by the Twenty-third Party Congress. Each Communist party congress drafts such a final summation of the business concluded at the congress. The Resolution for the 1966 C.P.Ş.U. congress contained the following fundamentals of the General Line on foreign policy and the world Communist movement (I have italicized key passages):

1. The international significance of the building of communism in the U.S.S.R. consists in the fact that this building progress *strengthens* the economic, political, and *defensive might* of the whole Socialist system and aids in the *spread and confirmation of the ideas of Socialism throughout the whole world.*

2. The Soviet Union has always supported and will continue to support the retention of normal relations between all countries of the world and the solution of contentious international issues by means of negotiation and not by means of war. *At the same time, it must be strongly emphasized that the principle of peaceful coexistence is inapplicable to relations between oppressor and oppressed nations and between colonizers and their victims.*

3. *Under conditions when the aggressive forces of imperialism are aggravating international tension, and creating hotbeds of war,* the C.P.S.U. will in the future *increase the vigilance of the Soviet people and strengthen the defense of the Motherland so that the Armed Forces of the U.S.S.R. will always be prepared . . . to deal a crushing blow to any imperialist aggressor.**

4. The period since the preceding congress [1961] has been characterized by an *increase of imperialist aggression and activization of reaction. The crisis of capitalism has deepened, its contradictions have grown sharper,* all of which in turn strengthen the *adventurism of imperialism* and its danger for the peoples, for the cause of peace and social progress. . . . *The main reactionary force* at the present time and one which plays the role of world gendarme *is American imperialism.* . . . The international situation urgently demands the unity of all anti-war and anti-imperialist forces [in the world] and above all, unity with the world Socialist system, all the branches of the international Communist, worker, and national-liberation movement and all the partisans of peace, *regardless of their political views and philosophies.* . . . *A crushing blow must be struck against the imperialists by the broad masses of the populations in peaceloving countries, and by political parties and mass organizations in these countries.* . . . *Unity within the great army of the world's Communists must be achieved.*

---

*The *double entendre* of Soviet wording requires the closest reading imaginable. Here, for example, the word "imperialist" is used after "any" ("*any* imperialist aggressor"). After the Ussuri River incidents of March 1969, however, the word "imperialist" was sometimes, dropped—*viz.*, ". . . a crushing blow to *any* aggressor," which would, presumably, include non-imperialist aggressors like Red China as well.

Developments Since the 1966 Party Congress

The two years following the Twenty-third Party Congress saw policies emanating from the Kremlin within the two areas of *U.S.-Soviet relations* and *Moscow's policy on world Communist strategy* which harmonized completely with the party line and the goals set by the Resolution and the reports at the 1966 congress. Out of the plethora of such events and policies from 1966 to 1969, two are worth singling out within the categories of Soviet policy toward America and world-Communist strategy.

First, the Kremlin's line on America continued to escalate in bitterness, as concerned the ideological expression of these relations from 1966 into mid-1969. Soviet media unceasingly attacked every aspect of American political life, saving, of course, the most abusive language to describe American policy in Vietnam ("piratical" being a much-used word). Moreover, accusations of perfidy were hurled at the U.S. for its alleged hypocritical behavior at the Paris peace talks, which opened in May 1968. At the same time, as mentioned above, the Soviet press on several occasions ran Ho Chi Minh's restatement of the basic position of the North Vietnamese Communists since early 1965: forcible liberation of the South by the North and description of the N.L.F. as the "sole, genuine representative of the South Vietnamese people." Simultaneously, on the diplomatic level, the Soviets were eager to give the impression that they were open to any changes in policy which might be forthcoming from Washington. Hints that an unconditional bombing halt might bring an end to the war were disseminated in typical Communist fashion—that is, on both official and "unofficial" levels. Frequently the impression given Western newsmen was that the Soviets would "give anything" to see the war end in Vietnam; that it was as much a burden to them as to the U.S.

In retrospect, however, it is extremely dubious that the Soviets had any such wish. First, the war in Vietnam was—and is—irresistibly valuable to them, and only modestly expensive compared to the American investment. Among the useful by-products of the war was the strong presence of the U.S. in Southeast Asia. This does not displease the Kremlin, because this presence frustrates Mao's efforts in the region to the south of China, thus distracting the Chinese from the north where the 4,592-mile border with the U.S.S.R. is located. Ironically, the U.S. thus assists the Kremlin in the latter's encirclement-of-China strategy. Second, the "internationalists" and "world Communists" of the stripe of Suslov, Ponomarev, and others, regard Vietnam as an excellent rallying point for achieving unity among the world's Communists. In his world-girdling travels to the major Communist capitals in 1967, American Communist Party chief Gus Hall evidently spread the word that his party intended to support these efforts of unity-'round-the-Vietnam-War. And to judge from the Communist and fellow-traveling press in the United States ever since, Vietnam *is* the "hottest issue" for rallying together "anti-war and anti-imperialist forces" (see excerpts from the Twenty-third Party Congress Resolution above) *since the Spanish Civil War of the 1930s*, which was a really small operation compared to the war in Vietnam where a half million American armed forces are involved with American expenditures of over $30 billion per year as compared to Soviet expenditures of from $1 billion to $3 billion.

Third, the post-Khrushchev leaders have attempted to use the rally-'round-Vietnam line to get the Soviet bloc more firmly into line—as the Soviet media phrase it, to "discipline" the Socialist forces. When this has not worked—as in post-January 1968 Czechoslovakia—the Soviets have resorted to military means to exact the desired unity. The invasion of Czechoslovakia in August 1968 has not been repeated in the case of other errant ex-satellites, like Yugoslavia and Rumania, or Albania, the one ex-satellite which has chosen to revolve about another mother-planet altogether, Maoist China. Instead of force, the Kremlin up to now has resorted to ideological and diplomatic pressure, which it puts on recalcitrant East European states to induce them to follow Kremlin policy more rigorously. It appears now that forcible means to "discipline" Rumania and Yugoslavia would likely incur a war between the invading Soviet disciplinarians and the Rumanians and Yugoslavs. Evidently, the Kremlin seeks to avoid this eventuality. Czechoslovakia, in fact, was the chosen target for demonstrating the seriousness of the Kremlin's call for unity because it was quite evident to the Kremlin that the Czechoslovaks would *not* take up arms, not only because they had not fought a war since 1620, as some Western observers noted, but because the Czechoslovaks had no desire to sacrifice soldiers in a hopeless conflict with an enemy that could overwhelm them in a matter of days or weeks.

One of the most revealing documents to be issued in the aftermath of the Soviet show of force in Czechoslovakia was the famous "Brezhnev Doctrine." The theory, expounded in a well-known article by a little-known C.P.S.U. publicist named S. Kovalev (*Pravda*, September 26, 1968), boiled down to one of updated Stalinism and Stalin's concepts of national sovereignty and national autonomy. Kovalev's essential thesis was that internationalism and Socialism take precedence over national sovereignty and national autonomy, as determined by Moscow. In other words, where a Socialist country chooses to go its own way, and should this autonomy clash with the current Socialist ideological *and* diplomatic line laid down by the

Kremlin, that country will be prohibited from taking an independent course. This doctrine was in striking contrast, of course, to the Khrushchev line of permitting "many roads to Socialism." (There were rumors, in fact, early in 1969 that the retired pensioner, Nikita Khrushchev, had sought an audience with the leaders in the Kremlin in order to criticize their Czechoslovak invasion and occupation policy and to recommend a different policy.)

At the Ninth Party Congress of the Chinese Communist Party, which met in mid-April 1969, Lin Piao, Mao's heir apparent, made the following characterization of the Brezhnev Doctrine in his congress report on April 24:

In order to justify its aggression and plunder, the Soviet revisionist renegade clique trumpets the so-called theory of 'limited sovereignty,' the theory of 'international dictatorship' and the theory of the 'Socialist commonwealth.' What does all this stuff mean? It means that your sovereignty is 'limited,' while his is unlimited. You won't obey him? Then he will exercise 'international dictatorship' over you—dictatorship over the people of other countries, in order to form the 'Socialist commonwealth' ruled by the new tsar, that is, colonies of social imperialism just like the 'new order of Europe' of Hitler, the 'Great East Asia Coprosperity Sphere' of Japan and the 'free world community' of the United States.[19]

Another recent development in U.S.-Soviet relations was an attack made on the usefulness of the sensitive Washington-Moscow Hot Line by a well-known Soviet publicist, Daniil Kraminov, editor of *Za Rubezhom (Abroad)* magazine. Kraminov, a reputed Suslov aide and one of the secretaries of the recently purged Union of (Soviet) Journalists, published a 2,000-word piece in *Za Rubezhom* (January 1968) in which he went into the delicate matter of U.S.-Soviet relations and President Johnson's allusion to them in his State of the Union message of 1968. Kraminov wrote:

Any truly 'important steps' toward international cooperation have still not been made and, in fact, are being frustrated deliberately by Washington. . . . Washington's sweet talk about U.S.-Soviet relations gives the undeniable impression that they are being exploited for other purposes. . . . They serve the interests of the anti-Soviet propagandists of the Peking splitters, the Trotskyites, and renegades in various countries. Moreover, the reference in Johnson's address to the 'Hot Line' between Washington and Moscow is grist for the mill of clever propagandists. The 'Hot Line,' which was established in order to keep events from going to tragic extremes, is now being exploited by American propaganda for anti-Soviet purposes.

Neither, it might be added, was the Hot Line established in 1963 between John F. Kennedy and Nikita Khrushchev for the purposes of a revived anti-U.S. propaganda campaign in Soviet media!

From 1966 to the present, both the Hot Line and the touted détente (touted only on *this* side of the world, by the way!*) between Russia and the United States have managed somehow to maintain a tenuous existence. But the relative thaw that produced them ended abruptly in October 1964. In the chilly climate that has since prevailed, it is not likely to be revived unless the "soft-line" trend which became noticeable in Soviet policy toward America in mid-1969 heralds a major *volte-face*.

Recall this statement from the 1966 congress Resolution: "The principle of peaceful coexistence is inapplicable to relations between oppressor and oppressed." Or Brezhnev's statement: "Our party and our state categorically renounce the absurd notion that the Great Powers can improve their relations at the expense of the interests of other countries." Substitute the word "détente" for "peaceful. coexistence" or "improve their relations," and the present chill in U.S.-Soviet relations will be better understood. An illustration of Soviet intransigence on the various Johnson-Nixon "bridges-to-the-U.S.S.R." proposals came recently when the Soviet U.N. representative Yakov A. Malik rejected the "linkage" principle in negotiating *as a package* outstanding issues between the U.S. and the Soviet Union. The Nixon Administration in February 1969 had sought to tie together a number of these problems which, it proposed, should be discussed together as a whole with the Soviets: the Middle East, Vietnam, even the German question. This, obviously, would be the most logical way to proceed, especially if the agenda of a summit conference were to be planned for some time in the foreseeable future. The Soviets rejected the proposal with a resounding *nyet*! From Mr. Malik's remarks, it was obvious that he thought such a packaged-discussion would tend to blur the "class-struggle" or "ideological" aspects of the current Soviet diplomatic line as it is applied to (1) the anti-Israel, Arab "national-liberation" movement in North Africa; (2) the war in Vietnam, "the fraternal struggle against American imperialism," the goal for spurring worldwide Communist unity; and (3) the German question, which Moscow obviously chooses *at present* to keep off the agendas of any foreign-ministers' or heads-of-state conferences between itself and the West, preferring instead to work toward a *pan-European Security Conference*. The question is: will such a conference exclude the United States? The Soviet position on this at present is obscure.

One closing remark about Soviet ideological reformationism so prevalent at the 1966 congress and since is in order. The party line on the war in

*The famous Glassboro mini-summit of June 23–25, 1967, fetched tall black headlines and front-page stories in the U.S. press and the press of other Western countries. But in the Soviet press, one-paragraph items, sometimes buried on inside pages, revealed the Kremlin's indifference to informing the Soviet people of this piece of U.S.-Soviet mini-summitry. It appears in retrospect that Kosygin's mission was not to conduct a meaningful negotiation on Vietnam or any other major issue, but rather to sound out Johnson personally, perhaps to assess the chances of America's changing its posture of persisting in Vietnam. It is interesting to recall a Russian diplomat's attributing "Anglo-Saxon *stubbornness*" to Americans (see Cassini quote above, p. 84).

Vietnam as applied to the "class struggle in America" is quite revealing in this respect. It is obvious that one of several spin-offs from the escalation of the Vietnam War (by both the Soviets and the U.S.) has been the ideological use of the expression "piratical U.S. imperialism in Vietnam" by Communists and fellow travelers. This ideologization of the war, moreover, has been used by Communists and their allies in the United States to attempt to forge a gigantic "all-people's anti-war, anti-imperialist *front*," as was recommended at the 1966 congress, which would embrace all kinds of people of a multitude of political complexions and backgrounds. Despite their differences, however, the people would be *united* on the central question of "getting out of Vietnam," thereby releasing untold billions of dollars to relieve the "plight of the American workers," and so on. They would unite in order to deal a "crushing blow" at U.S. imperialism. Who knows but that the Kremlin ideologists, including perhaps some of the top Politburo* leaders, may have thought (or may still think) that this "crushing blow" would eventually bring about a "Socialist America." The new Party Program of the C.P.U.S.A. intimates as much when it speaks of tying together the antiwar movement in America with the struggle for Socialism—thus following the Kremlin's ideological line on this point. A typical piece of writing for Soviet consumption illustrating the Kremlin's attitude toward the anti-Vietnam War movement in the U.S. appeared in *Pravda*, December 14, 1967, under the title "The Split Society" (*"Raskolotoye Obshchestvo"*) and was written by the veteran Soviet journalist G. Ratiani. Here are some excerpts:

This war [in Vietnam] is a nightmare for America. . . . It spits tongues of flame even when it arises by chance in a conversation about some topic. And there are almost no Americans who are indifferent to the war. The country is divided . . .

As the [peace] movement has developed, it has become impossible to call criticism of the Vietnam War a "Communist plot." If one does that, he merely imitates the McCarthyites who accused all heterodoxical opinion of being Communist. This may have been possible in the years of the 'great terror' when the organizers of the Cold War held *a majority of the American public under the control of their propaganda*. But now people who are far from holding Communist views demand an end to the aggression, and they are not afraid of being accused of treason. Likewise, they are not afraid of Communists who are marching in the ranks of the demonstrators, of Communist speakers at meetings, of speeches given by officials of the C.P.U.S.A. in universities, of the participation of Communists at conferences of the 'New Left.' This is a new phenomenon in America [italics mine].

Perhaps Mr. Ratiani exaggerates when he implies that this is an entirely

---

*It was decided at the 1966 party congress to change the name of the Party Presidium back to its old designation during the times of Lenin and Stalin: Politburo. By the same congress decision, the title of First Secretary was changed to the Stalinist-sounding "General-Secretary."

new phenomenon in America; after all, it happened in the 1930s. But on the scale it is happening today, Communist participation in the anti-Vietnam War "popular-front" movement is undoubtedly unprecedented in post-1917 American history. However, when the Communists have sought to interpenetrate or get command of labor unions or of radical or liberal groups in America in the past (for example, in their frustrated attempt to capture control of the American Veterans Committee after World War II), they have failed. Should they attempt this today they would doubtlessly fail again. Already there are signs of a "divided movement" among radicals which is far more serious for their revolutionary cause than a divided America is for the cause of liberal democracy. For liberal-democracy thrives on divided power, differences of opinion, and political heterodoxy. Radical movements, on the other hand, require centralized leadership, discipline, and orthodoxy.

An unexpected by-product of an overly ambitious Communist push for control could be a change of opinion in that same "American public" of which Ratiani spoke. Without (hopefully) returning to the outrages of the McCarthy period, American public opinion might once again support the exposure and destruction of the Communist movement in America through the courts and public action. Should they be made in the late 1960s or early 1970s, revelations of a "subversive Communist movement" in the U.S. could lead to a worsening of diplomatic relations between the two countries (as was the case in 1919–1933, 1940 to July 1941, and 1950–1954). There is already evidence that the Kremlin is pondering this question as it attempts to dissociate itself from the *extreme* leftwing radical elements in America; these, in any case, appear to the Kremlin to be violent "Maoists," or their equivalent. But it is by no means sure that the Kremlin ideologists, even when they are sensitive to unfavorable diplomatic fall-out which could result from extremist excesses, would necessarily rule out altogether the application of "nonpeaceful" means to reach Communist ends. The Moscow Communists have never disavowed the use of nonpeaceful means, under certain circumstances. This was, in fact, written into the resolutions of the two world conferences of Communists held in Moscow in 1957 and in 1960. The fact that Soviet media condemn the "anarchist" student radicals on various U.S. university campuses may not indicate Kremlin renunciation of the use of force, the occupation of buildings, and so forth. Rather, it may signify an admission on the part of the Kremlin internationalists that they do not (yet) have control over these American student movements. Therefore, they seek to polarize the movement, to split it, so that the men (the Communists with the Red flag) may be separated from the boys (the student Black-flag anarchists and radical nondescripts with their *non*-ideological points of view).*

*For an interesting description of the various currents within the New Left and how it contrasts with other liberal and radical movements of the past, see Irving Kristol, "The Old Politics, the *New* Politics, the New, New Politics," *The New York Times Magazine*, November 24, 1968, pp. 49–180.

As part of their coverage of the "increasingly revolutionary" American scene for Soviet readers, *Pravda* and *Izvestiya*, the two largest dailies, frequently employ the tactic of reprinting items published in the U.S. press. When this is done, however, there is usually considerable editing by Moscow. Very often, the published end-result is an out-and-out distortion of what was printed originally in the American publication. A recent example of this was *Izvestiya's* version (published on April 25, 1969) of the special issue of *Fortune* Magazine (January 1969) entitled "American Youth: Its Outlook Is Changing the World" (this title was omitted in the *Izvestiya* version, by the way). One of the articles, a declaration of radicalism written on the basis of 200 interviews with U.S. college students, was prefaced this way in the *Fortune* original (I have italicized the key phrases):

This declaration *never appeared any place but in these pages*. It is a free-form journalistic technique, synthesizing and codifying the views of student critics of U.S. society, most of whom are on the left. . . . It was written . . . on the basis of 200 interviews. . . . While students with these views were, in each case, *a campus minority*, they were not campus militants. It is Wierzynski's finding that they represent the principal intellectual thrust of the oncoming generation.

When *Izvestiya* got around to giving its version of *Fortune's* preface to the article, the Soviet government newspaper said (again, my italics):

Criticism of the 'American way of life' has become so large-scale that it has spilled over onto the pages of the *organs* of the bourgeois press. The declaration of American youth published on this page [of *Izvestiya*] was recently published in the magazine 'Fortune,' from which we have reproduced it with a few cuts. In its preface to the article, 'Fortune' asserts that the declaration was drawn up after a careful investigation of the views of a *representative group* of university youth in the United States. This group, the magazine said, is *'the basic intellectual force of the coming generation in the country.'*

By comparing the original with the *Izvestiya* version, one can see that *Izvestiya* has omitted *Fortune's* important phrase "a campus *minority*," *Izvestiya* substituting for it "representative group. . . ." This is a typical example of the "distorted mirror"* so often held up to America by Soviet media.

In a recent article written for *The New Leader,* the well-known Soviet specialist in America, Professor Zbigniew Brzezinski, had this to say about the current status of Soviet relations with the West:

[The Soviet leadership] has now concluded that peaceful coexistence, which meant that the Soviet Union exploited political openings in the West, and the United States, France and even West Germany probed for similar openings in the East—is more dangerous to it than to the West. Consequently, it has decided to opt for a policy of 'limited coexistence,' in which greater emphasis is put on hostility and ideological rigidity vis-à-vis the West. . . .

The rigid and hostile Communists prefer a rigid and hostile policy from the West; they fear more imaginative relations.[20]

*For a classic work on the subject of Soviet propaganda, see Frederick C. Barghoorn, *Soviet Foreign Propaganda* (Princeton, N.J.: Princeton University Press, 1964).

NOTES

1. *Today's Vital World Problems on Record*, vol. 2, no. 8 (1964), p. 35. Published by Keynote Publications, Inc., New York.
2. *Nepszabadsang*, (Budapest), October 20, 1964, quoted in *Bulletin* of the Study of the U.S.S.R., December 1964, p. 19.
3. *Bulletin*, December 1964, pp. 20–21.
4. *Ibid.*, p. 21.
5. *Pravda*, October 20, 1964.
6. I should like to single out some of the outstanding journalists who so attentively and conscientiously follow developments in the Communist world and who "nailed down" a number of post-Khrushchev policies long before the rest of the field was aware of them. E.g., Paul Wohl of *The Christian Science Monitor* was among the first to detect a definite trend away from Khrushchev's policies under the leadership of Brezhnev, Kosygin, *et al.* The same analytical acuteness applies to Anatole Shub of *The Washington Post*, Harry Schwartz of *The New York Times*, Michel Tatu of *Le Monde*, and Victor Zorza in Britain. There were others, of course, but by and large too many correspondents, columnists, and editorial writers failed to detect the signs of reorientation of Soviet policy, foreign and domestic, after October 1964, and *most particularly with regard to Soviet policy in Vietnam*.
7. *Pravda*, December 31, 1961, in an address to the U.S.S.R. Supreme Soviet.
8. William Zimmerman, "Soviet Perceptions of the United States," in Dallin and Larson (ed.), *op. cit.*, p. 165. I am indebted to this scholar at the University of Michigan for several of the facts that are given in the succeeding paragraphs. The analysis of Suslov's activities in purging Khrushchevism in Soviet writing about America is my own. I would, in fact, criticize Professor Zimmerman for rather too blithely accepting a continuation of Khrushchevism among academic publications without offering the caveat that this continuation *after* October 1964 was a sort of "cultural lag" which had not as yet been coped with by the C.P.S.U. ideologues. The lag had all but disappeared completely by the time of the Twenty-third Party Congress in 1966. For a brief summary of the Brezhnev-Suslov "ideological cleansing operation," see Wolfgang Leonhard "Politics and Ideology in the Post-Khrushchev Period," in Dallin and Larson (eds.), *op. cit.*, pp. 45–46, where Leonhard discusses the "little Zhdanov," Sergei P. Trapeznikov.
9. "Peaceful Coexistence—Two Diametrically Opposed Policies," *Peking Review*, VI, No. 51 (December 20, 1963), p. 16. Quoted in Zimmerman, *ibid.*, p. 168.
10. Aspaturian, "Foreign Policy Perspectives in the Sixties," Dallin and Larson (eds.), *op. cit.*, pp. 142–143; Zimmerman, *ibid.*, pp. 170–179.
11. Quoted in Zimmerman, *ibid.*, p. 174.
12. Col.-Gen. S. M. Shtemenko, "The Queen of the Battlefield Relinquishes Her Crown," *Nedelya* (Week), No. 6, issue for the week of January 31–February 6, 1965. The publication is a supplement of *Izvestiya*. Quotes are taken from

Thomas W. Wolfe, "Problems of Soviet Defense Policy Under the New Regime," published by the Rand Corporation (March 1965), p. 12.

13. E.g., see Marshal M. V. Zakharov, "Imperative Demand of the Times: On Improving Further the Scientific level of Military Leadership," *Krasnaya Zvezda* [*Red Star*] (February 4, 1965). Quoted in Wolfe, *ibid.*, p. 10.

14. *Pravda*, November 8, 1964.

15. Anatole Shub, "Russia Says West Plots War, Warns It Would Be Loser," *The Washington Post*, April 27, 1969, p. 1, and continued on p. A21.

16. The quotation and those following are taken from the full text of Brezhnev's address to the Twenty-third Congress of the C.P.S.U., published in *Pravda*, March 30, 1966.

17. The text of Suslov's congress addressed on Vietnam may be found in *Pravda*, April 9, 1966.

18. *Pravda*, March 30, 1966.

19. *The New York Times*, April 29, 1969, p. 12.

20. Zbigniew K. Brzezinski, "Meeting Moscow's 'Limited Coexistence,' " *The New Leader* (December 16, 1968), pp. 11 and 13.

CHAPTER X

The Shape of the Seventies

If the interests of the U.S.S.R. demand rapprochement with one or another country which is not bent upon breaking the peace, we take this step without hesitation.

—JOSEF STALIN to the Seventeenth Party
Congress, January 26, 1934

As it faces the 1970s, the Soviet Union is confronted with a *troika* of paradoxes—paradoxes, it seems, whose resolution the leaders of the Kremlin choose to postpone.

The Three Paradoxes

Paradox Number One

The country needs peace to advance its standard of living from a relatively low level for a major industrialized country and to prove thereby that Communism is the best system in the world. And yet, the regime pours a larger percentage of the Soviet G.N.P. into defense than does the United States, whose stronger economic position permits defense expenditures with a minimum of sacrifice. Moreover, the Soviet expenditures are directed into arms within a framework of a bellicose ideology which only aggravates tensions and provokes continuance of the arms race and even greater expenditures.

Paradox Number Two

In terms of grand strategy, the U.S.S.R. must, above all, avoid the predicament of a two-front war. Russia has always dreaded a situation in which enemies would appear simultaneously at the gates of its eastern and western marches. And yet, current Kremlin policy tends to aggravate tensions on both flanks, east and west, but without any determined effort to ward off these dangers by means of viable alliances. For example, there appears to be no discernible effort by Kremlin policy-makers to pick up the pieces of the "strange alliance" between the Russian East and the "Anglo-Saxon" West, which was shattered after 1945 as the Cold War set in. If the Soviets should stand in imminent danger of attack on either flank, they would surely wish to renew that alliance. The Anglo-Saxon–Russian core of the United Nations alliance upon which the Russians so desperately depended in their historical anguish of 1941–1945 languishes today.

As for Russia's present eastern adversary, mainland China, the Soviet alliance with that country, formalized between Stalin and Mao in 1950, is in shambles. There seems to be no concerted effort or desire, in either Peking or Moscow, to weld back together the broken shield of "fraternal Sino-Soviet friendship and solidarity."

Thus, current Soviet policy would appear to put the U.S.S.R. in the paradoxical position of being isolated from former allies while possibly needing those allies in the event of war.

Paradox Number Three

After Stalin's death in 1953, the "sword of terror" was largely sheathed and the Stalinist brand of outright bullying of the "satellites" came to an end because the Kremlin deemed it necessary to substitute persuasion and conciliation for unmitigated dictation. And yet, paradoxically, the post-Stalin rulers could also abruptly discard persuasion, as in the case of Hungary in 1956 and of Czechoslovakia in 1968. The Kremlin presumably seeks a genuine alliance with the peoples of the Soviet bloc should a common enemy (West Germany, for example) appear. But does it seriously imagine that these peoples could be *forced* into a friendly relationship with the Soviet Union? The method of persuasion, conciliation, and tolerance of the political and social particularities of each member of the bloc is obviously a better method than the application of brute force. Force brings only a phony, calico-thin "friendship" which would be torn to pieces if put to the test of war. Soviet military strategists are perfectly aware of this problem. A long war, which these strategists now say is likelier than a short "push-button war," would involve large conscript armies; mass armies enhance the factor of "political morale" and the peoples' conviction of the "justice of the goals that the Soviet Union and the entire Socialist Camp will pursue in the war."[1]

The present leaders in the Kremlin cannot be unaware of the three seeming paradoxes. But it is likely that they regard them as only "seeming." An examination of current Soviet foreign policy reveals that while the

Kremlin appears to be aware of paradoxes in its policy, it is even more sensitive to pre- and postrevolutionary Russian diplomatic history and the needs of preserving the dictatorship. The leaders seem to be bent upon a course of (1) "all-azimuth" defense of vital Russian national interests and national security; and (2) preserving the post-1917 Communist Party absolutism and Communist orthodoxy, while tabling resolution of the paradoxes in its policy. How the Kremlin may be able to proceed by indefinitely postponing this resolution will be examined in the Epilogue at the conclusion of this chapter.

Coexistence or Coextinction?

After late 1953, when the U.S.S.R. exploded its own first hydrogen bomb, Communist Party leaders in Moscow began to be cognizant of the dangers of waging an "anti-imperialist" Third World War, and in the face of ultimate weapons, aware of the necessity to redesign their entire grand strategy in its ideological, diplomatic, and military facets. However, it is part of the pathology of absolutism and encrusted bureaucracy, both of which plague the U.S.S.R., to suffer from what Nikita Khrushchev once called "bureaucratic inertia"—in other words, showing inflexibility in the face of changing circumstances. Thus, Soviet reappraisal of its strategy has come about only gradually since 1953. One of the first steps made by the post-Stalin leaders in this direction was to recognize the possibility of establishing a condominium with the United States, the largest superpower with "thermonuclear teeth." As one American specialist on Soviet diplomacy has put it:

the two superpowers would demarcate their respective areas of vital interest, define their area of common interest, delineate the status quo to be preserved, and establish the guidelines which would govern their competition in areas peripheral to their interests. . . . Such a condominium would, in effect, ensure American non-intervention in areas of Soviet vital interests and Soviet non-intervention in areas of American vital interests.[2]

The Geneva summit conference of 1955 was in large part a reflection of this dyarchical approach. The basic motivating factor doubtlessly was and is *fear*. The danger of a mutually devastating thermonuclear holocaust simply forced the two superpowers into some sort of mutually tolerable coexistence.

At the same time, while dreading coextinction, the Kremlin also fears *unlimited* coexistence with the West. Khrushchev, for all his alleged "revisionism," "softness," and so forth, was fully aware of the danger of ideological erosion and how this erosion might endanger the legitimization of one-party Communist rule. He never tired of emphasizing that peaceful coexistence with the capitalist West did not mean coexistence of the two ideologies,

Communist and "capitalist" (the latter meaning, essentially, a free market-place of *ideas* and *products*). The two ideologies, said Khrushchev and his successors, are mutually incompatible. In other words, the factor of mutual deterrence, enhanced by the terrifying stockpiles of nuclear bombs and hundreds of intercontinental missile carriers of the lethal weapons, did not rule out a continuing cold war between ideologies or the waging of "national-liberation wars" abroad. On the contrary. Deterrence opened up new avenues for revolutionary agitation and for exporting revolution to Third World "national bourgeoisies struggling against colonialism." Precisely because of the fear of an outbreak of thermonuclear war, "wars of national liberation" (local wars) have become feasible because the superpowers would be loath to escalate such wars into a world conflict.

Vietnam provides an example of a local war fought as a Soviet proxy war of "national liberation" with Soviet support. Restrained American escalation and continuing but also restrained Soviet military aid to the North Vietnamese and the Vietcong coact "in tandem," as it were, because of the unwritten understanding of the two superpowers that local wars, short of thermonuclear world wars, *can be* fought. At the same time, Vietnam and Soviet-backed Arab belligerency in the Near East are not motivated solely by ideology, or by the professed goal of "world revolution." As Gromyko pointed out in his Supreme Soviet address in 1968 (see above p. 153, Soviet foreign policy is at its ideal best when purely *raison d'état* or national interest considerations work in unison with ideological goals; the Soviet Foreign Minister himself gave Vietnam as a cardinal illustration of this coordination of diplomacy and ideology. Vietnam serves Soviet national interests in the traditional sense by giving the U.S.S.R. a position of strength in Southeast Asia. The strong military presence of the United States in the area is also in the Soviet interest; it is a formidable impediment blocking further Maoist expansion. The Soviets profit from this frustration of Maoist ambitions and reap the additional benefit of watching China become preoccupied to the south, that is, in a direction away from the Sino-Soviet border to the north.

That the Chinese and the Russians are rivals in East Asia was made explicit in an interesting article in the May 28, 1969, issue of *Izvestiya*. The leading commentator for *Izvestiya*, Vikenty Matveyev, wrote that the British pullout east of Suez had left a power vacuum in East Asia; this vacuum would become larger, he said, if the U.S. withdrew from South Vietnam. He pledged that the Soviet Union and other Communist countries would "contribute to every effort helping to insure firmer dependable peace and security in Asia despite the antipopular designs of bellicose reaction. . . . Mao and his henchmen entertain quite definite designs on a number of countries in this part of the world." Matveyev's words about Soviet efforts to block Mao's "designs" in Asia made a fitting accompaniment to the words of General-Secretary Brezhnev addressed to the conference of 75 Communist and Workers' parties held in St. George's Hall in the Great Kremlin Palace in June 1969. In a simple one-sentence paragraph, Brezhnev made the startling proposal—startling because it was unprecedented in the post-Stalin period—that *a collective security system be established in the Far East* (*Pravda*, June 8, 1969). Obviously, the cutting edge of such a security arrangement would be directed not so much against U.S. power positions in the West Pacific as against Maoist China.

In the Middle East—for two centuries, a sphere of attempted penetration by the Russians—the current Soviet pro-Arab policy is also motivated by traditional goals. The Mediterranean and Suez are obvious prizes in the East-West struggle for power and influence in the area. But also the dozen-plus Arab states of the Middle East represent a formidable force to the Soviets, an opportunity to work by means of foreign aid and diplomacy (including naval "showing of the flag") toward building a belt of friendly states in an area rich in oil and blessed—or perhaps cursed—with crucial strategic importance. Although of Moslem faith and with legal restrictions put on Communist Parties, the half-dozen most crucial Arab states of the Middle East are not totally without ideological importance, from the Kremlin's point of view. For the Soviets have developed the theory of the "national-bourgeois road to Socialism," a way station toward full-fledged Soviet-style "Socialism." The Kremlin reckons that ultimately Socialism will develop as Soviet aid, counsel, and power work toward convincing the ruling circles that one-party oligarchy and pro-Soviet policies provide more security and more internal stability.

Like it or not, the West is confronted with this dual diplomatic-ideological nature of Soviet foreign policy. It is a dangerous mix. But as long as the Communist oligarchy in the U.S.S.R. feels that ideologization of its foreign policy is useful while de-ideologization of its foreign policy threatens the legitimacy of its rule in Russia (see above, Chapter VI), it will continue to promote this type of dually motivated foreign policy. Ironically, as we saw, it is the very threat of a mutually destructive Third World War which, in a sense, helps make feasible Communist-backed local wars. Khrushchev's brinkmanship at the very door of the United States in Cuba in October 1962, Soviet support of Arab militancy, American intervention in Vietnam, the Brezhnev regime's support of North Vietnamese aggression ("the North will liberate the South") against South Vietnam and of North Korean brinkmanship in the *Pueblo* and EC–121 Incidents of 1968 and 1969 are evidence that mutual deterrence does not deter the two superpowers—especially not the U.S.S.R. and its friends—from taking dangerous steps in areas adjacent to the non-Communist and Communist worlds.

Despite risk-taking and brinkmanship, however, both powers are reluctant to court a Third World War. Even the Brezhnev regime, which boldly revised much of Khrushchev's latterday diplomatic and military strategy (see above, Chapter VIII) in a more militant direction, has nevertheless kept alive, although somewhat less enthusiastically than before 1965, Khrushchev's post-1956 principle that a thermonuclear world conflict would be detrimental to the interests of the working class. In early 1969, however, statements by the Brezhnev regime seemed to indicate that it might be being induced to revise even this principle, under pressure from the increasingly influential military bloc in the Kremlin (see the sections "Balloons and Straws in the Wind on May Day 1969" and "The Collectivumvirate," below). Should this be the case, even the balance of terror might not be enough to keep limited coexistence from escalating into unlimited coextinction. Taking the extreme step "over the brink" was made at least somewhat less suicidal from the Soviet standpoint as the Soviets embarked on their crash program to attain parity with the United States in stockpiles of nuclear weapons. This policy was inaugurated after the overthrow of Khrushchev and caused the U.S.S.R. to feel emboldened to venture even closer to the brink with the U.S. By 1970 the U.S.S.R undoubtedly will have attained full parity in ICBMs with the U.S.

Sino-Soviet and U.S.-Soviet Cold Wars

Communist China was the first Soviet-bloc state *bordering on the U.S.S.R.* to make a bold move in the direction of diplomatic and ideological independence from the Soviet empire in the post-Stalin period. Tito's Yugoslavia broke away from the Cominform in 1948 and has charted a largely independent course from that time to the present. But Yugoslavia is a small, only semi-industrialized country. Its population of 20 million is less than one tenth that of the Soviet Union, and its G.N.P. is less than 20 percent of the Soviet G.N.P. Although it possesses one of the best-trained and highly motivated armies in Europe, Yugoslavia represents no threat to the U.S.S.R., nor does it even border on the Soviet Union.

The case of Communist China is an altogether different matter. Although its economy is nowhere nearly as strong—either potentially or actually—as that of the Soviets, it is a large country, with a population three times that of the U.S.S.R. The Chinese army, although well trained, is not as well equipped at present as that of its neighbor to the north. But it is nonetheless a formidable threat numbering 3 million with a backup potential of 150 million males of military age eligible to be drafted. Added to this is the fact that China shares a 4,592-mile border with the U.S.S.R., and brandishes an ideological weapon that is pointed with equal hostility toward both Soviet "revisionism" and U.S. "imperialism." If this were not enough, China has territorial claims against Russia which add up to some 600,000 square miles of land now situated within Soviet borders. The bloody border clashes of March, May, June, and August 1969 indicated that the Sino-Soviet "paper war" between ideologies can also flare into a shooting war involving the flags of the two countries.

The world thus witnesses two gigantic cold wars being waged simultaneously, the Soviets being a party to both of them. On the one hand, the Soviets depict the United States as the "principal imperialist enemy" (see above, pp. 139–140). On the other hand, they adhere to a diplomatic policy of a "cold peace" or "limited coexistence" with the U.S. and of recognizing the danger implicit in unleashing a major war fought with nuclear-tipped ICBMs. Toward Communist China, the Soviets display a confusing ideological posture. On the one hand, they describe the rulers in Peking as phony Communists, a "bureaucratic-military clique around Mao Tse-tung," which is bent upon "military adventurism" and "leftwing extremism." On the other, they prophesy that the day will come when "true Chinese Communists" will throw off the Maoist yoke and rejoin China to the Socialist Camp headed by the U.S.S.R. Moscow's confusion arises from attempting to design an ideological treatment of Maoism which has no clear precedent in Marxism-Leninism. Meanwhile, the Maoists, by their ideological treatment of the "Soviet revisionists," attempt to adapt their anti-Russian position to Marxism-Leninism by terming the Soviet phenomenon one of *social imperialism* or of "rule by new Tsars." The former term, "social imperialism," is an old Comintern epithet that was applied by Stalin in the 1930s to Italian Fascism and German Nazism. But for some reason, the Kremlin ideologists have stopped short, up to now, of calling the Maoists "imperialists," of a "social" or any other type. The Soviets decline to use the Leninist term "imperialist," although there is a recent precedent for the use of this term in application to China, Cuba's Fidel Castro having called the Peking regime "imperialist"—perhaps in a rash moment, during a disagreement with China in 1967 over trade between the two countries.

Undoubtedly, the Soviets hesitate to brand the Chinese Communists as "imperialists" because of the havoc this would work for their dissemination of essential Marxism-Leninism *within the* U.S.S.R. It is evidently extremely vital to the Kremlin for the sharp, cutting edge of Marxism-Leninism to be aimed squarely at the "American and German imperialists," from whom the "principal threat to world peace" comes, according to the present Kremlin line. By diluting the concept of "imperialism" with "social imperialism" and hurling that concept in the direction of Peking, the Soviets would obviously confound their ideological treatment of alleged German *revanchism* and the "rebirth of neo-Nazism" and "Fascism" in West Germany. From the standpoint of Russian consumption, it would be difficult, if not impossible, to equate Chinese *Communist* "social imperialism" with Western *capitalist*

"American and German imperialism." This is true so long as the threat to the U.S.S.R. allegedly coming from the West, looms larger on the political horizon as scanned by the quadrumvirate of Brezhnev-Kosygin-Suslov-Podgorny than does the danger from the East. The anti-West Germany, anti-U.S. pitch of current Soviet propaganda would be seriously undercut by confronting Soviet citizens with *two* species of imperialism—one bred in a Communist state, the other in capitalist states!

At present, Soviet media under the editorial direction of the C.P.S.U. Central Committee and with the personal supervision of M. A. Suslov and his chain of command sometimes depict potential threats to Soviet security and Soviet retaliation with the following language: "No matter from *what point on the compass* the attempt to invade our country should come—east or west, north or south—*any* aggressor will suffer a crushing blow from our armed forces." (italics mine). A hint of de-ideologization is suggested by the expression *lyuboi agressor*, any aggressor. Thus, when the Sino-Soviet clashes took place on the Ussuri River in March 1969, Soviet media pulled out of the Soviet dictionary of epithets a term that had not been applied to a foreign state since the German attack on Russia in June 1941: *verolomnii*, or "treacherous." To a nonspecialist or a nonreader of the Soviet press, this might seem unimportant. However, under conditions of a heavily and thoughtfully edited press, where a single word may carry—and has carried —the hint of a change of policy or of leadership, the reintroduction of the word *verolomnii* in Soviet media had great significance. Moreover, this was the term's first reappearance in a quarter of a century. It was doubly significant that it should be applied to neighboring Communist China. It suggests that discussion may now be under way in the Kremlin to attempt some form of revision of Marxism-Leninism with which to cope ideologically with the danger of Russian national interest represented by Red China.*

Meanwhile, in the Soviet propaganda scale of values—or rather scale of evils—U.S. and German "imperialism" still rank ahead of Chinese adven-

---

*Soviet media opened another new chapter in the Sino-Soviet cold war by publishing for the first time, on March 18, 1969, a *cartoon* attacking the Maoists. Up to now, of the fourteen Communist states, only Yugoslavia had resorted to cartoon journalism to get its anti-Maoist point across. Unlike the Yugoslavs, however, the Soviet cartoonist so arranged the figures and objects in his cartoon so as not to show the epicanthic fold of the eyes of the advancing Maoist soldiers. The Chinese soldiers' faces are conveniently covered by the opened pages of the "little red book of Chairman Mao." Analogous cartoons appeared elsewhere in the European Soviet bloc, and the almond-shaped eyes of the Chinese (resembling those of millions of Soviet citizens as well) were likewise covered. The blatant *racial* note, in other words, has been kept out of anti-Maoist campaign up to now. However, the Soviets—through the "court poet" Yevgeny Yevtushenko —have not been beneath striking certain, almost racial, historical parallels. A poem by Yevtushenko which appeared in the spring of 1969 compared the Maoist soldiers on the Ussuri River to the Mongols of Genghis Khan. Andrei Voznesensky had made the same comparison in a poem written somewhat earlier.

turism" and "treachery." Interestingly, however, on the *Chinese* side it is Soviet "social imperialism" that is presently regarded by the Communist leaders in Peking as a greater danger than "U.S. imperialism." Analysis of Lin Piao's report to the Ninth Congress of the Chinese Communist Party in April 1969, for example, shows that Mao's heir apparent devoted 45 percent of his speech to attacks on the U.S.S.R., whereas he reserved only 7.5 percent for attacks on the U.S. About 33 percent of his attacks were directed against both the Soviets and the Americans.[3]

As yet, no such trend toward a greater condemnation of China than of the United States or of Germany can be discerned in Soviet media, despite the various 1969 border conflicts. That one or two straws now in the wind may suggest that such a trend might get under way later, will be explored below under the section "Balloons and Straws in the Wind on May Day 1969."

At present, invoking the devil of Western imperialism is still the primary Soviet ideological device for justifying the "efforts of the toilers in building Socialism," in accordance with the following recent exhortation in the Soviet press:

'Every blow of hammer in the cause of Socialist construction in the Soviet Union,' said the leader of the German workers years ago, Ernst Thälmann, 'is at the same time a mighty blow directed against capitalist class lordship in all other countries of the world.' . . . And the same situation prevails today. Wherever a Soviet person is found . . . he works in the name of the great common cause—the victory of the toilers throughout the whole world. Internationalism in deed, fraternal solidarity between laboring people, and unity and solidarity in the struggle against imperialism are the characteristics of Soviet man.[4]

One last point about China, the U.S.S.R., and the United States and the eventuality of a *Sino*-American détente. During the post-Khrushchev years —*but notably never during Khrushchev's reign*—Soviet commentators and Soviet leaders, including Brezhnev, have accused Washington and Peking of acting in collusion against the U.S.S.R. The latest occasion of this accusation came in the aftermath of the hints of such a détente that Western observers thought they detected in the remarks of a highly placed Chinese official, Chen Yi, at the end of 1968. As the traditional Sino-American talks were scheduled to reopen in Warsaw in early 1969, the Soviet press began to complain that American reaction to Chen Yi's remarks indicated that Washington might be playing the card of friendship with China. It mentioned the upcoming resumption of the talks in Warsaw as an example, as well as inept (in my opinion) remarks made by the late President's brother, Senator Edward Kennedy, calling upon the Nixon administration to normalize relations between the Chinese People's Republic and the United States manifestly for the purpose of exerting pressure on the U.S.S.R. The Soviets temporarily dropped their complaints when Peking abruptly canceled the Warsaw talks.

Similarly, some observers thought the aforementioned speech by Lin Piao at the Chinese party congress in April 1969 may have contained the hint of a Chinese initiative in the direction of normalization. Only a relatively small portion of Lin's speech, they pointed out, attacked America; the burden of the attacks was on the U.S.S.R. Moreover, at the conclusion of the party congress, and as the new leadership was presented to the conclave, the status of the moderates of the Chou En-lai type had not significantly dropped in standing in favor of the military headed by Lin.

Meanwhile, the Soviet press has made propaganda mileage out of hints of Sino-American reconciliation and favorable American reactions to them. For example, they duly condemned Senator Kennedy's recommendations. But whether the eventuality of such a détente between China and America is to Moscow a mere laughingstock or grist for the propaganda mill is worth considering. History may inform the Russians on this point. For at one juncture in U.S.-Russian relations, the United States defended another Asian power's territoriality in the face of a menacing Russia. Theodore Roosevelt came to Japan's defense, before and during the peace negotiations at Portsmouth, New Hampshire, in 1905, when he sensed an impending imbalance of power in Russia's favor. Similarly, mainland China in the 1970s and 1980s might need such protection. If China were threatened with invasion or occupation by the Russians and if it had by that time normalized relations with Washington, it might wish to depend upon as many friends, especially powerful ones, as it could muster.

Such a development, obviously, would seriously upset the Far Eastern balance of power, to Russian disadvantage. Under present conditions, therefore, Russia stands to gain by continuing to "cool" the situation between itself and Maoist (and post-Maoist) China. If Russia should permit relations to worsen, or should it lend a hand in their worsening, China might be driven into a course of normalization with the West. Indeed, China might find a receptive audience in the West, if not in Washington, then perhaps elsewhere. Thus, Premier Alexei Kosygin's attempted telephone call to Peking in late March (revealed by Lin Piao at the 1969 Peking party congress) takes on a deeper significance. Soviet initiatives toward Peking—proposing talks toward normalizing the situation on the navigable border rivers of the Ussuri and the Amur, and on Lake Khanka in the Far East*—suggest

---

*Recall the revealing series of events in March-May 1969: March 2 and 15—the bloody border clashes on the Ussuri River; March 20—Senator Edward Kennedy in an important speech said that the Ussuri fighting might lead Peking to reappraise its policy toward the U.S. in a favorable direction; March 21—Soviet Premier Kosygin tried to telephone Peking to arrange for Sino-Soviet talks; March 29—a formal written proposal for same was forwarded to Peking from Moscow; May 3—Soviets proposed a Sino-Soviet conference on insuring normal navigational conditions on Far Eastern border rivers; May 12—the Chinese agreed to meet. Until May 12, China had rebuffed these Soviet initiatives. So, the question remains: Did the Russians take these initiatives out of serious concern

that Moscow sees a definite disadvantage—in the long run—in exacerbating relations between itself and Peking. Moreover, it may appear to Moscow that once Mao leaves the scene, which is bound to occur within the next decade, the Soviets should exert every effort to close the diplomatic breach between themselves and the Chinese, and possibly, but not likely, also repair the ideological schism. Should that happen, it would be the Russians who would have acquired the advantage with respect to the balance of power in the Far East and with respect to the U.S. as well. For under conditions of restored Sino-Soviet cooperation, the U.S.S.R. would still remain the stronger of the two powers in Asia. At the same time, the Soviets would reap the political, ideological, and economic benefits flowing from renewed Sino-Soviet cooperation.

The chances of this occurring are dependent on too many contingencies to hazard any reasonable prediction. The biggest X-factor concerns the post-Maoist succession in Peking. If the moderates of the stripe of Chou En-lai and Chen Yi, or for that matter of the now disgraced Liu Shao-chi, should get hold of the reigns of power, the Soviets might see their dreams realized. If, on the other hand—and this presently seems more likely—Lin Piao and the "hard-liners" take over after Mao, the Russians will have to decide whether (1) to continue as before with a "no peace, no war" policy toward China accompanied by a Sino-Soviet "paper war" and occasional armed border clashes, or (2) to "give up on China" and work toward a serious understanding with the United States on major international problems and particularly on the matter of Red China, and by so doing, forestall a Sino-American understanding with respect to Russia.*

---

over possible alteration of the balance of power in the Far East resulting from a Sino-American détente? Or was it merely a Soviet pose in order to convince its East European allies and the world's Communist Parties of Soviet "goodwill" in the Sino-Soviet dispute? Did the Chinese agree on May 12 to a June convocation of the joint Commission for Navigation on Boundary Rivers also for a show of "goodwill"?

A Soviet announcement on June 14, 1969, as the 75 Communist and Workers' parties were meeting in Moscow, stated that the U.S.S.R. had called upon Communist China to begin negotiations on the river borders within two or three months. The statement rejected the Chinese contention that agreements on borders made between the two countries at the time of the Tsars and Mandarins were "unequal." Returning these former Chinese lands, now within Soviet borders, would be like demanding the return of the United States to Britain, the Soviet statement said.

*On several occasions from 1965 to 1968 during the Johnson Administration when Foreign Minister Gromyko was in Washington or New York at various times, there had been speculation in the U.S. press (in The Washington Post and The New York Times, for example) that China was one of the topics discussed by Gromyko and Secretary of State Rusk. The contents of such discussion would naturally be a closely guarded secret. Otherwise, the Chinese Communist press would have plenty of ammunition with which to mount an accusation of Washington-Moscow collusion and "Soviet revisionist treachery against the working class." The speculation was that Gromyko and Rusk voiced common concern over the growing military might of Red China.

At present, the Soviet course of action appears to be one of wait and see while at the same time following a policy of "encirclement" of China (see pp. 201–202). Meanwhile, American overtures to Peking seem to be an intelligent policy. Such initiatives by Washington might influence the post-Mao succession in a moderate direction which would eventually be more conducive to normal diplomatic and economic intercourse between *all* countries, including the U.S.S.R. Furthermore, Chinese receptiveness to American initiatives might spur the Russians into a more conciliatory attitude toward the United States. This, too, would perform a valuable service in the name of peace.

Balloons and Straws in the Wind on May Day 1969

The celebration throughout the Soviet bloc in 1969 of the "international workingmen's holiday" (May Day) revealed some noteworthy trends. They seemed to suggest that some new departures in Soviet policy might be in the offing. If true, Soviet foreign policy could be in for momentous alterations on the threshold of the 1970s.

First, just a few days before May Day when rehearsals with military equipment were already under way in dozens of Soviet cities, this joint decree of the C.P.S.U. Central Committee and Council of Ministers was published on page one of all Soviet newspapers:

The Central Committee of the C.P.S.U. and Council of Ministers of the U.S.S.R. have considered it expedient henceforth and commencing with the current year to conduct parades of military forces only on November 7, the anniversary of the October Socialist Revolution.[5]

No reasons were given for this decision either in the Soviet press or by Soviet Foreign Ministry officials, although they were pressed on the point by foreign correspondents in Moscow. But there was plenty of speculation in the Western press as to what this unprecedented decision meant, coming as it did in sudden, last-minute fashion.

Examining the May Day slogans published in the Soviet press in mid-April provides some hints. Unlike the slogans of the previous year or of 1967, the 1969 slogans minimized foreign affairs. The greetings to the foreign Communists, which were placed in the Number Five slot in the 1967 slogans, had been dropped to Thirty-ninth place by 1969. There was less mention in general of foreign parties and foreign affairs in 1969 than in either 1967 or 1968.

Furthermore, in the slogan pertaining to Vietnam, the word "piratical" (*razboinichii*) in application to American intervention in the 1968 slogan was significantly edited out in 1969. (I pointed out this trend in a published letter to *The Christian Science Monitor* in March in which I noted that *raz-*

boinichii had also been blue-penciled in Soviet press coverage of events in the Vietnam War.) There was, moreover, a generally less belligerent tone displayed in the 1969 slogans that dealt with "capitalist" themes.

A second change of tone in a moderate direction was evident in C.P.S.U. General-Secretary Brezhnev's May Day speech atop Lenin's Tomb in Red Square.[6] With a dozen or more bemedaled marshals and generals lined up on his right and who made no speeches (since there were no troops to whom to give the Order of the Day), the General-Secretary's bass voice intoned a short twenty-minute speech through the public-address system. The speech showed considerable moderation when compared to that of May Day, 1968. "Leninist principles of peaceful coexistence" and "solution of unsettled international problems by means of negotiations" were mentioned by Brezhnev as basic present-day Soviet foreign policy. In his single reference to the Vietnam War, "American" was omitted from Brezhnev's remark about "imperialist aggressors in Vietnam." He further designated the Middle East and Vietnam as areas ripe for negotiation. The overall bland tone of the party leader's speech was echoed in various other May Day items in the Soviet press.*

In all this, however, there were *two notable exceptions*. The daily of the U.S.S.R. Ministry of Defense, *Red Star*, took up a hard line on May Day. A blatantly anti-American item, under Viktor Mayevsky's by-line, was published in the military daily. Among other harsh things, the veteran *Pravda* writer declared rigidly that "capital and war are inseparable."[7] The same newspaper carried another type of hard-line item. The Soviet Writer's Union official, Anatoli Sofronov, condemned past "stupid statements" which deprecated the wartime leadership of Josef Stalin. Sofronov obviously had in mind, but did not name, Khrushchev and Khrushchev's de-Stalinization campaign. (The fact that immoderate tones are often found in the *military* press will be explored in a later section of this chapter subheaded "The Collectivumvirate.")

A second exception to the generally military-*less* May Day of 1969 occurred in East Berlin. East German Communist chief Walter Ulbricht was the only Soviet bloc leader to order military parades throughout his Communist state on May Day. With this East German deviation from the April 29, 1969, Soviet decree banning military parades on May Day and the apparent snubbing given Ulbricht on his visit to Moscow a few weeks previously, there arose the possibility that a trend toward moderation had set in within the Soviet Politburo. This was revealed earlier in the Soviets' "soft" handling of the potential "Berlin crisis" ostensibly caused by the pres-

---

*In reviewing the foreign press coverage of Brezhnev's May Day address, Soviet newspapers stressed the peace line which the foreign press had detected in the General-Secretary's speech. A picture that was run in May Day editions of Soviet newspapers showed Mikoyan among the members of the C.P.S.U. Politburo (of which he is not a member), an interesting departure from the practice of the last few years of placing Mikoyan at some distance from the ruling core or not in the scene at all.

ence of the West German presidential electors in Berlin. Soviet moderation with respect to the electors seemed moreover to put a strain on relations between Moscow and Pankow, the latter being the obvious supporter of several hard-line policies applied throughout the bloc during the post-Khrushchev period.

At the end of April and in early May 1969 there was also an evident softening in the Soviet press coverage of the rebellious radical students in U.S. universities. (The press had earlier condemned "extremist" elements in the Negro civil rights movement.) In an article that appeared in the Soviet journal *International Economy and International Relations,* the organ of the U.S.S.R. Academy of Sciences Institute of International Economy and International Relations (IMEMO) (see above, p. 216), the two authors, G. Diligensky and M. Novinskaya, commented unfavorably on the "romantic" actions by radical students on American campuses.[8] Although, said the authors, "the student movement keeps gaining in scope and spreading from one campus to the other," it is necessary to analyze the movement in a "sober-minded way." When so analyzed, this movement shows that many of the rebellious students protest on the basis of "tendentious theories." The "age and social traits of the demonstrators impart to the student protest a romantic and irrational character," the authors complained. Because of their "romantic" attachment to the "Che" Guevara cult and to Maoist propaganda, the article continued, the students often unwisely renounce all compromises, "parliamentary activity," temporary political alliances, and "similar methods of class struggle." "For many students it is psychologically more important to demonstrate their protests and their rejection of existing social practices than to gain concrete results of social significance." The authors continued by pointing out that the American students lack organizational skill and have no "clear-cut ideology or political platform." The authors used the term "extremist" to describe those students who fall under the influence of the Guevara cult or Maoist propaganda.

What motivated this hostile attack in a Soviet journal on the radical student movement in the United States? It certainly did not signify that Moscow had suddenly lost interest in supporting Communist activities among American youth. The Soviet press has, in fact, boasted on occasion of the fact that anti-Vietnam demonstrators of various political affiliations have allegedly welcomed Communists in their midsts. What the authors of the IMEMO journal article seemed to object to was that the students so often act in a disorganized way under the *black flag of anarchism* whereas they should organize themselves and close ranks under the *red flag of the Communists.* Although these remarks appeared in a journal that is known for its "sober-minded" view of things, the Diligensky-Novinskaya piece may nevertheless reveal a certain very recently changed disposition within high circles of the C.P.S.U. The Kremlin leaders, or at least some of them, may now seek to play down the irritating internationalist or "ideological" aspects of Soviet relations with the United States, especially if ending the war in Vietnam is actually on the Moscow-Hanoi agenda or if the danger of a Sino-Soviet military confrontation now seriously worries the Kremlin. This possibility was also suggested in Brezhnev's May Day 1969 speech, in the May Day slogans, in which a definite soft-pedaling of ideology as applied to diplomacy was evident, and in Foreign Minister Andrei Gromyko's address to the U.S.S.R. Supreme Soviet on July 10, 1969.

Another and opposite interpretation, however, should not be ignored. It is a long-standing principle of Leninist tactics not to risk exposure or arrest of Communist or fellow-traveler forces in a capitalist country by untimely or rash (ekstremistkiye) actions, such as the occupation-of-buildings technique used by the S.D.S. "anarchists," as the Soviet press calls them. These actions only bring about arrests and identification of Communist cadres and their eventual depletion, Leninism teaches. In addition, demonstrations should always include members of the working class. Otherwise, they hang in midair and are without roots in the toiling masses. The American student movement ignores the proletariat, say the Soviet ideologues.

.   .   .

In conclusion, May Day 1969 saw both balloons and straws in the wind as the weaponless parades (except for East Berlin) marched down city streets in the Communist states of the Soviet bloc and relatively moderate speeches were put on the airwaves. A nascent change in policy seemed to loom on the horizon, perhaps in the form of a belated repercussion from the bloody clashes along the Ussuri River in March, from the four-party Vietnam peace negotiations taking place in Paris, and from the encounter with Western and certain East European Communist leaders at the Kremlin conference in June 1969. If such a change is in the offing, it will undoubtedly be in the direction of policies that emphasize traditional Russian national interest and security, even if this necessitates a readjustment or deemphasis of ideology. Should the Vietnam War be resolved at the Paris peace negotiations in the near future—and events in late April and May 1969 suggested some minor initiatives toward that end were forthcoming from the Communist side—the way would then be opened for a rejuvenated American and Soviet dialogue of the type that was being inaugurated under Khrushchev after the Cuban Crisis of October 1962 and until his ouster two years later.

But there was also another possible course of events. The Communist side might use the Paris talks in order to gain time. As American forces were withdrawn unilaterally by the U.S. (by autumn 1969, this figure was to reach 50,000 troops, about 10 percent of the total American contingent) and as South Vietnamese soldiers replaced the Americans, the North and the Cong might continue building their strength for future battles in which, they might calculate, their chances for victory against South Vietnamese troops would be greater than when their opponent was American. Re-entry of the Americans into the war, should the Communists perpetuate this deceit, would appear highly unlikely to Hanoi and Moscow, especially as popular pressure continued to be applied back in the U.S. for continued and accelerated withdrawal. Talking-peace-while-continuing-to-fight, as the tactic was phrased in captured Vietnamese Communist documents in 1969, might well be the Communist plan. If so, continued and possibly escalated Soviet support for the North in the war would be a crucial necessity. With continued Soviet intransigence about finding ways to end the war (e.g., reconvening of the Geneva Conference which Moscow opposes despite her co-chairmanship of the conference with Great Britain) and ridicule by the Soviets of unilateral withdrawal of American troops, the war in Vietnam could go on indefinitely. In an article written for *The Washington Post* (September 7, 1969), Hugh Seton-Watson, noted British authority on international affairs, offered the opinion that if the war in Vietnam were to end, it would more than likely be *in spite* of Moscow rather than because of it.

Watch on the Reich

The May Day spirit of latent détente may also have penetrated the hard shell of relations between Bonn and Moscow. While to date there has been no visible abatement of the anti-West German line in the Soviet press—the "neo-Nazi"-type cartoons were still published into September 1969—a wrinkle or two was evident on the diplomatic or "state" level.

First, the Soviet government was careful to inform Bonn, along with other Western countries, of the events that took place along the Ussuri River in March 1969. In fact, between January 1968 and April 1969, and adding in several meetings held during both the Ussuri incidents and near-Berlin crisis of March 1969, no fewer than seventeen get-togethers took place between Soviet ambassador to Bonn Semyon Tsarapkin and West German Foreign Minister Willy Brandt. Moreover, during the same period Tsarapkin conferred with West German Chancellor Kurt Kiesinger more than a half-dozen times. The conversations apparently touched upon such problems as Berlin, the nonproliferation treaty (which Bonn had not yet signed), and a possible German-Soviet agreement mutually renouncing use of force in the two countries' relations.

Besides the talking, some German-Soviet movement toward rapprochement had taken place which mildly resembled the situation during Khrushchev's last months in office, First, plans for an unprecedented Frankfurt-to-Moscow air link were almost completed by the spring of 1969. (The link is to be established despite the many ticklish commercial and political questions arising from West German use of air corridors in and out of Berlin—in the absence of a German-Soviet peace treaty—and the question of East Germany's role in all this.) And extensive trade negotiations too were under way.* One Western correspondent has remarked on these recent German-Soviet developments:

Leading Bonn officials view the contacts with considerable curiosity as to Soviet intentions. . . . The new Soviet moderate [diplomatic] line toward Bonn coincides with a similar moderation in West German policy toward East Germany—a policy change which though accepted broadly by the Christian Democrats, bears the distinct stamp of the SPD [the East German Social Democrats].[9]

Another possible explanation for this moderate trend in the Soviet policy toward Bonn related to the West German parliamentary elections in September 1969. The Soviets presumably wanted to encourage more moderate opinion—and that meant above all the Social Democrats—in West Germany.** It is quite remarkable, however, that the Soviets should have felt so confident of the success of their overtures, coming as they had only nine months after the Soviet-led invasion of Czechoslovakia which resulted in numerous divisions of Warsaw Pact troops being put smack up against the West German border! More overtures can be expected in the aftermath of the election victory in West Germany of the Social Democrats under the leadership of Willy Brandt.

Another aspect of the Soviet attitude toward Germany relates to the fundamental problem of the Allied (including the Soviets') "Watch on the Reich," if I may coin a phrase.

We have already mentioned the manner in which Soviet propaganda exploits the alleged German menace as a bogey. It was so used as a pretext for the invasion and occupation of Czechoslovakia in 1969, and it underpins much of the foreign policy of East Germany and Poland. We have also made

*Moscow sent to Bonn its top authority on foreign trade, U.S.S.R. Minister of Foreign Trade N. S. Patolichev. He was the first major Soviet economic official to visit Bonn since Anastas Mikoyan signed a trade pact with West Germany back in 1958.

**During recent commemoration articles on the fiftieth anniversary of the Communist Third International in 1919, it was hinted rather strongly that the "cult of Stalin" has resulted in some grievous error with respect to the Comintern's position on pre-Hitlerite Germany. Instead of encouraging a popular front between the Communist and Social Democrats to oppose the Nazis, Stalin had ordered the German Communists to follow a policy of excluding the SDs. This abetted Hitler because the political forces opposing him had split. Now the policy of the Kremlin internationalists seems to be one of support for the West German SDs for the purpose, among other things, of winning ratification in the West German parliament of the nonproliferation treaty and of helping into power the Social Democratic Party which, Moscow may reckon, is somewhat more favorably inclined toward the Soviets than the Christian Democrats.

reference to the German problem in still another connection: West Germany *qua* the western extension of the current Soviet policy of "double encirclement." But there is still another consideration to keep in mind. This is the hypothesis that the salient feature of Soviet policy toward both West Germany and the United States is the Soviet desire to break up N.A.T.O. and by so doing, weaken the "Washington-Bonn axis"—which, the Soviets say, is the principal threat to their western flank—by ostracizing the U.S. from Europe and thereby pulling the American prop from under the West Germans. It is probably the consensus among most writers and scholars dealing with international affairs that this is, as it has been for many years, the Soviet goal in Western Europe. While the hypothesis at least sounds logical, it remains a *hypothesis* and is therefore worth careful and critical examination.

Consider for a moment what the consequences would be for the Soviets should the Americans withdraw from Europe, meaning in effect, abandoning of Germany. First, the Potsdam agreement on four-power responsibility for Germany—meaning for Russia particularly West Germany—would evaporate, as well as Articles 53 and 107 of the United Nations Charter providing for Allied prevention of a resurgence of Fascism and militarism in the defeated Axis countries. With the Potsdam and U.N.O. provisions a dead letter, West Germany would become a fully sovereign state, absolutely free to do what it wished, short of the limitations to which any state is normally subject by reason of the restraining power of its neighbors. West Germany, however, would be no "ordinary" state; it is the most powerful state in Europe (excluding the U.S.S.R., of course), and its central location makes it all the more crucial.

Second, West German freedom of action might well give encouragement to what the Russians above all consider to be a viable force in Germany: the inbred German *Geist* of militarism. No longer would the United States, Britain, France, and the U.S.S.R. have a formal say in whether, for example, Germany should be prohibited from acquiring nuclear weapons.

Third, American withdrawal from Europe and the breakup of N.A.T.O. would not be all that attractive to Moscow for several other reasons. For one thing, the Soviets apparently take to the idea of the West European economies being burdened and inflated with defense expenditures to meet the demands of N.A.T.O.; this in turn presumably aggravates the class struggle in these countries, since it is the working class—so say the Moscow internationalists and ideologues—which gets pinched the most by inflation and taxes. Secondly, are we sure that it is in the Soviet interest to have militarily weak states in the North Atlantic area? It would not take much imaginative "contingency planning" in Moscow to anticipate a situation—possibly by the 1970s, but certainly by the 1980s and 1990s—in which the Chinese will have built themselves up militarily to the point where they seriously menaced the Russians in the east. Suppose that the Chinese even mounted a large-scale military attack against Russia along the 4,592-mile Far Eastern border. Does it not seem plausible that the Soviets would wish to rely on European allies—meaning both Eastern and Western—in such a contigency? Would not Russia depict such a war as a Chinese threat to the *whole of European civilization?* Indeed, this is exactly the depiction that has begun to creep into some of the anti-Chinese documents emanating from Russia since the March 1969 clashes along the Ussuri River. An example of this is Yevtushenko's poem about the ravaging forces of Genghis Khan which were stopped by the Russians in the Battle of Kulikovo in A.D. 1380 and which he compares to the Maoist forces who threaten European civilization. Likewise, Soviet Foreign Minister Gromyko said in his July 10, 1969, address to the U.S.S.R. Supreme Soviet: "The security of the U.S.S.R. is bound up with the security of the whole of Europe."

In light of what has been said, then, consider the following *counter-*hypothesis. Moscow does *not* want to break up N.A.T.O. It wants and needs a U.S. presence in Europe in order, for one thing, to keep the Four-Power Statute on Germany intact, and for another, to keep all of Europe strong in the face of future trouble in the world—especially in the Far East—requiring police action. What, if any, "hard" facts are there to back up the counterhypothesis?

One tip-off that Moscow might not be irrevocably committed to the breakup of N.A.T.O. came with the invasion of Czechoslovakia in August 1968. The twenty-year term of the North Atlantic Treaty Organization was due to expire in 1969, only a few months later, in other words. In recent years there had been a gradual cooling of West European interest in N.A.T.O. France had all but completely withdrawn from the organization, and public opinion in many West European nations was growing increasingly anti-N.A.T.O. This trend must surely have been as obvious to the Russians as to West European observers. The Soviet press occasionally took note of the trend. But when the Russians and their four Warsaw Pact allies chose to move boldly and with great show of force into Czechoslovakia in the late summer of 1968, with dozens of heavily armed divisions bristling with late-model weapons, and some of which marched right up to the West German border, what reaction logically could be expected in N.A.T.O. capitals? And what reaction actually came? It can be boiled down to one short phrase: *girding up N.A.T.O.* Would it be wildly speculative to assume that Moscow *must have expected such a reaction before it made the momentous decision to move those many divisions into the heart of Europe?* Which raises the question: Why did Moscow choose such an apparently "unpropitious" moment to bring its errant satellite into line? Why was the prospect of a renewed and girded-up N.A.T.O. of obviously lower priority than an *overly* armed Communist presence in the center of Europe?

While not rushing to the conclusion that Moscow hoped for a bolstered N.A.T.O., we might at the very least assume that Moscow did not fear a refurbished N.A.T.O. so much that it would have avoided at almost any cost provoking a West European military buildup. Moscow, after all, did not even elect to wait until renewal of the N.A.T.O. treaty had become a *fait accompli*. It is possible, of course, that the Kremlin reasoned that the treaty would be continued in any case. Still, it must have expected that after its invasion of Czechoslovakia, the N.A.T.O. treaty would not only be renewed, but that the military strength of its members—perhaps including West Germany—would be sharply increased.

And this is not all. There have been several indications that Moscow still values the joint Allied Watch on the Reich represented by the Potsdam accords and Articles 53 and 107 of the U.N.O. Charter. The Potsdam Statute is continually referred to by the Russians as being very much in force. In fact, in recent years it has been brought up with greater frequency by Moscow than by the Western powers! Examples of this occurred in connection with the Russian protest against the presence of the Bonn presidential electors in West Berlin in the spring of 1969, the Russians objecting vehemently that this constituted a violation of the Potsdam accords and the U.N.O. Charter. On many other occasions as well, when trouble has been brewing in Berlin (much of it upon the instigation of the Russians or the East Germans), the Potsdam Four-Power Statute is brought up. Moscow also refers to the four-power controls whenever the topic concerns the alleged renascence of German neo-Nazism in West Germany, since part of the Potsdam agreements and the two U.N.O. Charter provisions concern denazification.

In short, the specter called "Germany," but meaning for the Russians particularly West Germany, still haunts the Kremlin. But it is by no means certain that the Russians take their own propaganda seriously when they treat the "Washington-Bonn axis" as though it were a threat to their security. While this may make good propaganda copy or a pretext for interference on influence in various countries of the Soviet bloc, it makes little sense from a *raison d'état* point of view. Moscow is perfectly aware of the fact that Washington (not to mention London and Paris) continues to serve as a check upon any extensive German rearmament up to and including strategic weapons or the German wherewithal to make them. The same applies to German reunification. Both Washington and Moscow oppose and have always opposed this *during the whole postwar period.* Paul Nitze, who took part in laying the foundations for N.A.T.O. in the late 1940s, once candidly assessed this convoluted American policy toward Germany which dovetails with the Russian position:

We did not see how the reunification of Germany in a form acceptable to the Bonn government could be *prevented* if Russian military forces were not directly present in support of the Eastern regime. Far from wishing Germany or any other part of Central Europe to become part of NATO, it was thought that the influence of the NATO powers would be directed to keeping Central Europe a buffer area, incapable of disturbing the security of the West or of challenging the East.[10]

To which George Bailey, former *Reporter* writer and now an editor at *Harper's*, commented after quoting Nitze's aforementioned remarks:

In short, in a peculiar, roundabout, and tortuous way, the creation of NATO was meant to provide a means of shoring up the *status quo minus* left by the Soviet blockade of Berlin [in 1948]. One of the principal but well-hidden functions of NATO throughout the postwar period was to act as a prop for the Four Power Statute of Germany, which had all but collapsed. . . . Thus the double purpose of NATO—crusade *with* the Germans against communism, but security *from* the Germans by incorporating them in a broader role.

Finally, Bailey astutely observes:

There are two remnants of the wartime alliance, both of which are being assiduously kept alive by the Americans and the Soviets: the Four Power Statute for Berlin, and by extension Germany, and the United Nations Organization.

Finally, in a letter published in *The Christian Science Monitor* (February 14, 1969) I made this rebuttal of a *Monitor* editorial:

Your Jan. 21, editorial, 'Moscow and Bonn,' erring both by commission and omission, fails to take cognizance of that perennial diplomatic play of forces known as the 'eternal quadrille' of Britain, France, Germany, and Russia.

You state that 'a constant thread in Russian diplomacy in Western Europe has been pressure . . . to drive a wedge between Washington and Bonn.' In your discussion, no mention is made of Russian policy toward Britain and France.

Contradictory—or should I say, 'dialectical'?—as it may seem, post-World War II Soviet policy toward the Washington-Bonn relationship can be read . . . as a Soviet attempt to preserve United States involvement in what remains of four-power control over both Germanys. The hub of this Allied supervision is, of course, Berlin. Far from wishing the United States to turn its back on European affairs and especially concern for Allied security in the face of a renewed and reunited Germany, Moscow has been satisfied with the following three developments: 1) a split and therefore weaker Germany; 2) a Western Allied watch on West Germany . . . 3) a Soviet and Western Allied understanding that Berlin remain an agreed-upon linchpin for maintaining a Watch on the Reich. *Most interestingly, in the recent Soviet pressure for pan-European security negotiations, Moscow made it explicit that she was not opposed to United States participation in the talks* . . .

As for the United States—Russia appears to be not altogether opposed to that transoceanic giant's remaining the 'fifth' member of the European quadrille [italics mine].

The Collectivumvirate

One can attribute political decisions to economic, social, and military factors and "imperatives" up to a point. But beyond that, the "subjective" factor of leadership becomes crucial. Just where to draw the line between personal and impersonal determinants of political decisions—and, indeed, for history as a whole—is a most complex problem. Historians themselves do not agree on the question, nor do political scientists. The most that can be said, probably, is that under certain circumstances and at certain times, the subjective factor may be of greater significance than such impersonal factors as "economic law," public opinion, "spirit of the times," and so on, although their strong influence should not be left out of the equation either. The political scientist might add that in a given regime or in a given species of regime, the subjective factor may tend to dominate over the others; this would undoubtedly be more true of a dictatorial than of a liberal-democratic regime, but not necessarily under all circumstances (see above p. 146).

As to the Soviet regime today, it is difficult to isolate *the* most important determining factor for the making and execution of Soviet foreign policy, assuming that only one existed—there are several, in fact. But it would probably not be one-sided of me to suggest that a system of committee rule, as in the case of the Soviet Politburo, backed up by a totally controlled press and in the complete absence of any substantive or effective social or political institutions representing or expressing popular opinion or the "popular will," gives the Soviet rulers an extraordinary degree of power and freedom of action. At the same time, the power is not always made or applied on the basis of totally unanimous decisions within the Politburo or Presidium of the Council of Ministers.* Khrushchev once admitted to Western correspondents that voting procedures were followed within the C.P.S.U. Politburo (then called the Presidium) and that majority rule, not unanimity, was the custom. Presumably, this practice continues today among the post-Khrushchev collectivirs. It may, in fact, be an even more commonly used procedure now than under Khrushchev because the "collective leadership" is today more "collective" than it was under the rule of the energetic and somewhat authoritarian First Secretary. This was confirmed in part by that fascinating and unprecedented occurrence from July 29 to August 1, 1968, when nearly the whole Soviet Politburo *as a body* got on a train and went to Cierna-nad-Tisou, Slovakia, to hold talks with the Czechoslovak leaders. This action suggested that nearly all Politburo members had to participate in the discussion if the resultant decisions were going to be truly collective.

*The Soviet Constitution makes no mention of a Presidium *of the Council of Ministers*, a kitchen cabinet within the top executive organs of the state apparatus. Still, such a body has functioned at various times in Soviet history, including the post-Stalin period. It is composed of the First and ordinary Deputy Premiers of the U.S.S.R. and the Premier Alexei Kosygin, as *primus inter pares*. The Premier and the *First* Deputy Premiers are customarily members of the C.P.S.U. Politburo, a ruling body which is also ignored by the Constitution.

This is not the place to journey into the labyrinth of Kremlinology, as respectable as that science has become of late,* beyond noting some recent trends in the perennial jockeying for position within the Kremlin.

Again, military figures loom large among the *dramatis personnae*. Toward the end of April—when the several trends noted above began to surface—various spokesmen for the military, and some of the outstanding military officials themselves, began to speak out in organs of the press where party control seems to be somewhat thin, or at least thinner than in the rest of the press. In *Krasnaya Zvezda (Red Star)*, in *Kommunist*, which is technically a C.P.S.U. journal but which is nevertheless obliged to give space on occasion to military points of view, in the Defense Ministry's *Kommunist Vooruzhennykh Sil (Communist of the Armed Forces)*, and in the R.S.F.S.R. daily, *Sovetskaya Rossiya*, articles began to appear which revealed an extraordinary degree of independence on the part of the military. The articles also displayed a certain deviation in a militant, even bellicose direction, from what appears to be a somewhat more moderate line of some of the civilian rulers within the C.P.S.U. Politburo today—a line upon which, there may not be unanimous concurrence within the Politburo itself. The situation suggests a parallel with the state of affairs which prevailed in the closing months of Khrushchev's reign. At that time, military spokesmen were getting their views into print despite the fact that they clearly did not harmonize with the ideas and policies promoted by the First Secretary.

On April 29, 1969, for example, *Red Star* ran an article written by an obscure military spokesman by the name of Major-General Vladimir N. Korshunov, identified only as a "non-staff contributor."[11] Korshunov emphasized the principal of *yedinonachaliye*, or "unitary leadership," within the armed forces. The implication was quite obvious. "Unitary leadership" is a Soviet euphemism for noninterference by nonprofessional-military "political commissars" in strictly military affairs. The most famous occurrence of the reassertion of the rights of the professional-military came in 1956–1957 when Marshal Georgi K. Zhukov unprecedentedly held the post of member of the C.P.S.U. Presidium and U.S.S.R. Minister of Defense. At that time, Zhukov spearheaded an effort by the military to carve out for itself wider authority in making military policy for the Soviet state. When Zhukov was ousted in October 1957, this was precisely the accusation made against him by the Khrushchev regime, which labeled him a "Bonapartist."

General Korshunov's article in *Red Star* suggests the possibility that the

*Henry Kamm's observation (*The New York Times*, May 4, 1969) is *apropos*: "To Kremlin watchers, these [events on May Day, etc.] are part of a perennial drama entitled 'The Power Struggle in the Kremlin.' They are taken the more seriously because in the dreary uniformity imposed by the cautious collective leadership almost no indication of a struggle comes to the surface."

professional military may again be on the warpath. This in turn suggests that major disagreements may exist between the military on the one hand and the civilian leaders of the C.P.S.U. Politburo on the other. There is also the likelihood that the military is able to get articles into print, as it was in 1963–1964, because of support coming from a part, at least, of the Politburo. One of the most likely sources is the office of Second Secretary Mikhail A. Suslov. It is he and his *apparat* which oversee the organs of the press—especially *Kommunist* and *Partiinaya Zhizn*, official C.P.S.U. publications, and also *Sovetskaya Rossiya*, all of which carried "hawkish" items authored by the military in April–May 1969 and in August 1969.

One of these harsh notes was struck by General Alexei A. Yepishev, a Brezhnev protegé and chief political commissar of the Soviet armed forces. Although not a professional military man and, in fact, a former careerist in the state security *apparat*, Yepishev has frequently adopted the line taken by more militant voices within the Soviet General Staff and Ministry of Defense. Like Korshunov and others, Yepishev may enjoy the backing of certain members of the Politburo and possibly but not necessarily that of General-Secretary Brezhnev, who had a hand in promoting Yepishev immediately after Khrushchev's ouster in October 1964 and who is himself an ex-political commissar. Yepishev wrote in the bimonthly *Kommunist* of the C.P.S.U. Central Committee in the second half of April 1969:

Certain ideologists of imperialism and political and military figures in the capitalist states are trying to prove that the Leninist formula characterizing war as the continuation of politics by forcible means is 'outdated,' that it is somehow incompatible with nuclear war, that such a war would not have a class-political content and would not represent the continuation of the politics of states and of various classes.[12]

"A third world war," Yepishev continued ominously, "if imperialism were permitted to start it, would be decisive [*reshitelnii*] class conflict between the two antagonistic social systems." Then Yepishev made this distinction:

From the side of the imperialist states, this war would be a continuation of the criminal reactionary and aggressive policies of imperialism. From the side of the Soviet Union and the countries of the Socialist Camp, it would mean the continuation of the revolutionary policies of freedom and independence of the Socialist state, a guarantee of the construction of socialism and communism, a legal and justified counteraction to aggression.

To a person unversed in the language of political commissars, the quotation above may not sound particularly earth shaking. But it was. Yepishev was, in fact, restoring the "ideological preparation of the Soviet armed forces" to the position taken by Stalin in 1948–1952 which had also charged that the West was preparing a Third World War. Yepishev's language and the trend of his thinking in the article did not appear to harmonize with the more moderate approach that began to be displayed in April–May 1969 by the civilian leaders of the C.P.S.U., or at least of the outspoken ones. Furthermore, Yepishev's remark that a Third World War would be the "decisive class conflict" between Socialism and capitalism was a chilling note and one that has lain mostly dormant since the days of Stalin. The identical militant line cropped up again in an article by Marshal N. I. Krylov, in *Sovetskaya Rossiya*, August 30, 1969. (Marshal Krylov, commander of Soviet missile forces, had been dismissed as Chief of the Soviet General Staff by Khrushchev, presumably for his radical "hawkism.") All of this suggests a revival of the Leninist-Stalinist essentials on war. Lenin had the following to say on the matter of wars:

We are not pacifists. We are opposed to imperialist wars for the division of spoils among the capitalists. But we have always declared it to be absurd for the revolutionary proletariat to renounce revolutionary wars that may prove necessary in the interests of Socialism.[13]

If war is waged by the proletariat after it has conquered power the bourgeoisie in its own country and is waged with the object of strengthening and extending Socialism, such a war is legitimate and 'holy.'[14]

Or Lenin, as quoted by Stalin:

'We are living,' Lenin writes, 'not merely in a state but in a *system* of states, and it is inconceivable that the Soviet Republic should continue to exist for a long period side by side with imperialist states. Ultimately, one or the other must conquer. Meanwhile, a number of terrible clashes between the Soviet Republic and the bourgeois states is inevitable.[15]

Yepishev's reference to war as a "continuation of politics by forcible means" was taken from Lenin's gloss on the writings of the Russian military theorist, Karl von Clausewitz (1780–1831). The concept of a Third World War as the "ultimate class conflict between the two antagonistic social systems" dates, as we noted, back to the Stalin period. But it also made a brief reappearance in the first and second editions (1962 and 1963) of Marshal V. D. Sokolovsky's book *Voennaya strategiya (Military Strategy)*, the controversy around which was discussed in a previous chapter (see pp. 175–176).

Not all the activities of the Soviet military in the spring of 1969 seemed outwardly belligerent or anti-U.S. in tendency. For example, the visit of Marshal Vasily I. Chuikov, head of Soviet Civil Defense, to Washington to attend the funeral of Dwight D. Eisenhower early in April 1969 deserves mention. During his brief stay, according to *The Washington Post* (April 13, 1969), Marshal Chuikov conferred at length with U.S. Secretary of Defense Melvin R. Laird and General Earle P. Wheeler, Chairman of the Joint Chiefs of Staff. *The Post* reported the following from Washington.

Although what was said is top secret, the Russian Marshal and Laird did more than engage in small talk. It is known that there was cordial, if not wholly productive, conversation about the intentions of Moscow in its present buildup of offensive missiles. In fact, the question of intentions was first raised by Chuikov. . . . Chuikov presented Wheeler with a personally inscribed copy of his book, *The Battle of Stalingrad*. In return, Wheeler presented the Russian with a medallion and then arranged for him to tour the National War College later in the day.

It may or may not be noteworthy that one of the statements made by Chuikov in his war memoirs in 1965 was the following:

They [the Nazi leaders] painstakingly sought to find a rift between the peoples of the Allied countries, and failed to find it. And if they did perceive waverings, a tendency on the part of certain personages of the Western powers to go as far as reconciliation with the Nazis and a separate peace, it was above all the people in the lands of those Powers which would not have allowed them to commit such a crime. . . . We showed him [General Krebs] that we would not retreat a step from the decisions of the Yalta and Teheran Conferences. Our loyalty and firmness restrained any expression of wavering among our Allies.[16]

Optimism over Chuikov's friendly visit to Washington and his conversation with Laird and General Wheeler and the attendant pleasantries should be cautious. For one thing, Chuikov is *not* one of the more influential military officers in the U.S.S.R. and today functions as a largely titular chief of national defense rather than as an important member of the Soviet high command. Still, Chuikov's brief encounter with American officials in Washington is not without interest and, possibly, significance.

Besides these and other stirrings within the military sector of the Kremlin hierarchy,* there are evidences of discord among the upper echelons of the C.P.S.U. The zigzagging course followed by the Politburo during the Czechoslovak crisis of 1968 provides some evidence of this. Moreover, the occasional references made by Politburo leaders to "certain comrades who . . .," followed then by a "mistaken" point of view held by these comrades, indicates dissension. One such article appeared in *Kommunist* in 1967 under the authorship of Politburo member and First Deputy Premier Dmitri S. Polyansky, a reputed "dove." Polyansky's complaint was that not enough funds and resources go into agriculture. The "certain com-

---

*E.g., Chief of the Soviet General Staff Marshal Matvei V. Zakharov's article in the C.P.S.U. cadres journal, *Partiinaya Zhizn* (*Party Life*) just before May Day 1969 made the point that Soviet missile defense possessed "a great number of new, and what is especially important, mobile launching installations. . . . Global rockets have unlimited range and are able to carry colossal payloads and overcome the anti-missile defense of an adversary." Marshal Zakharov did not, however, claim superiority over the United States, "possibly," as *The New York Times* Moscow correspondent Bernard Gwertzman pointed out (May 1, 1969), "to avoid alarming American officials [and] possibly to relieve fears within the Soviet Union about the dangers of arms control talks with the United States."

rades" were apparently some of Polyansky's colleagues on the Politburo who tend to place too much emphasis on military expenditures or expenditures within the heavy industry sector (an important part of whose production is related to defense). Stories occasionally appeared in the Western press in early 1969 predicting Brezhnev's "imminent" fall from power. But Kremlinologists are not entirely in agreement as to where Brezhnev fits into the factional spectrum of "hawks" vs. "doves" or "isolationists" vs. "disarmers" within the C.P.S.U. Politburo.[17] It is possible that Brezhnev nimbly avoids taking sides, attempting instead to steer a middle course while leaving the more concerted "hawkish" position to his deputy party secretary, Mikhail A. Suslov, the Second Secretary of the C.P.S.U. In any case, many of the "harder" post-Khrushchev policies we have discussed above and in preceding chapters were initiated under Brezhnev's leadership. His quasi-military background may be a factor in the policies that have been unfolded under his aegis since October 1964. It should also be added that Brezhnev probably now holds the position of Supreme Commander of the Armed Forces, as did his predecessor, or at least shares the post with Premier Kosygin.*

If a sharp turnabout in the direction of détente with America or a "softer" line in general (for example, settling the war in Vietnam, effective Soviet pressure toward cooling the tensions between Israel and the Arabs, agreement with the U.S. on ABMs, etc., softening toward West Germany), should be executed by the Kremlin, it appears unlikely that the present top leadership in the party and government would remain unchanged.

Foreign Policy and the Home Front

The intimate relationship between domestic policy and foreign policy should not escape our attention as we canvas Soviet problems on the threshold of the 1970s. A number of questions come to mind in this connection. For example, does insecurity at home cause stiffening of Soviet posture toward foreign countries? To quote the oversimplified question about the connection between the Soviet economy and foreign policy: Do "well-fed Communists" pursue a hard line, "hungry Communists" a soft one, or vice versa, in foreign policy?

We have already mentioned one or two advantages of the Soviet system in its dealings with non-Communist liberal democracies (see above, p. 148).

*The late Marshal Sokolovsky's book, *Military Strategy* (1962 and 1963 editions), discussed this point and stated that the post was held jointly by the head of the C.P.S.U. and the head of the government. At the time the book was published, Khrushchev held both positions as First Secretary and Chairman of the Council of Ministers of the U.S.S.R. Whether since Khrushchev's ouster, the post of Supreme Commander has been split between Brezhnev and Kosygin is not known.

The fact that the U.S.S.R. Supreme Soviet, the Soviet Union's "parliament," has no substantive power to "advise and consent" on foreign policy and in no way questions or interferes in the C.P.S.U. Politburo's and Secretariat's policy-making in foreign affairs, gives considerable leeway to the top leaders. Executives and foreign ministers in the non-Communist countries, meanwhile, must make their foreign policy decisions, not only on the basis of factors in the international arena, but also with an eye toward gaining approval in the public generally. Despite the advantages accruing to the totalitarian state in this regard, Soviet foreign policy-makers do not have freedom to do what they like in all respects and to ignore domestic factors altogether.

For one thing, consumer goods production in the U.S.S.R. is to a far greater degree than in most Western countries dependent upon government decisions on how natural resources will be allocated between Category A (heavy industry, including defense) and Category B (consumer goods). This stems from the fact that Soviet production of goods and services is less than half of the principal Western country, the United States, while the population is some 20 percent larger. In addition, Soviet agriculture, which produces most of the raw materials going into consumer goods, is notoriously capricious. Sometimes the culprit is weather—as it was in the winter of 1968/1969—which causes this production to flounder. Sometimes it is mainly the perennial factors of mismanagement and overcentralization within "socialized farming" which are at least equal to weather as major causes of "shortcomings."

Another factor should not be ignored: the state-plan system and the planners. Several *Communist* critics of the Soviet system have pointed out that the state planners *deliberately* keep consumer goods production at an almost-marginal level. They do this, not only because of the demands made on resources and production facilities by real or imagined defense needs of the country, but because to unleash a policy of "consumerism" within the planned economy would soon cause its own withering away. Popular demand for consumer goods would accelerate and with it, managerial pressures to dismantle the system of centralized planning and to switch over to a partially or wholly market-oriented economy *sans* the planners and party supervisors. This was precisely the program that the Czech "revisionist" economist and professor Ota Sik was evidently contemplating before he was dismissed, under Soviet pressure, from his post as state-planning chief and one-man economic brain trust in Prague soon after the Soviet-led August 1968 invasion and occupation.

Grand strategy, of which foreign policy is one of the main constitutents, makes various demands on the economy, depending upon what that strategy is. For example, should Soviet grand strategy become one of concerted effort toward East-West détente, Soviet foreign policy would change too.

Soviet diplomats would then begin working toward achievement of an understanding with the West—particularly with the U.S.—on such matters as for example, limiting production of ABMs. Soviet diplomats might also seek agreement with the West Europeans on an integrated pan-European security system, perhaps including the United States. These and other decisions like them would have an immediate effect upon the Soviet economy and the overall domestic situation in the U.S.S.R.

First, more consumer goods could be produced as greatly increased expenditures under Category B became possible once the Soviets felt more secure about their western flank, assuming that that is how they would react to East-West security pacts and the general atmosphere of relaxed tensions.

But, second, the one-party regime would then be confronted with the danger that the Soviet population would become increasingly restive as tensions relaxed and with it the ideological militancy toward "imperialism." The pleasure-bent Soviet people would then think only about the good life—traveling to the West, "conspicuous consumption," a free marketplace of ideas, and so on. The public would hardly be in a receptive state of mind should the Kremlin demand future sacrifices, say, in the face of mounting danger on the Soviets' Central Asian and Far Eastern flank facing Red China. Countervailing hard-line policies might then set in (see above, p. 148).

Thus, the regime must strike a delicate balance between the needs of the Soviet consumer and the drain on resources and production facilities necessitated by defense needs, and between a "reasonably contented" consuming public and one that has become unduly impatient for more nonessentials. The post-Khrushchev regime *has* given the populace a visible annual improvement in the standard of living. At the same time it has been able to meet the rather ambitious demands of the defense industry, which have been sharply increased since Khrushchev's overthrow. Some of the recent developments in the international arena have assisted, but at the same time have complicated, the harmonization of foreign policy and domestic policy.

When in March 1969 dozens of Soviet border guards lost their lives in skirmishes with the "Chinese adventurists," many border guards on duty in European Russia promptly requested reassignment to the Far East. Soviet workers and collective farmers began to promise greater feats of production and to pledge greater solidarity with "the foreign policy line set by our C.P.S.U. Central Committee and the government." Nor was all this enthusiasm fabricated by the Soviet press, like the forced smile on the faces of eager-beaver metalworkers and tractor drivers posing for front-page photographs in *Pravda* and *Izvestiya*.

But, on the other hand, when Soviet troops and those of the four other Warsaw Pact allies invaded and occupied Czechoslovakia in 1968, the popular reaction in the U.S.S.R. was certainly not as favorable as the Soviet press hoopla said it was. A small knot of protesters appeared unprecedentedly in

Red Square in front of St. Basil's Cathedral and carried signs defending Czechoslovak independence; they had to be dispersed by Soviet militiamen and the K.G.B. Moreover, open letters were sent to the Kremlin, some of them leaking out to the West.* The poet Yevgeny Yevtushenko reportedly wired the Soviet leaders:

I don't know how to sleep. I don't know how to continue living. All I know is that I have a moral duty to express to you the feelings that overpower me.

I am deeply convinced that our action in Czechoslovakia is a tragic mistake and bitter blow against Soviet-Czech friendship and the world Communist movement.

. . . We cannot forsee the consequences of this action.[17]

How limited and extensive this fall-out was among the Soviet population is, of course, impossible to determine. But it was certainly the first manifest disaffection to be provoked by a Soviet *foreign policy* decision in the whole 50-year history of the Soviet regime.** Despite its nonviolence and the apparently small scale upon which it was expressed, the negative reaction to the invasion and occupation of Czechoslovakia finds a parallel in the popular reaction to Tsarist foreign policy in the Far East in 1904–1905. In that case, however, the reaction was more widespread and was violent. Living conditions in Russia were worse than now, and the cause of the disaffection much graver: a hopeless and foolish war which took a large toll in Russian lives. Still, the 1968–1969 show of disaffection is analogous, although not identical, to the situation in Russia 65 years earlier.

Meanwhile, a sword of Damocles hangs over the Kremlin which would surely come down on the heads of the rulers should the regime get itself involved in any situation like the Russo-Japanese War and in which the lives of large number of Russian troops would be lost. In the peculiar way in which political absolutism in Russia—Tsarist and Soviet—"*hangs in the air*," to quote Peter Tkachev, the "first Bolshevik" of the 1870s, and sinks no deep roots in the population, causes a Russian regime to face the potential danger of widespread popular disaffection quite unlike the way in which liberal-democratic regimes face popular discontent. In the latter, such phenomena as popular antiwar street demonstrations, open television debates, the free

*For a fascinating insight into dissension among Soviet intellectuals, see Karl Van Het Reve (ed.), *Dear Comrade: Pavel Litvinov and the Voices of Soviet Citizens in Dissent* (New York: Pitman, 1969).

**Popular reaction, at least among many Soviet intellectuals, was likewise unfavorable with respect to Soviet policy toward the Arabs in the Israeli-Arab extensive June War of 1967. But the negative fall-out was more prevalent in Czechoslovakia, Poland, and particularly Rumania—the latter having the largest Jewish minority of any Communist country except the U.S.S.R. Ceausescu's regime in Rumania, unlike Moscow's other closest allies in Eastern Europe, did not break relations with Israel in 1967 and maintains relations with Israel that are at least as warm as those with the Arab countries.

press, multiparty competition, and the like, all act as safety valves releasing pent-up popular disgruntlement. But in the Byzantine atmosphere of the Russian police state, no such relief can be found. What the regime calls "spontaneous demonstrations" are programmed and rehearsed like performances at the Bolshoi. Truly spontaneous demonstrations are put down as fast as that of the 1968 pro-Czechoslovak protesters was in front of St. Basil's.

Should they become disaffected and aroused in the extreme, the Russian people would have to resort to other means, as indeed they have in their history, and in not very remote history at that. As Lenin remarked when he was in a more populistic frame of mind before 1917: When sufficiently angered by their regime, Lenin said, the Russian people will "vote with their legs."

World Communist Conference III

The Kremlin and the "internationalists" headed by Suslov succeeded, after several frustrated attempts, in holding a conference of Communist and Workers' parties June 5–17, 1969. Representing 75 parties, the conference in St. George's Hall in the Great Kremlin Palace was the third such gathering of the clan in the post-Stalin era (Conference I was held in 1957; II, in 1960). Several traditional diplomatic problems were aired by the Soviet leaders for the benefit of the foreign comrades; some of them hardly contributed to "Communist unity," a catch phrase of the conference. In his June 7 address to the 300 delegates, Brezhnev, for example, went right ahead and condemned the Maoists, despite an agreement at preparatory meetings earlier in the spring *not* to "read out" the Chinese. True, the General-Secretary said that the "changing situation" had warranted the C.P.S.U. decision to excoriate the "messianism" and "evil anti-Sovietism" of the Maoists in Peking. Moreover, the Paraguayans had taken on the onus of condemning the Chinese a few speeches before Brezhnev's. But the decision of the C.P.S.U. Secretariat was hardly calculated to contribute to international solidarity, although it undoubtedly served Russian national interests.

The Italian Communists, the Rumanians, the British, the Australians, and several other delegations all let it be known that they opposed a number of the positions taken by a majority of the Communists headed by the C.P.S.U. Ceausescu, head of the Rumanian Communist Party, said that his delegation had considered walking out of the conference over the issue of the condemnation by the Soviets and others of the Chinese Communist Party but had decided to stay in order to try to reverse the anti-Chinese trend. Similarly, Ceausescu made a strong appeal for the inviolability of national sovereignty and thus subtly repudiated the "Brezhnev Doctrine," which justifies interference by Communist states into the affairs of other Communist states. The Italians, harking back to Togliatti's theory of "polycentrism," stated their opposition to any type of "hegemonism" within the international Communist movement. This clashed with the C.P.S.U. bloc's view—particularly as voiced at the conference by East German Communist leader Ulbricht—that the third conference should have agreed unanimously on a number of issues, among them condemnation of Red China and support for the Soviet-led invasion and occupation of Czechoslovakia.

The behavior of the Russian hosts at the conference gave clear indication that the Sino-Soviet dispute, which has lately turned into a shooting mini-war along the Far Eastern and Central Asian borders between the two huge countries, occupies a central position in Kremlin policy. It may be said in the light of the conference that the Soviet flag leads while C.P.S.U. ideological shibboleths follow. Put another way, it is Russian national interest and security that are attaining, at present, first priority; world Communist unity is slipping to a lower priority. As was shown by the Russian decision to invade and occupy Czechoslovakia in August 1968, Communist internationalism and "international solidarity" must sometimes be sacrificed on the altar of Soviet *raison d'état*. Even the location of the conference smacked of this priority. As originally planned, the delegates were to convene in a large hall on the outskirts of Moscow in the Lenin Hills region. Instead, the Soviets chose to hold meetings in St. George's Hall in the Great Kremlin Palace. Its white marble plaques celebrate the knights who won fame and honor in the Tsarist army, and there is a sculptured display of Russian victories in wars fought from the fifteenth to the nineteenth century. The 300 leaders of the 75 delegations who strode past these memorials could scarcely have ignored the symbolism. Brezhnev, incidentally, referred to another kind of symbolism attaching to the hall. It was here, said the General-Secretary in his June 7 speech to the conference, that Mao Tse-tung indulged himself in the most bloodthirsty misanthropy at Conference I in 1957. "With despicable heedlessness and cynicism," said Brezhnev, "Mao Tse-tung spoke in this same hall about the possible destruction of half of mankind in the case of atomic war. The fact is that Mao Tse-tungism calls for a struggle not against war, but for war, which is regarded as having positive historical significance."

Hints of U.S.-Soviet Rapprochement

A variety of developments in mid-1969, when added to the earlier straws in the wind sent aloft by the Kremlin around May Day, pointed in the direction of a more moderate Soviet line on relations with the United States. Whether it is a tangible or illusory change of line remains to be seen. Two factors seemed influential in bringing about this possibly emerging change of attitude toward America. The first was the escalating danger represented by a militant Red China. The other factor seemed related to the world Communist conference and to the influence many of the foreign Communist leaders may have exerted on the Kremlin leaders in their private discussions with the *troika* of Brezhnev, Kosygin, and Podgorny before and during the conference of the 75 parties.

Besides his propitious call for a Far Eastern security system, C.P.S.U. General-Secretary Brezhnev also made an important revision, in his June 7 opening speech to the world Communist conference, of the peaceful coexistence line. Heretofore,. during the post-Khrushchev period, peaceful coexistence was construed officially to apply mainly to non-Communist nations of the Third World. Only secondarily or by implication did it apply to relations between the U.S. and the Soviet Union per se (see discussion in Chapter IX). However, on this occasion Brezhnev made a direct and unequivocal application of peaceful coexistence to U.S.-Soviet relations:

We make here no exceptions [in the application of the policy of peaceful coexistence] to any of the capitalist states, including the U.S.A. Peaceful coexistence is for us not a temporary tactical device but an important principle of a consistently peace-loving Socialist foreign policy.[18]

Then in the first half of July came the daily Soviet press coverage of American astronaut and Apollo 8 commander Colonel Frank Borman's nine-day visit in the U.S.S.R. (including an audience with President Podgorny). While not playing it as a page-one item, the Soviet press nonetheless printed many friendly remarks made by the American military officer. At one point, according to TASS, Colonel Borman even made the traditional if somewhat inaccurate comparison between the American West and Soviet Siberia. The frequent mention of the Soviet hosts, the Union of Soviet Friendship Societies and the Institute for Soviet-American Relations, and Borman's encounters with Soviet cosmonauts and top-level academicians culminating in his visit with President Podgorny were indications that a "blip" had appeared on the U.S.-Soviet friendship screen. When added to another more profound development, the July 10, 1969, speech by Foreign Minister Gromyko, a major Soviet *volte-face* with respect to America seemed in the offing.

Gromyko, the personification of Soviet *raison d'état*, made a wide-ranging review of conditions throughout the world in his mid-1969 speech to the U.S.S.R. Supreme Soviet and found grounds for optimism when it came to U.S.-Soviet relations. (The speech was favorably received in U.S. official circles.) The Foreign Minister said that his government "had always attached great importance to relations with the United States." Although the two countries are divided by "profound class differences" (the ideological motif) Gromyko said, "The Soviet Union has always believed that the U.S.S.R. and the U.S.A. can find a common language on questions of maintaining peace."

With the obvious approval of the top leaders of the party and government who sat on the raised platform behind Gromyko, the Foreign Minister also spoke favorably of relations between Yugoslavia and the Soviet Union which had been somewhat strained since the invasion and occupation of Czechoslovakia by the Soviets and their Warsaw Pact allies. As to Vietnam, Gromyko spoke rather predictably of the U.S. war effort as "hopeless" and called upon "sober elements" in the U.S. to make the U.S. government end its intervention in Vietnam. Still, the Soviet official's language was mild compared to his previous foreign-policy reports to the Supreme Soviet in recent years. Similarly mild language was used with respect to West Germany. Finally, Gromyko expressed interest in a future summit conference between President Nixon and the Soviet leaders (presumably including all three members of the Soviet troika—Brezhnev, Kosygin, and Podgorny!). This section of the Foreign Minister's report may have been the most significant one of all in terms of long-term U.S.-Soviet relations. Cold War peace feelers emanating from the Kremlin in 1969 hinted at the opening of an era of détente. More tangible evidence of change might have to wait until 1970, the year of the celebration of the Lenin Centennial and the expected convening of the Twenty-fourth Party Congress.

NOTES

1. V. D. Sokolovsky, *Voennaya strategiya (Military Strategy)*, 2nd ed. (Moscow: Voennoye Izdatelstvo Ministerstva Oborony SSSR, 1963), p. 437.
2. Aspaturian, "Foreign Policy Perspectives in the Sixties," in Dallin and Larson (eds.), *op. cit.*, p. 141.
3. *The New York Times*, May 1, 1969, p. 1.
4. *Izvestiya*, May 1, 1969, p. 1.
5. *Izvestiya*, April 29, 1969, p. 1.
6. *Pravda*, May 2, 1969, pp. 1–2. Joseph C. Harsch, special correspondent for *The Christian Science Monitor*, speculated (CSM, May 3–5, 1969) that President Nixon's decision to disperse Task Force 71 in the Sea of Japan which had been sent to the Sea of Japan following the EC–121 incident, took the military parade off the Moscow May Day agenda.
7. *The Washington Post*, May 2, 1969, p. A15.
8. *The New York Times*, May 2, 1969, p. 27.
9. Dan Morgan, "Trade Talks Rekindle Bonn-Moscow Dialogue," *The Washington Post*, May 1, 1969, p. A20.
10. Seymour Freidin and George Bailey, *The Experts* (New York: Macmillan, 1968), pp. 152–153 and 374. Nitze, interestingly, was one of the key Ameri-

can negotiators at the American-Soviet SALT (Strategic Arms Limitation Talks) meetings in Helsinki which began on Nov. 17, 1969.

11. *The Washington Post*, April 30, 1969, p. A15.

12. *Ibid.*, April 27, 1969, pp. 1 and A21.

13. V. I. Lenin, "Farewell Letter to the Swiss Workers, 1917," in *Selected Works* (New York: International Publishers, 1943) vol. VI, p. 16.

14. V. I. Lenin, "Leftwing Childishness and Petty-Bourgeois Mentality" May 3–5, 1918, in *Selected Works* (New York: International Publishers, 1943), vol. VII, p. 357.

15. J. V. Stalin, *Voprosy leninizma*, 11th ed. (Moscow: Gosudarstvennoye Izdatelstvo Politicheskoi Literatury, 1947), p. 140. Stalin quotes from Lenin's *Sochineniya (Works)*, 1st ed. vol. XXIV, p. 122.

16. Chuikov, *op. cit.*, p. 255.

17. David Binder, "Opposition to Brezhnev in the Soviet Leadership Is Reported," *The New York Times*, May 1, 1969, p. 10. See also Paul Wohl, "Rising Role for Military Seen in U.S.S.R.," *The Christian Science Monitor*, April 25, p. 1, and the stories filed from Moscow by *The Washington Post* correspondent Anatole Shub during April and May 1969. Shub was thereafter expelled from the Soviet Union.

18. Stephen S. Rosenfeld, "Hints of Sociability Come Out of Cuba," *The Washington Post*, May 4, 1969, p. B6.

Epilogue

The year 1969 found Soviet foreign policy at a crossroads. A trio of paradoxes confronted the Kremlin (see pp. 238–240, above) and several alternative courses of action lay before the leaders as they began their agonizing discussion of priorities and allocation of resources within the upcoming Five-year Plan, 1970–1974. (Brezhnev revealed in his May Day address that discussion of the new plan was under way.)

The "guns *vs.* butter" paradox is, indeed, a tough one for the Kremlin. We have discussed at several places in this book Russia's extreme need for national security. This demand, as we saw, persistently confronts Russia largely because of its geopolitical position in the world and the legacy of concern for national security stemming from Russian history, which was made more tragic whenever Russian protection of national security was slackened in the slightest. But the paradox may be only seeming after all. For should a desperate pinch or new-style "scissors crisis" confront the Soviets in which they literally could not make ends meet, the Soviet deck nevertheless contains a number of trump cards. One of them is the tradition of American and Russian cooperation.

Russia has called upon America before, and America has responded. Even before official recognition was extended to the Soviet regime by F.D.R. in 1933, many-sided assistance was given to the Soviets by American businessmen and humanitarians (see Chapter V). After recognition, trade and assistance continued until the period of Lend-Lease during World War II when American-Soviet collaboration reached a post-1917 peak. This cooperation, especially from the American side, is indelibly etched in the history of Soviet-U.S. relations. And it surely has not been forgotten by the leadership in Moscow, as was suggested by Foreign Minister Gromyko's remarks in his July 10, 1969 speech. Should the need arise—whether economic or military —these leaders are apparently confident that bridges to the U.S. could be erected in rather short order, just as fast as they had been after June 1941.

But the key word here is "apparently." For if Moscow should permit U.S.-Soviet relations to deteriorate into a refrozen cold war, as has been suggested more than once since the ouster of Khrushchev, it might not be so easy to re-erect those bridges. Nonetheless, the administrations of Kennedy, Johnson, and Nixon have all stated the wish to improve Soviet-American relations. A similar wish has been expressed, although much more rarely and weakly, from the Soviet side, even since 1964. This "invisible" bridge, or reserve of traditional friendship, may figure in the present calculations of the Kremlin leaders as they put their heads together in late 1969 at the threshold of a new Five-Year Plan and a new decade and make what appears to be an "agonizing reappraisal" of a number of their policies.

And there are other reasons why Paradox Number One—the problem of producing *both* tanks and tractors—may be only "seeming" or latent. Soviet resources have evidently not been strained marginally, even with the post-1964 modernization of the Soviet armed forces. One reason is that the military modernization program, although impressive, has not been all that sweeping. Another is that the regime has been blessed with reasonably good harvests since 1964—the one possible exception being 1969 which followed an unusually cold and long winter in 1968/1969 damaging much of the winter wheat crop. Industrial production, too, advanced reasonably well in 1965–1969. Again, with this exception: the plan fulfillment in 1969 revealed that the harsh winter had adversely affected industry as well as agriculture. Labor productivity was also disappointing.

But no really serious shortages or pinches evidently developed in 1969, nor had they in the other four post-Khrushchev years. This suggests that the increased expenditures on arms in 1966–1969 have not unduly pressed the Soviets. However, it is worth speculating that the moderate tone which was detectable in Soviet policy in spring 1969 may well have reflected the somewhat poorer-than-usual showing by the Soviet economy in the same period. Which raises the question: Do economically pressed Communists make peaceful Communists? Perhaps so.

Real or imagined, seeming or concrete, Paradox Number One appears to be under control. It is not likely to cause an abandonment of the basic goals of Soviet foreign policy. It does, however, constitute a potential threat to a continuity of that policy, as it is presently designed.

Paradox Number Two—of coping with a two-front predicament and alienating potential allies—also appears to be under control and may be, in any case, more seeming than tangible. Since Khrushchev's overthrow, the Kremlin leaders have undertaken a number of measures which are obviously intended to give up their defenses should a danger arise from the Chinese side of the 4,592-mile frontier. First, there has been no more frequent visitor to the Russian capital from 1965 to the present than the 53-year-old leader of the Mongolian People's Republic, Yumzhagin Tsedenbal,* the force behind

*Tsedenbal made a stop in Moscow on his way home from East Germany the day before Khrushchev was ousted from his several posts. The Mongolian leader stayed throughout the tumultuous days of completion of Khrushchev's ouster, October 13–14, and then left on the 14th without being seen off, in the usual Soviet manner, by a single Soviet official!

the Outer Mongolian Communists for the past thirty years. Obviously, Mongol-Soviet secret talks have concerned the building up of defenses along the 2,500-mile frontier which the M.P.R. shares with Communist China. On hand, too, for most of their discussions were high officials of the Soviet army, air force, and rocket forces. Top civilian Soviet leaders as well have gone to the Mongolian capital of Ulan Bator since 1965, Brezhnev and Podgorny being among these Russian visitors. And there have been military visitors also.

Another post-Khrushchev phenomenon—one that was also manifest but to a somewhat lesser degree in the Khrushchev period—involves among others India, Japan, North Vietnam, North Korea, Pakistan. As part of the current policy of "double encirclement" (of West Germany and Red China —see above, pp. 197–201), the U.S.S.R. has sought to ring Communist China with strengthened interstate relations between the U.S.S.R. and the several aforementioned neighbors of Maoist China. Moscow may even soon resort to repairing its relations with Nationalist China! Victor Louis, a Soviet citizen and "journalist" based in London and who functions in the semiofficial capacity of a go-between for Western publishers of controversial Soviet literature and Moscow, recently turned up in Taiwan. Louis had some complimentary things to say about the Formosans and the Nationalist Chinese, and little good to say about the Maoists on the mainland. Speculation ran that Louis's visit might have been a Moscow-instigated trial balloon looking toward possible opening of Soviet diplomatic relations with Nationalist China. Peking duly voiced its suspicions of Louis's motives.*

The extensive courting of India, Japan, Pakistan, Afghanistan, Australia, North Korea, Cambodia, Laos, and North Vietnam by Moscow since 1964 seems also to fit into the pattern of double encirclement, Far Eastern division. The latest development in this connection was Premier Alexei Kosygin's rather unexpected visit to New Delhi for the funeral of Indian President Dr. Zakir Husain in May 1969. Kosygin was the only head of government of a large nation-state to come to the funeral.

To the West, or the other half of a potential two-front predicament, Moscow has been busy too and will likely continue to be in the years ahead, not alienating potential allies, but probably doing just the opposite. At times since 1964 it has seemed that the Kremlin has aggravated relations with West Germany and its "overseas protectors, the U.S. imperialists" rather than trying to come to realistic and unhysterical grips with the problem. But Moscow has by no means cut its ties to Bonn altogether. Its diplomatic recognition of the German Federal Republic goes back deep in the Khrushchev period.

*Louis also hinted strongly in September 1969 that the Soviets were contemplating a "preventive war" or "preemptive attack" against Red China and its nuclear facilities. Presumably, a letter to this effect was earlier circulated throughout the Soviet bloc by the Russians. At the same time, a Chinese reaction to this became evident: an order signed by Mao to increase combat readiness for an "inevitable" Soviet attack.

And although the Kremlin looked on bitterly as Rumania joined Yugoslavia in establishing full-fledged diplomatic relations with West Germany, it did nothing—if indeed it could—to arrest this process.

By its invasion of Czechoslovakia, the Soviet Union temporarily stopped whatever trend there may have been toward a sweeping Prague-Bonn détente which had set in after Antonin Novotny's ouster and the coming to power of the young Alexander Dubcek. But even here, the principal aim of the Soviet intervention in Czechoslovakia seemed to be motivated more by *imperial* considerations than by an alleged "threat" from West Germany, which, in any case, was grossly manufactured by Soviet propaganda as a pretext for the invasion. Not the German Federal Republic, but *unity of the Soviet bloc* and *bloc loyalty to Moscow*—military, economic, and diplomatic—seemed to be the principal goads urging the Russians and their four Warsaw Pact allies into the invasion to stop a Czechoslovak drift toward Yugoslav-style Communism, Sik-ism and consumerism in Czech economic policy, and the eventual defection of Czechoslovakia from the rest of the Soviet bloc.

By its bridge-to-Paris policy, moreover, Moscow seemed to be coping with West Germany by means of encircling her. But in spring 1969, when so many other developments took place, President Charles de Gaulle resigned. Suddenly the rug was pulled from under Soviet policy toward France in the post-Khrushchev period unless, of course, Gaullism in this respect should continue under M. Pompidou. With France passing through an uncertain period of interregnum, Moscow was expected to reappraise its French *and* its German policy. This may be part of the explanation as to why spring 1969 saw several initiatives by Moscow in the direction of normalizing relations between itself and Bonn (see above, pp. 253–258).

In any case, at the present juncture, the Far Eastern expression of the Soviet policy of double encirclement continues to broaden. But in the West, too, new departures may be under way. If the United States is to be included in a Soviet initiative toward détente in 1969–1970, the paradox mentioned above in the first section of this chapter may tend to disappear. To the Kremlin, the paradox involved in aggravating tensions east and west without taking measures to cope with the danger of a two-front war may be only chimerical, or at the very least an only remotely concrete paradox. Instead of being trapped in a paradox, the Kremlin may reason, several measures are being undertaken precisely to cope with this problem. Not the least of them concerns some future move toward rapprochement with West Germany and the United States while at the same time forging a band of friendship with China's neighbors in the Far East—in short, adoption of an all-azimuth policy of disciplining Moscow's adjoining Communist allies in Eastern Europe while forming relationships with many other non-Communist countries at every point on the compass.

The Russians' third paradox concerns the means that Moscow uses to weld together its imperial quasi-duchies in the Warsaw Alliance in order to guarantee their friendship and loyalty. This ticklish problem confronts the Kremlin with a host of subsidiary Gordian knots involving the personalities of the Communist leaders of these states, the particular national characters of the various peoples of the bloc, the generation gap, and the "Western" cultural and democratic traditions of at least two of them—Czechoslovakia, and to a lesser extent, Hungary. When faced with the danger of defection by one or another of these Soviet duchies, how should Moscow proceed? With the carrot or the stick? If it overuses the carrot, the given quasi-satellite will begin to behave like the Soviet child in the *Krokodil* cartoon who wants more and more candy from his doting parents and finally gets it. Eventually the "spoiled" child, like the given East European country, gets out from under parental authority altogether. Moscow obviously thought that this was what was going to happen in the case of Czechoslovakia, if Dubcek and his youngish liberal "brain trust" were not stopped forcibly. Hungary also drank the milk of independence in 1956 while the Kremlin looked on with dread and then abruptly decided to intervene with Soviet troops, apparently upon the advice of a clique of Soviet marshals.

If, however, the stick (in the form of Soviet troops) is used, how can any firmly based friendship be established between the U.S.S.R. and its bullied East European neighbors? This paradox seems to have occurred to the Kremlin after it faced and considered the consequences of its August 1968 invasion of Czechoslovakia. By this action the Russians had unleashed a hornet's nest of opposition, not only in Czechoslovakia, but in most other countries as well, and within most foreign Communist Party *apparats* throughout the world. Some of this fall-out was still raining down at the time of Communist Conference III in Moscow in June 1969. It did not seem unlikely that some Soviet officials may have well asked themselves, "Was the invasion worth it?"

This paradox is, then, very real. But the leaders in the Kremlin give no indication as yet that they know how to cope with it, least of all resolve it. With over half the populations of these countries under the age of 21 and with a largely optimistic outlook in their young souls and a desire for the good life, a neo-Stalinist policy of forcible collaboration can scarcely get results from these citizens, or perhaps even from their rulers in the 1970s and in the decades to come. Moscow must now take serious measure of how badly it needs this friendship and cooperation—should adversity confront the Russians in the Far East, for example. In the talks between the Soviet Politburo and the East European leaders in April 1969, the final communique contained no reference to pledges made by Russia's satellites to help the Soviet Union in a future confrontation with Communist China. East European informants and Western correspondents, however, reported that the Russians *had expected* such pledges; that, in fact, Brezhnev, the leader of the Soviet delegation to the talks, became so furious over hesitation on the part of his allies to make such a pledge that he pounded the table and shouted angrily at them.

Quite obviously, banging the table or rolling Soviet tanks through the streets of satellite capitals is not going to produce wholehearted support or loyalty for Mother Russia by Moscow's allies! Clearly, a new and more realistic tactic will have to be tried, and there is evidence that one may be in the offing. Several trade deals made by Moscow in 1969 with the other members of COMECON display a certain generosity or at least willingness on the part of Moscow to respond to pressures from the other side. A fair-sized credit was granted to Czechoslovakia in early 1969 and a number of flexible commercial arrangements have been established between the U.S.S.R. and the other East European members of COMECON. Many problems still confront the "Communist Market" countries, not the least of which is the adoption of common exchange currency and effective banking and credit arrangements, meeting contracted obligations punctually, assuring high quality of delivered merchandise, and so forth. Whether Moscow will "listen" to its satraps and respect the national sovereignty of each of its allies remains to be seen.

A special case, and a difficult one at that, is presented by Yugoslavia. Like Albania, Yugoslavia ceased some time ago to be a full-fledged member of the Soviet bloc. A post-Czechoslovak invasion development has been the steady worsening of the *party* relations between the C.P.S.U. and the Yugoslav Communist League. Even on the state level President Tito has not been subtle in his condemnation of the Soviet invasion and occupation of Czechoslovakia or what the Yugoslav press calls the "drift toward neo-Stalinism" in general in the Kremlin. On the Russian side, however, comes evidence of a desire to heal an impending new breach with Belgrade; witness Foreign Minister Gromyko's trip to Belgrade in mid-1969. Meanwhile, an exchange of visits by Tito and Brezhnev may be in the works. In the latter half of 1969, both the Soviet and Yugoslav press showed signs of toning down the bitterness toward each other's policies, ideologies, and political systems; earlier in 1969, however, the term "revisionist" had been used in application to Yugoslavia in not too subtle fashion by *Pravda, Izvestiya*, and other Soviet publications. (As might be expected, the most vitriolic attacks on the Yugoslavs appeared in the military press of the U.S.S.R.) Comments by *Pravda* on April 30, 1969 marked a peak in Soviet needling of the Yugoslavs, with language that was more embittered than it had been some months earlier. To wit:

Anyone who tries, by means of nationalist demagogy [an implied attack on Tito] about alleged 'limited sovereignty,' to undermine brotherly solidarity and mutual support to Socialist countries in the struggle against external and internal reaction, plays into the hands of the enemies of Socialism. . . . There are essentially no neutrals in the struggle between the two world systems. All classes, parties, and states express their relations toward that struggle. The pretense of standing outside that struggle, presenting it as some kind of clash between two military-political blocs, is in fact a petty bourgeois-nationalist maneuver whose purpose is to exploit contemporary contradictions and for promoting one's limited and falsely understood national interests.

Significantly, no major vituperation has been leveled at the Yugoslavs by the Soviet press since then. Meanwhile, Albania, which formally withdrew from the Warsaw Alliance at the end of 1968, has made some friendly overtures toward its neighbor and erstwhile adversary, Yugoslavia. Albania will come to the defense of its Yugoslav neighbor, says Tirana, should its sovereignty be threatened: a clear implication that neither Peking (which has warned of the same cooperative action with respect to Albania and Rumania) nor Tirana would stand aside should the Russians attempt "another Czechoslovakia" at either Yugoslavia's or Albania's expense. The same applies to Rumania. Meanwhile, all of this must be noted with some concern in Moscow and may account in part for the Kremlin's efforts in mid-1969 to repair relations between itself and Belgrade, not to mention Peking.

In distant Communist Cuba, there were also signs of an effort on the part of Havana to improve relations with the U.S.S.R. Cuban-Soviet relations have been somewhat strained in recent years by niggardly Soviet assistance to the "Island of Freedom" and Soviet displeasure with Cuban promotion of "romantic," Guevaraesque guerrilla warfare tactics for exporting Communism to the other countries of Latin America. (Soviet trade with South American countries, particularly the relatively more prosperous ones, is evidently too valuable to Moscow for it to endorse a Cuban-inspired policy of disrupting normal social and economic life in those countries.) From Havana came hints of "sociability."[18] An important speech delivered on April 17, 1969, by a top Castro aide, Rafael Rodriguez, contained the implication that Cuba had now abandoned its policy of fomenting revolution in Latin America. Another development was a pastoral letter read by eight Catholic bishops in Cuba on April 20. The same bishops who warned in 1960 of an "enemy within the gates" were now, nine years later, protesting against the "unnecessary suffering" incurred by the blockade established by the Organization of American States in 1964. Since the bishops' statements are closely edited by the Cuban Communists, lest they contain any politicisms, the presumption is that Havana may be hinting in this curious manner that it has an interest in normalizing relations with the non-Communist Latin states and perhaps eventually also those with the United States as well.

Interesting possibilities for U.S.-Soviet détente were opened by two developments which occurred late in 1969: SALT (Strategic Arms Limitation Talks) negotiations in Helsinki and indications from Moscow that the U.S.

would *not* be excluded from an all European security conference. The Soviets had been giving increasing attention to both subjects since the Sino-Soviet border clashes earlier in the year. The seriousness of the present détente-mindedness of the Kremlin will be tested by the ultimate outcome of SALT begun in mid-November. Moreover, if an all European security conference, said by Moscow to be scheduled for "early 1970" expressed a new-found attitude toward the U.S., it could lend support to the hypothesis (discussed above, p. 256) that Soviet contingency planning for Europe by no means leaves N.A.T.O. or the United States out of the picture.

Many of the trends and developments canvassed in this book all point a quizzical finger at the Kremlin as if to ask: "Well, what are you going to do next?" The Soviets stand at a danger-ridden crossroads at the beginning of a new decade. The flexibility that they must demonstrate in the face of new situations and complex problems is at a premium.

Times are changing, and changing with dazzling speed. It remains to be seen whether the encrusted party and state bureaucracy of the Soviet Union will be able to measure up to the task. Or whether for the Kremlin, time will continue to be out of joint.

BIBLIOGRAPHY

Bibliography

Allen, Richard V. *Peace or Peaceful Coexistence?* Chicago: American Bar Association, 1966.

Babey, Anna M. *Americans in Russia (1776–1917)*. New York: Comet Press, 1938.

Bain, Chester. *Vietnam—The Roots of the Conflict*. Englewood Cliffs, N.J.: Prentice-Hall, 1967.

Baldwin, Hanson W. *Great Mistakes of the War*. New York: Harper & Row, 1950.

Beloff, Max. *The Foreign Policy of Soviet Russia*, 2 vols. London: Oxford University Press, 1947.

Bishop, Joseph Bucklin. *Theodore Roosevelt and His Time*. New York: Scribner, 1920.

Bloomfield, Lincoln P., Clemens, Walter C., Jr., and Griffiths, Franklyn. *Khrushchev and the Arms Race—Soviet Interests in Arms Control and Disarmament 1954–1964*. Cambridge, Mass.: M.I.T. Press, 1966.

Brzezinski, Zbigniew K. *Ideology and Power in Soviet Politics*. New York: Praeger, 1962.

Brzezinski, Zbigniew K. *The Soviet Bloc—Unity and Conflict*. New York: Praeger, 1961.

Bullitt, William C. *The Great Globe Itself*. New York: Scribner, 1946.

Buzek, Antony. *How the Communist Press Works*. New York: Praeger, 1964.

Byrnes, James F. *Speaking Frankly*. New York: Harper & Row, 1947.

Carr, Edward Hallet. *The Bolshevik Revolution, 1917–1923*, 2 vols. New York: Macmillan, 1951.

Chuikov, Vasili I. *The Fall of Berlin*. New York: Ballantine, 1967.

Churchill, Winston. *The Gathering Storm*. Boston: Houghton Mifflin, 1948.

Churchill, Winston. *The Grand Alliance*. Boston: Houghton Mifflin, 1950.

Churchill, Winston. *The Hinge of Fate*. Boston: Houghton Mifflin, 1950.

Churchill, Winston. *Triumph and Tragedy*. Boston: Houghton Mifflin, 1953.

Conquest, Robert. *Russia After Khrushchev*. New York: Praeger, 1965.

Crankshaw, Edward. *Khrushchev: A Career*. New York: Viking Press, 1966.

Dallin, Alexander, and Larson, Thomas B. (eds.). *Soviet Politics Since Khrushchev*. Englewood Cliffs, N.J.: Prentice-Hall, 1968.

Dallin, David J. *Rise of Russia in Asia*. New Haven, Conn.: Yale University Press, 1949.

Dallin, David J. *Russia and Postwar Europe*. New Haven, Conn.: Yale University Press, 1943.

Dallin, David J. *Soviet Russia's Foreign Policy 1939–1942*. New Haven, Conn.: Yale University Press, 1942.

Davies, Joseph E. *Mission to Moscow*. New York: Simon & Schuster, 1941.

Deane, John R. *The Strange Alliance*. New York: Viking Press, 1946.

Dinerstein, Herbert S. *Fifty Years of Soviet Foreign Policy*. Baltimore: Johns Hopkins Press, 1968.

Doolin, Dennis J. *Territorial Claims in the Sino-Soviet Conflict*. The Hoover Institution on War, Revolution and Peace. Stanford, Calif.: Stanford University, 1965.

Dulles, Foster R., *The Road to Teheran—The Story of Russia and America*. Princeton, N.J.: Princeton University Press, 1944.

Fainsod, Merle. *How Russia Is Ruled.* Cambridge, Mass.: Harvard University Press, 1963.

Filene, Peter G. *Americans and the Soviet Experiment, 1917–1933*. Cambridge, Mass.: Harvard University Press, 1967.

Fischer, Louis. *Machines and Men in Russia*. NewYork: H. Smith, 1932.

Francis, David R. *Russia from the American Embassy*. New York: Scribner, 1921.

Frankland, Mark. *Khrushchev*. New York: Stein and Day, 1967.

Freidin, Seymour, and Bailey, George. *The Experts*. New York: Macmillan, 1968.

Friedman, Elisha. *Russia in Transition: A Businessman's Appraisal*. New York: Viking Press, 1932.

Gehlen, Michael P. *The Politics of Coexistence—Soviet Methods and Motives*. Bloomington: Indiana University Press, 1967.

Hazard, John N. *The Soviet System of Government*. Chicago: University of Chicago Press, 1964.

Hirsch, Alcan. *Industrialized Russia*. New York: The Chemical Catalogue Company, 1934.

Hoover, J. Edgar. *Masters of Deceit*. New York: Holt, Rinehart and Winston, 1958.

Horelick, Arnold L., and Rush, Myron. *Strategic Power and Soviet Foreign Policy*. Chicago: University of Chicago Press, 1965.

Hyland, William, and Shryock, Richard W. *The Fall of Khrushchev*. New York: Funk & Wagnalls, 1968.

Jelavich, Barbara. *A Century of Russian Foreign Policy—1814–1914*. Boston: Lippincott, 1964.

Johnston, Erich Allen. *We're All in It*. New York: Dutton, 1948.

Kennan, George F. *Russia and the West Under Lenin and Stalin*. Boston: Little, Brown, 1960.

Kerensky, Alexander. *Russia and History's Turning Point*. New York: Duell, Sloan, & Pearce, 1965.

Laserson, Max M. *The American Impact on Russia—Diplomatic and Ideological.* New York: Macmillan, 1950.

Lenin, V. I. *Selected Works.* New York: International Publishers, 1943.

Librach, Jan. *The Rise of the Soviet Empire—A Study of Soviet Foreign Policy.* New York: Praeger, 1964.

London, Kurt. *The Soviet Union—A Half Century of Communism.* Baltimore: Johns Hopkins Press, 1968.

Mamatey, Victor S. *Soviet Russian Imperialism.* Princeton, N.J.: Van Nostrand, 1964.

Manning, Clarence A. *Twentieth Century Ukraine.* New York: Bookman Associates, 1951.

Massie, Robert K. *Nicholas and Alexandra.* New York: Atheneum, 1967.

Maxwell, John S. *The Czar, His Court and People.* New York: Baker and Scribner, 1848.

Mazour, Anatole G. *Russia—Past and Present.* Princeton, N.J.: Van Nostrand, 1951.

McNeal, Robert H. (ed.). *International Relations Among Communists.* Englewood Cliffs, N.J.: Prentice-Hall, 1967.

Pares, Richard, and Taylor, A. J. P. (eds.). *Essays Presented to Sir Lewis Namier.* London: Macmillan & Co., 1956.

Penkovsky, Oleg. *The Penkovsky Papers.* Garden City, N.Y.: Doubleday, 1965.

Petony, DeVere E. (ed.). *Soviet Behavior in World Affairs: Communist Foreign Policies.* San Francisco: Chandler, 1962.

Pistrak, Lazar. *The Grand Tactician—Khrushchev's Rise to Power.* New York: Praeger, 1961.

Raymond, Ellsworth. *The Soviet State.* New York: Macmillan, 1968.

Riha, Thomas. *Readings in Russian Civilization,* Vols. II and III. Chicago: University of Chicago Press, 1964.

Robinson, Geroid T. *Rural Russia Under the Old Regime.* New York: Macmillan, 1949.

Rossi, A. *The Russo-German Alliance—August 1939—June 1941.* Boston: Beacon Press, 1951.

Sakharov, Andrei D. *Progress, Coexistence, and Intellectual Freedom.* New York: Norton, 1968.

Seton-Watson, Hugh. *The East European Revolution.* New York: Praeger, 1950.

Shabad, Theodore. *Geography of the U.S.S.R.—A Regional Survey.* New York: Columbia University Press, 1951.

Sherwood, Robert E. *Roosevelt and Hopkins.* New York: Harper & Row, 1948.

Sokolovsky, V. D. *Voennaya strategiya (Military Strategy).* 2nd ed. Moscow: Voennoye Izdatelstvo Ministerstva Oborony SSSR, 1963.

Sorokin, Pitirim A. *Russia and the United States.* New York: Dutton, 1944.

Stalin, J. V. *Voprosy Leninizma (Problems of Leninism)*, 11th ed. Moscow: Gosudarstvennoye Izdatelstvo Politicheskoi Literatury, 1947.

Stalin, J. V. *Sochineniya (Works)*, 1st ed. Moscow: Gosudarstvennoye Izdatelstvo Politicheskoi Literatury, 1946–1952.

Steinbeck, John. *The Russian Journal*. New York: New York Herald Tribune Syndicate, 1948.

Stettinius, Edward R. *Roosevelt and the Russians: The Yalta Conference*. Garden City, N.Y.: Doubleday, 1949.

Stillman, Edmund, and Pfaff, William. *The Politics of Hysteria—The Source of Twentieth-Century Conflict*. New York: Harper & Row, 1964.

Tatu, Michel. *Power in the Kremlin from Khrushchev to Kosygin*. New York: Viking Press, 1969.

Thiel, Erich. *The Soviet Far East—A Survey of Its Physical and Economic Geography*. London: Methuen, n.d.

Ulam, Adam B. *Expansion and Coexistence*. New York: Praeger, 1968.

Vernadsky, George. *A History of Russia*. New Haven, Conn.: Yale University Press, 1961.

Ward, Harry F. *The Story of American-Soviet Relations—1917–1959*. New York: National Council of American-Soviet Friendship, 1959.

Werth, Alexander. *Russia Under Khrushchev*. New York: Hill & Wang, 1961.

Werth, Alexander. *Russia at War—1941–1945*. New York: Dutton, 1964.

Wolfe, Thomas W. *Soviet Strategy at the Crossroads*. Cambridge, Mass.: Harvard University Press, 1965.

Zabriskie, Edward H. *American-Russian Rivalry in the Far East 1895–1914—A Study in Diplomacy and Power Politics*. Philadelphia: University of Pennsylvania Press, 1946.

Zagoria, Donald S. *Vietnam Triangle—Moscow/Peking/Hanoi*. New York: Western Publishing, 1967.

Newspapers and Periodicals

Annals of the American Academy of Political and Social Science

Atlas

Automotive Industries

Bulletin of the Institute for the Study of the USSR

Current History

East Europe

Economic Review of the Soviet Union

Ekonomicheskaya Zhizn (Economic Life)

Foreign Affairs

Interplay

Izvestiya (News)

Journal of International Affairs
Kommunist Vooruzhennikh Sil (Communist of the Armed Forces)
Krasnaya Zvezda (Red Star)
Nedelya (Week)
Newsweek
Novoye Russkoye Slovo (New Russian Word)
Peking Review
Pravda (Truth)
Pravitelstvennii Vestnik (Government Messenger)
Problems of Communism
Survey
The New Leader
The Reporter
The Washington Post
Time
U.S. News & World Report
Voennaya Mysl (Military Thought)

INDEX